C0-ATA-813

THE MARYKNOLL SISTERS IN HONG KONG,
1921–1969

The Maryknoll Sisters in Hong Kong, 1921–1969

In Love with the Chinese

Cindy Yik-yi Chu

0401073

THE MARYKNOLL SISTERS IN HONG KONG, 1921–1969
© Cindy Yik-yi Chu, 2004

All rights reserved. No part of this book may be used or reproduced in any manner whatsoever without written permission except in the case of brief quotations embodied in critical articles or reviews.

First published 2004 by
PALGRAVE MACMILLAN™
175 Fifth Avenue, New York, N.Y. 10010 and
Houndmills, Basingstoke, Hampshire, England RG21 6XS
Companies and representatives throughout the world

PALGRAVE MACMILLAN is the global academic imprint of the Palgrave Macmillan division of St. Martin's Press, LLC and of Palgrave Macmillan Ltd. Macmillan® is a registered trademark in the United States, United Kingdom and other countries. Palgrave is a registered trademark in the European Union and other countries.

ISBN 1–4039–6586–2 hardback

Library of Congress Cataloging-in-Publication Data
Chu, Cindy Yik-yi
    The Maryknoll Sisters in Hong Kong, 1921–1969 : In love with the Chinese / Cindy Yik-yi Chu.
        p. cm.
    Includes bibliographical references and index.
    ISBN 1–4039–6586–2 (cloth)
    1. Catholic Foreign Mission Society of America—Missions—China—Hong Kong—History—20th century. 2. Maryknoll Sisters—Missions—China—Hong Kong—History—20th century. I. Title.
BV2300.C35C49 2004
266'.25125—dc22   2004044460

A catalogue record for this book is available from the British Library.

Design by Newgen Imaging Systems (P) Ltd., Chennai, India.

First edition: November 2004
10 9 8 7 6 5 4 3 2 1

Printed in the United States of America.

To my parents

CONTENTS

040103

LIST OF TABLES AND FIGURES

Tables

Figures

PREFACE

This book is the product of my own research project. I came up with the idea of looking into Maryknoll history in summer 2000; the American Sisters had left me the impression of being independent, outgoing, optimistic, and socially conscious, very different from stereotyped images of conservative and reserved nuns seen on T.V. and in news magazines. When I approached the Maryknoll Sisters in August that year, they were enthusiastic about the project and showed no hesitancy in answering my queries, giving me a very good start. The more I read about Maryknoll history, through books written by the women themselves and others, the more I was amazed by the courage they had in going to foreign lands with languages and cultures they knew very little about. When the six pioneers came to Hong Kong in 1921, they had to get through tremendous cultural shock, not to mention the responsibilities of opening a mission field and making important decisions in a situation they were still trying to adjust to. They had to persevere, and foreign mission was a life-long task simply because the congregation did not have plans for the missionaries to return home until 1946. Those who arrived in the colony after World War II were often shocked by the appalling poverty of most people. A Sister described her experience in the Chinese culture as equivalent to one of "reincarnation."

I made two research trips to the Maryknoll Mission Archives in Maryknoll, New York, the first one in summer 2001 and the second one in summer 2003. The records of the Sisters were very detailed, as they probably did quite a lot of writing during their stay in Hong Kong; it seemed as if I were able to see with my own eyes their daily work, living, and people around them. Their description of Hong Kong society resembled a first-hand history book, tracing developments of the place through different times of the twentieth century. As a Hong Kong person, I almost thought that I could go back to history, and I appreciated the unbelievable sacrifices and hard work of the Chinese people, making Hong Kong what it is today.

In my research in the Maryknoll Mission Archives, I received much help from Sister Martha Bourne and I am particularly grateful to her for answering every question of mine, no matter how unimportant it was. I thank the Maryknoll Mission Archives for permission to publish photos and quotations in this book, and for the kindness of its staff. Also, I appreciate the Hong Kong Catholic Diocesan Archives for permission to use its material, the assistance of staff at the Hong Kong Public Records Office, Hong Kong Collection of the Main Library of the University of Hong Kong, Archives on the History of Christianity in China of the Hong Kong Baptist University Library, and Map Library of the Hong Kong Central Library.

When I asked individual Sisters for interviews, every one of them was willing to grant me opportunities, for which I am truly grateful. I also thank the Sisters for their hospitality during my visits in Maryknoll, and the generous support of Sisters Rose Duchesne Debrecht, Betty Ann Maheu, and Mary Lou Martin in Hong Kong. There are people I should thank for their advice: Professors Stephen Uhalley, Hok-lam Chan, Ka-che Yip, Joseph Yick, Gerald Chan, Timothy Man-kong Wong, Lisa Leung, Yin-lee Wong, Elisabeth Koll, Marilyn Levine, and Odoric Wou. I also thank Ms. Lisa Yang for her expertise on land issues, Ms. Angela Choi, and Ms. Law Yuen-han for their diligent work as research assistants. Grants from the Hong Kong Research Grants Committee and the Hong Kong Baptist University paid for research trips and the work of research assistants.

A Note on the Names of People and Places

In the late 1960s, the Maryknoll Sisters could choose to return to their baptismal names instead of using their religious names. For Sisters whose names changed in the Hong Kong archival records owing to this reason, their religious names are put in parentheses when their names are first mentioned in the text.

For people and places in Hong Kong, this book spells the names in the same way they have been spelled officially in Hong Kong (close to Cantonese pronunciation). As for names of people and places in China, *pinyin* is used instead.

Cindy Yik-yi Chu
May 2004
Hong Kong

CHAPTER ONE

INTRODUCTION

We do not go anywhere with the sense of remaining permanently. That is why Maryknoll does not build big buildings, big centers, in the missions. We will never be ambitious to build up lasting monuments to ourselves. We are building only that the Church of Christ may be extended and extended as Christ wanted it to be, ... and when that is done in one place we must go on and do it over and over again elsewhere.

Mother Mary Joseph Rogers, 1948[1]

By the beginning of the twenty-first century, the Maryknoll Sisters had been in Hong Kong for more than eighty years. In November 1921 when the pioneering group arrived in what was then a British colony, they had to adapt to a totally new environment. The population was primarily Chinese with the Cantonese dialect as the spoken language. On the top of the social hierarchy were the British, who acquired Hong Kong and ruled over the people through the highest authority of the appointed governor. Foreigners were a minority in the place, and often occupied the best positions in government and companies. Besides foreign officials and business-men, missionaries also came from abroad to preach and to serve. Since 1841 the Catholic Church has been present in Hong Kong, the earliest foreign Catholic missionaries being either Italian or French. There were not that many Catholics in Hong Kong, most of whom were Portuguese. In 1918 the Maryknoll Fathers arrived. As Americans, the Maryknoll men and women were new to the small number of foreign Catholics. In a Chinese society, the Maryknoll Sisters needed to learn the language, customs, and culture. Under the British administration, they had to adapt to another style of governance. As Catholics, they tried to find ways to spread their faith. As women, they struggled in a conservative and patriarchal society. In 1921 the Maryknoll Sisters naturally "felt like strangers" in Hong Kong.[2]

Maryknoll was the third community of Catholic nuns in Hong Kong, after the French St. Paul de Chartres Sisters and the Italian Canossian Sisters. As a congrega-tion of American Sisters, they made a new start in life, like being "reincarnated." From the beginning, the Sisters were poor and had to find the means to support themselves. They created a mail-order business and produced hand-embroidered vestments to be sold to priests in the United States. They also made use of the oppor-tunities to convert Chinese women into Christians. In 1925 they started a kinder-garten in their convent; and since then, education turned out to be their major endeavor. Unintended when they arrived in 1921, Hong Kong remained a part of their overseas mission.[3] Their temporary departure during the Japanese occupation did not prevent them from returning after World War II. In the 1950s and 1960s, the poverty of the society was appalling. The Sisters expanded the scope of their work, providing relief and service to refugees from mainland China. As missioners of the poor, they found joy in their service. Throughout the years, they adapted to changing circumstances, achieved their goals in education, social service, and welfare, and became a household name in society. According to Mother Mary Joseph Rogers, who founded the congregation, the Sisters did not build monuments for themselves in their mission areas. They came to serve the people and were ready to leave if they had fulfilled their goal. They did not receive financial rewards but the Maryknoll spirit—showing compassion to the people who would then do the same to others—guided their mission. Looking back into their history in Hong Kong, they would agree that they were always in love with the Chinese people.

As a Study of Cross-Cultural Relations

The Maryknoll Sisters of St. Dominic (formerly known as the Foreign Mission Sisters of St. Dominic) were the first American Catholic congregation, whose women religious were committed to missionary service abroad. In 1912 the community came into being, and in 1920 it received permission from Rome for sending mission-ers to faraway lands. The motherhouse situated on what was originally farmland in Ossining, New York, overlooked the Hudson River. While its entrance requirements, training, and religious life were nothing extraordinary compared to other groups, historian Jean-Paul Wiest points out, Maryknoll was unique in two ways—its members embraced the eagerness, expectations, and preparations for mission; and its candidates had a humorous and cheerful disposition.[4]

In the beginning, the Maryknoll Sisters were Americans who went to Hong Kong in their twenties and thirties. They were mainly of Irish and German descent. As their mission grew, they accepted their first Portuguese and Chinese members in the colony. Later on, they also included Canadians and Filipinas. Well educated, some of them finished college and joined Maryknoll. In those days, as it was not very common for American women to go to university, some were high school graduates when they entered the Congregation. During their training, they obtained their first degrees from colleges such as Maryknoll Teachers' College. Some received their master's and doctoral degrees after they became nuns. The Maryknollers were profes-sionals, and served as teachers, social workers, doctors, and medical personnel in Hong Kong.

This book is a study of cross-cultural relations. It describes how a community of largely American women adapted to a Chinese society, and through the passage of time grew and matured with the local people. Recently, historians of foreign relations have shown an increasing interest in cross-cultural exchanges.[5] As Harvard professor Akira Iriye points out, American–Asian interactions have been the focus of the cultural dimension of foreign relations. According to him, historians discuss "how individual Americans, mostly on private initiative, have reached across national boundaries to engage in commercial, religious, educational, and other activities over-seas."[6] They "deal with American-Asian interactions, for cross-cultural relations are nowhere more fascinating than in the meeting of Americans, imbued with a sense of mission and proud of the best legacies of Western civilization, and Asians with their own traditional heritage."[7]

There are studies on foreign missionaries and missions in China. *The role* of the Christian missionaries aroused the most attention. Initial efforts examined the self-perception of these sojourners, their objectives, and work. John K. Fairbank, as editor of *The Missionary Enterprise in China and America* made the pioneering attempt in analyzing the impact of American Protestant missions in China.[8] Other works soon followed. Among the scholarship, relations between missions and foreign treaties had produced mixed evaluations. While some praised missionaries for their strong motivation to serve, others criticized them for being so "mission-centered" that they were insensitive to local needs.[9] *The process of adaptation* is the main thrust in cross-cultural relations; and stories were that of adjustment, transformation, and sometimes, indigenization. In Chinese society, foreigners learned the language, customs, and culture; many scholarly works are on such individual men and women.[10] There are also personal accounts and reflections of former missionaries to China.[11] While the adjustment of missionaries is a theme in the works, the experience of Chinese Christians has caught increasing attention. In Daniel H. Bays' recently edited volume, *Christianity in China*, the contributors discuss the interactions between the Christian and Chinese cultures.[12]

Another theme of cross-cultural relations is *evolution of missionary work*. Historians emphasize secular activities of foreign missionaries in China. In *United States Attitudes and Policies toward China*, edited by Patricia Neils, the contributors assess the evolution of missionary activities at the turn of the century.[13] They stress three dimensions: from protection of foreign powers to rejection of dependence on foreign treaties; from Bible-centered approach to expansion of secular activities; and contribution of missionaries in arousing public interest in China back at home. Besides individuals, scholars also look into institutions established by foreign missionaries in China. They were mainly educational institutes, serving as a bridge between cultures—native and foreign, as well as Confucian and Christian.[14] In *Yenching University and Sino-Western Relations, 1916–1952*, Philip West studied the role Yanjing University played in Chinese–American relations, between the governments and the people.[15]

The Catholic missionary movement came later than the Protestant endeavor.[16] The literature focuses on the twentieth century and the indigenization of Catholic missionaries. In his study of the Catholic University of Beijing, Xiaoxin Wu examines the early history of a Catholic institution established by American Benedictine missionaries and local educators.[17] The adjustment and evangelization methods of three Catholic priests in a Chinese province in the 1920s added to the cross-cultural history and regional history.[18] Focusing on the formation of native women congregations, Sue Bradshaw is positive about the contribution of both European and American Catholic nuns.[19] Nevertheless, scholars also identify Catholic missions with foreign power and protection.[20] In *China, American Catholicism, and the Missionary*, Thomas A. Breslin surveys developments of American Catholic missions from 1918 to 1949. According to him, Chinese fields were "outlets and dumping grounds for enthusiasts, mavericks, and misfits."[21] While Protestants concentrated in cities, he says that American Catholics were on the periphery, the countryside of China. Jeroom Heyndrickx's edited book, *Historiography of the Chinese Catholic Church, Nineteenth and Twentieth Centuries*, is a more recent study of Catholicism in China from a variety of perspectives—historiographical themes, personalities, institutions, and so forth. If more research waits to be done for the China missions, one of the contributors of the volume, Bernard Hung-kay Luk, claims that the Catholic Church in Hong Kong, which is the largest Chinese-speaking diocese worldwide, receives little attention.[22]

However, there has been some output on the contribution of the Catholic Church in Hong Kong. Among the graduate research works is Father Louis Ha's doctoral dissertation on its early history.[23] A chapter in Wang Gungwu's edited volumes, *Xianggangshi xinbian (Hong Kong History: New Perspectives)*, offers a concise survey of its historical developments.[24] Articles in the edited volume of Stephen Uhalley, Jr. and Xiaoxin Wu, *China and Christianity*, are useful.[25] In 1997 the Hong Kong Diocese produced the *Historical Documents of the Hong Kong Catholic Church*.[26] Its Chinese version was published by the local Holy Spirit Study Centre in 1983, and this updated English collection covers information after 1983.[27] A recent attempt of Beatrice Leung and Shun-hing Chan, *Changing Church and State Relations in Hong Kong, 1950–2000*, analyzes the transition of Churches in Hong Kong, including the Catholic Church, in their relations with government and the wider community.[28] Nevertheless, there are still many topics that deserve close attention from historians. One example is the role of the Catholic Church in providing social relief, welfare, and education in the two decades after World War II. The present book on the Maryknoll Sisters will surely fill an important gap in this history.

The Maryknoll Sisters witnessed the tremendous changes in Hong Kong society for the most part of the twentieth century. Indeed, they contributed to the making of modern Hong Kong history. Maryknoll Sisters had their own vision of an ideal society, but they had to respond to local needs and circumstances. Their history was that of cross-cultural exchanges, and concerned some important questions. The first question was that of cultural adaptation—how they transformed their ideals in the process and how they continued to lead the social services. As foreigners, they encountered a different culture. They learned the language and customs, to serve the ordinary people. As Americans living in a Chinese environment, they adjusted every bit of their life, unavoidably affecting their own identity and self-perception. The second question was that of politics, their relations with the government, local religious and nonreligious groups. The third question was that of gender. In a conservative society, Maryknoll Sisters learned to handle sexual biases and fought for recognition. At the same time, they hoped to present a different image of women through their service to the community. They introduced more positive values of women in their education and social work. Through the years, the Sisters grew and changed with the local people.

There has been a rising awareness for women missionaries in China. Missionary work allowed single women to lead a professional life independent of their families, and wives to develop meaningful work apart from their domestic responsibilities, as in the case of Protestant women at the turn of the century. Jane Hunter's *The Gospel of Gentility* is a readable account of women missionaries in China. According to

Hunter, "Single women came to discover social autonomy in shared spinsterhood, while married women struggled to balance their missionary vocation with maternal responsibilities."[29] Patricia R. Hill's *The World Their Household* studies American women's missionary movement overseas from 1870 to 1920. In the late nineteenth century, women societies attracted a huge influx of applicants, who filled their minds with romanticism for mission abroad. As Hill points out, the women's boards allowed for development of a separate mission and the expansion of the outlook of the members.[30] In *Educating the Women of Hainan*, Kathleen Lodwick describes the cultural transformation of a Presbyterian-sponsored missionary to Hainan Province from World War I to the outbreak of the Pacific War. The woman received a splendid education in the Chinese language and culture. Her letters showed her absorption into the local society, as well as her adventurous attitude and professional orientation.[31] Maria Cristina Zaccarini even argues in *The Sino-American Friendship as Tradition and Challenge* that missionary women challenged traditional male authority by assuming key roles in foreign fields.[32]

In *American Women in Mission*, Dana L. Robert describes the evolution of the roles of American missionary women, from Protestant wives and teachers in the early nineteenth century to the emergence of missionary Sisters in the early twentieth century.[33] Catholic nuns are also the research topic for others.[34] In *Havoc in Hunan*, Mary Carita Pendergast, who had served in Hunan, writes about American Sisters of Charity there from 1924 to 1951.[35] In her article, Sue Bradshaw studies the work of four American congregations, including Maryknoll Sisters, out of the total number of twenty-five in China in the years between the two world wars. According to Bradshaw, the nuns contributed to an effort to raise the status of local women, and in her other article, she argues that American Sisters developed native women congregations, which assumed an independent and leading role in the Chinese Catholic Church.[36] The missionary days abroad opened women to more opportunities, new perspectives, and independent decision-making possibilities.

Such was true of Maryknoll Sisters, who belonged to a young congregation, more willing to venture into different areas, to get rid of excessive formalities and to reach out to society. The argument was particularly applicable to this single-gender group in Hong Kong, a place with mounting demands. As a community of women only, the Sisters had freedom to move into "open fields" of education and social service in Hong Kong, to make use of their expertise, and to realize their own potential. They became a force in society, and shouldered their responsibilities as capable individuals. Within their community, the nuns had chances to prove themselves and to take up any openings without sexual biases. When asked whether "Maryknoll offered American Catholic women at that time, an opportunity to be professional persons and to be of service distinctly as a woman long before the emphasis was put on that by women's liberation," a Sister readily agreed.[37]

Revealing the Social History of Hong Kong

Maryknoll Sisters were socially active. As social activists, they were in the forefront of service to society. Their work fell into three main areas—education, social services, and welfare. This book describes the philosophy of education of the Maryknoll

Sisters and the achievement of their schools. After their arrival in Hong Kong, they concentrated on education. Maryknoll Convent School and Holy Spirit School (later known as Maryknoll School/Maryknoll Sisters School) were among the first grant-in-aid schools, which received government recognition for their high standards. Also, both were among the earliest schools to offer respectable education for women. Subsequently, in the 1950s and 1960s relief and service became another dimension of their work. As missioners of the poor, Maryknoll Sisters spearheaded efforts for poor refugee communities. They traveled the hillsides of wooden shacks and cared for the needy. In 1952, the Sisters established a social welfare center in the resettlement area of King's Park. It was a pioneering project to relieve problems related to postwar housing, sickness, and employment. They also facilitated the construction of fireproof stone cottages for the homeless in King's Park and Tung Tau Tsuen. In order to promote social welfare, the Sisters set up youth centers, clinics, and a hospital, and served in squatter areas, resettlement estates, and working-class neighborhoods. In the 1960s and 1970s, they helped train local social workers. Today, their service continues for those in need.

Further, this book contributes to a more sophisticated approach to Hong Kong history. The revisionist theory describes "the complexity of British colonial rule" on the one hand, and people as "active agents of Hong Kong's history" on the other hand.[38] It negates orthodox interpretation that the colonial government was always benevolent and people were by nature submissive. The traditional wisdom, that government interference was only minimal and the society was by and large hard-working but apathetic, has been put to the test. As Tak-Wing Ngo points out, the nature of British colonial rule was complicated and Chinese society was far from homogenous. The relationship between ruler and ruled, in fact, differed at different times. Ngo argues that the government used many ways to maintain its rule. Sometimes it was "benevolent," other times it was "manipulative," and occasionally it could be "oppressive." At the same time, "social cleavages did exist and were manifested in various forms."[39] The government tried to "manage and accommodate" conflicts by playing one group against another in society. The influence of the administration was "far more penetrating," not only confined to the common understanding of the close connections with big business.

While the colonial government could be benevolent, manipulative as well as oppressive, this book adds a fourth dimension to its rule, that of being incompetent at times. In the early twentieth century, it relied on foreign religious groups to provide education for the needy. After the Communist takeover of China in 1949, Hong Kong experienced a flood of refugees from the mainland. There were shortages of food, housing, medical care, schools, and jobs. Unlike what the government originally thought, newcomers did not leave, but stayed in Hong Kong and set up new homes there. The government was too ready to support foreign missionaries, to cater to the all-encompassing needs of the rapidly growing population. As this book shows, the colonial administration was often incompetent and social anxieties were evident. In the state of extreme poverty, the refugee community required immediate attention. The foreign religious groups took up the tasks that should have been government responsibilities, offering whatever assistance was possible to the poor and the needy.

While scholars talk about the relationship between ruler and ruled, there was "another force" present in society. The "first force" was the government, whose ultimate objective was to maintain order and stability in the colony. Under colonial administration, Hong Kong people were the "second force" and were concerned about their own livelihood. Like other foreign missionaries, Maryknoll Sisters played the role of a "third force," providing service to people and preventing the escalation of social tensions. The third force was independent of the government, but had cooperation of the latter. As foreigners, they assumed a different identity from the Chinese population, but at the same time were equally sensitive to the pressing needs of society. They made available opportunities of education, social welfare, and service to the poor. The Sisters did not have political power, but they shared government responsibilities. They were obviously a minority in society, but unlike foreign expatriates in the government and in companies, they lived and worked with ordinary people. They provided professional expertise without asking for financial rewards. Maryknoll Sisters shouldered tasks that were government responsibilities, and resolved inherent social tensions. Not only does this book study the objectives and work of Maryknoll Sisters, it also examines their relations with other communities and the responses of the government and people. It aims to show that the nuns were successful in relief, services, and welfare activities, contributing their part to ensure the stability of the local administration and for resolution of conflicts in society.

The social history of Hong Kong concerned the identity of its people. Society was far from being homogeneous. Social tensions were rampant, as elaborated in Chan Wai Kwan's *The Making of Hong Kong Society*, which reveals contradictions between merchants and laborers.[40] Other works also emphasize a closer look at development of the local community. They pay particular attention to the contribution of the various sectors of society. They include Wong Siu-Lun's *Emigrant Entrepreneurs*, Carl T. Smith's *A Sense of History*, Wang Gangwu's edited volumes of *Xianggangshi xinbian (Hong Kong History: New Perspectives)*, Jung-fang Tsai's *Hong Kong in Chinese History* and the subsequent expanded Chinese version, *Xianggangren zhi Xianggangshi 1841–1945 (The Hong Kong People's History of Hong Kong)*, and the edited book of Lau Yee-cheung and Wong Man-kong, *Xianggang shehui yu wenhuashi lunji (Studies in the Social and Cultural History of Hong Kong)*.[41] At the same time while Hong Kong was under colonial rule, contrasting political opinions and forces were present. Taking on different profiles at different times, historians point out, leftists had their supporters in the colony and their activities could be traced back to pre–World War II years.[42]

In the 1950s and 1960s, there were floods of refugees from mainland China. The newcomers regarded Hong Kong as their temporary place of residence. Since many of them arrived almost empty-handed with only a bundle of clothes, they started their life from nothing. Working as hard as they could, they tried to gain the most within the shortest time. While Hong Kong retained its precarious colonial status after the world war, people were in "a borrowed place in a borrowed time." Huge Baker describes society as living "life in the short term," very often with the hope of "getting rich quick."[43] As other works depict, people were industrious and were willing to seize whatever opportunities were available to them.[44]

Although the huge majority of the Hong Kong population were ethnic Chinese, foreigners played a role in shaping local history. Foreign influence also penetrated the lower strata of society. As Nicole Constable explains in *Christian Souls and Chinese Spirits*, a sub-ethnic minority was converted, and maintained an identity as both Hakka and Christian, different from that of the materialistic Cantonese.[45] In the process, there was accommodation of Christian beliefs to local customs and culture. In *Hong Kong Remembers*, edited by Sally Blyth and Ian Wotherspoon, thirty-one people, foreigners and Chinese, retell their stories in the British colony.[46] From all walks of life, they include administrators, social activists, businessmen, journalists, and a Maryknoll nun. Expatriates, who were in Hong Kong for many years, write their personal accounts of people they met and places they visited.[47] At the same time, there are studies on the foreign communities in Hong Kong;[48] these studies concern not only Western communities but also other ethnic minorities.[49] Within Chinese society, and the once immigrant community, there were cultural diversities and exchanges. Identity was a mixed one, fundamentally Chinese but infused by the foreign presence. As Gordon Mathews argues, Hong Kong Chinese embraced their "Chineseness" as well as Western education, political, social, and economic values.[50]

The relationship between ruler and ruled had many dimensions. Colonial rule was complicated. For a long time in Hong Kong history, there was a collaborative relationship between Chinese businessmen and colonial administration, both aiming to make the place a commercial center. As John M. Carroll elaborates, mutual interests existed.[51] From this perspective, government and business could be "active agents" in society. Scholars even argue that government was conscious of the needs for social welfare in the early twentieth century, though they disagreed among themselves on the extent of government intervention.[52] Debates were from minimal government involvement to active social relief. Within the confines of its ability, colonial administration was interventionist, very different from the conventional image of playing a minimal role in the economy. In *The Shek Kip Mei Syndrome* by M. Castells, L. Goh, and R. Y.-W. Kwok, the authors argue that, Hong Kong was not a laissez faire model as commonly asserted and there was government intervention in postwar public housing.[53] While some scholars focus on interventionist policies, others recognize that the colonial government could be chaotic in its policymaking and was in some circumstances powerless in solving crises.[54] While colonial rule was sometimes active and interventionist, it could be hesitant and powerless as well.

This book is the first in-depth study of the adaptation and contribution of Maryknoll Sisters in Hong Kong. Maryknoll Sisters were in Hong Kong for so long that their story provides much insight into local society. There are very few works that focus on Maryknoll men and women in Hong Kong, and of these, two unpublished papers written by missioners themselves examine the contribution of the Sisters.[55] As a historical account, this book hopes to fill an important gap in the literature of Hong Kong history. It reveals the significance of the contribution of Maryknoll Sisters, who not only provided relief for the poor but also helped people to improve themselves and to secure a respectful status in society. They were not satisfied with piecemeal measures. They aimed not only at remedial measures but also sought to establish social awareness and progress. Through the establishment of service and welfare centers, clinics, nurseries, schools, and cottage industries, they provided material and emotional support for the needy. Service for the poor is an apt description of their work throughout the years. This book should be of interest to scholars, social workers, and government administrators, who try to find solutions to the current problems of Hong Kong society.

The History of Maryknoll

The foreign mission of Maryknoll Sisters has been the topic of some research works. In her doctoral dissertation "First Choice: Mission," Maryknoll Sister Joan Chatfield puts forth a sociological analysis of personnel deployment from the perspective of both the congregation administrators and individual members.[56] Maryknoll was the first American congregation founded with the purpose of conducting mission work abroad. Since the sending of its first overseas missioners, who arrived in Hong Kong in 1921, the nuns worked in Asia, Africa, Latin America, Eastern Europe, and the Central Pacific. After World War II, there were astonishing numbers of applicants and intakes, which reflected the surmounting fervor for religious life and service. By the mid-1960s, Maryknoll Sisters reached the peak of its membership at over 1,660. In the 1970s they numbered about 1,000–1,200.[57] Looking into the congregational documents, Sister Joan denies that a plan or plans for personnel deployment existed within the administration. However, feedback from her questionnaires to individual nuns revealed that a predominant number of them chose *mission* as their lifetime work when they entered Maryknoll. As Chatfield says: "It became clear that the women who chose Maryknoll chose mission." While members of other congregations considered religious life their principal reason for becoming nuns, Maryknollers saw that "being a religious was a conditional aspect of their life." Therefore, they were willing to accept "the additional factors which were constitutive to being a nun" since "going to the missions, having a part in the entire missionary enterprise" was "their first choice."[58]

Recently, Penny Lernoux's *Hearts on Fire* was written with the collaboration of Maryknoll Sisters. It aims at a larger readership, not only religious and academics, and describes the lives of the Sisters worldwide. An award-winning journalist, Lernoux traveled to all the mission places but died before completing the book. The final product includes the work of others, and is an illuminating survey of Maryknoll's changing outlook, organization, and purposes—from an initially America-centered perspective to becoming highly critical of U.S. world policy; from a close adherence to rules and senior leadership to a democratic representation of their members; and from seeking to convert "pagans" to emphasizing service for the poor. Lernoux conveys a distinct impression of the independent character of these American women, unbound by gender restrictions of their society and times. As she writes: "they discovered that the real objective of their often perilous journeys was not to change the world, or even a small portion of it, but to go beyond themselves and do something important in life."[59]

There were books written by Maryknollers about their general history. Many of them were widely read after the world war, especially those written by the famous Sister-writer Maria del Rey Danforth. Sister Maria del Rey's portrayal of fun-loving and fearless nuns going off for overseas mission was a reason explaining the numerous applications to Maryknoll in the 1950s and early 1960s. A prolific writer, her books were all bestsellers. Some of her works covered the early China mission, such as *Pacific Hopscotch, Safari by Jet: Through Africa and Asia*, and *No Two Alike: Those Maryknoll Sisters!*[60] In addition, Sister Jeanne Marie Lyons' *Maryknoll's First Lady* and Sister Camilla Kennedy's *To the Uttermost Parts of the Earth* studied the founding lady of the Maryknoll Sisters.[61] To commemorate the work of the Sisters after their departure from China, Maryknollers produced a number of accounts on their stories in the mainland. The titles included Sister Maria del Rey's *Nun in Red China*, Sister M. Marcelline Grondin's *Sisters Carry the Gospel*, and Sister Mary Francis Louise Logan's *Maryknoll Sisters.*[62]

In its early years, China *was* the dream of Maryknoll, and until 1951, the most important mission area. Studies center on the theme that the mission offered Maryknoll Sisters and their local women trainees an independent and professional career in China. As Sue Bradshaw points out in her article, Maryknollers were the second group of American nuns in China. According to her, the formation of a novitiate for Chinese Sisters was their major work in the mainland.[63] The policy was to advise those who were interested in becoming nuns to enter the native congregations if available. Or else, Maryknoll Sisters worked toward the creation of such communities in the localities. This was what happened in the provinces of Guangdong and Guangxi. As Bradshaw elaborates, Chinese Sisters were expected to shoulder the same tasks as Maryknollers. Responsible for "direct ministry among the women and children," their training "was not confined to the cloister but was combined with practical field experience in the missions."[64] These included catechumenal work, assignments in hospitals, leprosaria, dispensaries, and orphanages, and visits to the sick and prisoners. Not only Maryknollers, but Chinese Sisters also enjoyed a status, higher than society commonly ascribed to women, in their religious career. Patricia Hughes Ponzi looks into "The Maryknoll Sisters in South China, 1920–1938," and believes that cultural experience was beneficial to an understanding between the Americans and Chinese.[65] In "Maryknoll in Manchuria, 1927–1947," Kathleen Kelly argues that Maryknoll placed strong emphases on the establishment of an indigenous Catholic Church and on training native religious personnel.[66] While they adapted to local culture and society, American Sisters used their own ways to develop the leadership qualities of the trainees. As a result, their mission maintained its unique characteristics and the local Church was able to survive turbulent years in the Northeast. Also, Mary Ann Schintz examined "the modernizing role" of Maryknoll Sisters in China and Hong Kong through secular and religious education, medical work, and social welfare services.[67] The Maryknoll Sisters were mainly involved in institutional tasks in "schools, novitiates, industrial workrooms, dispensaries, clinics, hospitals, orphanages, and asylums for the aged, physically handicapped, and lepers."[68]

Jean-Paul Wiest's *Maryknoll in China* is a very well-researched work on the Maryknoll mission in China.[69] It is a product of extensive as well as intensive archival research, and more importantly, the interviews of two hundred Maryknoll missioners who served in China and fifty-six Chinese Catholics. Wiest had the support of Maryknoll in his research. The Maryknoll Joint Advisory Board explained the objectives of the Maryknoll China History Project thus: "to seek to understand the past history of the mission work" and "as a guide for the future service of the two societies [the Fathers and Brothers and the Sisters]."[70] As Wiest points out, Maryknollers went to China for two purposes, evangelization and establishment of the native church. Evangelization involved education of local catechists, direct apostolate, and in the process providing social services. In order to train Chinese priests and nuns, Maryknoll also set up seminaries and novitiates in the various localities. According to Wiest, Maryknoll Sisters played a rather independent and active role, as opposed to the traditional image and reality of other women religious in those days, in two aspects, reaching out to people and converting them and preparing for future nuns in the novitiates. However, he devotes very little coverage to Hong Kong.

There are very few works entirely on the history of Maryknoll Sisters in Hong Kong. Sister Miriam Xavier Mug's "Maryknoll Sisters, Hong Kong-Macau Region" is an unpublished account of fifty-five pages kept at the Maryknoll Mission Archives in Maryknoll, New York. It is essentially a factual and ministry-oriented survey for keeping a record of the Hong Kong mission. In addition, the present author provides a scholarly outline of the Sisters' work in her article "From the Pursuit of Converts to the Relief of Refugees: The Maryknoll Sisters in Twentieth-Century Hong Kong." Another work focuses on both the Maryknoll men and women in Hong Kong— Father Peter Barry's paper on "Maryknoll in Hong Kong, 1918 to the Present."[71] As a recollection of days in the Stanley Internment Camp under Japanese occupation in the 1940s, Father James Smith and Father William Downs wrote "The Maryknoll Mission, Hong Kong 1941–1946."[72] Some descriptions throw light on the life of the Sisters who were also interned. The papers offer some guidance for further research and analyses. Though a little outdated, Bill Surface and Jim Hart's *Freedom Bridge*, published in the early 1960s, was an account of Maryknoll in Hong Kong.[73] It was mainly about Maryknoll Fathers, and occasionally touched upon Maryknoll Sisters.

Historical Material Used and Time Span of This Book

This book depends heavily on material kept at Maryknoll Mission Archives in Maryknoll, New York. The Archives have a wealth of information on the topic, most of which has not been explored by researchers. China was Maryknollers' first overseas mission, and Hong Kong was the first place where they settled after having traveled a long way from the United States. Renowned for their archival records, Maryknollers preserve Hong Kong material so well that it is possibly one of the best collections of their mission histories. The Archives still keep in excellent condition the letter from the Sisters to the New York Motherhouse, written in pencil on their first night in Hong Kong on November 3, 1921! This was the first letter of the Maryknoll Sisters from their first overseas mission house. The records are treasures not only to researchers of Maryknoll history, but also to those interested in the social developments of Hong Kong. This book makes use of archival material, most of which has not been studied before, such as South China Region (Hong Kong/Macau Region) records, Regional Correspondence (South China), Personal Narratives of World War II, Diaries, and Hong Kong Chronicles.

In addition, this book uses material kept at the Hong Kong Catholic Diocesan Archives, Hong Kong's Public Records Office, Hong Kong Collection of the University of Hong Kong Main Library, Archives on the History of Christianity in

China of Hong Kong Baptist University Library, and Map Library of Hong Kong Central Library. Besides archival research, it draws information from interviews with thirty-four Maryknoll Sisters who were engaged in various aspects of work in Hong Kong. Some of them are still in active service at the moment, while others were already retired during the interviews. Considering the many years of service with the local community, their oral history is an irreplaceable source of reference. Mission history and social development of Hong Kong were so intertwined that both stories become one in the telling of this book.

This book covers the history of the Sisters in Hong Kong from their first presence in the colony in 1921 to 1969, when a special chapter/meeting of the Maryknoll Congregation responded to decisions of Vatican Council II and made corresponding changes to the missionary objectives of the nuns. From 1969 onward, missioners were no longer required to engage in institutional tasks, but could take up positions outside the Maryknoll establishment, to provide service to local people. Moreover, evangelization/conversion was no longer seen as the primary objective of the missioners. Instead, they came to believe that their objective was to promote the well-being of individuals and to support their efforts to be better persons. In the second half of the 1960s, the nuns began to wear suits and simplified veils, and in 1969, they began wearing ordinary clothes. Instead of using their religious names (given to them when they began their novitiate), they could choose to return to their baptismal names. At the turn of the 1970s, Hong Kong also entered another stage of development, as society became more well off and more confident of itself. It was more capable of taking care of its own needs, and became less reliant on foreign missioners for professional and social services. From 1969 onward, both Maryknoll and the local society moved into a new phase of history.

The present chapter explains the focus and analytical framework of this book, and at the same time, draws lessons from related literature in explaining the historical context of the study. It also traces the history of the Maryknoll Congregation and the sending of the first group of nuns to Hong Kong. Chapter two describes the early years of Maryknoll Sisters in Hong Kong from 1921 to 1937. It explains how the women decided to establish themselves as a community in the colony, and how education turned out to be the major component of their work. Focusing on 1937 to 1951, chapter three describes difficulties during the Japanese takeover and subsequently, tremendous effort in rebuilding the mission after the world war. It makes use of the personal narratives of the nuns, and reveals life at the Stanley Internment Camp during the Japanese occupation of Hong Kong. In the 1950s Maryknoll Sisters expanded the scope of their work, and provided relief and social service to refugee communities of Hong Kong. This is the theme of chapter four, which examines housing and welfare projects in King's Park, Homantin, and Tung Tau Tsuen. Chapter five traces the origins of the Sisters' work in Chai Wan in the 1950s, and describes the general livelihood of refugee families there. The following two chapters focus on the 1960s. Chapter six describes the establishment of Our Lady of Maryknoll Hospital in Wong Tai Sin and its subsequent development. Chapter seven continues the Chai Wan story, and introduces Maryknoll's work in Kwun Tong and its long-term social service program in the 1960s. Finally, chapter eight highlights the evolutionary aspect of the objectives and work of the nuns, and provides an evaluation of the Maryknoll mission in Hong Kong.

Birth of the Maryknoll Mission

Maryknoll was born in the 1910s when the American Catholic Church had grown to maturity and was able to accept greater responsibilities overseas. Starting June 1908, the United States was no longer considered mission territory by Rome. In the next decade, Maryknoll founders looked for a "foundation for foreign missions," a national movement to "enkindle the mission spirit" among American Catholics.[74] They soon became leaders of the cause. In the nineteenth century, American Catholics began to notice the demands of overseas missions,[75] and responded to the calls of Rome, which in 1841 asked for assistance from American bishops for the mission in Liberia. In 1860 when the same request was made for Bahamas, religious men and women from the United States took up the tasks. Also, congregations with European heritage heeded their superiors general/major superiors, and sent missioners abroad. For example, Passionist Fathers started their work in Mexico City in the 1860s, and in Buenos Aires and other places in the 1880s. When the Franciscan Sisters of Allegany, New York, headed for Jamaica in 1879, they became the first community of nuns founded in the United States to assign women overseas. In the 1890s the Jesuits and the Sisters of the Holy Family began their service in British Honduras. So far, the idea of spreading Christian faith in foreign lands had attracted some attention. Nevertheless, the American Catholic missionary effort was still passive and infrequent.

Unlike Protestants, Catholics could not find any groups to join in the United States if they wanted to preach abroad. While American Catholics worked overseas before the 1900s, there was not even one religious congregation that was committed to a foreign mission program. This was the case before the founding of Maryknoll in the 1910s. The director of the Boston branch of the Society for the Propagation of the Faith, Father James Anthony Walsh, felt the need to educate Americans about missionary service abroad.[76] To serve the purpose, he launched the first issue of the magazine *The Field Afar* in January 1907. Father Walsh had become the spokesperson for foreign missions. He was the authority whom anyone interested in the subject should approach. It was under such circumstances that Mary Josephine (Mollie) Rogers, who was then a demonstrator in the Zoology Department at Smith College, visited him in December 1906. At that time, Father Walsh was proofreading essays for *The Field Afar*, which was soon to be published. Many more meetings resulted from their first encounter. In the following years, she contributed to the magazine and was involved in its publication.

Mollie Rogers was Irish, born in Roxbury, a suburb of Boston, on October 27, 1882. She studied in Boston's public schools, and furthered her education at Smith College, which was a famous women's college in Northampton.[77] Majoring in Zoology, Rogers obtained her university degree in June 1905. Hoping to secure some working experience for possible graduate studies, she began work as a Zoology demonstrator when the academic year began in 1906.[78] With a position at college,

Rogers felt secure. However, an incident "was to change her life forever," and she was haunted with queries afterward:

> One day, a group of students came knocking at her door.
> Girls: Hi, Mollie! We've come to sign you up for one of the mission study classes. Which one would you like to join? Come with us. Join us. We have a wonderful class on mission study. There's a wonderful plan for us. If we do well in these classes, some of us will be sent out to fields afar. Next September some of us will leave for China. ...
> Mollie: I'd love to, but I'm afraid I can't join you just now. I'm a Catholic. So I'll have to join the Catholic group.
> Girls: Mollie, there isn't any. But you would be welcome at any of the others, so if you'd like to join one.
> Mollie: Thanks, that's very kind of you, but I'm afraid I have to decline.[79]

The absence of study groups among Catholic students was an issue among the faculty at Smith as well. The advisor of the College Association for Christian Work proposed that Rogers arrange a mission study class so that Catholic girls had "some kind of religious organization, activity" like "every other group."[80] Upon the suggestion of her pastor, Rogers wrote to Father Walsh for information about preparation of missioners, mission orders, overseas missions, and sources of funding. She received an encouraging reply from him, which led to her visit at his Boston office. On that occasion, both were impressed with the other. Rogers then proceeded with the planning of her class. In October 1907, *The Field Afar* introduced her program as a guide for other Catholic study groups.[81]

Father Walsh and Father Thomas Frederick Price obtained approval from the American Church authority for a foreign mission seminary in April 1911, seven months after the two men decided to combine efforts toward the goal. In June they secured authorization in Rome, and the Catholic Foreign Mission Society of America came into being. Originally, Walsh and Price wanted to establish a society for secular priests for foreign mission, later, they decided to include also Brothers.[82] The year 1911 marked the beginning of the commonly known Maryknoll Fathers and Brothers. Jean-Paul Wiest explains the origins of the name Maryknoll—"Father Walsh had vacationed in a beautiful resort in New Hampshire called 'The Knolls.' This designation was combined with Father Price's profound devotion for Our Lady, and 'Maryknoll' became the name of the large farm on Sunset Hill in Ossining that they purchased to launch their missionary enterprise."[83] In fall 1912 Walsh and Price set up the seminary in Maryknoll, on the hill in Ossining along Hudson River. Before moving there, they located temporary offices of the Society and *The Field Afar* in Hawthorne, New York. In a small rented cottage in Hawthorne, Mary Louise Wholean, Mary Dwyer, and Sara Sullivan celebrated their new start. Their feast on January 6, 1912 began the story of future Maryknoll Sisters. Together with Nora Shea, who later joined them, they volunteered to be "secretaries" for the magazine. Having received help for her family's financial difficulties, Rogers brought Margaret Shea along with her to Hawthorne in September. Shortly afterward, the priests and students moved to Maryknoll.

The property, now named Maryknoll, was "fifty-two acres of farmland with several colonial-style houses."[84] The secretaries occupied one of the houses on

October 15, 1912, on the feast of St. Teresa of Avila. Their place became known as St. Teresa's Lodge and they themselves the Teresians. The lodge had twenty-two rooms and was a few hundred feet away from the seminary house.[85] Besides secretaries in Hawthorne, there was a newcomer Anna Towle, making a total of seven women in St. Teresa's. Except Dwyer, they were to be the first Maryknoll Sisters. When we read Maryknoll history, we are bound to come across their picture, with Wholean, Towle, Rogers, and Sullivan sitting in the front row, Dwyer and the two Sheas (not related) standing behind. Although they aspired to be religious women, they did not have "any real knowledge of religious life." Occupied with the establishment of the seminary, Father Walsh did not have "the experience or the time to direct such a formation of a religious order of women missioners."[86] From 1914 to 1916, the Teresians received training from the Immaculate Heart of Mary Sisters of Scranton, Pennsylvania. Rogers had been known by her religious name, Mary Joseph, and acted as directress of the Teresians.[87] Some others joined the group later.

The Teresians decided to follow the Dominican Constitutions. Between 1916 and 1920, they petitioned thrice for authorization to become a religious congregation. To the Roman Catholic Church, the idea of sending women missioners abroad required careful consideration. The United States had just ceased to be its mission territory in 1908, and Maryknoll was still young. The first petition was unsuccessful, and Rome only recognized the Teresians as a Pious Society without vows in January 1917.[88] A year later, the second petition failed on the ground that the nature of the mission work and the sources of funding were not well laid out.[89] In 1918 the Maryknoll Fathers started their first overseas mission in Yangjiang in Guangdong Province, China. Father Walsh then wrote to the Society of the Propagation of the Faith in Rome, saying that his missioners needed women helpers. His concern was that the mission in China "awaited the Teresians who were held fast by Rome and unable to move."[90] Finally, in early 1920 Rome gave its approval to the Foreign Mission Sisters of St. Dominic. They were to be commonly known as Maryknoll Sisters. That year, almost sixty women entered as postulants. In a small chapel at St. Teresa's, twenty-three women attended the first profession ceremony in February 1921. Among them was Rogers, who then became Mother Mary Joseph, Mother General of the community. In August 1921, another group of novices professed their vows.

For the first time in American Catholic history, a congregation of Sisters committed themselves entirely to service abroad. As Teresians, they had emphasized their religious life and the spirit of prayer; and as Dominicans, they sought for equilibrium between contemplation and missionary activities.[91] Maryknollers were the only community of nuns in the United States founded for foreign mission. As Americans they differed from their European counterparts by their atmosphere of flexibility, individualism, equality, and openness to Protestantism and the lay people.[92] Often, they referred to the "Maryknoll Spirit" as the guiding philosophy. Some years later, Mother Mary Joseph reflected on the Maryknoll mission. She said the Sisters should maintain an "apostolic spirit"—"As one lamp lights another nor grows less, so nobleness enkindleth nobleness."[93] It was "a foreign mission spirit." She described: "Each one of us, in her own work, with her own particular little sweetness or attractiveness, is to be used by God as a particular tool to do particular work and to save particular souls."[94] In those days, the Sisters were to "seek those lost sheep of the fold." They spoke of looking for the pagans and converting them to Christianity. Such were the missionary perspectives before Vatican Council II of the 1960s. At the same time, Mother Mary Joseph stressed the importance of adaptability in foreign places. She explained: "Train yourself to go up or down, in or out, with this person or that, in any work whatsoever, and to accept these changes readily, easily and quickly."[95]

After the General Chapter in 1925, the *Tentative Constitutions of the Foreign Mission Sisters of St. Dominic (Third Order), Congregation of the Immaculate Conception* was in use. Drafted in 1917 and later revised, it was the first constitution of the Maryknoll Sisters. The first chapter denotes the "nature and end of the Congregation," which "was instituted especially for the sanctification of its members and the salvation of souls." The Sisters should always "have this double object in mind and endeavor"—the "chief and essential object" was their "personal sanctification"; and the "secondary or special object" was "the cooperation with the work" of the Maryknoll Fathers and Brothers and other foreign mission groups "for the conversion of pagans in heathen lands."[96] Founded for foreign mission work, the Congregation asked that all Sisters be ready "to go out to any missions in heathen countries" to which they were assigned. They should be aware of the significance of their mission, and assumed "very great prudence with regard to their conduct during the voyage." The reason was: "Their behavior will be closely observed, both by those who are disposed to be friendly to them and those who will be glad to see in some defect in their actions, a matter of reproach to the Catholic Church or to the Religious state."[97]

The Congregation had strict requirements for its Sisters. Before being admitted into the community as a postulant, an applicant must satisfy the close enquiries regarding her family, her personal history, as well as her physical and psychological well-being.[98] She had to present documents on these matters. Later on, a postulant was tested on her knowledge of Christian doctrine, her faith, and her intentions. If she passed, she received her habit and religious name while keeping her family and baptismal names. She became a novice, wore the habit, and began her novitiate. Before profession, the novice must understand her obligations.[99] Profession comprised the three vows of poverty, chastity, and obedience. As the Constitutions explained: "The novices make these three vows at first for one year, at the expiration of which the professed, if they are deemed worthy, may renew without delay, for two successive years, these annual vows, after which they make their vows for a period of three years."[100] The temporary vows lasted for six years, after which she made her final profession of vows according to the Constitutions. Every profession was a "public act" performed in the presence of other Sisters.[101] As their chief objective, the Sisters sought "personal sanctification" through adherence to the three vows of religion and the Constitutions.[102]

After authorization in 1920, Maryknoll Sisters established their first mission houses in the Japanese communities in Los Angeles and Seattle. On September 12, 1921 their first departure ceremony took place—for the first time American Sisters embarked on a foreign mission under the patronage of an American congregation.[103] China was the dream of Maryknoll Sisters, as they thought that the country did not have many missioners.[104] Their dream came true that day, as the pioneering group of six Sisters ascended the altar, repeated the vows they earlier took, and received the crucifixes, which signified their willingness to commit to foreign mission work. They were Sisters Mary Paul McKenna, Mary Lawrence Foley, Mary Barbara Froehlich, Mary Rose Leifels, Mary Monica Moffat, and Mary Imelda Sheridan. In November they reached Hong Kong, which they considered only a point of transit. They were supposed to go to Yangjiang, where the Maryknoll Fathers had already started the mission, to work with Chinese women there. China was *the* destination, promising much excitement. In those days, Catholic and Protestant missionaries alike believed that China was an open ground for evangelization. Beyond the original anticipation of pioneers, the colony of Hong Kong, which the British took from China, turned out to be "a permanent part" of the Maryknoll mission.[105] The year 1921 began the history of these American nuns there.

CHAPTER TWO

EARLY ARRIVAL, 1921–1937

Every one is eager to do what is right and all are surely earnest in keeping the Rule. We are thrown much among ourselves with few distractions beyond mail from the home land and it is bringing out the best in each. We are happy and our recreations are gay. It seems to me to be a year of special grace—we are removed from the world and we have time to think of our meditations and our resolutions—and it is doing us good.
Sister Mary Paul McKenna, 19 Chatham Road, February 1, 1922[1]

In 1921 the pioneering group of Maryknoll Sisters embarked on their foreign mission. Arriving in Hong Kong, they established the first overseas house of Maryknoll Sisters. Everything was unforeseen and unknown to them. There was so much unexpected from the people and surroundings that it almost resembled a so-called "reincarnation experience." Even the faces of foreigners looked unfamiliar, as they were mostly Europeans. Americans and Catholics were supposed to be two different groups in the colony. The common thinking was that Americans were Protestants and Europeans were Catholics. The Maryknollers were the first community of American nuns to appear on the scene. They did not speak Cantonese and were ignorant of Chinese culture. Besides cultural differences, they struggled with the greatest and most immediate problem, how to support themselves. In contrast to the impression of the local people that Americans were rich, the Sisters were not. To survive, they started an industrial department and gave lessons to children in their convent. However, they suffered a setback as their American background prevented them from taking up positions in a hospital. They made a successful start in education though; and coincidentally, the Catholic Church was opening up a new parish and looking for somebody to set up a school nearby to correspond with the development. Maryknoll Sisters were the obvious choice, and eventually, they moved Maryknoll Convent School to its permanent location in Kowloon Tong. Education turned out to be their major endeavor.

The Maryknoll mission in Hong Kong was not pre-planned, and the way in which it came into being was a response to local needs and circumstances. Originally, the nuns regarded Hong Kong as a point of transit. The pioneering group thought of Yangjiang, Guangdong Province, as their final destination. However, the need to study the Chinese language and culture before moving to China became too apparent. They decided to stay in Hong Kong for mission preparation, and as a result, had to find means to support themselves. Later on, they had an extra concern. With the opening of the house in Yangjiang, the colony became useful as an outpost for those in China. They believed there would be more mission areas in future. With the responsibility of servicing the interior, the Hong Kong house became important not only as a resting place for travelers, but as a permanent part of the China mission. Missioners always considered Hong Kong a part of their mission in China, despite the fact that it was a British colony. Its close vicinity to the interior merited special attention. Only after many trials and errors would the Maryknoll Sisters establish their foothold in Hong Kong. By the 1930s, they had made their name in education, winning the respect and trust of society. They were a group of well-qualified teachers, recognized as energetic and devoted to their tasks. While Maryknoll Sisters embarked on their journey to China for the purpose of converting people to Christianity, some of them settled in Hong Kong, and evangelization was but one of their goals in the mission. As professionals, they acquired a status higher than what was commonly ascribed to women.

First Year in Hong Kong

In June 1921 Maryknoll Sisters assigned their pioneers to China. Foreign mission was their dream; and they waited eagerly "in prayerful hope" when Father Superior James Anthony Walsh read out the names of six of them in the small chapel of the Sisters' Motherhouse.[2] They were Mary Paul McKenna, Mary Lawrence Foley, Mary Barbara Froehlich, Mary Rose Leifels, Mary Monica Moffat, and Mary Imelda Sheridan. Two of them were already professed; the other four were novices and were soon to take their first vows. Nine years had passed since the women volunteered to be secretaries for *The Field Afar*, and finally they realized the very reason for their founding. They were excited and enthusiastic about the endeavor. In August the four novices professed their vows. Almost a month later, on September 12 the pioneers departed for the faraway land. "Friends came from far and near" on this important day, "to be present at the first departure of the Maryknoll Sisters to foreign shores."[3] The missioners left without thinking of returning and the Congregation did not yet have any plans for future home visits.[4] The date marked a bold attempt of the women, who made a lifelong commitment to mission in China.

A friend of Maryknoll, a priest, went with the group to the stopover at St. Paul, Minnesota. The Sisters were joined by the father superior and other priests.[5] In October they reached Japan and were ashore for two days, enjoying the company of Japanese and French acquaintances, who met them at the dock. They went to two Catholic schools as well as the Shinto shrines—an exploration of a mixed nature that was to prepare them for their days ahead. Later they stopped at Shanghai, where they visited two communities of nuns and saw the developments of the Catholic Church. They also got to know the Christian leader, Lu Bohong (Lo Pa Hong in the original documents), who gave them an introduction to Chinese culture. On this occasion, the Sisters learned about "the deep inner refinement," which they later believed explained the industriousness so characteristic of Chinese people.[6] Their last stopover before Hong Kong was Manila. On November 3, five priests welcomed them at the Kowloon Wharf. At last, they had arrived in the British colony.

Originally, the Sisters planned to join the mission of Maryknoll Fathers in Yangjiang, Guangdong Province. They would work for the evangelization of Chinese women; and for them, China was *the* place to go, a "wonderful adventure."[7] Therefore, they assumed that their residence in Hong Kong was temporary and that they would soon leave. They did not plan "to be established there as a community."[8] As events turned out, however, Maryknoll Sisters were to begin a mission in the colony. On the southeast coast of mainland China, Hong Kong, the island itself, was ceded to the British after the Opium War in 1842; Kowloon Peninsula was ceded in 1860, and New Territories (also covering the remainder of the peninsula, which gradually became known as New Kowloon) were leased for ninety-nine years in 1898. The colony emerged as an important port of Chinese–foreign trade. Hong Kong was rather rugged with ridges of hills, and people usually settled on the low lands around Victoria Harbor and near the tip of the peninsula. In 1921 trade was in a "depressed state" and improvement in sale of rice was short-lived.[9] Nevertheless, the development of the Kowloon Peninsula had gone on quite well, with the construction of more buildings, reclamation on the harbor front, and leveling of hillsides. In the census of April 1921, the Chinese population was 610,368 and the non-Chinese 14,798, adding to a figure of 625,166.[10] By mid-year, the number of people living in Kowloon and New Kowloon was about 120,000.[11]

The nuns stayed in a five-room cottage that Maryknoll Fathers had rented. Adjacent to Rosary Church and the Italian Canossian Sisters' convent and school, the location was 19 Chatham Road, Kowloon (see figure 2.1). It overlooked the Victoria Harbor and the Canton Railroad tracks; as Sister Mary Paul described— "It is a red brick house, of two stories, a little weather-beaten because it faces the sea and this is a typhoon country."[12] As a Vicariate Apostolic, Hong Kong was under the jurisdiction of priests from the Seminary for Foreign Missions in Milan (which in 1926 became the Pontifical Institute for Foreign Missions, P.I.M.E.).[13] Rosary Parish was under an Italian pastor. The Maryknoll Fathers tried hard to find suitable accommodations, as there was a shortage of houses, and they had to buy furniture as well. The furnishings reflected the fact that the French previously occupied the cottage. In the reception room, there were white enamel chairs with canary colored upholstery. As Sister Mary Paul still remembered so vividly many decades later—"The rug on the floor was pink with blue roses on one side and blue with pink roses on the reverse."[14] There were many mirrors on the corridor walls. Enough for only six people, the dining room was decorated with wallpaper of pink and gray stripes and with a horizontal band of flying birds around the ceiling. On the second floor, there were three bedrooms; beds and mosquito nets took up much space. The nun said, "We never forgot that house." Indeed, it was their first experience of long-term residence overseas.

Sister Mary Paul was the leader of the group. From an Irish family in Reading, Pennsylvania, she finished her studies at Reading High School and Reading Normal School. She had been a headmistress. Having entered Maryknoll in 1917 she was professed four years later; she was thirty-three when she arrived in Hong Kong. As the other members of the group remembered, she had been the most outstanding in the Maryknoll Motherhouse and had been the postulant mistress.[15] With a strong and commanding character, she was the unquestionable choice to lead the pioneers. None dared to ignore her orders. She did not falter, not before the Sisters, the bishops, or anybody. Nevertheless, the early days required quite a bit of adaptation from anybody.

Figure 2.1 The Maryknoll Sisters on their day of arrival in Hong Kong on November 3, 1921 in front of Rosary Church, Kowloon. The front row, left to right, Sisters Mary Paul McKenna, Mary Rose Leifels, and Mary Lawrence Foley; the back row, left to right, Sisters Mary Barbara Froehlich, Mary Imelda Sheridan, and Mary Monica Moffat. Also present were Father James Anthony Walsh (next to Sister Mary Paul), Maryknoll men, other priests and people in Hong Kong.

Source: Sisters Photo Collection, Maryknoll Mission Archives.

On their first night, Mary Paul wrote to Mother Mary Joseph.[16] Written in pencil, this letter from the first overseas mission house of the Maryknoll Sisters read:

> Foundation Day (underlined)
> Nov. 3, 1921 (underlined)

My own dear Mother,

Greetings from our Convent home! This is our first night and we are sharing our recreation with our dear sisters at Maryknoll. They came in so easily and Sister Baptista's "weekly" added to the time after dinner when we gathered in the community room—the upper half of the refectory.

We have some elegant things—lovely little tables and carved Chinese cabinets. All is unlike so many other beginnings when Chinese houses were the first homes. There was a lovely letter here from the Providence Sisters at Honan [Henan] welcoming us to our new field.

We wish we were back home for a few moments and you would find some crucifixes and holy pictures among the missing after we ran back to our Kowloon homes. We have our Blessed Mother in the hall and the Sacred Heart upstairs and that is all.

Pray for your far-away Maryknollers. They will keep close to you.

> Your loving,
> Sister M. Paul

These paragraphs took up two pages, front and back, of a paper. The paper used was a bit smaller than the current letter pads, already with the heading "Convent of the Maryknoll Sisters—19 Chatham Road—Kowloon, Hongkong." This letter had two sheets; and on the third page of the second sheet, Mary Paul talked about "The Funnies on Chatham Road." She recounted:

> The Maryknoll Sisters have an "ahmah" Anna by name. She wears trousers, slippers without stockings, a pajama-suit coat, a crochet needle in the Grecian coil. Sister [Mary] Barbara is training her and Sister [Mary] Paul asked, "Does Anna understand you?" And bright Sister [Mary] Barbara said, "She misunderstands me."

The fourth page included a picture, which was entitled "wall paper in refectory." Flying birds marked the boundary of the wallpaper, and vertical stripes alternated in two different colors. Here, she drew one of the funnies in the house—a cockroach climbing on the wall—calling it "the species of bugs that travels around our Convent." The surroundings were so unfamiliar to the American nuns that the first letter included even the slightest detail.

On November 8, Sister Mary Paul wrote again and marked "Personal" on the front page.[17] She said, "We did not feel at home—poor lost children without a chapel." Very much unlike herself, she admitted her anxieties—"And, Mother, I was a baby and the tears came—not when anyone was around—when I saw the strange combination which was to be called a convent." As the superior, Mary Paul felt tremendous responsibilities. She expressed herself truly—"Pray for us, Mother, that we may not spoil this big work before us and it presents more problems than I ever dreamed and I foresaw many." The Sisters wanted to study Cantonese; otherwise it was impossible to communicate. Indeed, the first month was lonely and they lacked a sense of direction. The cottage stood facing the harbor, which separated Hong Kong Island from Kowloon Peninsula. It was near the tip of the Peninsula, and one of their activities was to walk along the waterfront "about three minutes' distance" away. They were homesick. As Mary Paul wrote two weeks later:

> It is good to be here but we miss every one of you. Poor Sister [Mary] Lawrence missed them hard last night but I think it was because the day brought no diversion. Today, I've given all the children some money and we are going to ferry over to Hong Kong and then see the sights. . . . I'm going to Happy Valley or up the Peak tram which is too steep for many.
> We found a place—King's Park—where we can play "Maryknoll Woods" and take our lunch. It is not so nice, of course, nor is there a St. Christopher's along the edge but it holds now what we hope to have for Christmas—a *contented* [underlined in the original letter] pine tree which we are going to dress up with—nothing and around which we'll sit and have our doughnuts and coffee after midnight Mass. Air castles!
> Dear Mother, we miss you and when you come next year we are going to keep and keep and keep you and I know you'll want to stay always because it's good to be here.[18]

King's Park where they went to picnic was to the north, and at that time was covered with trees and undergrowth.[19] The Sisters lived in a mostly Portuguese and Chinese area. The Chinese referred to them as "the six American Sisters" and looked at them "as curiosities."[20] In those days, the Chinese word for Sister(s) was *gou leung* (in Cantonese pronunciation) or *guniang* (in *pinyin*), which meant unmarried lady (or ladies).

Staying in the cottage, they decided to sell some of the furniture and use a room as the chapel. The convent was not proper without a chapel. Mary Paul asked the bishop for approval, but the initial reply was that they already had two people in one room and they had no space. Determined to get what she wanted, she said, "We won't mind going three in a room. We'd rather have a chapel."[21] Six of them squeezed into two bedrooms, and a room was available for the purpose. They made some adjustments and catered to the unusual circumstances:

> So we arranged that the room that had been a children's nursery [of the previous occupants], would be chapel. That room had been color-washed in preparation for our coming. Then one, wet, damp day, (and there were many wet, damp days) illustrations of nursery rhymes came out on the top of the chapel wall. There was Little Bo Beep, and there was Little Red Riding Hood.... We enjoyed it very much. We had matting on the floor and knelt on the floor. There was no altar, at first, no candle sticks, nothing.... But when we knew we had permission for the chapel we borrowed them from the church. And we asked a Maryknoll Brother, Brother Albert [Staubli], who did a lot of construction work, to make us an altar. So he made us a box-like altar that we could open on the side and use the inside space for storage. It cost us $5.00 Hong Kong currency, our altar!...Then we borrowed the tabernacle and candlesticks, from Rosary Church. Well, the tabernacle was almost as big as the altar! It was made for the parish church and the candle sticks, too, were huge.[22]

In those days, altar equipment was not available for sale in Hong Kong. The Sisters borrowed the items from the Church.[23]

Like the Sisters at Maryknoll, the women had a regular timetable. Sister Mary Paul made known her desire for strict discipline in the house. As the superior, she gave directions for the daily schedule, and set the rules and regulations for the house. While she assumed the responsibilities, others followed her orders without questions.[24] Their timetable was as follows:[25]

Morning 5:10	Rose from bed; meditation; The Little Office of the Blessed Virgin (A common prayer recited together for about five minutes)
6:30	Mass
After Mass	The Office of the Dead (Finished saying the prayer on Friday morning); Breakfast; Charges (household tasks)
8:45	Study
9:45	Class
11:00	Work
Noon	Examen (Noon prayer—Examination of Conscience); Dinner (as they called it; lunch in fact); Vespers and Rosary (prayers)
Afternoon 1:30	Recreation
2:00	Work
3:45 / 4:30	Class (usually ended at 5:15)
5:30	Matins (prayer); Short walk
6:10	Supper
6:45	Spiritual reading
7:00	Study (for half an hour, then free for fifteen minutes)
7:45	Recreation
9:00	Bed

Their spiritual exercises followed the Congregation's draft constitutions, which became official in 1925. According to the 1917 draft, the Sisters recited the Little Office of the Blessed Virgin Mary in common everyday, and in Latin according to the Dominican rite. Every week, excluding those of Easter and Pentecost, they recited the Office of the Dead, also in accordance with the Dominican rite.[26]

Besides religious exercises and meals, they had about six hours for use, three for studying Chinese and three for work. As Mary Paul pointed out, the amount of time was like that in Maryknoll. Regarding the learning of Chinese, her impression was that three hours were enough, and more than that was "stupefying" as the Sisters were still repeating the tones. The language was not easy, she explained, "you can't learn rapidly no matter how eager you are."[27] Time and practice were necessary, but the Sisters had very little contact with the Chinese people. In those days, they could not stand around after Sunday Mass and talk to folks. They followed strict rules, greeted others, and then returned home.[28] Nevertheless, they recognized the need to learn the Chinese language, culture, and customs. As for work, father superior wanted them to take up office duties so that Maryknoll priests could concentrate on the mission. In turn, they received a salary for their clerical work. For calculation, Mary Paul asked for the Sisters' pay scale in Maryknoll.[29] Three months after their arrival, she realized she had no previous examples to follow. Despite her natural leadership qualities, she was uncertain. She had to make all sorts of decisions, regarding the health care, religious life, and other concerns of the Sisters.[30] As she wrote to Mother Mary Joseph, "please know that any suggestions you make will be welcome, so welcome." "Please criticize freely anything I have done so that I may not do the same again," she said, "I feel as though I am walking through trackless spaces and it is not always easy to know where to step."[31]

The Sisters faced a serious problem—lack of money—and they had to pay their bills. In the first year, they concentrated on language learning and mission preparation.[32] They depended on simplicity and were responsible for their own expenses. The Sisters lived on the money they brought from the Motherhouse; they did typewriting, mimeographing, and dictation for the priests, and received payment in return. Sister Mary Paul suggested offering English tutorials for pupils in the convent.[33] They had to pay for the rent, furnishings, and retreat. With no choice, they borrowed from the Maryknoll Fathers. A second group of missioners arrived in 1922, which meant greater expenses in the house. Writing to Mother Mary Joseph, Mary Paul asked for money to cover the debts.[34] Later on, when Sister Mary Lawrence reported to the Motherhouse, she forgot to indicate whether the indebted sum was in Hong Kong dollars or U.S. dollars. The absentmindedness was of help this time. Exchange was always high, four or five to one. Therefore, as soon as the money came, in U.S. dollars, the Sisters were overjoyed.[35]

By the end of 1922, the Maryknoll Sisters had been in Hong Kong for a year. Despite their difficulties of adaptation, they got to know some local women. The Sisters tried to keep the place clean. Very soon they became "a unique sight" for people, who went to the 7:30 Mass at Rosary Church every morning and saw them washing windows of their house that was right on the street. They were recognized as the American Sisters who just came. Living nearby, a Chinese priest, who was an assistant in the Rosary parish, offered to introduce some Chinese and Portuguese girls to help with the work. One of them was Teresa Yeung and another was Laura Marie Carvalho. Both of them later entered Maryknoll, and became Sister Maria Teresa and Sister Cecilia Marie.[36]

Teresa Yeung was the first Chinese to join the congregation. Her example was the first close contact the American nuns had with a local Chinese. She was eager to provide assistance to the Sisters, to get around, to shop, and to know the "so many curious." Yeung had long wished to become a nun, and had applied to the Little Sisters of the Poor, a French congregation whose work she admired. She later developed affection for the Maryknoll Sisters, and changed her mind. At the beginning, Sister Mary Paul had some reservations as to whether Yeung could lead the disciplined life of a woman religious. Yeung's background was unusual. From a well-to-do family with three generations of Catholics, she belonged to the very few Chinese who could speak English. While Yeung was "quick and quite a leader," she seemed to be "very strong willed" and "had little exercise in curbing it." "Her qualities of leadership and the freedom of her life—her mother died when she was born and her father when she was eleven leaving her more than enough money—would make the restraint of a Rule a trifle hard, I am afraid"—Sister Mary Paul wrote.[37] In addition, Mary Paul wrote, "ever since she knew us she seemed attracted but I judged it rather a personal attraction because she used to come in to me and tell me her difficulties." While Yeung had not yet submitted her application, she was rather open to the Sisters. On an occasion, Mary Paul cautioned her—"I told her I fear that her fondness for us might have influenced her and that she must know that she would be sent here and there without any regard for her fondness for any Sister." What the Sister said had implications for the qualities of a Maryknoll missioner, that she must be confident, independent, and daring to act.

While the Sister had her doubts, she was not against the idea of accepting Chinese into Maryknoll. She referred the case to Father James Edward Walsh (superior of the Maryknoll Fathers in China, to be distinguished from the Father Superior James Anthony Walsh). He believed missioners should know more about the Chinese community before considering applications from local people. "An organization that takes Chinese vocations after one year in China," he thought was "venturesome" and must have "a lot of faith." As Maryknoll was committed to foreign mission work, he wondered whether it was "much of a test for a Chinese girl" to serve in her own culture. Instead, he suggested starting an order in Hong Kong. He wrote—"Start a native order. Let them work under you as catechists. Give them vows, as soon as we have a Bishop. Then recruit from them from time to time for your own Order as you get more experience and are able to size them up better."[38] His suggestion remained forever a suggestion only. Eventually, Yeung entered Maryknoll in 1927 and spent her novitiate period in the Maryknoll Motherhouse in New York State.[39] In later years, however, the Maryknoll Sisters were able to establish local novitiates in mission fields in China.

The Maryknoll Sisters received permission from the local bishop to establish the house in Hong Kong as a "procure" for their future houses in China.[40] This was not the original plan of Mother Mary Joseph or the Sisters.[41] There was a rejuvenation of spirit when the second group of missioners arrived in Hong Kong in October 1922. Led by Mary Magdalen Doelger, they were Mary Francis Davis, Mary Dolores

Cruise, Mary Cecilia Cruickshank, Mary Thomas Bresnahan, and Mary Gertrude Moore. The five-room cottage on Chatham Road "was bursting at the seams" with the newcomers, who slept on temporary beds in the reception room. Some of them were to move on to the interior. Their luggage included personal wardrobes, dishes, table utensils, books, and "bolts and bolts of mosquito netting."[42] A few weeks later, the Sisters headed for Yangjiang and established their first mission house in China.[43] Opened on November 21, it was occupied by members of the first and second groups. With Mary Magdalen as superior in the Yangjiang house, they were Mary Barbara, Mary Rose, and Mary Lawrence of the pioneering group, and Mary Francis and Mary Gertrude of the second group.[44] After their departure to the interior, the number of Sisters in the Hong Kong house was still six, but it grew to twelve in 1923 with more of them coming from the United States.[45]

Sister Mary Paul recognized the usefulness of studying Cantonese in Hong Kong, after having accompanied the six of them to Yangjiang.[46] Arriving there, the Sisters spent four hours a day on language. Father Francis X. Ford was in Yangjiang and stressed the importance of language in the mission. Since the Sisters of the pioneering group already had some Chinese vocabulary, they were helpful even though Cantonese and the Yangjiang dialect were not the same. The local people were able to understand when the Sisters spoke in Cantonese. Also, Father James Edward Walsh did not advise studying the Yangjiang dialect because it was not useful in other mission fields. The Sisters were to keep their Cantonese tones. At the same time, Sister Mary Paul recognized the sharp contrast of life between Hong Kong and Yangjiang where there was "terrible poverty." She suggested the center of the Sisters' mission in future to be in China, though a permanent house in Hong Kong was necessary.

Early Struggles

Sister Mary Paul felt that the Hong Kong house should be a service center for the future expanded mission in China. As her letter to Mother Mary Joseph explained, a Sister acted as a "procurator" to pass on news, mail, and supplies from Hong Kong to those working in Guangdong. She thought a house should always be in the colony—"there will always be at least one Sister here who will have to act as procurator for the Sisters in the interior—looking up things, getting information, sending personal things if the general mission attends to food, etc., and this sister could be supported by the mission houses."[47] However, she was aware of the financial difficulties of the Hong Kong house, which did not have a steady source of income. The Sisters were just starting out in Yangjiang; and it would need several houses to support the Hong Kong house in future. When the mission was mature, the houses in the interior could pay for the expenses in the colony. However, she recognized it would take a very long time before such a scenario came true. This was her understanding in January 1923, which meant that so far she did not have *a plan* for the mission in Hong Kong. She had to find out soon how to meet the expenses, and what work the Sisters should do. The only certain thing was that they were to continue to stay in Hong Kong, to establish a foothold for the coming endeavors in the interior.[48] The search for direction for the mission locally was understandable, as the Sisters were still trying their best to survive in the new environment. Their concerns were basic, namely how to maintain their livelihood.

In her recollection many years later, Sister Mary Paul emphasized the tough beginnings in Hong Kong. The pioneers had no precedents or any sort of instructions to follow. Mother Mary Joseph had not been to China, and father superior who accompanied them on their trip had not been in Hong Kong since 1918. In the words of Sister Mary Paul—"I said to Father General, when we got to Kowloon, 'What should we do?' He said, 'Didn't Mother Mary Joseph tell you?' And I said, 'No.' Mother Mary Joseph, when I asked her, before we left what we should do, she said, 'Oh Father General will be with you.' So that was the message we got."[49] According to her, the six of them did not question much before they embarked on their journey. They thought they were heading for China and would see what other people were doing. As she explained, Maryknoll was still young and they just went off in "simplicity and faith."[50] They did not have special preparation for Chinese mission, history, and culture. As the pioneering group, they presumed they could learn the language from the local people, and then try to convert them. The nuns did not even think of the financial question before they left.[51]

They had to find means to support themselves, as Hong Kong very probably became "a permanent part" of the Sisters' mission.[52] On New Year's Day 1923, they moved the convent to 103 Austin Road, a house owned by the Maryknoll Fathers and rented to them at a nominal rate. The lease of the cottage on Chatham Road had expired, the place was on sale, and therefore the Sisters had to move.[53] Unlike the Sisters in Yangjiang, those in Hong Kong did not have "viatique," which meant subsidies from the Maryknoll Fathers.[54] In Yangjiang, the Sisters took care of the school, the blind children, the orphans, the abandoned babies, and the elderly in Father Ford's "Old Folks Home." They were fully occupied with the mission work, and as a result, received subsidies from the priest. In Hong Kong, however, the Sisters managed their own finances and were on their own. They explored several options in this difficult situation. The possibilities were private tutorials, music classes, the running of a religious store, the sending of Asian crafts and artifacts for sale in the United States, and secretarial tasks for the Maryknoll Fathers. Besides a source of revenue, the private classes were also a way for the Sisters to get to know more people. Chinese thought Americans were very rich, and could not believe that the Maryknoll nuns had no regular income.[55] Indeed, it was a challenge to be self-supporting in a foreign place, and there was "no room for the unnecessary."[56] In March Mother Mary Joseph wrote to Sister Mary Paul, and agreed that a period of transition was necessary before the Hong Kong house could be fully on its own. As she said, "I agree with you that in time Hongkong should be self-supporting and its up-keep contributed to by our mission houses, because Hongkong will act as Procure for all our missions. This is of course ideal; but while there is the heavy debt on the house we shall look forward to sending money to you as we have during the past year."[57] Having said that, she believed the Sisters should be a help rather than a burden to the mission work, and should provide service far greater than the worth of their salary.

Besides the uncertainties ahead, the Maryknoll Sisters struggled hard in a foreign land where they had very little experience. "In addition to the problems of adjustment to a new climate, strange food, different customs and a different language, these pioneer Sisters had to contend with a very definite prejudice against Americans, as unfitted for mission life"—these were the perceptions of Maryknoll Sisters in their mission records. They "found themselves, if not welcome, certainly not sought after" when they arrived in the colony.[58] This was an apt description of the situation; and in her book in 1964 Sister Jeanne Marie raised the questions—"Was it because they were occidental, or because they were American, or because they were Roman Catholic, or because they were new and untried, or because they were all these things together?"[59] In 1993 Penny Lernoux's *Hearts on Fire* seems to respond by saying— "The European Sisters also distrusted the new arrivals, . . . The Chinese looked on them as curiosities; the British colonials ignored them as socially unimportant."[60] Maryknollers were on the fringe of society, foreigners to the Chinese, outsiders to the British colonial government, and possibly a new experience to European Catholic communities. They were the third Catholic community of Sisters in Hong Kong— the French St. Paul de Chartres Sisters arrived in 1848 and the Italian Canossian nuns in 1860—but the first American Catholic religious women to start a mission. At that time, missioners from the United States were supposed to be Protestants. These were the circumstances that made them feel like strangers in Hong Kong.[61]

In 1923 Mother Mary Joseph made a trip to Asia. Traveling with her were the third group of Sisters assigned to China, as well as the sixth group of Maryknoll Fathers and Brothers to the mission. In September, they headed for Hong Kong and China. The trip was the mother general's first "visitation" overseas. A large and imposing woman, Mother Mary Joseph always had a welcoming smile and showed no hesitance in reaching out to people. She was able to develop a personal touch with the persons she met. When she saw Teresa Yeung in Hong Kong, she said, "Oh, this is the Tessie that I have been hearing about. How about going shopping with me?"[62] Mother Mary Joseph had some unusual moments in China. In Guangzhou, people were asking who the "foreign devil" "occupying the whole street" was.[63] To some of them, she looked like a big Buddha. While she was not used to the way they shopped, Yeung insisted bargaining for the right price before buying, explaining it was appropriate to do so. The trip provided the mother general with first-hand experiences of mainland China. She acquired an understanding of the chaotic circumstances, and more in-depth knowledge of missionary work. For five months she traveled to Hong Kong, Guangzhou, Shanghai, Nanjing, Beijing, and the Northeast. She even managed to visit the Sisters' mission in Korea. "By every possible means— steamers, trains, river boats, junks, sampans, sedan-chairs, and rickshaws," she completed her journey.[64] Her presence had a consoling effect on the Sisters, who were eager to tell her what they saw and heard, and were in turn encouraged to go on. After her visit to China, she felt the need for greater development of the mission. She agreed to Father Ford's "a bit novel" idea of sending Sisters in pairs to the villages, to live with the people for weeks at a time for the purpose of direct apostolate.[65] In later years, the method turned out to be quite successful; and historian Jean-Paul Wiest coins it the "Jiaying method."[66]

A remark made about Maryknoll Sisters was that they tried to make light of difficult circumstances. Although they felt anxiety and uncertainty in new environments, they were always prepared for the unexpected and learned many new things. They lived like ordinary Chinese; and during their first days in Hong Kong shocked Father James Anthony Walsh who was planning to visit mission fields in the interior, as he saw Sister Mary Barbara carrying a fish (or meat in another account) on a piece of string after having been to the market with the cook Anna (who was mentioned in Mary Paul's first letter to the Motherhouse). While the nuns tried to be like everybody else, they were advised that they sometimes had to be different. According to the priest, foreigners had to be careful with their behavior or they would lose respect among Chinese people. He said they should not carry such bundles around. A Chinese boy did the food shopping for them afterward, and no matter how Sister Mary Paul asked him for more, "he would count the family and then buy one portion for each Sister."[67] In some accounts, the strangeness of the place was like "storybook" adventures to them.[68] They enjoyed dried fish and rice for breakfast, and this was true even for Sister Mary Paul. Strict and commanding, she turned out to be rather adaptable to local society. As she said, "we used to laugh about the things that happened that showed our ignorance."[69] For Thanksgiving, speaking their best Chinese, they told Anna to prepare chicken. They were surprised to see the whole chicken, with the head, on the table, and were more surprised when she cooked the same dish the next week, having misunderstood that the nuns wanted chicken every Thursday. When Hong Kong had very damp weather, it took a long time to dry the washed habits. A Chinese woman helped with the laundry, boiled water on the stove, and then washed the clothes in tubs in the backyard. Returning home one day, the nuns found their white and gray scapulars hanging on the backs of chairs in the chapel, as there were no other places available for drying clothes. There were many things they had to learn and get used to.

Industrial Department, and Conversion of Chinese Women to Christianity

Gradually, the mission of Maryknoll Sisters grew. In 1924 the number of Sisters in Hong Kong was fourteen; and in September another house opened in Luoding, north of Yangjiang, with six missioners. In order to adapt to the circumstances, the Sisters had to be innovative. While in company with Mother Mary Joseph in China, Sister Mary Paul realized that many religious communities supported themselves and their charity work by making vestments. She then obtained the approval of the mother general for starting the same endeavor in Hong Kong. At first, she arranged for Teresa Yeung to work in the convent dining room. Yeung was skillful with needlework and knew the various kinds of Italian embroidery. Further, Mary Paul set up a workroom for training poor young girls to do the job.[70] In 1924, she began the Industrial Department in the convent garage on Austin Road. It produced hand-embroidered vestments, which were made of lightweight silk. Through the Motherhouse, the Sisters in Hong Kong received mail orders and sold the garments to priests in the United States.

Sister Mary Liguori Quinlan took charge of the Industrial Department. She designed the vestments and chose the colors. Supervising the work was Yeung, who was responsible for hiring and paying the women workers. The women were good at Chinese embroidery, but they learnt from Yeung how to combine the stitches, to be careful with the colors, and to do the metal and silver parts. The vestments sold very well, and the Industrial Department turned out to be a major source of income for the nuns. Many American priests preferred the lighter products to the heavy European ones. Also, the garments were of superb quality and reasonably priced as they were imported duty-free. A Sister even traveled back to the United States to show the vestment samples and receive orders. In 1926 and 1927 the department moved temporarily to rented flats in Yaumati, as the Sisters built an extension in the garage to teach school kids. While Chinese women slept on the second floor, the production was on the third floor.[71] Subsequently, they moved back to Austin Road; then moved again to Kowloon Tong in 1937. Including the sections for embroidery, vestments, and church linens, the industrial department employed up to ninety workers at a time by the 1930s. This mail-order business was so successful that it continued into the 1960s.

Not only was the Industrial Department a stable source of income for the Sisters, it also provided an occasion for the conversion of Chinese women to Christianity. Conversion was the goal of missioners at the time. According to Sister Mary Liguori, all workers in the embroidery section were "pagans" but most of them were converted to Christianity. Some of them became nuns of other Orders, for example, the local Chinese community of Precious Blood Sisters. The daily schedule of the Industrial Department was prayers at 8:10 a.m., followed by work until a 15-minute break at 10 a.m. for an explanation of the Gospel. Noon dismissal was at 12:25; work resumed at 1 o'clock, and a 10-minute afternoon recess was at 4 p.m. Rosary, litany, and reading of the Old Testament commenced at 4.10 p.m.[72] As a Christian practice, the women took care of the embroidery room shrine. They also gave voluntary offerings for flowers. At the same time, priests provided a weekly talk on the Bible and timely matters. The Catholics joined groups like the Children of Mary and Catholic Action, and contributed to religious activities.

Baptism was a big event in the Industrial Department, and the Sisters made sure that it was "a big party." Besides godmothers and sponsors for Confirmation, other Catholics and catechumens were also present. It was a party for the baptized as well as the department. For Lent and Advent, the practices were—"To say the Stations of the Cross that day; To say an extra rosary that day; To go to Mass the following morning; To say a special prayer a number of times."[73] During Easter, the women "had an egg hunt, games and a party but the big thing was a big SHRINE with lilies, potted palms...and a big statue" of the Risen Christ.[74] Another event of the year was the Christmas celebration, when the place was decorated with a Christmas tree and gifts. Every woman got "a face cloth, a towel and a piece of nice toilet soap (a special gift)."[75] Also, the department celebrated Chinese New Year.

The Industrial Department provided many opportunities for Sisters to reach out to local people. Besides daily encounters in the workplace, the Sisters also paid home visits to Chinese women, caring for their physical and psychological needs. Many embroidery workers aged from twenty to thirty or over, stayed in a place that was rented by the pastor of St. Teresa's Church in Kowloon Tong. The women workers were from very poor families and got the job through recommendation. Indeed, they received little education, and the majority of them could only read a few Chinese characters. Therefore, the Sisters also set up a library for these girls so that they could acquire some basic literacy.[76]

Under the administration of Sister Mary Reginald Silva who arrived in 1925, the cassock section provided another source of income for the nuns. At first, there was only one table, one shelf, and one sewing machine for Sister Mary Reginald and another Chinese woman hired for making cassocks. By 1937 when the entire Industrial Department moved to Kowloon Tong, there were nineteen workers and three sewing machines in the cassock section. Philomena Wong was the name of the Chinese woman, who was there from the very first day. A long-time Catholic, she later became the supervisor of the workers and her position gave her "lots of face." The women included both "pagans" and Catholics. Besides work, the activities were the recitation of Rosary, spiritual reading in Chinese, talks given by priests, and the singing of hymns. The women were able to read more through the religious instruction, and could borrow books, including fiction, from the library. Their daily schedule was similar to that of the embroidery workers.[77]

The Sisters' mission in Hong Kong really got a start with the Industrial Department. As it turned out, the Sisters had the occasion to be in close contact with the local people, to know what they thought, and to bring them to the Christian faith. At the same time, Chinese women learned to trust their own abilities, to be independent, and not to be a burden to their families. Through the department, the Sisters secured a steady income and financed their next move, opening a kindergarten in the convent. Therefore, cooperation with local women enabled the Sisters to continue in Hong Kong. It was a cross-cultural endeavor, and there were to be many examples of this kind in future. Both sides benefited, practically and as a life experience. In one of the photos of that time, three workers in Chinese suits and trousers sat around the table while a nun in full habit was examining their piece of work. The women were young, their braids tied at the back. It was a scene of two cultures, not related in any way but somehow together. While the Chinese women depended on the nuns to a certain extent, the same thing could also be said vice-versa. As written in the Tentative Constitutions, the Congregation aimed at the personal development of the Sisters and preaching the Gospel in faraway lands. The mission began in Hong Kong with the poor and women, to whom the Maryknoll Sisters were to dedicate their service. In 1924 the mission came into being with the operation of the Industrial Department. Nevertheless, the Sisters lacked a long-term plan for mission in Hong Kong. They were adapting to circumstances, exploring possibilities, and making use of opportunities open to them. Sometimes they succeeded in their ventures, and sometimes they failed, as in the staffing of the Kowloon Hospital in 1924 and 1925.

Kowloon Hospital Incident of 1924–1925

For a few years, Bishop Dominic Pozzoni, then vicar apostolic, had been suggesting to the government that the Catholic Sisters serve as the nursing staff of a hospital being planned in Kowloon. In April 1923 he recommended that Maryknoll Sisters could provide suitable personnel to the proposed Kowloon Hospital. The recommendation was successful, and the news reached the superiors in Maryknoll, New York.[78] Coincidentally, toward the end of the year when Mother Mary Joseph visited Hong Kong and China, she met with Lu Bohong in Shanghai and got to know local medical facilities. A decade later she sent her Sisters to work in a new mental hospital there.[79] The Hong Kong endeavor seemed agreeable to her. In 1924 Sisters in Hong Kong were getting ready for their positions in the hospital, to be in service the following year. Writing to the mother general in October, Sister Mary Paul included an unsigned contract between the government and the Sisters. According to the document, "the Foreign Mission Sisters of St. Dominic, Incorporated, a corporation incorporated under the laws of the State of New York" was "prepared to provide and undertake the carrying out of all the duties of the trained staff of nursing sisters for the hospital."[80] For the time being, the hospital needed eight qualified nurses. Maryknoll Sisters took up the nursing duties, and the government paid their monthly salary. As a secular institute, the hospital was not a place for Sisters to preach or to convert people to Christianity. The corporation, not the government, was responsible for the acts of the Sisters.

After the government published its budget and made known the staffing of Maryknoll Sisters at the hospital, there was immediate condemnation in a local English-language paper, the *South China Morning Post*. Sister Mary Paul subsequently described the attacks as bigotry. In October and November, criticisms flooded the correspondence columns, which were against the appointment of American Sisters, and bombarded the government for ignoring the high unemployment rate in England. The paper revealed ill feelings, and some of the quotations were as follows:[81]

Quotation 1. I gather that feeling has been aroused by the suggestion to import nursing sisters from the Maryknoll Mission of New York, which, I presume, is a Roman Catholic institute. The Hospital is, of course, a H.K. Government building, and will be controlled by Government authorities. I should like to know the reason for importing non-British service, more especially Sisters of a connection not generally acceptable to the Britishers likely to become patients.

Quotation 2. The fact that our splendid British nurses are among the lowest paid of the Government servants makes this attack seem the more unjustifiable. The policy of the Government of this Colony in the past has not been altogether divorced from common-sense—it would be a sad thing if it should part company in this particular instance.

Quotation 3. From an "Ex. Soldier": There will be a certain sadness when it is recollected that there are over a million unemployed men and women in England.
And yet, how are we dealing with the matter practically? There are hundreds of trained nurses in England out of work, many of whom have seen service. It would appear that we are about to overlook their plight and to staff a new Government Hospital with nurses from the most prosperous country in the world.

There were also suspicions that Maryknoll Sisters would take advantage of the situation to solicit converts:[82]

Quotation 4. From "Britisher": it is interesting to observe that the Government is not only building and equipping what is in reality a Medical Mission for the American Roman Catholic nuns of the Maryknoll Mission, but if Dame Rumor is correct, they have also set apart one room for their use as a Chapel.

Quotation 5. There can be no doubt that the purpose of the Roman Catholic sisterhood is to exercise its religious influence. Anyone who knows religion knows that its object is to disciple whenever and wherever possible and these sisters who have given up home and other things one holds dear in obedience to religious calling, will not exclude what they have given up these things for.

With the discontent expressed by British residents in the newspaper, there was a petition to the government to withdraw its proposal. In mid-November, the Kowloon Residents' Association sent a letter to the local colonial secretary with signatures of a few hundred British residents. The petition argued against hiring of non-British staff in a British governmental institute and granting responsibilities to a religious group. Also, it warned that the proposed action would produce unwanted implications and send wrong signals to outside people.[83]

Resentment was expressed, but there were also other opinions. For example, a letter to the editor said that Catholic Sisters had provided high-standard medical service in Shanghai, and that opposition so far represented feelings of a minority of people. Signed as "Broadminded," a reader used strong words against the prevailing prejudice—"people of Kowloon are, if necessary, prepared to prove to this small noisy section of bigots that there is to-day no room in our broad Empire for the vile methods of those who would spread the poison of religious hatred. The men who would introduce the principles of the Ku Klux Klan into Hongkong must know that their work is absolutely opposed to the spirit of Christ." Another reader, signed as "Anti-Bigot," described the whole incident as a "disgraceful exhibition of narrowminded bigotry which has been disfiguring the pages of the local press for some time."[84]

Throughout the ordeal, the Maryknoll Sisters remained quiet. They refused to withdraw from the plan though some people had advised them to do so. Sister Mary Paul claimed that the proposal had provoked endless controversies, which pointed specifically to the American and religious background of the nuns. The situation generated "a lot of bigotry" and had "not been most pleasant." Writing on November 19, she said that the government had not taken part in the debates, but at the same time, it had not been in touch with the Sisters. According to her, the objections were not only local but from England as well. With the high unemployment rate, British nurses were eager for foreign assignments, which were usually for three years and very well paid.[85] Mary Paul decided to wait and see. Unwilling to pull out from the agreement with the authorities, the Sisters did not want to act in a way that would make them lose face in Chinese society.[86] The government finally broke its promise; and the severe criticism from the British population was the main reason for its decision.[87] Subsequently, the *South China Morning Post* reported that the government had withdrawn its proposal to staff the Kowloon Hospital with Sister nurses of Maryknoll. The newspaper explained the action as a response to "strong agitation" and "outcry aroused by the Government's proposal."[88] On December 30, Mother Mary Joseph wrote to the colonial secretary in Hong Kong, regretting the situation but asking for a public statement to clarify that Maryknoll Sisters "had no ulterior motive in accepting the government's offer."[89] Later, she decided not to pursue the matter though the Sisters deserved "a plan and clear statement." While it was "unwise to antagonize" the authorities, she believed it was difficult for the government to admit its own "weakness" in the incident.[90]

Education Endeavor

Education became a major endeavor of Maryknoll Sisters. In 1929 the Sisters came up with *a plan* for the mission to focus on their two schools. It took them quite some time to make the commitment, which had not been proposed nor even thought of when they first arrived in Hong Kong.[91] By 1923 they began to look for openings in education. While they had considered a number of possibilities, the chances were not promising. In 1925 they opened a kindergarten in their convent on Austin Road, as a means to secure additional income. It grew and became Maryknoll Convent School. Two years later, they started Holy Spirit School on Hong Kong Island. The Sisters were uncertain of the prospects of the schools, which started from humble beginnings. It was only in 1929 that they believed education could develop into a long-term endeavor. A plan for the mission was then possible. Through the years, the local Catholic Church played a significant role.

There were rumors that Maryknoll Sisters were about to establish a school in Hong Kong. In January 1923, when she wrote to the mother general, Sister Mary Paul argued it was *not* the right time for them to do so. She was against the timing, not the idea. Although she was not denying such possibility in future, she thought the Sisters so far did not have enough preparation for the task. As a former head-mistress in the United States, she was fond of school work. However, she was well aware of the lack of trained teachers to run a school. The Sisters had not yet decided whether they would pursue the field of education. In case they finally made up their mind, they should study the local situation and know the needs of the people. As she said, this should be done before the Motherhouse sent out Sister teachers to Hong Kong.[92] So far, the Sisters saw the school as a source of support for their house. As Mary Paul commented—"*Good* because we need it, but I think if we started this year, we will be making a mistake."[93] She thought that the school, if opened, should be for the Chinese. Moreover, she did not want to appear as competing with the Italian Canossian Sisters, whose school was close by on Chatham Road.[94] In her correspondence to Bishop Pozzoni in February, Sister Mary Paul said that she had been "much disturbed" by rumors. "We have done nothing in this movement," she emphasized and "if we contemplated taking up educational work, we would consult with you directly and immediately."[95] She repeated that Maryknoll did not wish to interfere with the existing work of any community.

Soon the Church, which had been keen on the expansion of Catholic education after the First World War, took a position and made a proposal to the Maryknoll Sisters.[96] In May, John Spada, the Milan priest who was a friend of the nuns, approached Sister Mary Paul with a map of Kowloon Tong. Most of the area of Kowloon Tong lay north of Boundary Street, and it extended up to Lion Rock and was leased to the British for ninety-nine years in 1898. In the early 1920s, Boundary Street began to come into being. It was the Old Frontier Line that marked the boundary of the leased territories in the northernmost part of Kowloon Peninsula.[97] The government was leveling hillsides and cutting down streets but Kowloon Tong was still waiting to be developed.

Father Spada revealed the decision to build a church and open a parish there. Eventually, he said, Kowloon Tong would become a Chinese settlement with 220 families. He wanted Maryknoll to establish a school in the parish, to correspond with the development. According to Mary Paul, a parish school in Hong Kong was differ-ent from those in the United States, which were established and operated by the parish. It provided education for the children of the neighborhood, but was entirely independent of the parish and was under the administration of responsible Sisters. It also followed the government's education regulations. Spada asked Mary Paul to obtain a government grant (for the land) for building a school in two to three years' time. Both of them made a trip to Kowloon Tong, to check on the location of the church and the suggested site for the school, which was on the opposite side of the road. Mary Paul's impression was that the area was still "in a raw state."[98] The government was opening roads and removing high grounds. However, progress was quite slow since much of it was manual labor.

Subsequently, she consulted Father Léon Robert who also knew about the settlement plan in Kowloon Tong. Father Robert was the procurator for the Paris Foreign Missionary Society in Hong Kong and was a close friend of James Anthony Walsh.[99] Upon hearing the proposal, he advised her to buy the land at once before waiting for the approval of the mother general.[100] He was against accepting a grant from the government, which then had the right to reclaim at any time land presented on such basis. Moreover, Robert expected an increase in land value in future. He told the Sisters not to worry about the huge expenditure involved, as he could lend them money, to be paid back whenever they wanted to. He suggested having the bishop represent them in the land deal with authorities. His reason was that "the Bishop could obtain anything from the Government, but that we [the Sisters], as a new community without having done any work here, would not meet with the same ready acquiescence."[101] On the site, Maryknoll could build a school and a convent. The school should accommodate at least 200 students, who came from Kowloon Tong and the neighboring areas of Homantin and Yaumati. The convent would become the center and rest house for Sisters in the interior as well. Previously, Mary Paul was against commitment to school work. She then changed her mind and decided to accept the offer. She felt that the Catholic Church wanted Sisters to take up the task. Since it would take a few years before Kowloon Tong could be developed and the school be built, there was enough time to look for trained teachers. The school would also attract the attention of Chinese families. In all probability, land price would rise, and the deal involved no risk at all.[102]

Twice in May and June, Bishop Pozzoni asked the government to grant the land (near the impending Kowloon Hospital) for the church, Maryknoll school, and houses for the Portuguese community.[103] The bishop died the following year, and Spada became pro-vicar apostolic (meaning, for the vicar apostolic when the bishop was not in residence). Sister Mary Paul tried to deal with the authorities, but was not successful. She gathered from sources that the government was reluctant to sell to a religious body.[104] In September 1924, the colonial secretary turned down the Church's request for land "in the neighborhood of the Kowloon Hospital," which was south of Prince Edward Road, but suggested considering sites north of the traffic instead.[105] A month later, Spada made a new proposal, asking for land for the church, school, and houses for a Catholic population on the north side of Prince Edward Road. However, the government rejected the plan again.[106]

While the Kowloon Tong proposal was still hanging in the air, the Sisters needed additional revenue. They made a profit from the Industrial Department, which allowed them to open a kindergarten inside the convent on Austin Road. With an enrolment of twelve Portuguese children, the kindergarten was not in the original plan of the missioners. There were demands from the Portuguese for English-language education (some of whom were relatives of the future Sister Cecilia Marie Carvalho), and the bishop agreed to such undertaking. In February 1925 the kindergarten opened; however, at that time, the Sisters were still unsure of its future. With limited space in the community room, it could only take fifteen to twenty children. The tuition fee was Hong Kong currency $8 a month.[107] Sister Mary Paul did not expect this small kindergarten to develop into a school, like the one she envisaged for Kowloon Tong. As she explained to Mother Mary Joseph, "this work is practically among the Portuguese and you may wonder why I undertake this when I have held aloof from undertaking a school here in this house."[108] She continued—"A kindergarten finishes automatically, but a school opens possibilities and to be anything worthwhile, should carry the pupils on for a longer period than the kindergarten would. People are willing to pay for the kindergarten but it would be more difficult to open up a private school for older girls with the same convenience of hours and the equivalent amount of revenue."[109] The Sisters were trying their best to run the house and to survive. The kindergarten came into existence as a source of income.

It was very well received. Adding a higher class each year, the kindergarten grew to a school of five classes by 1928. Originally, Maryknoll Convent School started as a kindergarten in the convent's community room. It expanded to occupy the convent's unused garage and even a portion of the industrial room. In 1928 the Sisters rented a flat in King's Terrace, next to the convent, for the school. One year later, the school moved to Torres Building, 2 Kimberly Road, and housed kindergarten through Class 6.[110] Expansion of the school was beyond the anticipation of the Sisters. In early years, the children came from many different backgrounds. As a Sister recalled, "we could claim 12 nationalities among our members in the kindergarten: Chinese, Japanese, English, Portuguese, Irish, French, German, Scotch, Russian, American, Peruvian and Hindu Indian."[111] Their parents were government officials, army officers, and business people. There were some from poor families as well.

It was in 1927 that the Sisters opened another school, located on 41 Robinson Road on Hong Kong Island. With a student body of over one hundred, Holy Spirit School was situated in a purely Chinese neighborhood.[112] The Sisters had much difficulty even after the first school year. They had to learn how to adapt to the local circumstances. While they had to meet the standards of the government, there were no specific guidelines or textbooks they could follow. On the one hand, the field of education seemed to hold great potential, promising many opportunities ahead. They recognized the significance of a good start—education in Hong Kong could be "a wide field" if it was done properly.[113] On the other hand, they did not receive much guidance from the government or the bishop, and had to proceed with caution. After the first year, the Sisters admitted that they had made "a very serious mistake" in using American textbooks with "entirely different standards" at Holy Spirit School.[114] In the second academic year, they used American books only as additional references. Even selection of English texts was not easy, and the Sisters were venturing into a new territory. Their feelings were—"The field is entirely new and you have a feeling of reaching out into space.... we have an additional difficulty of trying to pull it up without letting anybody know that we made some serious mistakes last year."[115]

Hong Kong: A Different Agenda in the China Mission

The 1920s was a decade of strikes and demonstrations, with the outbreak of the large seamen's strike in Hong Kong in 1922 winning sympathy and support in Guangzhou as well. In 1925, demonstrations in Shanghai sparked off heated nationalistic sentiments across the country. Antiforeign activities erupted from time to time; as James Edward Walsh warned "No foreigner's life is safe in the interior. One walks the streets these days half expecting a brick or a shot in the back and very few foreigners venture out at all."[116] In April 1927 the Luoding Sisters left their mission for Hong Kong, following Walsh's advice.[117] By the end of the 1920s, Maryknoll Sisters had already expanded their overseas endeavor. There were over one hundred and twenty of them abroad—in South China (including Hong Kong since 1921, Yangjiang since 1922, and Luoding since 1924), the Northeast (since 1925), Korea (since 1924), the Philippines (since 1926), and Hawaii (since 1927).[118] In August 1929, in the Maryknoll Motherhouse, Mother Mary Joseph drafted a mission policy for Asia. While the Sisters were responding to local circumstances, she believed they could acquire more independent roles and shoulder the same tasks as those of priests. As she said, Maryknoll had grown "in such a way that it might be said to have developed out of the needs which arose rather than by prearranged policies and ideals."[119] The statement was particularly applicable to Sisters in Hong Kong, whose convent on Austin Road had eighteen members, and could be said to be a precise evaluation of their work so far.[120]

Nevertheless, what the Mother general envisioned for the Sisters in Asia was to be very different from the agenda of those in the colony. Putting much emphasis on "catechetical work and direct evangelization," she requested the Sisters to live in villages in groups of two, in an environment without daily Mass in church and the company of a larger Christian community. They should "undertake direct catechetical and evangelical work and for that purpose will expect to go from station to station for visitations comparable to those of the priests."[121] Here, she supported Father Ford's idea of direct apostolate, which had been experimented with in Yangjiang before the priest was assigned to Jiaying, also in Guangdong Province, in 1925.[122] At the same time, the document was meant for discussion among superiors in the Asian missions. As events turned out, Maryknoll Sisters in Hong Kong devoted themselves primarily to education. While it belonged to the South China region, Hong Kong was an outpost that demanded different attention.

Bishop Henry Valtorta, vicar apostolic since 1926, was eager to pursue the plan for Kowloon Tong after he took office. In May 1928, he mentioned the requests of the Church in 1923 and 1924, and asked the government to respond to the matter. In reply, the colonial secretary said that the grant of land on the north side of Prince Edward Road was "no longer available." Instead, the government pointed to two lots of land, each 150,000 square feet, for the church and school, at the corner of Boundary Street and Waterloo Road, for consideration.[123] The lot for the Maryknoll school became its permanent location (since 1937). The church ended up in the earlier proposed site on Prince Edward Road, as the bishop insisted on that location and was willing to buy it at auction, instead of receiving a government grant.[124] In November 1928, the Church purchased at auction a lot of 76,500 square feet at the junction of Prince Edward Road, Waterloo Road, and Boundary Street for the erection of St. Teresa's Church. After many years of negotiation and a few proposals, the land for the church was settled; and Spada, "Parish Priest of Kowloon," would supervise the construction of St. Teresa's.[125]

In 1929 the Sisters committed themselves to *a long-term plan* in Hong Kong. Bishop Valtorta urged them to reconsider the proposal for Kowloon Tong.[126] With the support of the Church, they were ready to take up the challenge. Spada spoke with the authorities, who then agreed to hold the land for Maryknoll. The government reiterated its previous proposal. The area was about 150,000 square feet, situated at the corner of Boundary Street and Waterloo Road. On the opposite side of Boundary Street was China Light & Power, already completed; and on the other side across Waterloo Road were bungalows and the location for the new St. Teresa's Church. Land for the school was "quite uneven," but "could be leveled for ten cents per foot or less."[127] The surroundings were like this—Waterloo Road was cut down, but 20–30 feet were to be cut down for Boundary Street, which extended back about 80–100 feet.[128] Further, Waterloo Road was very wide, and in the middle there was a nullah with stone walls on both sides.[129] The land opposite was low, with bungalows, but the frontage for the school land was high, about 30 feet. In June 1930, the education director indicated his support for a girls' school in the location in his communication within the government.[130] Four months later, the governor wrote to London concurring with the opinion, saying that Maryknoll Sisters had done "much good educational work in the Colony" and it was desirable to sell them the land for the construction of a girls' school.[131]

By January 1931 the Sisters secured the site in Kowloon Tong, then 200,000 square feet. After paying for the land, the Sisters also needed to pay HK$1,000 for Crown Rent each year.[132] Proposed by Father Spada in 1923, the plan of a parish school in Kowloon Tong became a reality. Maryknoll Convent School fitted into the scheme at the right time. With the purchase of the land, the Sisters had accepted a long-term commitment. Soon the School needed a larger site. In 1932, it required more space and moved again, this time to 248 Prince Edward Road. The move corresponded with the completion of St. Teresa's Church and the opening of the parish. The School provided both primary and secondary education. Hong Kong was developing three streams of schools, and Maryknoll schools belonged to the type of Anglo-Chinese schools, which were run by either the government or missionary bodies, putting emphasis on Western knowledge and the use of English as the teaching medium (except for Chinese language classes). The other two types were modern Chinese schools and traditional vernacular schools, both of which used Chinese as the teaching medium.[133]

Maryknoll Convent School (M.C.S.) and Holy Spirit School were the first schools of Maryknoll Sisters in Hong Kong; and they continued after World War II. Holy Spirit was different from M.C.S., "which was open to any nationality, where all subjects were taught in English, with Chinese, Portuguese or French as a language."[134] In 1930 Holy Spirit was resituated in an old three-story building on 140 Caine Road. The Sisters leased that place for the School, and subsequently bought it as well.[135] By then, education was their plan. The schools were to stay, and the purchase of the property on Caine Road was to avoid troublesome moving from time to time. The only doubt was whether Holy Spirit would consolidate with the plan in Kowloon Tong within a few years or would continue to develop on its own. In the 1930s M.C.S. was more successful than Holy Spirit in attracting students. In 1932 M.C.S. had 185 students and Holy Spirit had 136.[136] One year later, the former had 274 and the latter had 127.[137] M.C.S. had less competition in Kowloon Tong while Holy Spirit was close to a number of well-established schools.

Maryknoll schools were atypical with their native English-speaking staff of post–high school/college qualifications. The Sisters constituted a significant part of the staff of both schools, and were well trained in different disciplines. Further, Sister Mary Paul often asked the Motherhouse for Sister teachers to Hong Kong. An example was her letter to the mother general in 1933. With more than two hundred students, M.C.S. had become "extremely crowded." She particularly requested a Sister with teacher's training and experience, who was to serve as a senior staff, to conduct higher classes and to teach French.[138] Indeed, the Sisters were very highly educated; and in the 1930s this was particular impressive. The qualifications of some of them before teaching in Hong Kong were as follows:[139]

(1) Sister Ann Mary Farrell
—Graduate from Catholic University of America and Pittsburgh Training School for Teachers. Finished a summer session at University of Pittsburgh.
—One year of teaching experience at Franklin School, Pittsburgh, Pennsylvania.

(2) Sister Henrietta Marie Cunningham
—Graduate from Framington Academy & High School, Framington, Massachusetts; and State Teachers College, Framingham, Massachusetts.

(3) Sister Matthew Marie Stapleton
—Graduate from Marquette University and Milwaukee State Teachers' College in Milwaukee, Wisconsin; and St. Mary's School in Rhinelander, Wisconsin. Also received additional credits in the disciplines of Education, History, and English at various institutes.
—Two years of teaching experience in Ludington School, Wauwatosa, Wisconsin; and six years in public schools in Milwaukee, Wisconsin.

(4) Sister Frances Marion Gardner
—Graduate from Holy Names Academy and Holy Names Normal, Seattle, Washington. Also received additional credits for Music at the Pius X School of Liturgical Music, New York City.
—One year of teaching experience at United States Territorial Service, Atka, Alaska.

(5) Sister Santa Maria Manning
—Graduate from South Boston High School and Boston Normal School. Received additional credits and certificates for Music, General Science, Drawing, Geography, Education, Reading, Psychology, and Philosophy.
—Thirteen years of teaching experience in Sarah Greenwood School, Boston, Massachusetts; and one year in St. Anthony's School, Honolulu, Hawaii.

(6) Sister Mary Camillus Reynolds
—Graduate from Brushton High School, Brushton, New York; and trained as a nurse at the Ogdensburg City Hospital, Ogdensburg, New York. Received additional credits from St. Joseph's Maternity Hospital, Troy, New York, as a registered nurse.
—Had two years of teaching experience in each of the following schools: Moira School, Moira, New York; school at Fort Covington, New York; and Riverside School, Livermore Falls, Maine.

(7) Sister Anne Clements (Mary Famula)
—Graduate from St. Vincent Academy, High School, Nelson Co., Kentucky; and Catholic Sisters' College, Catholic University, Washington, D.C. Received additional credits in Education, Geography, History, Reading, and Arithmetic.
—Two years of teaching experience in Maryknoll School, Seattle, Washington; and seven years of experience at schools in Dalian (Dairen), China Northeast.

(8) Sister Rosemary de Felice
—Graduate from St. John's Parochial School, New Haven, Connecticut. Received additional credits through summer sessions in Los Angeles. Four extension courses in Hawaii on "English Literature of Child Life," "Practice Teaching," "Receiving Room and Kindergarten Procedure and Materials," and American History.
—Six years of teaching experience in St. Francis Xavier School, Los Angeles, California; and two years in St. Augustine's School in Waikiki, Honolulu, Hawaii.

(9) Sister M. de Ricci Cain (Canadian with British citizenship)
—Graduate from Prince of Wales College and Provincial Normal School, Charlottetown, Prince Edward Island, Canada. Spent one year in St. Francis Xavier University, Antigonish, Nova Scotia, Canada. Received her Bachelor of Arts degree from College of Mt. St. Vincent, Riverdale, New York.

Becoming "Local"

In 1934 Maryknoll Sisters were incorporated in Hong Kong. According to the "Foreign Mission Sisters of St. Dominic" Incorporation Ordinance, No. 20 of 1934 of the Legislative Council: "The Regional Superior for the time being in the Colony of Hong Kong of the Foreign Mission Sisters of St. Dominic shall be a corporation... and shall have the name of 'The Regional Superior in Hong Kong of the Foreign Mission Sisters of St. Dominic' and in that name shall have perpetual succession and shall and may sue and be sued in all courts in the Colony and shall and may have and use a common seal."[140] Since the "Foreign Mission Sisters of St. Dominic" was incorporated under the laws of New York State, the local corporation in Hong Kong was under the title of the "Regional Superior." In fact, three years ago, Sister Mary Paul was already thinking of getting incorporated locally. As a foreign corporation then, Maryknoll Sisters had to obtain the approval of the Legislative Council for every purchase and every sale. When acquiring the building on Caine Road, they realized the government process was very slow. If the Sisters bought or sold property as a local corporation, it could avoid unnecessary bureaucracy, additional taxes, and the request for official permissions.[141]

Maryknoll Sisters were establishing their foothold in Hong Kong. The same year they got incorporated locally, they also won the recognition of the government for the high standards of M.C.S. The Board of Education agreed to put M.C.S. in the list of grant-in-aid schools, which meant that the School would receive government subsidies. It was estimated that each grant-in-aid school would receive HK$10,000 in the year 1935. In other words, the government supported HK$2 or more for each student each month with the understanding that the school was up to the standard.[142] In 1935 the construction of the M.C.S. building began. This represented the first stage of the work in Kowloon Tong, as the land was bought for both the school and convent. For the moment, the school building, auditorium, covered playground, and industrial department occupied one half of the site. As Sister Mary Paul described, the building would be completed in eighteen months and would be in "solid, reinforced concrete frame[s]."[143] Teak was used for the classroom floors and doors. Windows were steel, which were quite often seen in Hong Kong. As for the face tiling, the roof tiling, the dado, and the paving tiling, the materials were Japanese. In 1936 the foundation stone was laid; and in 1937 the Sisters and the School moved into the new building. The M.C.S. building was an imitation of the Maryknoll Motherhouse in Ossining, New York; and it eventually turned out to be more impressive and breathtaking! At present, it is still a landmark in Hong Kong. The M.C.S. building had images of "a children's book":

> The russet tiled roofs topping a patchwork exterior in shades of *café au lait*, the gables and sweeping cobbled drive, the dormers and tall narrow casements that let in slanting shafts of sunlight, the arches and buttresses and broad verandahs are the stuff of a child's dream. Behind the heavy doors rise elegant wrought-iron banisters and wooden staircases. None the worse for wear after years of scraping and scuffing by young hands and feet, they are a happy marriage of style and material. Where they lead is not always important. Only the eccentric baron is missing and we deeply regret that no wayward heiress was ever imprisoned in the tower.[144]

It was in such an atmosphere that the Sisters continued their dream for Hong Kong.

CHAPTER THREE
DIFFICULT YEARS, 1937–1951

Just at the last Gospel, the air raid siren blew. We pricked up our ears but, as the buses still ran, we thought it was a "rehearsal" as we have had a few recently. On leaving the Church, we saw about 30 planes circling about like beautiful silver birds against a deep blue sky. The crack of anti-aircraft guns and machine gun fire, told us it was no display. Men were flat against walls and we rushed for the convent with the now scattered planes nearly overhead. Somehow, we got across the street and gathered together many frightened children standing by the gate and under the archway. We took them quickly to the laundry, until some one from inside opened the "tiffin room," a partly underground room, a made-to-order shelter.
Sister Santa Maria Manning, Boundary Street, Kowloon Tong, December 8, 1941[1]

In 1937 Maryknoll Sisters' Convent and Maryknoll Convent School relocated to the new building on Waterloo Road at Boundary Street, Kowloon Tong. The Sisters had moved before, and the location was their third residence since they arrived in Hong Kong. The house could take in more newcomers, and promised greater opportunities for expansion of the mission. Also, it was the fifth address of the School. The larger space and better facilities allowed for the future development of the School. Finally, the Sisters thought they had settled down. Education was the focus of their work. In mid-1937, the local population increased to an estimated figure of 1,006,982, out of which about 22,582 were non-Chinese.[2] Unfortunately, the outbreak of the Sino-Japanese War (1937–1945) cast a dark shadow over China and Hong Kong. In December 1941 the Japanese invaded the colony, and began the occupation, which lasted for three years and eight months. During the ordeal, the Sisters were interned for quite some time, and were subsequently released. Some were repatriated, and some headed for the interior of China. When the war ended in 1945, they returned to the colony, only to find the School full of sick soldiers, furniture gone and repairs necessary. They had to start all over again, and had to face the tremendous challenges ahead. Like the local people they were subjected to political upheavals beyond their anticipation and control. The conclusion of the war brought different problems and ushered in a new period of Hong Kong history.

Sister Mary Paul McKenna

Sister Mary Paul led the pioneering group to Hong Kong and was then superior of the Sisters in the colony and the interior. In 1931 when the General Chapter set up the Regions, the missions in Guangdong, Guangxi, and Hong Kong came under the South China Region.[3] Mary Paul was regional superior, a post she held until 1946 when she was elected to the Congregation's General Council. She had leadership qualities, and retained much of her "schoolmarm manner," as she had been a school-teacher and principal in Pennsylvania.[4] Penny Lernoux gives a vivid description of the Sister of such authoritative character—"Short and bespectacled, with a promi-nent chin and prim-looking mouth, she showed no shyness or hesitancy. Many who came in contact with her were overawed, whether young Sisters, bishops, or Japanese military commanders.... when Mary Paul rang a bell, absolute silence ensued, none daring to speak as she gave orders. Nor did she mince words when dealing with church and government officials: ..."[5]

When Mary Paul first arrived in Hong Kong, she was in her early thirties. In 1937, she was forty-nine. For twenty-five years Mary Paul was superior of the Sisters in Hong Kong. Strict and commanding, her rule was coined the "Manchu Dynasty."[6] She ventured into education, took care of the Sisters during the Japanese occupation, and got back Maryknoll Convent School (M.C.S.) in 1946. Born to be a leader, she made an enormous contribution to the mission. At the same time, her emphases on discipline and obedience made a strong impression on many Maryknollers. A Sister once described Mary Paul as the "benevolent empress dowa-ger." Her significance was undeniable and she was also an imposing figure. Up till now, there is still a story circulating among fellow Maryknollers. Its authenticity was hard to prove, but many, who had known Mary Paul before, were quite ready to believe it. It happened in late 1941 when the Japanese began their occupation of Hong Kong. When the Japanese soldiers asked a Sister to open the gate of the M.C.S. compound, she insisted that they enter through another entrance on the side street. She was following the instruction of her superior, and explained that it was better to disobey the Japanese than to disobey Mary Paul.

Mary Paul demanded that everyone in the house closely follow rules and regula-tions. Even Sister Mary Gemma Shea (Margaret Shea), one of the founding women of Maryknoll, was no exception. In the late 1920s and early 1930s Mary Gemma was in the Northeast of China; and in the late 1930s she was in Tokyo, Japan. One time, she was in Hong Kong for three months. She was not familiar with the schedule of the house. The Sisters had to take a "siesta" in the afternoon. Mary Paul made this a rule considering the hot and humid weather in Hong Kong. Instead of taking a nap, Mary Gemma began reading a book. After a while, Mary Paul came and just grabbed the book from her without a word. She then realized that she was not supposed to read.[7] Also, she found it hard to walk for an hour or do an hour of exercise everyday, as the rule required. She understood the reason for the strictness of Mary Paul. Well acquainted in their early years in Maryknoll, she got to know some of the McKenna family. Coming from a family of army officers, Mary Paul was used to a very disci-plined life. As Sister Mary Gemma explained, Mary Paul was demanding not only of others but of herself as well. Mary Gemma once visited the house of Mary Paul's elderly uncle in Vancouver, Washington State, and thought the place to be very different from the other places she had been. The uncle was a retired army officer, staying at an army post where the military lived. The family had similar traits—"He talked more or less like Sister Paul; very decided when he had something to say." She began to understand Mary Paul better—"when I saw for myself how strict Sister Paul was, I thought, 'No wonder!' There are army people in her family and I suppose that was where she got that kind of discipline, strong discipline."[8]

In an interview many years later, Mary Paul looked back at the work of the pioneers in Hong Kong and China. She said Maryknoll Sisters lived out the goals of a missionary life. They spread Christian faith not only by words, but also by their own examples and deeds. She said, they used means that they saw fit to express Christ's message. By showing others how they lived a Christian life, others would understand and do the same. Through their own examples, services, and affection for others, the Sisters preached the Good News in a practical way. When asked what the most successful achievement in Hong Kong was, Mary Paul answered education.[9]

School Years

Under the leadership of Sister Mary Paul, the convent moved to the new M.C.S. building on Waterloo Road in May 1937. A year earlier, Sir Andrew Caldecott, British governor, laid the cornerstone. The Sisters occupied two wings on the upper floor. Having completed this first stage, the second stage was expected to follow with the construction of the permanent convent building nearby on the same plot of land. The future convent building would serve as a center house for Sisters in the interior as well.[10] The M.C.S. building was an imitation of the new Maryknoll Sisters' Motherhouse in New York, which was completed a few years earlier in 1932. In fact, it was a more outstanding design and structure:[11]

> It was a two story building of brown facing brick with a high pitched gable roof covered with tiles, and it was built around a large open court. Verandahs on all four sides of this court served as corridors, for this school was in the sub-tropics and every room had cross ventilation on east and west, or north and south. The kindergarten was an extension of the south-west corner; the chapel flanked it on the northwest. The covered playground was a prolongation of the north side; the Industrial Department was an additional wing attached to the east side. There were ground floor, second floor, basement rooms and a wonderful attic. Below the auditorium was the wash court, open on one side; below the stage, the "tiffin" room where the children ate their noon lunch....
>
> For the time being, until a separate convent could be built, the Sisters were sleeping in three classrooms, cooking in a section of the domestic science room, and dining in a section of the vestment workroom. They were using the gallery of the auditorium as their community room, and a second floor corridor as library.

By 1937, Maryknoll educational principles were already instituted. M.C.S. provided all classes up to matriculation. As a grant-in-aid school, its students took the examination for entering university. The Maryknoll Sisters had adapted to the local educational needs. In 1937, Sisters Mary Paul and Mary Imelda attended the General Chapter at the Motherhouse. On their return trip, they deliberately traveled via Europe to check on British schools and relevant schoolbooks.[12] Besides regular classes and schoolwork, the School encouraged extracurricular activities, which were particularly important for students. Through these functions, the girls explored their talents, learned to work with others, and knew more about the place where they lived. Activities of the Brownie Pack and Girl Guides Troop provided the girls with opportunities to get out on their own, to be independent, and to develop a close friendship with their schoolmates. They had "a chance to get out and know their city."[13]

When M.C.S. moved to the building in Kowloon Tong, it was a gala day for students. Classes were from kindergarten to matriculation; and there was enough space for students, including regular classrooms, a domestic science room, a science laboratory, and a large auditorium. The covered playground also made possible the offering of physical education. Besides English, French, and Portuguese, the Chinese language was also offered as a subject. After matriculation, students hopefully waited for chances to enter the University of Hong Kong and Lingnan University in Guangzhou.[14] The extracurricular activities in the school were growing. The students performed plays like "Hansel and Gretel." The Girl Guides belonged to the 6th Kowloon Guides, and received honors such as the Prince of Wales Banner and the Guide Shield. The students regularly visited patients and crippled children at Lai Chi Kok Hospital. Many years later, a Sister said the school life of Maryknoll students was specially designed to provide "opportunities for enjoying optimism and happiness."

Recognized for its high standards, M.C.S. was on the government's grant-in-aid list. At the same time, it was under the supervision of the director of education. At the Maryknoll Mission Archives, a business card was found that read—"THE MARYKNOLL SISTERS—WATERLOO ROAD AT BOUNDARY STREET—KOWLOON TONG—HONG KONG." On the card, Sister Mary Paul wrote—"Dear Mother: Herewith a copy of the School Code under which M.C.S. will work from Sept. '41. If later there are any questions, I shall be glad to answer them. Now I don't know what to explain. Keep well, dear Mother. Sr. M Paul." She attached the Grant Code of September 1941, which governed all the grant-in-aid schools in Hong Kong. In three possible ways, the government supported these schools: recurrent grants to pay for salary, rent, and other expenses; contributions to provident and superannuation funds; and capital grants for buildings and equipment. There were two types of schools receiving government subsidies, English Schools and Higher Grade Vernacular Schools. M.C.S. belonged to the first category, which meant that it used English as the basic medium of instruction. M.C.S., therefore, participated in the government's scheme for "public education," and could not refuse applications on "other than reasonable grounds," with preferences given to children born in Hong Kong or whose parents resided in Hong Kong.[15] It accepted students of both Catholic and non-Catholic backgrounds, which was also the policy of Holy Spirit School on Hong Kong Island (see table 3.1). In 1941, M.C.S. had 651 students. More than half of them were Chinese, and the rest were Portuguese, Europeans, Americans, and Indians. Of the twenty-one teachers, twelve were nuns.[16]

The number of classes and age limits of students of English Schools (different from those of Vernacular Schools) were as follows.[17] There were four classes for kindergarten. Class 1 was for children over 4 and not yet 7; Class 2 for over 5 and not yet 8; Class 3 for over 6 and not yet 9; and Class 4 for over 7 and not yet 10. There were ten regular classes:

Class 10 was for those over 8 and not yet 11;
Class 9 for over 9 and not yet 12;
Class 8 for over 10 and not yet 13;

Table 3.1   The enrolment figures for M.C.S., 1936–1939[a]

	Boys		Girls		Total
	Catholics	Non-Catholics	Catholics	Non-Catholics	
1936–1937					
Classes 7–8	55	16	100	109	280
Classes 3–6			75	84	159
Classes 1–2			12	9	21
					(460)
1937–1938					
Infant classes	55	13	58	43	169
Classes 4–8			124	117	241
Classes 1–3			19	9	28
					(438)
1938–1939					
Infant classes	43	17	64	43	167
Classes 4–8			118	152	270
Classes 1–3			22	11	33
					(470)

Note: [a]"Yearly Report from July 1st, 1936 to June 30th, 1937 to be sent to the Vicar Apostolic of Hong Kong," July 1937, p. 2; "Yearly Report from July 1st, 1937 to June 30th, 1938," July 1938, p. 2; "Yearly Report from July 1st, 1938 to June 30th, 1939," July 1939, p. 2, Folder 1, Box 43: Religious Sisters Congregation—Maryknoll Sisters, Section V: Mission Personnel, Hong Kong Catholic Diocesan Archives.

Class 7 for over 11 and not yet 14;
Class 6 for over 12 and not yet 15;
Class 5 for over 13 and not yet 16;
Class 4 for over 14 and not yet 17;
Class 3 for over 15 and not yet 18;
Class 2 for over 16 and not yet 19;
Class 1 for over 17 and not yet 20.

As a member of the public education scheme, M.C.S. followed the government curriculum, which prepared students to take the Hong Kong School Certificate Examination in Class 2 and the matriculation examination for entering the University of Hong Kong in Class 1. The first M.C.S. student was admitted into the University of Hong Kong in 1937, with a full scholarship. Between 1937 and 1941, there was a steady number of matriculated students and some continued their studies at the University. The languages taught in school were "English, Chinese, Kwok Yu [*guoyu*, Mandarin], Cantonese, or Portuguese."[18] The government stressed the importance of learning Chinese even in an English School—"All Chinese pupils in Class 2 are required to take the paper in Chinese at the School Certificate Examination, unless specially exempted by the Director [of Education]."[19] The curriculum also included "physical training," and "instruction in practical hygiene," and "teaching of Art, Handwork and Music or Singing."

The First Two Months of Japanese Occupation

In 1940 when Mother Mary Joseph visited Hong Kong, she found that the colony was already preparing for war. There were "blackouts and mock battles."[20] From the roof of the M.C.S. building, Sisters watched the simulated attack—"invading planes, sweeping searchlights, and the *phoom-phoom-phoom* of antiaircraft fire."[21] At the same time, refugees were flooding into Hong Kong to escape from Japanese attacks in the interior. Some of them settled in temporary camps set up by the government.[22] Outside the convent gates were lines of refugees eagerly waiting for food.[23] Carrying babies on their backs, they looked everywhere for work and accommodation. Some were homeless, sleeping on the street. The situation forced the mother general to make a difficult decision, as she had to decide whether Maryknoll Sisters should continue their missions in the midst of turmoil in Asia.[24] She sadly bade farewell to the Sisters, who were returning to Jiaying (or Meixian), Guangdong Province, from Hong Kong. With foreseeable dangers ahead of them, the Sisters prepared for the worst in China. In 1940, the mother general managed to see some of them who were stationed in northern China and Korea. They traveled from Dalian, in the Northeast, to Shanghai to see her. Some from Fushun, in the Northeast, and others from Korea met with the mother general in Kobe, Japan. At that time, the U.S. government urged Americans to leave Asia. However, the Roman Catholic Church requested pastors to stay in their mission areas unless the situation turned extremely critical. Although the Sisters were not pastors, Mother Mary Joseph decided to follow the Church policy. In spring 1941, she returned to the Motherhouse.

Despite the uncertainties ahead, the policy was to establish a center house for the Sisters of the South China Region. Therefore, the work on the site for the convent continued. By then, traveling to and from missions in the interior came to a halt. The American government did not allow its people to travel to China, and the Sisters did not leave their missions for fear that they could not return afterward.[25] By December 1941, before the outbreak of the Pacific War, the Maryknoll houses in Hong Kong were located as follows (table 3.2).

Maryknoll Sisters produced very detailed records of happenings prior and during the Japanese occupation of Hong Kong. Their personal narratives, presently kept at Maryknoll Mission Archives, are precious information about this critical period of history. According to Sister Santa Maria Manning, the first alarms came on December 7 when the government announced by radio the advance of the Japanese and ordered the volunteers to report for active duty for at least three months. At that time, the nuns did not think the threat was immediate. The next day was the Feast of Our Lady, and in the morning they attended Mass with the school children but were interrupted by the air raid siren. This time, it was not a drill or a "rehearsal," as

Table 3.2 Maryknoll houses in Hong Kong before the Japanese occupation in 1941[a]

	Opened	Closed
19 Chatham Road, Kowloon	11/3/1921	
(moved to 103 Austin Road)	1923	
(moved to Waterloo Road)	5/17/1937	12/1941
Holy Spirit School, Robinson Road	1/10/1927	
(moved to 140 Caine Road)	12/30/1930	
Holy Spirit School established as a separate Community	1937	during the war

Note: [a] Sister Mary Eunice Tolan and Sister Mary Incarnata Farrelly, comp., *Maryknoll Distaff—1932–1941* (Unpublished, 1970), p. 35, Maryknoll Mission Archives. This is a modified version of the original chart, which also contained information on the Motherhouse and the convents in the United States, Hawaii, and other parts of Asia.

they had been having recently. They realized the warning was real:

> On leaving the [St. Teresa's] Church, we saw about 30 planes circling about like beautiful silver birds against a deep blue sky. The crack of anti-aircraft guns and machine gun fire, told us it was no display. Men were flat against walls and we rushed for the convent with the now scattered planes nearly overhead. Somehow, we got across the street and gathered together many frightened children standing by the gate and under the archway [of M.C.S.]. We took them quickly to . . . a partly underground room, a made-to-order shelter.[26]

Hiding in the shelter, the nuns prayed and sang hymns with the children, but their voices were trembling. It took an hour for the planes to leave; and at once M.C.S. became a first-aid post. By noon about twenty auxiliary nurses, who were foreign nationals, arrived. St. John's Ambulance Brigade doctors were to be on duty also. The Sisters packed their suitcases and were ready to leave if they had to. Meanwhile, they took eight-hour shifts for the patients, who were foreigners coming in individually (four of them) or with their families (four families).[27] Too many things happened this day—the eighth—fighting between the Japanese and the British soldiers had broken out. The Sisters heard that Italian priests were to be interned at Stanley prison. Around 11:30 at night, another siren blew, and all rushed to the shelter. The air raid was about half an hour and there was the noise of overhead planes. The nuns who were not on duty returned to bed afterward, "but few slept, even though it had been a most exhausting day."[28]

The next day—the ninth—air raids continued. Their nerves were "jumpy."[29] Many times, the Sisters rushed and hid—"We would drop what we were doing, rush to our shelter, say a complete rosary and a few extra prayers, and the all-clear signal would sound."[30] Although each attack did not last very long, the situation persisted throughout the day. From the students who managed to return (between the raids), they learned about the seriousness of the situation. Oil stations at Lai Chi Kok and a military post on Stonecutters Island suffered from bombing. Two miles to the northeast, the airport was another target. So were the docks on both the Kowloon and Hong Kong sides. Also, the Sisters realized that planes had taken prominent Chinese to the interior the night before. Among those who fled were two students of M.C.S., one was the granddaughter of the late Nationalist leader, Dr. Sun Yat-sen.[31] On the tenth, there were rumors that the Japanese were getting close.

On the eleventh, a shell hit the north side of the M.C.S. building, creating a hole in the wall of the middle classroom on the second floor. The Japanese were trying to silence the anti-aircraft gun near St. Teresa's Church. Already, the British soldiers were abandoning Kowloon and retreating to Hong Kong Island. That morning, the Sisters saw "the lorries with English soldiers and guns withdrawing from the Kowloon Hills."[32] That afternoon, the first-aid post at M.C.S. was disbanded. Instead, the nearby La Salle College of the Christian Brothers was to house the Red Cross. Auxiliary nurses and the Sisters were advised to seek refuge there. While some of the Sisters left temporarily for La Salle, the remaining ones stayed and held on. Policemen were leaving and the Chinese began looting. At night, the Sisters heard "the cars of looters and later the steady tread of the Japanese troops with the roll of tanks and motor lorries, but not a voice."[33] Marching into Kowloon, the Japanese had come on foot, in trucks, and on horses and mules. They carried guns, bayonets, shells, and heavy artillery. Hour after hour that night, they passed the M.C.S. building in the direction of the airport, which was their destination. The atmosphere was "uncanny and nerve racking," and the nuns could hardly sleep.[34] When British soldiers withdrew, they destroyed telephone lines, electricity and water supplies, and sank boats and ferries in the harbor. In the following two weeks, the nuns got water only from an outside well.

On the afternoon of the twelfth, three Japanese soldiers appeared with a Christian Brother and a doctor from La Salle. The Japanese were to billet their soldiers in the M.C.S. building. While they demanded "sheets, bedding, towels and face cloths" for 400 men, Sister Mary Paul did not hesitate to say there were extras for only six. Nevertheless, the Japanese occupied two classrooms on the first floor on the south side and the auditorium that held about 300 people.[35] The advice for the nuns was to stay at the other side of the building, which they readily accepted. They communicated with the soldiers through the writing of Chinese characters, and Sister Anne Clements (Mary Famula), who had served for a few years in Dalian in the Northeast and knew Japanese, was to be the interpreter for the coming months. At dusk when the troops eventually arrived, the Sisters retreated to the northwest corner of the building. Three priests and a foreign man were in the room across from the Sisters, "giving at least a feeling of protection." As the Sisters explained—"The northwest corner of the building could be locked and cut off from the rest of the building with an entrance through the music room, where [Maryknoll] Father [Maurice A.] Feeney stayed, and, as we were permitted to hold the pass keys, was fairly secure."[36] Shortly afterward, the six Sisters who had gone off to La Salle returned.[37] La Salle continued to be a relief hospital, with both foreign and Chinese medical staff and Chinese menial workers, numbering over two hundred.[38]

For almost two months, the Sisters stayed in the M.C.S. building. They were safe though they had very limited freedom and the place was in disorder. The Americans were usually "kept out of sight," occasionally getting out on the covered playground and a few times to the swimming pool.[39] Only the Portuguese and the Chinese Sisters were permitted to go out. The Japanese troops came and went. The first group were engineers, who behaved properly. Once, they presented a chicken to the Sisters; and when they left, they gave away their provisions—rice, flour, onions, sugar, and soy sauce.[40] However, the groups that followed deteriorated in type. The soldiers looted the building and took away materials from the industrial workroom. Soon, the Sisters saw Japanese truck drivers wearing "silk shirts in all liturgical colors."[41] Another group included Chinese coolies, who stayed for a week in the wash court next to the Sisters' room. The last group of Japanese troops was the worst—"the 'Ali Babas' who were the official thieves"—and they removed furniture, clothing, machinery, and anything worthwhile, and sent them all to Japan.[42] With the coming and going, what remained was the filth the soldiers left behind. There were also dozens of horses in the school compound, feeding on the grass, shrubbery, and vegetables. The Japanese had created a mess, but for most of the time, did not show any signs of hostility. Some of them "came in to talk to Sister Famula, either a social call, or to tell of their victories, or to discuss religion."[43] Despite the hectic situation, the Sisters had Midnight Mass and a quiet Christmas. During their stay in the M.C.S. building, they survived despite scarcity and uncertainties, but were not mistreated.

During this period, there was an unexpected and "very pathetic happening."[44] On the evening of December 21, the Japanese brought in 700 prisoners, including British, Canadians, Portuguese, Indians, and Chinese. Many were volunteers, wounded and without any care. Most of them had dysentery and had not eaten for at least three days. As the Sisters saw them standing in lines in the garden and waiting to enter, they felt pity for them as they had suffered from exhaustion and starvation. The Japanese ordered the prisoners to the court, and took their pictures.[45] The next day, the Sisters obtained permission to take care of the wounded and the sick. Two Sisters who were registered nurses and one who was a doctor tried to lessen the pain of the prisoners. Having lost much blood, some of them had clothes that were "as stiff as boards."[46] They did not stay for long though, and by late afternoon left for a former refugee camp nearby. Their presence also raised the possibility of the outbreak of disease. As described, "the filth in the bathrooms was inches deep."[47] Sister Mary Paul asked to have Chinese coolies, who were in the building, to clean up the place. If not, disease was likely to break out. Under the instruction of Sister Anne, "the fire hose was turned on the floors and all the filth was swept out onto the verandah and down the drains." This was done in every bathroom, and afterward "lysol was sprinkled over all the floors and another drastic sweeping was in order." Having repeated the same procedure for a few times, the Sisters felt less nervous about the situation.

The Stanley Internment Camp, 1942

Hong Kong fell to the Japanese on Christmas Day 1941. Far away, in the New York Motherhouse, the Sisters heard the news on the radio on Christmas afternoon.[48] There were altogether twenty-eight Maryknoll Sisters in the colony. They were among the almost three thousand foreign civilians (of the Allied Powers) who stayed behind.[49] The Sisters included twenty-two Americans, one Canadian, three Portuguese, one Chinese, and one Filipina. In the Kowloon Tong convent, there were twenty-one of them. They were:

Mary Paul McKenna—Regional Superior (from Reading, Pennsylvania);
Mary Regina Reardon—House Superior (from Boston, Massachusetts);
Ann Mary Farrell—Assistant (from Pittsburgh, Pennsylvania);
Cecilia Marie Carvalho (Portuguese from Hong Kong);
Anne Clements (Mary Famula) (from Detroit, Michigan);
Henrietta Marie Cunningham (from Framingham, Massachusetts);
Mary St. Bernard Donnelly (from Chicago, Illinois);
Mary Christella Furey (from Omaha, Nebraska);
Frances Marion Gardner (from Seattle, Washington);
Maria Corazon Jaramillo (Filipina from Manila, Philippines);
Joseph Marie Kane (from St. Louis, Missouri);
Santa Maria Manning (from South Boston, Massachusetts);
Mary Liguori Quinlan (from Brooklyn, New York);
Mary Clement Quinn (from Brooklyn, New York);
Mary Camillus Reynolds (from Brushton, New York);
Mary Gonzaga Rizzardi (from New Rochelle, New York);

Mary Reginald Silva (from San Francisco, California);
Rose Olive Skehan (from Watertown, Massachusetts);
Beatrice Ann Stapleton (Matthew Marie) (from Milwaukee, Wisconsin);
Mary Dorothy Walsh (from Kokomo, Indiana); and
Maria Teresa Yeung (from Hong Kong).

On the Hong Kong side, five Sisters stayed in the convent in Holy Spirit School on Caine Road. They were:

Mary de Ricci Cain—House Superior (Canadian from Prince Edward Island, with British citizenship);
Mary Amata Brachtesende (from St. Louis, Missouri);
Mary Eucharista Coupe (from Lonsdale, Rhode Island);
Maria Regis Murphy (from New York City, New York); and
Mary Chanel Xavier (Portuguese from Hong Kong).[50]

There were also two Sisters who were assigned to China but were in Hong Kong at that time for medical care. They were:

Candida Maria Basto (Portuguese from Macau); and
Mary St. Dominic Kelly (from Chicago, Illinois).

On the morning of February 8, 1942, the Sisters in Kowloon Tong had three hours to pack as the Japanese were going to turn the M.C.S. building into a hospital. Bishop Henry Valtorta and Father Andrew Granelli (of P.I.M.E.), who was the pastor at St. Teresa's Church, came before the Sisters left. The bishop explained that he had begged the Japanese not to intern the religious, instead to confine them in their own houses, but he was not successful. At last, the Sisters had to go—"we left with heavy hearts, but resigned to accept whatever God had in store for us, having had numerous proofs of His Divine Providence during the past two months."[51] They were Americans, eighteen of them, and they headed for Stanley on the south side of Hong Kong Island. Sisters Cecilia Marie and Candida Maria were Portuguese, Sister Maria Teresa was Chinese, and Sister Maria Corazon was Filipina. They were not interned because they were Asians or third nationals. Sister Mary Chanel, a Portuguese, was originally in the convent on Caine Road but had come over to the Kowloon side. She was in the Kowloon Tong convent when the Sisters left for Stanley. It turned out the five of them stayed behind in the M.C.S. building for less than two weeks and later moved to an outside apartment. Also, Maryknoll Father Feeney "was not taken that day and within the next three days he was able to obtain a Third National Pass because of his Irish origin."[52]

Leaving the Kowloon Tong convent, the American Sisters rode on a lorry, a ferry, and a bus to the Stanley Internment Camp. For the first time in almost two months, they were out on the street and saw the damage in the city. The scene was "most depressing" as most buildings "had large shell holes, or were badly smashed, and windows broken from shrapnel." "A barren and deserted look," the trees had no leaves or were "burned from fire or the whiz of flying shells."[53] They reached the camp around 5 o'clock, and found the other five Maryknoll Sisters already there. After the fall of Hong Kong, the women from the Caine Road convent had worked in Queen Mary Hospital. They were

Sisters Mary de Ricci, Mary Eucharista, Mary Amata, and Maria Regis. All were subsequently interned. Being on the Hong Kong side for surgical operation, Sister St. Dominic was also sent with the Caine Road Sisters to the camp. The five Sisters had been there since January 21, the day when the Japanese commandeered Queen Mary Hospital for their soldiers and interned all foreign doctors and nurses.[54]

The camp included the grounds of Stanley Prison (but not the prison itself) and the adjacent grounds of St. Stephen's College. The Japanese headquarters were situated on the hill overlooking the prison grounds, and were the former residence of the prison superintendent and doctor.[55] The camp was close to the Maryknoll Fathers' house, and was on "a small peninsula." There was "a narrow strip of land—just a narrow beach on the left, then a road, and a Chinese village; on the right, another beach."[56] Behind the barbed wire, there were the prison warders' apartments, St. Stephen's College, and buildings. Maryknoll Father William Downs, also interned, gave an idea of the camp's layout. It consisted of (1) seven blocks of prison warders' apartments, (2) St. Stephen's College, with two main buildings and some small bungalows, (3) six blocks of flats of the Indian prison guards and their families, (4) a block for single warders, (5) the prison officers' club, (6) a building, then serving as the camp hospital, and (7) another building, then allocated for the British doctors.[57] There were also the cemetery, which became a popular place for reading and chatting, and Tweed Bay Beach, where swimming was allowed but watched over.

The internees mostly lived on the prison grounds, with only a few hundred over at St. Stephen's. In February there were about 2,400 British internees, approximately 300 Americans, and 60 Dutch.[58] Before they arrived in Stanley, most internees had already been interned for weeks in various places. Therefore, they were in a poor condition.[59] Since the Americans were interned rather early, they took up three blocks of the warders' apartments, and were in more favorable accommodations, furnished with at least the minimum, camp cots and some furniture. The Sisters from the Caine Road convent lived in one of the blocks. Besides the "American blocks," the Americans also used the main hall of the prison officers' club for Church and recreational activities. Camp cots were limited and quickly ran out. Many of the later internees had nothing but their own belongings to count on. The buildings had been looted when hostilities broke out in December, and thus latecomers could only sleep on the floor in the Indian flats and St. Stephen's College.

February 8 was "a rainy, drizzly Sunday" when the Sisters moved from Kowloon Tong to Stanley. There were "a huge lorry piled sky high" with baggage and "a bus full of Sisters" riding to the camp.[60] When they arrived, the American blocks were already full. The chairman of the American community did not want to see them sleeping on the cement floor in the Indian flats. He got hold of two rooms in the British section, just a five-minute walking distance away, as "temporary quarters" for the eighteen newly arrived nuns.[61] Eleven Sisters slept in one room and seven in the other. They stored their baggage in the room of the seven Sisters; and while there was space between mattresses in one room, the other was completely occupied and they "just stepped on one another in passing." They placed the bedding on the mattresses, and since it was cold they did not mind very much being crowded together. The first days in the camp were hard to forget—"Very few people in the camp had beds. We rolled the mattresses up into little settees around the room during the day and could not have looked more like refugees sitting shivering on our rolls."[62] As theft was common under the circumstances, they always had at least one Sister in the room to look after their belongings.

After staying there for about two weeks, the Sisters moved to the American blocks. As Sister Mary Liguori recollected, they would have waited longer had Sister Mary Paul not put pressure on the chairman whenever she saw him.[63] The latter tried her best to take care of the others—"Sister knew there were a number of rooms in the American blocks with only two, three or four in them. It did mean some changing around which was a bother for all."[64] At last, the Sisters moved to the ground floor of the same block where the Sisters from the Caine Road convent were staying. In every block of the prison warders, there were six apartments, each with three rooms, two servants' rooms, a kitchen and pantry, bath, and a small laundry room.[65] The Sisters took up the entire apartment on the ground floor. As Sister Santa Maria described, they then felt "fairly comfortable, though crowded."[66] They used the small middle room as the chapel with the Blessed Sacrament reserved. "Curtains were pulled across the width of the room in front of the Blessed Sacrament," and the rest of the room was crowded with camp cots.[67] In the morning, the Sisters in this room rose a bit earlier to clear the beds and to prepare the chapel. They placed boards between chairs and managed to come up with four rows of benches. Used as a chapel, it "was open to the public during the afternoon and it meant much to the Catholics and some non-Catholics also, to have a place to pray in peace and quiet and gather spiritual strength to 'carry on.'"[68] Catholics from the American, British, and Dutch sections visited the chapel; so did priests, Brothers, and the Canadian Immaculate Conception Sisters.

Religious life continued inside the camp. There was public Mass every Sunday and Masses in the quarters everyday. On Sundays and holidays, Masses began at eight, nine, and ten in the morning in the "American Club," the main hall of the prison officers' club.[69] On Sunday afternoons there were religious conferences followed by Benediction. In their own small chapel, the Maryknoll Sisters had two Masses every day. There were also daily Masses in several places—the Immaculate Conception Sisters' quarters in one of the "British blocks," the place of the Salesian Fathers, the "Dutch block," and a cottage not far away from the American blocks. During Lent, Catholics were able to have the Stations of the Cross. Maryknoll Sisters held their May devotions on the lawn in front of their block. Other religious activities were possible too. Three of the Sisters—Mary Dorothy, Mary St. Bernard, and Santa Maria—offered religious classes to the Catholic children in the school of the camp.[70] Some Sisters found opportunities to spread the faith among non-Catholics, especially women. They also had moments of sharing with the Protestant missionaries, who lived right next to them. Baptism and Confirmation were allowed inside the camp.

There were unforgettable memories; and food became the most common subject they talked about. It was always rice—at 9:30 a.m., the kitchen served rice with fish stew or beef stew; at 12:30 p.m., lunch was rice soup; and at 5:00 p.m., rice and meat stew and a few vegetables for supper.[71] The Sisters had "gooey, gummy, dirty, wormy rice with *goo*," which was something between thick gravy and stew.[72] They managed to have some vegetables, though in small portions. Those kinds were "sweet potatoes, carrots, carrot tops, alfalfa, cooked lettuce, beets, popcorn soup."[73] Sometimes, they had bread though they preferred their own bread to that being provided by the camp.

When they received flour rations, they baked their bread. "A slice of real bread was a tonic," Sister Beatrice Ann remembered, and "if we had butter or jam to even brush over it, we were almost delirious." It was dessert, and some even saved the bread to eat later but that "took will power."[74] Nevertheless, there were bad times. Occasionally, the internees queued up for hours under the sun or in the rain outside the canteen. They stood "in lines 2,000 long and waited from six in the morning until their turn came [at] about three in the afternoon when they were able to draw a can of jam and maybe a can of bean sprouts, depending upon what was left."[75] For two weeks, there was not enough food and the nuns had to bear the hunger.

Because of the scarcity of food and necessities, the "political life of the American Camp was intense."[76] The Americans organized the American Club, and met twice a month to discuss their needs and problems. Their chairman was a wealthy businessman, who was very skillful in handling the Japanese and the Chinese go-betweens. On topics of food, furniture, and practically anything, the meetings could become very heated.[77] Speaking up and asking for whatever they wanted, the Americans did not hide their feelings against those who had a bit more supplies or got ahead in the queue outside the canteen. The stressful situation inside the camp sometimes turned even worse. Once, for a while, the Japanese became suspicious. On a day in February, the internees gathered at the athletic field while the Japanese searched their belongings for radios or communication devices. Standing in the "drizzly rain" for hours, many were without umbrellas or raincoats. After each one of them was frisked, they returned to their quarters. "Almost every-one's shoes leaked" after the search.[78] The Japanese took away the typewriter that the Sisters had borrowed from the Maryknoll Fathers. Mary Paul did not hesitate to act, she went and got it back. At times, she made requests to the Japanese. Some were heeded, and she was allowed to send messages to the Sisters in the interior, to allay their worries.[79]

Always, Mary Paul maintained a regular timetable. Mass was at 7:00 in the morning in their own small chapel. Afterward they had breakfast; and then worked until noon when they had prayers, Examen, and Rosary. They had rice soup if it was still being served by the kitchen. In the afternoon, the women used twenty minutes for mending. They also had one hour of free time from 4:00 to 5:00. At 5:00, they had prayer (Compline) and supper. From 7:30 to 8:30, they had community recreation. At 8:30 there were night prayers, and at 9:30 all went to bed.[80] There were no dull moments. Besides the "mending squad," the Sisters also arranged their "washing squad" and "ironing squad." They washed their clothing, sheets, and pillowcases in a bathtub with the wooden Chinese scrub-board. They also did some washing and mending for friends and the Maryknoll Fathers. Their clothes were hung outside the house, and they had to be careful with their things. People even stole clothes pins.[81] With the scarcity of things, the nuns improvised, for example, they ran a very hot iron over a sheet, then, rubbed the candle over the sheet and the melted wax slowly covered the entire surface. Adding a few tapes, they then had a shower curtain for use![82] For recreation, reading was a choice. The American Club kept more than one thousand books of various types, and maintained a small library for the American and British internees. Sisters Mary Amata and Mary Eucharista worked there three afternoons a week, and made some acquaintances.[83]

Releases and Repatriation

The five Maryknoll Sisters who were not interned moved out of the convent to an apartment nearby. They knew on February 8, 1942 when the others were interned that the M.C.S. building would soon become a hospital for Japanese soldiers. After the others left, they tried to save the remaining furniture by moving as much as they could to the St. Teresa's Church's compound until they were told not to do so on February 12. The Japanese asked them the same questions everyday—their age, nationality, and their passes. On February 20, they moved out in two trucks, taking away as much as possible. In the following months, they had to make many business trips. Since there were very few buses, and when they came they were overcrowded, the Sisters usually walked to town. Almost everyday, the Japanese stopped all traffic on the main streets to search entire blocks. This took over two hours, and thus no matter how early the Sisters headed for town, they never knew when they could return home.[84]

They made repeated attempts to ask for the release of four interned Sisters. As Sister Candida Marie justified her request to the Japanese—"All the Maryknoll Sisters now at Stanley are of Irish descent, with the exception of two who are of German and Portuguese descent respectively, and one Italian by birth. However, the four Sisters for whom we are now making application are not only of Irish descent but are actually Irish, their parents having been born and brought up in Ireland, . . ."[85] After many trips to town, their efforts bore fruit. On April 21, 1942, Sisters Mary Paul, Anne, Ann Mary, and Maria Regis were released. As the bishop conveyed to the Japanese foreign affairs office, they were "Irish born of Irish parents from Ireland," and were "therefore comparable to Japanese, Italians or Germans . . . born of Japanese, Italian or German parents who from Japan, Italy or Germany went to settle down in the United States."[86] The Sisters were overjoyed and almost could not believe the good news. In May, Sister Candida Maria left for Yangjiang, Guangdong, and Sister Mary Chanel for Wuzhou, Guangxi—these areas in the interior were not under Japanese occupation.

On June 5, another three were released. They were Sisters Mary Clement, Mary de Ricci, and Mary St. Dominic. They, with their belongings, rode away in a truck. An excited camp had assembled to see them off. Sister Mary Clement described what happened after they had left the camp. They rode off on a lorry with their baggage, and there seemed to be "no movement of any kind" on the road. When they passed Repulse Bay, the area was completely deserted, except for military guards at Repulse Bay Hotel. Gardens and lawns lay in ruins and the beach was covered with garbage. They headed for the Hong Kong-Shanghai Bank Building in Central, where the Japanese headquarters were situated. In half an hour, they arrived in the foreign affairs office, where they received their temporary passes. Sister Mary Paul accompanied them to Holy Spirit School, which they reached in another twenty minutes. The newly released stayed in the convent on Caine Road.

The next morning, they went to get their ration cards. As Mary Clement reported, Caine Road was no longer what it used to be, without any of its previous excitement, but just like one of the other "dori" (*toori* in Japanese, meaning street or road) in the occupied colony.[87] On the streets, English signs and prints were removed or painted over. The miserable begged for food. In a corner, there was "a poor woman crying with hunger and eating some scraps she had salvaged from a garbage pile."[88]

Not far away, "two men, too weak to stand, were lying in the street crying piteously to the passers-by for help."[89] As people suffered from hunger, the Sisters had to be careful with the food they carried or else it would be snatched from them. If caught by Japanese, the snatchers could be beaten, bitten by police dogs, locked up in a cage, and even killed.[90]

Prices rose beyond imagination. Before the war, a bag of flour had cost HK$6; but then under government control, it was HK$70; on the black market, it was HK$200. The Japanese rationed the supply of flour, rice, and sugar. Each day, a person could only get six ounces of flour; and each month, one pound of sugar. As for gas and light, the prices increased by over 500 percent. To forestall looting, shops opened late in the morning and closed early in the evening. There was organized robbery of bombed and empty houses, and that usually happened at night. The nuns were well aware of the situation. There were steps that led from Caine Road to Seymour Road, and were on the side of their house, providing easy access to the lower floors. At night, they were often disturbed by movements along the steps. Burglars removed windows, doorframes, pipes, fixtures, staircases, and floorboards. When the inside was finished, they started with the outside, taking away iron gratings and bars, roof tiles, and then brick by brick, the walls.

In the colony, everything was in the state of alert. In front of public buildings, military guards were on duty. People who passed by bowed to the guards. If they wanted to enter, they had to wash their hands in a basin of antiseptic solution and wipe their feet on a mat with the same solution. When riding ferries and getting on buses at stations, people and baggage had to be searched. The nuns were able to get some exemptions. While they had to bow to the guards, they did not need to wash and wipe. Although they were not searched, their baggage was looked into. Later, some schools reopened but teachers could only speak in Japanese and Chinese. There were English papers and news bulletins, however, to propagandize the success of the Axis Powers to the third nationals. Many decided to go elsewhere. Every day, friends and students went to say goodbye to the Sisters, who were also leaving in groups.[91] Toward the end of June, Sisters Mary de Ricci and Mary St. Dominic left for Guilin, Guangxi.

Rumors about repatriation had long been spreading and finally they came true. Americans and Canadians were repatriated in exchange for Japanese internees elsewhere. The first repatriation took place June 29, when twelve Maryknoll Sisters left Stanley Camp and boarded the Japanese ship *Asama Maru*. They were Sisters Mary Regina, Mary Camillus, Mary Reginald, Mary Liguori, Mary Gonzaga, Mary St. Bernard, Santa Maria, Joseph Marie, Rose Olive, Beatrice Ann, Frances Marion, and Mary Amata. Besides the internees, diplomats and Americans who had not been interned in Stanley also left that morning. As Sister Frances Marion described, "The *Asama Maru* was anchored outside of Stanley, which gave us a slight disappointment in that we did not see Hong Kong before leaving."[92] The repatriated were mostly Americans. On July 23, they were exchanged for Japanese repatriates in Lourenco Marques, East Africa, and went on board the Swedish vessel *Gripsholm*, which had carried Japanese from the United States.[93] On August 25 they arrived in Hoboken, New Jersey. Soon they returned to the Maryknoll Motherhouse. The second repatriation took place more than a year later, and the repatriated were mainly Canadians.

After her release, Sister Mary Paul estimated the loss of Maryknoll property during the Japanese occupation. In Kowloon Tong convent, the Japanese took away all the furniture and clothing. Only a few beds remained. From the chapel, they removed furnishings, the altar, the organ, stalls, and vestments. The loss amounted to HK$25,000. The M.C.S. building became a military hospital for the Japanese, without any remuneration or concessions to the Sisters. Almost all the furniture and science equipment of the school, costing HK$50,000, were looted. The Japanese also burnt the furniture and the small library in the industrial workroom. They confiscated the silk, linen, and brocades for vestments, amounting to HK$60,000. Occupied earlier by the Japanese and subsequently serving as headquarters for the released nuns, the Holy Spirit School building suffered from tremendous damage. The loss of school equipment was HK$8,000, and of the convent HK$2,000.[94]

After repatriation, four Maryknoll Sisters remained interned. Outside the camp, there were eight others staying behind. Two and a half months later, on September 12, Sisters Mary Dorothy and Henrietta Marie were released. That day the Maryknoll Fathers were also released, except Donald L. Hessler and Bernard F. Meyer. Sisters Mary Christella and Mary Eucharista stayed to assist the priests in Catholic Action, and continued their religious classes, choir practice, hospital visits, and management of the library. They spent Christmas in the camp. Sister Mary Christella remembered some small Christmas gifts they could offer, which were still very much appreciated—a woman who was known to be from a very wealthy family cried after receiving a small bar of soap. Midnight Mass was conducted outdoors. The specials for Christmas dinner were a bit of pork wrapped in cabbage leaves and a slice of fruitcake received from Red Cross. By then about twenty Americans were left in the camp.[95] The Sisters noticed the difference between the Americans and British—"The 'Merry Christmas' as rendered by the American internees was spontaneous, hearty, and well meant; on the other hand, the British recoiled and, . . . demanded why it was a 'merry Christmas.'"[96]

Toward the end of 1942, the Maryknoll community was preparing to leave Hong Kong. In September, Sister Mary Paul received a cable, which read "Maryknoll orders all priests, brothers, Sisters home except free China. Communicate message Toomey. Cable receipt. Bishop James Walsh."[97] The "harrowing tales" of the repatriated in Maryknoll were the reason for the decision. Although there were no definite plans, the nuns knew they had to make the necessary arrangements for departure.[98] Shortly afterward, Sister Maria Regis headed for Guilin, Guangxi and Sister Ann Mary for Macau.

By January 1943, the remaining two Sisters were released from the camp. Sister Mary Eucharista described the situation outside. Their truck passed Wanchai, and they noticed the absence of cars or buses on the road. At the foreign affairs office, the Sisters received temporary passes and applied for regular passes.[99] In the beginning, Mary Eucharista was not sure how much freedom she could have though she was released. Soon, she realized that, "if you walked alone as if you were sure no one would question your right to do so, there was much less danger of being troubled than if you looked the least bit uneasy or frightened."[100] Only once when she was out on the street she was asked for her pass. There were more damages of war in Wanchai than Central. The further "along the water front toward St. Paul's Hospital and North Point, where the Japanese made their first landing on Hong Kong, the more war scars there were."[101] On the Kowloon side, it was a tragic scene. As described—"Shells of once lovely houses now stand stripped of doors, window frames, floors, not to mention furniture."[102] The shops were looted of everything. This was their last glimpse of Hong Kong. All Maryknoll Sisters left Hong Kong in January 1943. There were ten of them. Sister Mary Eucharista left for Luoding; Sister Henrietta Marie for Wuzhou; and Sisters Mary Paul, Mary Clement, Mary Dorothy, Christella, and Cecilia Marie for Guilin. Sisters Anne, Maria Teresa, and Maria Corazon joined Ann Mary who had earlier arrived in Macau. Only after the war in September 1945 did the Maryknoll community return.

Return of the Maryknoll Sisters

The Japanese surrendered in August 1945. Sister Ann Mary and Sister Anne were the first to return. The M.C.S. building was still a hospital for Japanese soldiers. Therefore, they stayed temporarily at St. Mary's School, Tsimshatsui, and later moved to a small bungalow on Prince Edward Road, Kowloon Tong. In October, Sisters Mary Clement, Mary Christella, and Henrietta Marie arrived. Shortly afterward, Sisters Mary Paul and Cecilia Marie also returned. Everywhere—the M.C.S. building, the convent, and the La Salle building—there had been looting. It was wise of the Sisters to have brought a few cots, blankets, and mosquito nets from the interior. When Sister Mary Paul returned, she immediately looked for possibilities of regaining the M.C.S. building, which now housed 1,200 Japanese soldiers. All the school furniture was gone and patients slept on the floor. Sister Mary Paul learned that the British had requisitioned large buildings for the wounded; the same had happened to La Salle College. The British were still searching for places to hospitalize their sick soldiers.[103]

In November, 800 more Japanese soldiers were hospitalized, increasing the number of patients in the M.C.S. building to 2,000. By then Sister Mary Paul had abandoned the idea of reopening M.C.S. somewhere else in the neighborhood, as this might give the authorities an excuse to delay the return of the building. Although Hong Kong was under military rule, she thought it was "unfair" that Maryknoll was denied its own property. She wrote to the Chief of Civil Affairs, Brigadier D. M. MacDougall, but the response was not encouraging. Unwilling to give up, Sister wrote again to the General Officer Commanding, Major-General F. W. Festing, who happened to be a Catholic.[104] In both letters, dated November 16 and 19, she argued that M.C.S. should start as soon as possible, as there were presently no schools in the neighborhood. According to her, the Education Department and the local community were anxious to see the School reopen. In addition, the building was Maryknoll property and was not built on a government grant. The Sisters should regain the building. For the time being, they were staying in a small bungalow with very difficult living conditions. The M.C.S. building was also the location of the Maryknoll convent, the regional center of the Sisters in South China. Being deprived of their building, the Sisters could not take up any work. They found it hard to understand why their situation after the war was no different from that during the Japanese occupation. Sister Mary Paul said that despite the bishop's intention to protect Church property, Maryknoll Sisters had been forced to leave the building and to seek refuge in the interior of China;[105] on their return they were not being permitted to live in their own house. Without any hesitancy, she claimed that the authorities were "depriving a neighbourhood of a badly needed school, a religious community of its home, of resumption of any work and that after more than three years of refugee existence."[106] Subsequently, she received an appointment with Festing.

In the meeting with Festing, she understood the British tried to keep hospitals and most troops on the Kowloon side. She made a number of suggestions. Instead of asking for the entire building, she suggested that the Sisters occupy a part of it while the sick soldiers continued to stay there. The next day, the British officers took the nuns to a vacated Chinese school but they thought the place was not suitable to restart M.C.S. Without any alternatives, they indicated that they were willing to use the top floor of the M.C.S. building, except certain rooms, and to let the soldiers stay in the rest of the place. The Sisters were to have their own entrance and chapel. Finally, Festing agreed.[107] Mary Paul thought if they moved into the building it would be easier for them to get rid of the Japanese and prevent the British soldiers from getting in. After the war, she was surprised to see large numbers of military personnel—air, army, and navy—in Hong Kong. The admiral of the British naval fleet was there. As she observed, Hong Kong served as a military post for the British who were unsure of the development in China and the future of the colony.

Walking into the M.C.S. building, the Sisters appraised the damage. They were lucky that the doors and windows were still there despite the serious looting.[108] When they moved back in December, they were able to occupy more areas than they had originally asked for. Sister Mary Paul pressed hard and succeeded. They took up the building except the covered playground and the basement underneath, the auditorium, and the gallery.[109] The industrial workroom was reserved for sick soldiers. The Sisters could not help but cheer over her achievement, as the nearby buildings were still being requisitioned. The British military had offered assistance and provided trucks for the moving on December 18 and the following few days. Under the direction of the Sisters, the Japanese war prisoners moved furniture and cleaned the place. For a few days, the Sisters collected the belongings they had stored elsewhere—in the Italian convent, hall and attic of St. Teresa's Church, and the basement of a priest—but often found them rotten and damaged by dampness. Even books, which had remained in the School, were rotten and eaten by white ants. Cleaning tasks were unbelievably difficult, as the Japanese had been packed into the building and the dirt seemed impossible to remove. The building had "floors thick with dirt, so thick it could be scraped off, doors jammed and sometimes burnt open, lights twisted and turned, with additional electric wire[s] running around everywhere; the chapel denuded, coats of dirt on whatever fixtures were left behind."[110] The swimming pool and the changing rooms were intact. However, the garden was in ruins, heaps of yellow clay lay on the lawn; the covered playground had become a kitchen and another playground had an incinerator. Sweet potatoes were growing on the school ground. The covered playground was still used by the military—"all enclosed and divided up with heavy concrete walls and is used for dental clinic, dining room, kitchen where a big concrete kitchen has been built in."[111] The neighborhood was taken over by the military and was rather dark and isolated from the rest of the city at night. While there was still looting, the building was guarded by British and then Indian guards and was quite safe. Sisters and visitors used the Waterloo Road gate, and guards prevented entry from the Boundary Street gate. Until May 1946, the Sisters lived with 600 Japanese soldiers in the building. Subsequently, they took possession of the entire building (see figure 3.1).

Figure 3.1 Maryknoll Convent School on Waterloo Road in 1950. In the middle of Waterloo Road was a nullah with stone walls on both sides.
Source: Sisters Photo Collection, Maryknoll Mission Archives.

After the war, there was scarcity of everything. The Sisters in Hong Kong made requests to the Motherhouse. Some of these items were a sandpaper machine, which would be resold after use, and varnish for the floors of the M.C.S. building. In January 1946, Mary Paul sent out a purchase order to the Motherhouse. The two-page list included canned vegetables, preserved meat, fish, fruits, dried fruits, jam, cereals, pasta, and all kinds of household needs! The supplies were to be sent through the United Nations Refugee and Relief Administration (U.N.R.R.A.), which meant free transportation. They even asked for prayer books. In earlier correspondence, some of the Sisters requested habits and sent in their measurements. They had been wearing their habits for a long time, and Sister Maria Teresa was doing the mending. Some of them had stayed in China during the war and the condition of their clothing was unacceptable. Another needed item was shoes, in the right sizes.[112] As Mary Paul wrote to Mother Mary Joseph, the nuns had tried to "look respectable, which is quite a problem these days and would have been impossible if it hadn't been for your goodness in sending those grey cotton habits to us."[113] Hong Kong society was experiencing appalling poverty, and the nuns could not afford to buy anything and could only ask the Motherhouse.

Two weeks before reopening M.C.S., the nuns spent "extra busy days scrubbing, cleaning floors, windows, furniture," and everyday there was a squad of about twenty Japanese to help them with the work.[114] On January 8, the School reopened, and for the time being, it also accepted boys to the upper classes.[115] As Sister Marie Corinne Rost, who was among the first group of Maryknollers to go abroad for mission after the world war in 1946, recalled, M.C.S. was taking in some boys of La Salle College because the Christian Brothers were not yet able to return to their school building.[116] The M.C.S. enrolment was 450. The students sat in substandard classrooms, with inadequate furniture, equipment, and facilities. Everybody was desperate to make up for lost time; anything handy was used—"file drawers were used as chairs, some pupils brought their own stools, collapsible tables (which often collapsed during class!) served as desks, and classes were often held on the playground or lawn...."[117] In the next three years, the building underwent repairs and renewal. The School now took up to almost seven hundred students. In 1948 government inspectors wrote up their report on M.C.S. By then the School had undergone rehabilitation. Much progress had been made since it reopened two years ago. There were altogether twenty-seven teachers. Points four to eleven of the report read:[118]

MARYKNOLL CONVENT SCHOOL
INSPECTION REPORT 1947/48

4. *Buildings and Accommodation.*   The buildings which were used as a hospital by the Japanese during the occupation are now in an excellent state and exceptionally well kept. The classrooms are spacious and well lighted. There is a covered playground which is used for physical training. There is an excellent Assembly Hall with a platform that can be used as a stage for school dramatic performances. The playground is spacious enough for a netball court and basket ball court. The swimming pool completed in 1941 unfortunately suffered at the hands of the Japanese but when funds are available it is hoped to put it into use.

The Science laboratory has recently been fitted with well designed benches particularly suited to the teaching of biology.

5. *Equipment.*   The new school desks are of an excellent design, in three sizes, and can be adjusted to individual needs.

The school is well supplied with pictures and the classrooms have ample blackboards and panels for the display of students' handwork.

The laboratory equipment is adequate and the students themselves have supplied live-stock for the study of biology.

The Kindergarten equipment is very good and sufficient for each child to enjoy.

6. *Libraries.*   The staff reference library has a good supply of books and there is a central library for students. Each class has its own library of interesting reading books.

7. *Class Organization.*

Class	No. of Divisions	No. of Pupils
2	1	10
3	1	22
4	1	31
5	2	77
6	2	79
7	2	80
8	2	81
9	1	40
10	1	41
Kindergarten	5	209
		Total 670

8. *School Discipline and Order.* The girls conduct themselves in a pleasant well mannered fashion and are bright and responsive in class. The school uniform is neat and comfortable and suitable for all ages.

9. *Curriculum.* The school curriculum has been well planned and the general standard of the work is high.

10. *Examination Results.*

School Leaving Certificate Examination, June 1948.

No. Entered	No. Passed	No. Failed	% Passed
10	8	2	80

The School Certificate Examination results were very good and above the average. In all Subjects uniformly good marks were obtained.

11. *Extra-Curricular Activities.* The school has its own Girl Guide Company, the 6th Kowloon, the captain being an old girl of the school. This company was successful in winning the shield in 1948.

The School Science Club which meets each Saturday reflects the keen interest of the girls in this subject and much credit should be given to the teacher of biology whose own enthusiasm is responsible. Many specimens of local insects and animal life have been collected during the past year by members of the class.

(s) E. M. Gray
Lady Inspector of Schools
7.12.48.

(s) L. G. Morgan
Senior Inspector of Schools
7.12.48.

The report concluded with the observation that there was "a general air of lively activity in the school."

At the same time, the Sisters also engaged in services for the less fortunate children. They took care of the Boys and Girls Clubs for school-age children who could not afford formal education. The objective was to educate them in social responsibility, their responsibilities to themselves and to others. Meeting in the afternoon at M.C.S., the Sisters arranged the hiring of teachers for the children. The children managed to acquire some basic literacy and mathematics.[119] With government encouragement, the Club was the first of its kind in the colony. There was the urgent need to take care of the children who had arrived recently with their parents from China. With the help of the Sisters, some of them were able to obtain financial support and later attended regular schools.[120]

In 1946, Sister Mary Paul was elected to the General Council and returned to the United States. Sister Imelda became superior of the Sisters in the South China region. In December the first group of Maryknoll Sisters to embark on foreign mission after the war, reached Hong Kong. The community had twenty-four members, who stayed in the convent in Kowloon Tong.[121] The new arrivals were in their early twenties, and right away, the next month, they were in the classrooms. With the need for teachers, there was no time to lose. Among them was Sister Rose Duchesne Debrecht, who was surprised to know that the medium of instruction was

English. Before her arrival, she thought she would study Cantonese and communicate with the students in their mother tongue. At that time, English schools were more prestigious and students acquired a satisfactory command of English, so as to allow them to find better jobs in the future. Having understood the circumstances, she concluded—"The students were so able to learn English that we realized too that, if you were really going to fulfill your own objective of being a great help to them that you'd need to sacrifice your own personal interests in the second language in order to give them every opportunity to speak."[122] Indeed, there were no leisure moments to think further as the Sister teachers had long timetables (thirty periods a week, and forty minutes a period) and large classes (forty students or more) to handle.[123] They followed a tight schedule everyday:[124]

Morning	5:15	Getting up
	Twenty minutes later, morning prayers together	
		(Prime from the Divine Office)
	Half an hour of meditation, then Mass, breakfast	
	8:20	School started—assembly, teaching
Noon	Rosary together, lunch	
Afternoon	1:20	Classes began
	3:30	School ended
After school	Correcting students' work, preparing next day's classes	
	5:00	A compulsory 15-minute walk,
		Spiritual reading, Vespers (prayers),
		15-minute reading about Chinese culture
Evening	6:00	Supper
	After supper, an hour of recreation together	
	Community prayer ended with Compline (which was sung)	
	9:30	Bedtime, lights out

At the age of twenty-four when she arrived in Hong Kong, Rose Duchesne came to realize that her students were not very much younger than herself. The Chinese had lost the opportunity to study during the world war, and most of them registered with the school five years younger than their real age. During home visits, the mothers usually asked the nun whether she wanted to know the "school age" or the "real age" of their daughters. Teaching upper classes, her students could actually be twenty-one or twenty-two. This was quite common in schools in the postwar years. In her fourth year of teaching, she felt the pressure. As she recalled: "It suddenly hit me that the responsibility of teaching was a very great one and how had I the audacity for three years, to stand in front of a group of people, some of them were my own age."[125] All at once, crisis struck. "It took every atom of my strength to get me into the classroom and after about five minutes I would forget myself in the interest that I had in them," she said.[126]

In 1948, Holy Spirit School on Caine Road also reopened. It acquired grant-in-aid status and came under the new name Maryknoll School, as the government requested the change of name to reflect the sponsorship of the School. Since the end of the war, the Sisters had been negotiating for its opening. Like the Canossian Sisters trying to get back their school also on Caine Road, Maryknoll appealed to the court for recovery of the premises for teaching purposes.[127] Nevertheless, any plans could only be "verbal" as families who occupied the building were unwilling to leave.

With the shortage of houses, there was great difficulty in persuading occupants to find other places to stay. Earlier in the year when some of the residents moved out, the Sisters knew they could act. During the summer, they started repairing the building. In August, they made use of two vacated rooms for registering girls who wanted to begin their studies the next month.[128] Reflecting on the lack of education opportunities, about seven hundred girls (plus a few boys) lined up that morning to apply for admission. They took both written and oral exams. The Sisters could only accept six classes; one of them had 36 students, the others 39, 37, 30, 28, and 13.

While there was enough enrolment, there was much anxiety as to whether the building could be used on time. Since the beginning of summer, much work was being done on the war-torn building. The outside was covered with bamboo scaffolding; so were the inside stairways and rooms. The roof "was scattered all over three floors in the form of termite-eaten beams, decaying rafters, tiles, mud, plaster and bricks."[129] There were no roofs, no lights, no icebox, no plumbing, no phone service, and few helpers. As the Sisters were involved in the manual work, they found it difficult—they had to "crawl under bamboo scaffolding, squeeze between the wall and bamboo poles, step through two feet of shavings, into a tub of mud plaster"; and one of them might find her veil brushed against a newly painted wall or her apron caught on a projecting nail. At night, they got accustomed to their "various trundle beds," luckily without falling off as they were "surrounded by saws and nails hammers and logs."[130] Two of them "spread their bohookas over two carpenters' horses," another's "bohooka on two boxes could not stand the strain and she came stumbling in for morning prayers," and another slept "on chairs between the table and the wall." At last, with hard labor, the school reopened after seven years on September 6.

After opening their schools, the Sisters were gradually getting on their feet. However, the Communist victory in 1949 soon had a terminating effect on Maryknoll endeavors in China. Communists took over Yangjiang, Luoding, and Jiaying in Guangdong, and Wuzhou and Guilin in Guangxi, where missions were situated. In December 1950, the Communists declared martial law in Wuzhou and occupied the convent. This was also the case in other mission locations.[131] From 1950 to 1952, Maryknoll Sisters in China were under house arrest; finally they left China. Having been in confinement in Jiaying, Sister Joan Marie Ryan was released in 1952. When she crossed the border to Hong Kong, she told the British soldier on guard: "I don't have a passport, but I'm a Maryknoll Sister and my Sisters in the Colony will identify me." The reply she got was: "You don't need a passport, Sister. Your face is passport enough."[132]

Meanwhile, Hong Kong experienced a flood of refugees from the interior. At the turn of the 1950s, Hong Kong faced new circumstances and problems—"hills became literally honey-combed with all sorts of lean-to shacks made from anything obtainable. The lucky ones had shelters made from old five-gallon kerosene tins; others were not so fortunate and had to be content with paper cartons, gunny sacks, or, in many cases . . . , holes dug in the hillside."[133] Newcomers, who fled from different places in China, brought with them nothing but a bundle of clothes, and could only live in wooden shacks, which were in appalling conditions. With the dramatic increase of the population in millions, demands for relief, housing, medical care, and education posed a tremendous burden to society and the government. Together with refugees from the interior, Maryknoll Sisters faced the challenges of another period of history in Hong Kong. The Sisters were to develop elaborate welfare, medical, social, and educational services in the community, and it was through new endeavors that their role as a third force became more apparent.

CHAPTER FOUR

EXTREME POVERTY OF THE 1950S, KING'S PARK AND TUNG TAU TSUEN

The movement towards organized work by the Maryknoll Sisters in refugee resettlement areas in Hong Kong began with a fire which swept the densely populated area known as "Tung Tau"—just twenty minutes walk from Maryknoll Convent School, on the eve of Thanksgiving Day 1951. And yet, paradoxically, the work did not start with the fire, as for years the Sisters had been visiting the homes which had given them many contacts for apostolic work among the people. These openings in the homes of the people again went back to the opening of a little free school for the poor known as the Boys and Girls Club on Maryknoll Convent School premises. . . . It was through the apostolic work which our Sisters took up in their free time in becoming acquainted with the parents of the poor school students that made the fire in Tung Tau the turning point for us in our work for the poor, and was as it were, the stepping stone to more and more work for the refugees.

Maryknoll Sisters, Hong Kong, 1954[1]

The 1950s were the refugee years of Hong Kong, which witnessed a dramatic upsurge in population. People were fleeing from China and settling in the colony. At first, the government thought newcomers would stay temporarily, but it was wrong. The plight of the poor necessitated immediate attention and actions. Without sufficient means to handle the situation, the government had to rely on the assistance of voluntary groups. As one of "those colonies in the residue of the old empire" of the British, Hong Kong could not expect anything from the foreign master but had to count on its "own devices in social affairs."[2] Pessimists believed that the colony was suffocating from the problems and was in a state of despair. Indeed, difficulties were too immense for the government to handle by itself, and it was more than willing to have religious groups share the responsibilities. In 1946 when the Catholic hierarchy was established in China, the Hong Kong vicariate became a diocese with parishes formally created.[3] Catholic missioners who recently left the interior became "part of the Church's answer to the problem."[4] Surely, circumstances provided a fertile ground for the organized social service of Maryknoll Sisters. With the departure of all of them from China, the four houses in Hong Kong had altogether forty-three Sisters in 1953.[5]

The early 1950s marked another phase in the history of Hong Kong and the Maryknoll Sisters. In the local refugee communities, nuns began their organized work, providing accommodation, relief, and social service to the poor. Demands were all embracing—food, clothing, shelter, medical care, and education. Trying to offer the people basic support, the Sisters encountered new challenges and pioneered in new fields. In King's Park and Tung Tau Tsuen, they launched their welfare program for the homeless and needy. At the same time, they continued their commitment in education. Besides the two existing schools, they opened new ones for poor children. Parish work was another focus of attention, as the Hong Kong diocese became one of the fastest growing in the world. Through the years, the Maryknoll mission expanded its scope and reached out to more people and localities. Working in a desperate environment, the Sisters were missioners of the deprived and less fortunate. Circumstances were unprecedented, and proved to be a test of their ability, perseverance, and even talents. Shouldering the responsibilities, which should be those of the authorities, they provided relief, welfare, and social services to the poor refugee community of Hong Kong. In doing so, they took up the role of a "third force," mediating between the "first force" of the government and the "second force" of the Chinese people.

The Sisters found the situation after the war incredible, as Hong Kong suddenly became a society with millions of people. Whereas the population was about half a million in 1945, it grew to over two million in 1951. The influx of refugees increased the complexity of the population, with people coming from almost everywhere in the interior and speaking almost every Chinese dialect.[6] The small colony became very crowded. The impossible seemed to be happening, as the nuns found thousands and thousands of new arrivals without work and accommodation, squatting on the hillsides. When the refugees crossed the border some just carried a bundle of clothes tied with a rope. "One wonders how they actually exist[ed]."[7] Those from northern China had never been to the south and were forced to live in a miserable environment. Those from the South could be intellectuals, former government officials, and military officers. They were among the first groups who fled to Hong Kong, and were under circumstances that they had never imagined or comprehended.

Since many of the refugees came with very little belongings, they lived in very shabby squatter huts made of tin plates and wooden boards, clustered together on hill slopes and abandoned lands. While the squatter problem was small in the immediate postwar years, "only minor expressions of the postwar housing shortage," the situation quickly got out of hand after 1949.[8] "It was mostly during the years of 1949, '50 and '51 [that] people with no homes began to find some vacant hill side and built a shack of wood or tin. . . . until a whole hill-side and its valley were crowded with such dwellings."[9] Between 1949 and 1956, the number of squatters expanded from 30,000 to 300,000.[10] Five or six people stayed in a wooden shack of only forty square feet, and the density of the squatter areas could be up to 5,000 people per hectare. The landscape changed quickly—"Here you find mountain after mountain side, or hill-top after hill-top crowded with such little one room huts," which then formed into villages.[11] In the early 1950s, these villages were huge and began to be self-supporting. As described, many were "with their own shops, schools and small industrial units as well as a variety of illegal enterprises."[12] The various businesses were housed in temporary huts or one-story village-type structures that survived ravages of the Japanese occupation. The wooden shacks were so close to each other that a fire could spread through an entire village very swiftly. Such tragedies happened rather often in the colony, putting the government to the test and offering openings to missioners for relief work.

"Maryknoll Sisters' Scheme Cottages"

The Church responded faster than the government in meeting the needs of society. An incident demonstrated the ability of missioners to shoulder some of the government's responsibilities. In January 1950 a fire broke out in the refugee settlement of Tung Tau Tsuen, which was close to the Maryknoll convent in Kowloon Tong, and had devastating consequences. Many people were thrown out on the street, as their homes were destroyed. Concerned about the plight of fire victims, Maryknoll Sisters provided shelter for over eighty of them in the M.C.S. building for almost a month. With assistance from the Catholic Action of St. Teresa's Parish, including voluntary groups of both Chinese and foreigners, beds and meals were already available before government relief arrived.[13] Some of the M.C.S. students also donated their clothes. Subsequently, the authorities managed to supply food and clothing to the people. The event left a strong impression on the Sisters; the suffering of the poor became "a constant preoccupation" of their thinking, especially as some of them were already involved in catechetical work in Tung Tau Tsuen and got to know the residents there. Soon, the nuns found their answer to the situation in organized relief and social work.[14]

In 1950, Tung Tau Tsuen had a population of 78,000 people who lived in squatter huts on the hillside. There were also "village type structures or old apartment type buildings" that suffered from war damages.[15] Tung Tau Tsuen found "the Old Walled City with its dark, dirty alleys, drug and gambling dens, a hideout for criminals and vice."[16] Already living in a highly undesirable situation, people there knew the worst could happen once a fire broke out.

In November 1951, Tung Tau Tsuen suffered from another fire, which was more destructive than the previous one. The word "tsuen" means village and all of a sudden 1,700 people of the village became homeless. Immediately, the Sisters hurried there—twenty minutes of walk from the convent—with the hope of offering help. They had been teaching catechumens in the area, and were very familiar with the surroundings. Chaos was all they saw; they could do nothing but take with them a girl whose home was destroyed. Her parents were not around, and when the nuns saw her, she was "trudging ahead . . . along the road lugging a heavy suit case and her bedding."[17] That night, she was taken care of in the convent. The next day, the Sisters were back again to the depressing site. Some of their catechumens had been crowded together on the second floor of a small shop—"some exhausted and covered with mud trying to get some rest while others just sat there on the floor looking into space."[18] The shop owner was generous enough to offer at least a temporary shelter. Nevertheless, the poor people had no permanent place to stay. It was clear that relief work was necessary.

Sister Mary Imelda succeeded Mary Paul as regional superior of the Maryknoll Sisters. She was to be called "the carbon copy of Mary Paul" as she retained very much the administrative style of her predecessor. After the fire, Mary Imelda looked for possibilities for providing accommodation for the victims. Resettlement was the most urgent task. She made contacts for donations, and at the same time, discussed the matter with Maryknoll Father Paul J. Duchesne, who was in charge of the National Catholic Welfare Conference (N.C.W.C.), an organization founded by bishops in the United States. The provision of some kind of permanent housing was needed, and the families could then relocate to the new homes. Anxious to implement the housing project, Sister Mary Imelda and Father Duchesne approached the Resettlement Office, which was then basically responsible for granting land sites to the refugees. The officer in charge of resettlement, James Tinker Wakefield, accompanied Mary Imelda to possible areas for the project. At last, the government supported the plan and allocated an area, stretching over King's Park and the adjacent Homantin Villages, for the homeless. As a response to the refugee problem and the chaotic situation, the government assigned certain areas on hillsides where people built their wooden huts and other possible accommodations; and these areas were known as resettlement areas.[19] In 1952, the Urban Council formulated regulations for the resettlement areas, which required a renewable permit (and the accompanied fee) to erect and maintain any structure in such localities.[20] King's Park was one of the resettlement areas.

At that time, the government defined King's Park as bounded by Waterloo Road (in the northwest), Nathan Road (in the west), Austin Road (in the south), and the Kowloon Canton Railway track (in the east and northeast), whereas Homantin was just north of King's Park over the other side of the track. A decade later, in the early 1960s, King's Park was redefined and reduced to land north of Gascoigne Road.[21] In 1951 in the assigned area of about one square mile, Sisters began their work.[22] King's Park was "mostly a grave yard with a few wooden shacks in one spot; no roads, no water, except from a few wells; all hills and just waste land."[23] Almost everything was lacking. Although Sisters were able to make a start, they foresaw many difficulties ahead. Writing to Mother Mary Columba Tarpey, then Mother General who succeeded Mother Mary Joseph, Sister Mary Imelda reported the amount of funding solicited and asked if the Motherhouse could obtain further donations from the United States.[24] Mary Imelda also launched a public fund-raising campaign, and made multiple trips to local schools to seek contributions for the fire victims.

The housing project was officially registered as "Maryknoll Sisters' Scheme Cottages." Designed and supervised by Maryknoll Brother Albert Staubli, who was an architect, the cottages were built of stone bricks and were fireproof. They were made of granite, which was quarried on the site, abundant locally and thus very low in cost.[25] In a few months, twenty stone cottages were ready for the new occupants of King's Park. They were the first of its kind in Hong Kong, and Maryknoll's housing project was also the first attempt to provide accommodation to newcomers after the war, as a remedy to the problem of squatters.[26] Screened by the government for their eligibility for resettlement, inhabitants were fire victims or legal squatters whose huts were demolished by the authorities for various reasons. As the Sisters explained, refugees came in a rush and had no ready income. Without money or even belongings, they could only "secure a few old tins or in some cases corrugated boxes and put up a shanty on the side of one of the many hills in the colony."[27] They were then known as squatters, and because of pressing circumstances, were considered legal squatters. Indeed, the problem of housing was acute. Later on, forty-two more stone cottages were erected on the hillside and two others were scattered on isolated spots.[28] From individuals and firms, the Sisters secured donations of over HK$150,000 for construction of these stone cottages. More of them were to be built to cater to growing demands; but the total number of stone cottages differed in the different accounts of the nuns. The number most often quoted in their records was seventy-one, which was mentioned in the 1953 report.[29] During the screening process, the poorest and most desperate were accommodated. Inhabitants did not pay for or rent the cottages. Nor did they own the property, and they had to return the cottages when moving out.

By July the 71 stone cottages housed 71 families of 326 people in King's Park and Homantin. The stone cottages had one/two room(s), a small kitchen, and a bathroom. Later, with further donations, the Sisters erected another type of cottage, a total of eight. Made of pounded mud (rather than stones) and with only one room, the other group of cottages cost HK$850 or about US$160 each, which meant more than 50 percent reduction in construction cost. These cottages were provided free-of-charge to the homeless. The Sisters supplied beds to families who had been sleeping on the floor. Also, they created a modest housing cooperative with two larger house units, and offered it to families whom they employed. These families had a steady income, and were required to make some contribution. Paying a small amount every month, the money would be reinvested for the developing of more co-ops.[30]

With donations secured, the Sisters were able to carry out their housing project on government land. At the beginning, the immediate objective was rehabilitation of the fire victims of Tung Tau Tsuen and the homeless who had been coming from China. The project in King's Park was the first of its kind in Hong Kong, after which other religious bodies and private companies also launched similar endeavors. Soon, the resettlement area grew in size. By the end of the 1950s, the inhabitants in King's Park and Homantin increased to 40,000. They spoke different dialects, mostly Cantonese (*Guangdonghua*) but also Hakka (*Kejiahua*), Swatonese (*Shantouhua*), and Mandarin (*Guoyu*). Initially, they paid an annual land tax of HK$25 to the government. It was necessary to appoint district officers to the areas and to improve facilities and transportation. In King's Park and Homantin, the government assigned officers to take care of local demands. It also built roads, arranged bus routes, and began to supply electricity and water to residents. Subsequently, the authorities raised the land tax to HK$160. Speaking for local people, the Sisters were against the tax increase. They argued that occupants needed more time to rehabilitate and to settle down. As they explained, the people were not only fire victims but also refugees from the interior. Many of them were from the quiet, peaceful life of the country, and had difficulty adapting to the city life of Hong Kong. Nevertheless, the protests went unheeded; and occupants of the cottages often sub-let their places and used the rent to pay the land tax.[31]

The housing project also covered Tung Tau Tsuen, where rehabilitation was starting. Since 1947 the Sisters had been working there—with catechumens and most children of the Boys and Girls Club. The accounts recorded that ten stone cottages were built for the fire victims in 1952; many occupants were catechumens. The Sisters used a room for religious instructions, and later rented part of a shop close to the residence of the catechumens on the main street.[32]

Desperate Need for Resettlement in Hong Kong

Gradually, the government realized that it had to formulate a policy to deal with impending problems of refugees. Besides socioeconomic concerns, the situation created sources of tension for different political groups.[33] These were poor refugees, the colonial administration, former Nationalist officials, and leftist forces. As anxieties were rampant and conflicts sparked off easily, stability of the society could be at stake. For political purposes, any incident could be manipulated, as Sister Agnes Cazale (Maria Petra) recorded in a story of the Kowloon Riot in 1952:

> On Saturday it was learned that a committee of about thirty Communist Officials were coming to Kowloon from Canton [Guangzhou]. They termed themselves the "Comfort Mission" and their mission was to "comfort" and help the people who recently lost all their possessions because of fire. They were going to present a check in the amount of Hong Kong dollars 102,000.00 to the people of Tung Tau Village to help them rebuild their homes. . . . A group of about two or three hundred set out [from the Kowloon side] via train Saturday morning to go to the border and welcome this committee. However, when the train reached the last stop before the border all in said company were told they could go no further. After much loss of time over disputes, etc., they finally disconnected one coach that was full of these people and others were made to get off the train. Only one man was allowed to go to the border to announce to the Officials that they were not being permitted to come into the Colony. At the Kowloon station waiting for the party to return were thousands of Communists, mostly young boys and girls . . . with banners and flags. In fact the streets were lined with these kind[s] of people. When they received the news that the Committee was not allowed in they began to protest! Police cars were overturned and one or two plus a police motorcycle were burned and the people began to scream and fight with anyone that opposed them.[34]

The incident continued for a few hours; and police and British soldiers moved in to disperse the people. Discontent and poverty bred social unrest and violence. The homeless problem did not only create immediate pressure on society and the administration, but if not taken care of, could also be a threat to law and order and legitimacy of the ruling authority.

In fact, fires broke out quite often and became regular news items. A fire started one night in 1953 in one of the villages about half-an-hour's walk from the Maryknoll convent in Kowloon Tong. It was the fourth happening in the last seven months. "A dangerous night," as seen from the nuns' place, the wind was strong and sparks were flying in the air.[35] A few thousand people were thrown out on the streets as their homes were burnt to the ground. Learning from past experiences, the government was quick to build temporary mat huts for these people and on supply them with food. There was growth of community spirit among the poor. Since the location was close to King's Park, the inhabitants there took all the food they could collect to feed the fire victims. Nevertheless, such incidents were hard to prevent. Shortly afterward, another fire broke out:

> The village that was burnt is not very far from our Convent here [in Kowloon Tong], so we knew how large a fire it was from the smoke. . . . The fire started about 6:00 in the evening and lasted till about 10:00. Because of a wind at that time the fire spread

farther than was expected. The police, boy scouts and volunteers tried to stop the progress of the fire by getting ahead and tearing down wooden shacks in order to make a break, but the fire spread so rapidly only part of the house[s] would be down and the men would have to leave because of the terrible amount of smoke and heat and in no time those houses were in flames. There was just no stopping it. About 20,000 are said to be homeless. This is the third or fourth time this village has had a fire, I guess by now there aren't anymore wooden shacks there.[36]

The biggest disaster happened on Christmas Day of 1953, when the fire in Shek Kip Mei cost 53,000 people their homes and the little belongings they had. A year later, the government began a major resettlement program, which involved construction of H-shaped seven-story resettlement blocks, providing minimal accommodation facilities for the homeless. There was always a limitation to how much the government could do. Not everybody could benefit from the government program, nor could the authority, entirely on its own, deal with the severe circumstances. In the 1950s, the government engaged in measures of social relief, while supporting services of religious groups. Although it could not "avoid a portion of responsibility for their relief," its scanty resources and income did "not really provide the strength for shouldering the entire responsibility of aid to the refugees."[37]

King's Park Social Welfare Center

There was a desperate demand for social work in Hong Kong. Social services in King's Park were representative of the work of Maryknoll Sisters in the 1950s.[38] The different areas included relief, housing, medical care, nursery, social welfare, employment, education, and catechetical work. Suddenly, the Sisters realized that they had so much to do. Reporting to the Motherhouse, Sister Mary Imelda pointed to open fields in Hong Kong:

> The opportunities seem unlimited. We have been invited to take over work in five of the nineteen or more refugee settlements. It was our hope that Maryknoll would consider at least three of the areas offered us; namely, King's Park, Chai Wan, and Tung Tau. Government hopes that missionary Societies will engage in the work. . . . I hardly need to repeat that the need is tremendous. The people are ready and in need of the spiritual and moral uplift we hope to be able to give them. If we do not act now, other elements less desirable or harmful will take over.[39]

Begun in 1952, the Social Welfare Center in King's Park was an original project to tackle the problems of housing, health, education, and employment in the community.[40] Only the Canossian Daughters of Charity were experimenting with a similar program in Hunghom. Despite changes in personnel and sickness of some of them, Maryknoll Sisters maintained a close working relationship with Father Duchesne. With the flood of refugees into the colony, everything was in great demand. Scarcity was the norm of the day. Concentration of the refugee settlement in King's Park offered "the advantage of compactness" for the existence of a social welfare center.[41] According to the Sisters' report, the Center started "as a place to minister to the needs of the people independent of, but in conjunction with, the Government Social Welfare Office, by dividing the Sister's time about 50–50 between relief of physical sufferings and religion."[42]

In February Sister Mary Imelda was confident of "possibilities for definite work with refugees."[43] She moved ahead to establish a welfare center and a vernacular primary school in King's Park. The government granted land for the Social Welfare Center, but did not offer any financial help for construction of the building. Out of the initial cost of US$8,000, the local Church (through Archbishop Antonio Riberi, Apostolic Internuncio to China) provided US$5,000 and the Maryknoll Sisters had to cover the rest of the expenses.[44] For the school, the Education Department was willing to consider government subsidization. The local Church also agreed to the idea. Through Father Duchesne and Monsignor Martin T. Gilligan of the Catholic Welfare Committee of China (formed in Shanghai in 1946 and subsequently established branch offices in other cities),[45] Sister Mary Imelda obtained financial support for part of the cost of the school building.[46]

In June 1952 the Sisters opened the Social Welfare Center, which was situated on the road leading to the settlement.[47] A stone building, it served as a chapel, a recreation and catechetical center, and convent of the Maryknoll nuns. Sisters Antonia Maria Guerrieri and Dorothy Rubner (Barbara Marie) were its first occupants. Indeed, the Center became multifunctional. With a large hall that could accommodate two hundred people, it provided activities for nearby residents. A heavy curtain separated the hall from the sanctuary, and the place was also a chapel. On the right side of the sanctuary was the sacristy, and on the left was the oratory (and also a quiet work room) for the nuns. The convent was at the other end of the hall. At the entrance of the hall, the Sisters used a small room for meeting with people, conducting Sunday and evening classes, distributing and collecting handwork of the industrial cottage. The average monthly activities in the Center in 1952 are shown in table 4.1.

The Center served as a gathering place for children and families. The Sisters described the life in King's Park—"a ping-pong table was a 'must' from the very start and proves its worth on holidays and during vacation season."[48] Also, "homework and family chores, i.e., the carrying of water from the public water supply, going to the market, or minding younger members of the family, keep the children well occupied on school days."[49] In the evening, children gathered in the recreational room. Some also used the library. Their homes were small, and they went out for fun or study. At Christmas, the Sisters arranged "a successful Christmas play with borrowed costumes and another very enjoyable entertainment for the parents, consisting of several skits and action songs requiring only simple costuming."[50] Religious services

Table 4.1 Average monthly activities in King's Park in 1952[a]

Daily catechism classes (taught by Sisters and the catechist)	107 classes
Average attendance at these classes	53
Private instructions	49 classes
Number of pupils	12
Letters for help written	90
People interviewed	184
Visits to homes	159
Clothing and food given to	130 families
School enrolment	480 pupils

Note: [a] Excerpt of the Report on the Catholic Social Welfare Center in King's Park (to Bishop Fulton Sheen), July 12, 1953, p. 4, Folder 1, Box 8, South China Region: Hong Kong/Macau Region, 1921– , Maryknoll Mission Archives.

were provided, as the chaplain held daily and Sunday Masses, and services for catechumens. With Sister Moira Riehl as superior in King's Park, one Sister was responsible for welfare work, two for catechetical work, and one for the management of the primary school. Sister Moira had been superior of the Sisters in Wuzhou, Guangxi before coming to Hong Kong. There were also lay helpers—a qualified social worker, a woman for the industrial cottages, catechists, and an assistant. This was the situation in 1954. Other groups volunteered their services—the M.C.S. Girl Guides, Kowloon Scouts, Legion of Mary, Our Lady of Sodality, Blessed Sacrament Sodality, Apostleship of Prayer, and so on.[51]

Relief—Food, Clothing, Health Care, and Other Needs

Inhabitants lived in surroundings, which were "urban" but "not regarded as a city," "rather a board-tin-tar-paper-hut village" "with no paved roads."[52] This was the description in 1953. Most of them were "casual manual laborers" while some were factory workers, clerks, and schoolteachers. Although many had their professional expertise, they could not continue in their own professions. They lost all they had in China while seeking refuge in Hong Kong. Sisters estimated that the percentage of inhabitants in King's Park, who were employed at one time, never went beyond sixty. Usually, family incomes could not cover living costs or were barely enough for survival. Men were casual laborers, night watchmen, hawkers, coolies, sailors, and street sweepers. Mechanics, carpenters, painters, electricians, and carriers earned HK$5–6 a day; and for some helpers, HK$3.50 a day. Most of them only had work three days a week, further bringing down their salaries. Therefore, wives had to look for additional income and became washwomen, workwomen, and part-timers for handicraft work.[53]

Relief was the priority; also, health care was particularly important. As the Sisters described, malnutrition was "the prevailing disease in the area."[54] Distribution of food was necessary. The 1953 report listed out their initial activities in King's Park. The Sisters gave out almost five thousand pounds of milk powder to one hundred families for a period of five weeks and to some occasionally. To more than sixty families, they distributed vitamins. In addition, to inhabitants they re-distributed food, which the police confiscated from illegal hawkers.[55] With rapidly expanding population, local medical service was under strain. The King's Park settlement was close to several hospitals—two Catholic, one government, and one Chinese supported by public donations—where children received vitamins and the needy obtained special medical attention. In order to cater to growing needs, Sisters arranged a Catholic doctor to offer more convenient services to inhabitants. They also taught personal hygiene to children in school and to adults in special classes. A voluntary dentist paid weekly visits to the neighborhood. At the same time, the Sisters provided material aid to expectant mothers and wrote introduction letters for them to hospitals, usually to nearby Kwong Wah Hospital on Waterloo Road.[56] Maryknoll's Social Welfare Center also had health relief services, such as provision of prenatal vitamins, and afterbirth milk for both mothers and babies.[57]

In all possible ways, no matter how small, the Sisters took care of local needs. Reports of work in the second half of 1953 listed quite a number of items. The Sisters helped people apply for dry rations, licenses, rescinding of prison or deportation sentences, birth and marriage certificates, resident cards, loans, and scholarships. Moreover, they offered assistance to those who had difficulty in paying rent, raising babies, starting a business, repairing their homes, and even paying bills. They wrote letters for those seeking jobs and for those in need of medical care.[58] There was special concern for the living conditions of the poor. Even short-term measures were very much welcomed. Since wooden shacks could not stand frequent and heavy rainstorms, the problem of "leaking roofs" was common. The Sisters studied the situation, and supplied tar-paper, tin, and asbestos sheeting for repairs and roofing. Through "Adopt a Family" aid program in the United States, American Catholics sponsored welfare service abroad. Therefore, the Sisters were able to secure donations for winter clothing and blankets for families in need.[59] They offered the most they could, and worked in any of the areas that needed attention (see table 4.2).

In 1955 Sisters opened the new Social Welfare Center building on Nairn Road, which led to Homantin Villages north of the Kowloon Canton Railroad track.[60] Not far away from its previous location, the Center was also the Sisters' convent. Under the supervision of Sister Moira, Sisters Frances Murphy (Maria Regis), Margaret Marie Jung, and Marie Thomas Connolly were the staff from 1955 to 1957. Sister Moira was in charge of the Social Welfare Center, Sister Frances was the school principal, Sister Margaret Marie took care of catechetical work and home visiting, and Sister Marie Thomas was responsible for the local women's cottage industries.[61] Other names—Sisters Miriam Schmitt, Josephine Marie Isaac, Mary Heath (Maria Crucis), and Monica Marie Boyle—were also added to the personnel list in following years.[62] The Center continued its relief service, which it had been providing for many years. For relief, Catholic Relief Services (C.R.S.) of the N.C.W.C. supplied flour and oil to the poor. Bishops of the United States established the C.R.S., a worldwide organization formerly known as War Relief Services, for temporary purposes shortly after World War II. Nevertheless, with the postwar refugee problems around the world, it underwent reorganization and came under the N.C.W.C. After 1949, the C.R.S. moved its branch office from Shanghai to Hong Kong.[63]

By 1957, 7,227 families had registered with the Social Welfare Center. The amount of relief items was indeed staggering. For three times that year, a family received rice rations, twenty pounds, ten pounds, and ten pounds, and might be given an additional ten pounds. In 1957, 350,000 pounds of rice were distributed. Also, the Center arranged "Five distributions of 10 lbs. each to every family, plus a further 10 lbs. to 1,150 families."[64] Other kinds of food for distribution were beans, cornmeal, and vegetable oil. Not listed as relief goods, powdered milk was only offered to families with young children. That year, thousands of tins of powdered milk were supplied on regular basis.[65] Later on, people began to sell the supplies on the black market. As Chinese consumed boiled rice and vegetables, they did not need flour and preferred to sell it for some extra money. Sister Moira then came up with an idea, asking people to submit flour and oil to a "noodle factory," and they then received noodles in return (see figure 4.1).[66] Monsignor John Romaniello, of Maryknoll, who supported the suggestion, facilitated the famous "noodle factories," and he was affectionately called the "noodle king." For many years the Sisters were the distributing agency for C.R.S., which gave out clothing as well. In 1957 "110 bales of clothing were sorted and distributed to over 1,700 families, also 200 bundles of babies' clothing and 117 blankets."[67]

Table 4.2   General survey of work at King's Park[a] (June 1–December 31, 1953)

Application for dry rations 30—23 received; 3 families received rice tickets; 4 cases still under investigation	
Application for licenses 30—8 received; Government willing to issue but uncontrollable circumstances hindered 6; 10 still under investigation; 6 not granted	
Application for rescinding of prison or deportation sentences 3—3 granted	
Application for extension of period of time to pay taxes 6—6 granted	
Application for obtaining S.W.O. Card 3—2 received, 1 refused	
Application for birth certificates 2—2 received	Fees 3.00
Application for marriage certificates 3—3 granted	10.00
Application for resident cards 3—3 received	5.00
Application for securing loans from Family Welfare Association for people seven applications—5 received, 2 refused	
Application for hospitalization for 12 patients—12 granted	
Application for care for expectant mothers 7—7 granted	
Application for scholarship 1—1 received	
Aid in paying rent—1 family	15.00
Aid in securing schooling for 13 children	
Aid in redeeming bedding and clothing 8 families	72.00
Aid in starting a business 14 families	990.00
Aid in raising babies 17 (one of those, we persuaded one mother to raise her child after she had abandoned it)	
We bought some milk before we had milk powder	110.90
Now we give milk powder—clothes are also given	
Aid in repairing huts 5	85.00
Aid in paying license fees 2	35.00
Loan to folks 6 families	320.00
Beds bought for families 8	189.60
Clothing bought for those seeking positions 2	42.20
Medical bills paid for folks	174.00
Aid to expectant mothers 15 women	280.00
Hospital bills	66.00
Tickets to destination	55.00
Two houses bought, placed 3 families	1,690.00
Aid to another family to obtain a house drawn by lottery	110.00
Letter or phone calls for positions 108—17 received jobs	
Families placed in houses 4	
Requests for houses 13—none to give	
Charity (June to September 15; 426.55)—(September 15–December 31; 98.50)	525.05
Interviews 1,133	
Letters to doctors 314	
4,860 lbs. of milk powder distributed—about one hundred families received the milk powder for five weeks running, other families received it only once or twice	
Food received from police (taken from unlicensed hawkers) supplying about 500 families. Times received 10	
Vitamins given to 62 families (these families are followed up)	
Money paid out for food	747.70
Varia	27.00
Office supplies and books	191.70
Handwork supplies to 12 girls and 8 women, capital for this comes from friends of the Sisters mostly	
Furnishings	324.55
Electric bill 8	287.70
Christmas party—cloth for children	624.00
Christmas party—candy and cookies	25.00

Note: [a] "General Survey of Work at King's Park, June 1st–December 31st, 1953," n.d. [1953?], pp. 1–2, Folder 1, Box 8, South China Region: Hong Kong/Macau Region, 1921– , Maryknoll Mission Archives.

Figure 4.1   Sister Moira Riehl distributing noodles to residents in King's Park, ca. 1951.
Source: Sisters Photo Collection, Maryknoll Mission Archives.

Health relief remained another concern. A mobile clinic visited twice a week and the Sisters also began a medical clinic in a rented building. In 1958 a new day nursery and clinic building opened very close to the Center.[68] Each month, the clinic treated around 1,500–1,600 patients. Five volunteer doctors worked one afternoon a week, and a pediatrician also visited once a week. The nursery took care of boys and girls, 115 of them, aged 2 to 7. It gave priority to children of widows/ widowers, single parents, and very poor families. In these cases, parents had a job, and most of the day, were not at home with their children. Families paid a modest fee of 20 cents per day for a child, and sometimes half the charge. For very poor parents, the service was free of charge.[69] In the nursery, children obtained meals and medical care. Daily activities included "play, singing, dancing, drawing, simple reading, writing of Chinese characters, religion, elementary etiquette and hygiene."[70]

Community Welfare and Service

Besides relief, the Sisters' work in King's Park targeted many different aspects. Sister Mary Imelda outlined their objectives in a work plan, which she submitted to

Lawrence Bianchi, Second Bishop of Hong Kong Diocese. The tasks were as follows: (1) to minister to needs of people, concerning relief, jobs, education, and medical attention; (2) to provide educational, cultural, and recreational activities; and (3) to offer useful training classes such as embroidery and painting.[71] Sisters worked along these lines: employment for the people, material and spiritual rehabilitation, catechumen classes, and fostering religious family life.[72] Every day, they visited homes of residents, whose problems were lack of food, jobs, money, and morale.[73] For large families on the brink of starvation, the Sisters immediately contacted the government's Social Welfare Office, which provided them with dry rations. The basic solution was to help the father or mother find a job or a means of living. Usually, the government was cooperative in granting peddlers' licenses to people whom Sisters recommended. As described—"The very poor are content if they have work and sufficient food to be healthy and strong, plus a few changes of clothing and perhaps a little extra for an occasional cigarette, or candy or a toy for the children."[74]

Many times, women also earned money for the family. In the very beginning of the Social Welfare Center, the Sisters organized sewing classes for girls. Classes later developed into cottage industries, in which women earned a living through embroidery work. Wives worked because husbands could not find a job or did not have enough income to support the families. At the same time, daughters took part in cottage industries, some of them worked after school. It was a way to protect young girls who would have otherwise gone to factories with adverse conditions. They also earned money for school. In the Social Welfare Center, Sisters offered two types of work to these women. The first kind was embroidery work, which was already designed and then distributed to the women to do at home. The Sisters marketed finished products, and the entire earnings (after deducting the cost of the raw materials) were the women's salaries. The second kind was handicrafts, which could be paper flowers, plastic bags and toys, brocade purses and albums, and knitting.[75] Sister Marie Thomas was in charge of the cottage industry, and recalled women from Suzhou producing excellent embroidery work. They sewed linen towels, tablecloths, and hand towels, and were able to earn some money through mail orders from American servicemen in Okinawa.[76] Unlike American families, Chinese women worked not for leisure but for survival. In 1952, Sister Miriam Schmitt arranged work for about ninety families, providing a solution to their financial difficulties.[77] By 1959, the Sisters sponsored five cottage industries, which were "Embroidery and Hemstitching, Brocade and Plastic, Knitting, Sewing gloves, and Making wrist-watch straps." Here 371 adults worked, and altogether earned more than $12,000 a month.[78]

In order to help people to be self-supportive, the Sisters opened "an unofficial employment bureau."[79] They looked for job openings in newspapers and assisted people in writing application letters. Whenever the government needed laborers for work projects, the Sisters handed in lists of names to the offices. They did not miss any chance. For example, after heavy rain, the Resettlement Office employed extra people to clean roads and villages. The work then offered a source of income for residents. There were at least five people competing for one job. Unfortunately, many were even university graduates who had fled from China.[80] In six months, the Sisters wrote letters or made phone calls for more than one hundred people looking for jobs. Sometimes, they bought clothing for people to attend interviews and took care of traveling expenses. If families wanted to start a small business, the Sisters were willing to help. In the general survey of work in the second half of 1953, they reported providing loans to six families and capital to fourteen families, and securing loans for five families from an outside source. The Sisters obtained licenses for some, and paid fees for a few.[81]

Nevertheless, inhabitants suffered from a low standard of living. This was true even for those who had a job and a steady income, and effects were upsetting. The Sisters observed undesirable consequences—poor morale, declining moral standards, borrowing, pawning, gambling, children delinquencies, broken families, and domestic violence. There were frequently occurring illnesses, like tuberculosis and encephalitis, and serious problems of miscarriages and infant mortality. Psychologically, poverty might lead to discontent with government, "mobs and unreasonableness."[82] Often family income was not enough to pay for all expenses. For example, a street-sweeper was a government employee and had a reliable job. In 1954, he earned HK$105 a month, but was less than the family expenditure (see table 4.3). That year, Sisters surveyed a number of families with different occupations, and produced some useful data. Some of them earned an income, which was just adequate for their daily expenses, and their needs were kept to a minimum. There were those families whose income was not enough for living (see table 4.4). According to the Sisters, "a normal standard of living for a family of six members, including school, primary and high school expenses, travel, little extras now and then" should be about HK$500.[83] Therefore, inhabitants were living at a level of mere subsistence.

Besides looking for employment for people, the Sisters also aimed at emotional and psychological rehabilitation. The population in King's Park and Homantin was around 17,000 in 1953; through instruction and welfare, the Sisters reached more than one half of the people.[84] The following years recorded greater progress. In daily visits and interviews, they were more aware of the difficulties of individual families. During 1957, they made visits to almost three thousand homes. At the same time, the Social Welfare Center offered advice and counseling service, to handle marriage problems and sometimes drug addiction.[85] With the objectives of fostering family life and preventing broken families, it organized yearlong monthly seminars on "Marriage and the Family," and had an attendance of about sixty parents.[86] The

Table 4.3 The living standard of the family of a government-employed street-sweeper in 1954[a]

Father, mother and four children		Average per month (in HK$)
Rice	100 lbs. @ .70	70.00
Salt	2 lbs. @ .10	.20
Oil	5 lbs. @ 1.80	9.00
Kerosene	1 tin @ 7.00	7.00
Vegetables	1.00 per day	30.00
Toilet articles		2.00
Taxes 60.00 per year		5.00
Hair cut twice per month		2.00
Street-sweeper and family-ordinary expenses		*125.20 monthly*

Note: [a] "Standard of Living of Government Workers," October 1954, Folder 1, Box 8, South China Region: Hong Kong/Macau Region, 1921– , Maryknoll Mission Archives.

Table 4.4 Standard of living in 1954[a]

Occupation		Income (HK$)	C. of L. (Cost of Living) (HK$)	Members in family	
				Adults	Children
Casual laborer		60.00	94.25	2	1
Cobbler (2 men)	110.00				
Dish maker	60.00	170.00	151.00	4	2
Night watchman	120.00				
(wife workwoman)	40.00	160.00	154.70	2	1
Washwoman		90.00	123.50	2	2
(husband not working)					
Hawker		90.00	105.99	2	3
Coolie	80.00				
(wife and daughter)	15.00	95.00	135.30	3	3
Sailor	140.00				
(wife sews)	47.00	187.00	162.00	2	5
Street-sweeper		103.00	158.80	2	4
Policeman		250.00	200.80	3	2

Note: [a] "Standard of Living of Poorer Families," October 1954, Folder 1, Box 8, South China Region: Hong Kong/Macau Region, 1921– , Maryknoll Mission Archives.

Sisters educated families on parental responsibilities.[87] Every month, they held women's meetings, with an attendance of over two hundred. They arranged parents and teachers meetings. Movies, picnics, and game contests were part of the activities. Library facilities and English classes were also available. Indeed, the Center was the first of its kind in providing long-term social service to the community. It became a model for similar welfare centers; twenty others followed after its establishment. Through Father Duchesne and the N.C.W.C., it obtained most of the funding for its regular expenses. Local and foreign benefactors also contributed, and made possible work for the poor.[88]

Catechetical Services

In those days before Vatican Council II, conversion was supposedly the primary objective of a missioner. Sisters emphasized catechetical services, and when asked none would have denied that catechetical work remained "the center" and "the main focus" of their commitments. As Sister Miriam Xavier Mug explained:

> If mission is to make present the Kingdom of God in this world and to make Jesus Christ known to the people, catechesis is an essential and vital portion of mission. If Christ is to be proclaimed, there must be those whose major activities are proclamation, telling of and about Jesus. This is the time-honored role of the teacher, the catechist. While witness through our lives is necessary, it does not eliminate the need of verbal announcement. Rather it makes it more urgent.[89]

The Sisters advocated active preaching and were eager to spread Christian faith. As they stressed—"Unless the active apostolate is based on solid spiritual and intellectual foundations and consistently nourished by a spirit of prayer, the spirit of activism would soon pervade our work."[90] They regarded such principles as "the guiding impetus" of catechetical work, and development in King's Park. Initially, in

1952, Sisters Antonia Maria and Dorothy grouped new Catholics into the Apostleship of Prayer, as a way to strengthen their faith. The association continued to grow into two branches, one for men and one for women. Throughout the years, the Social Welfare Center served as the catechetical center, with catechumen classes and religious instruction for women and children. As reported in 1955, there were day and evening classes for women to prepare for Baptism, and for children of different age groups and needs.[91] There were follow-up visits to their homes; and after Baptism, the Sisters also organized group gathering and more in-depth classes. By that year, they recorded the conversion of almost seven hundred people to Christianity.[92]

In fact, the Sisters started their catechetical work many years earlier in Tung Tau Tsuen. There, the agenda was basically offering catechumen classes. In 1952, Maryknoll Sisters worked with the people in a small rented shop. Subsequently, they rented a larger store. Afterward they secured land from government for the erection of a new building; the construction was completed in two months' time. The Maryknoll women's center then served the purpose of direct apostolate, among women and children. It provided doctrine instruction to local residents, who spoke four different dialects. Because the Sisters had been in China before, they spoke either Cantonese or Hakka. On alternate days of the week, they taught in Cantonese and Hakka. Their convent in Tung Tau Tsuen lasted from December 1954 to August 1958, and Mary Ignatia McNally and Agnes Cazale were the two Sisters staying there.[93]

In 1954, the women's center had five catechetical staff, two Maryknoll Sisters, two lay catechists and one lay companion for home visiting. Women catechumens numbered around forty to fifty monthly. For several years, the total number of baptisms for men, women, and children was 1,000.[94] In Tung Tau Tsuen, the Sisters met with different people; some were even university graduates and teachers who had lost everything they had in China.[95] Among the destitute, a religious community developed. Maryknoll's catechetical service always began with the poor, and Tung Tau Tsuen represented their earliest effort. The local population also changed quite a bit after the fire in 1951. A Sister later described their catechetical work and the people whom they served:

> During the years that have elapsed since the Sisters first went to Tung Tau the work has developed in many ways. Of primary importance, however, has been the direct apostolate through which the Sisters have sought out and instructed catechumens in preparation for baptism. The area has changed in many ways too. Fires, subsequent to that of November 1951, have destroyed many wooden huts some of which have been rebuilt while others have been replaced by the seven storey flats of which there are now six in "Tiger's Cave Village." In addition to the wicker work, cloth weaving is carrying on. Many of the Catholics have moved away or been resettled in other areas, but those who live near enough come back for a visit now and then. At the present time, 1958, catechumens number about three hundred. Some are wicker workers; some cloth weavers. Others sew or embroider for a living, while a few are teachers. Many are housewives. All our people are Chinese and there are few who speak English.
>
> ...On the whole, the people are poor and barely make ends meet. Some refugees have been able to get jobs and live a little better than they did when they first came to Hong Kong, but most of them are poorly paid and none of them able to live as well as they did up-country.[96]

Living in community was the most effective way to spread religion. The Sisters moved into Tung Tau Tsuen after the convent was completed in 1954. As Sister Mary Ignatia wrote in an aerogramme—"We moved into our new convent on December 16th and it is really wonderful to be living among the people." Close contacts with people provided more opportunities for mutual understanding. There were memorable moments:

> We too are glad that we have it [the convent] furnished with everything done by the Refugees and the people love to come in and see the cloth they wove on our windows and the wicker furniture, etc. They are all so good. Our first morning in the village they all came to Mass and Holy Communion and gave a generous Mass stipend to Father to have the Mass sung for us....
>
> We had a wonderful Xmas here in Tung Tau with many Baptisms the afternoon of the Eve and Solemn High Mass at midnight with most of the people making their First Holy Communion at midnight Mass. Those who had babies had to wait until the morning Mass as it was too cold to bring infants out in the middle of the night.
>
> We also gave our first play—the children's sodality had to give the play three times to three different groups, but they loved the acting, you may be sure!...Our catechumens fill the room now as we have the four different dialects, but of course we can't have them together except for Sodality meeting and parties, then we have to give a short talk in the four different dialects in order to make sure everyone is understanding. Cantonese is becoming the one dialect for all and they understand quite a bit of every day language in Cantonese, but of course they cannot understand the doctrine terms.[97]

The Sisters had a fixed weekly schedule. When one of them was giving the catechumen class, the other was out to the village for visiting. Every week, a Sister spent three days on religious instruction and three days on home visits.[98] "We are here for those whom God sends to us"—that was the spirit—and missioners carried the message that the individual had his/her own special value:

> ...we do all we can to convey this idea to every Catholic, catechumen, prospective catechumen, pagan, and in fact every individual with whom we come in contact. Interest in the embroidery being done by the pagan woman as she squats on a tiny stool in front of her wooden hut; interest in a little child who doesn't look well; interest in a cut finger; interest in a child bending over a wooden horse tracing his characters; all these help us in our efforts to bring Christ to these villagers.[99]

Catechumens spent at least six months on doctrine instruction, and attended Sunday Masses as well. For catechumen classes, the women were divided into two groups, those who knew some Chinese characters and those who were illiterate. On Saturdays, the children had their classes. The newly baptized took a yearlong course on more thorough discussions on the Sacraments, Commandments, and Gospels.[100] Though a small community, Tung Tau Tsuen proved to be the "cradle" for catechetical work. In July 1955, the Sisters reported 830 baptisms yearly. The local population in 1954 was 87,000.[101]

Establishment of a Vernacular School in King's Park

When the Sisters began their refugee work in King's Park in 1952, they envisaged the establishment of a vernacular primary school. Sister Mary Imelda had the approval of the local Church and the government's Education Department. In April 1953, Lok Tak School (or Maryknoll Primary School as its English name) opened with 300 students. "Lok Tak" meant "joyous virtue." The inscription on the cornerstone of the building, as well as the name of the school, paid tribute to Bishop Patrick Byrne, of Maryknoll, who died in the Korean death march, for his "happy disposition and joyous sacrifice."[102] Its establishment would not have been possible without government granted land and subsidies. While the government paid for one half the school building and equipment, Archbishop Riberi and Monsignor Gilligan took care of the remaining expenses. Lok Tak was the first of its kind in a resettlement area. Soon, some smaller schools appeared on the hillsides of King's Park. Nevertheless, educational facilities were always in demand, considering the growing needs of poor children.

Maryknoll's refugee work in King's Park had three dimensions—housing, the Social Welfare Center, and education. The Sisters visualized a triangle, with the housing project forming the base and the Center forming one of the sides. In the poor community, relief and welfare were essential; but to really help children, education was the long-term task. "Realizing that the little children, growing up in the village would be a prey to everything undesirable in social life, unless provided with an education fitted to equip them mentally and morally for a useful life in the future," the Sisters decided to engage in education, forming the other side of the triangle.[103] This was their understanding of motives and responsibilities of education in King's Park. By the end of 1953, 480 pupils sat in the classes in the morning and afternoon sessions. Out of the six initial classes, four were for first-graders, demonstrating great needs for education in the resettlement area. Lok Tak was a vernacular primary school under the guidelines of the Hong Kong (and essentially British) educational system. While it charged a monthly fee, ten percent of the pupils obtained free tuition from the government, and twenty-five percent of them were supported by private donations.

Not only did Lok Tak offer educational opportunities for children; it was also *their* school where they could be temporarily away from family problems and concentrate on studies. It was their "own school," as the "wide eyed, happy youngsters wended their way up the stone steps."[104] Lok Tak provided a safe environment, and they "could be unburdened of family troubles which they carry deep down in their hearts."[105] As principal, Sister Frances realized that many children could not afford to continue secondary education. It was not unusual to find students overage, as they had lost many years of schooling. Some deliberately lied about their age so as to be admitted.[106] Therefore, Lok Tak was possibly their only chance to receive normal education. Afterward, they had to earn their own living and for their families. The Sisters decided to teach the students practical skills in school so that they could secure a job in future. Lok Tak targeted needs of the local community. In 1955, the Sisters sought permission from the Education Department to build a school extension, so as to provide workrooms for both boys and girls. In the following year, the construction began on the original campus; and when completed in September the enrolment increased to 810. As described:

> The object of the new extension has been achieved—boys of all ages can learn wood craft, wire, rattan and wicker work. Boys and girls can learn the art of using plastic thread to advantage in making objects. The girls are taught all they need to know in

sewing, such as patching, mending, darning, as well as cutting and sewing garments by hand and machine. They also learn knitting, crochetting, embroidery, weaving on a weave-o-ette and the art of making stuffed animals and dolls. These trades and skills give the boys and girls the assurance that they "can" use their hands in earning a livelihood, as well as giving them a practical opportunity of trying their hand at a trade before making the final decision. The work rooms are open to the students after school hours and there is a teacher there to help them in every way if they wish to return to learn more about their hobby.[107]

At least, it was hoped that children had pleasant memories of schooldays, had learned to trust their own abilities, and acquired some skills for a living.

New Kowloon Tong Convent, Parish Work, and Maryknoll Schools

The Church was developing rapidly in Hong Kong. Different orders were erecting buildings, expanding their schools and actively engaging in the community. Maryknoll Sisters were no exception. In her letters to the mother general in the early 1950s, Sister Mary Imelda could not help mentioning local Catholic circles. By then, the political situation in Hong Kong was rather stable; and with the influx of refugees in the past years, there were great demands for almost everything in society. The Church was eager to capture golden opportunities ahead, for education, catechetical work, and expansion.

Writing to Mother Mary Columba in January 1952, Sister Mary Imelda explained that the Church was well aware of various government projects and was ready to respond. For the moment, the government was engaging in a HK$6,000,000 housing project and a number of plans for new schools. Authorities were also considering provision of loans to other organizations for expansion of existent school buildings. Indeed, many religious institutions were investing in Hong Kong, recognizing chances in front of them. Sister Mary Imelda listed the ventures— new building of the French Procuration; extension of French Convent's school in Happy Valley; Canossian Sisters building an extension to their school; industrial school of the Salesians; Good Shepherd Sisters trying to obtain government support; and work of Salesian Sisters in the squatters' settlement of Diamond Hill.[108] Meanwhile, she asked Mother Mary Columba to approve floor plans for the Kowloon Tong convent. Maryknoll Sisters were aware of tremendous opportunities as well as competition in Hong Kong. In building the convent, they recognized the need for a center house and possibilities for future expansion.

When Maryknoll Sisters bought the land on Waterloo Road at Boundary Street, they had in mind two phases of development. In 1937, the first phase was completed with erection of the M.C.S. building; the Sisters moved into the building with the understanding that the second phase would soon start with the construction of the convent on the same lot. Before the Japanese occupation, site formation for the convent had already begun. Nevertheless, construction came to a halt during the war. With emerging opportunities in Hong Kong, the convent would become the Center House for Maryknoll Sisters locally and in Taiwan. The Sisters were eager to go ahead.

Construction of the convent proceeded after the mother general had approved the plans. Much energy was devoted to the project. Indeed, the Sisters were careful to make sure that the convent matched the M.C.S. building.[109] They ensured that style and materials of the two structures were alike. The emphasis was "the harmony of the whole building, considering it as well in connection with the structure already erected."[110] Both buildings had an inner court, which resembled the Maryknoll Sisters' Motherhouse in Ossining, New York. The exterior of the convent maintained the colorings of *café au lait*, and was built with similar bricks and tiles. It proved to be quite an investment for the Sisters in Hong Kong. Japanese goods were imported duty-free; therefore tiles of the building were of reasonable price. Nevertheless, the Sisters expected huge expenditures. They asked the Motherhouse to sell all their securities, as the market was high for the moment, and to deposit the cash in their account in the National City Bank. They knew they would soon need money, and should have funds ready for use.[111] As Sister Imelda emphasized, they requested an immediate sale of all assets, and it was urgent. Erection of the Center House signified the beginning of a new phase of work in Hong Kong. At last, in 1953 Sisters moved into the newly completed convent on Waterloo Road next to the M.C.S. building.

In the 1950s, parish work became an expanded and specialized field. There were discussions on the role of "The Sister Missioner in Direct Apostolate." The direct apostolate sent the Sisters to the locality, to work with women and children for conversion and Baptism. The Sisters provided religious instruction for people. There was a close relationship between Sisters and lay catechists. As described—"The Sister-Apostle does not supersede or oust the lay catechist, but rather becomes the answer to a well-trained body of Catholic Action workers, guiding them, working with them, inspiring them and at all times encouraging them in the often arduous and discouraging work for souls."[112] This was the religious' perception of their role in catechetical work, that there should be a mutual supportive relationship between them and catechists. In those days, non-Christians were still known as "pagans." There must be ways to arouse their curiosity. The Sisters believed the religious habit was able to attract the curious, and to invite many enquiries. Living among people was most effective in spreading Christian faith. Sisters had "a place in this specialized field" of direct apostolate—"That the well-trained Sister deeply imbued with the significance of her vocation can live so closely with the people and yet retain her dignity and a healthy combination of the contemplative and active life is nothing to be wondered at."[113] With the influx of refugees to Hong Kong, catechetical work was of tremendous potential. Just across Waterloo Road from St. Teresa's Church, Maryknoll Convent was located in the midst of the rapidly growing Chinese communities of Kowloon Tong and Homantin. Having left China, some Maryknoll Sisters took openings at St. Teresa's. In 1951 they joined the catechetical staff of the parish, bringing a new change to local apostolic work.[114] It marked the beginning of full-time parish work of Catholic Sisters in Hong Kong. M. Rosalia Kettl and Mary Lou Martin (Regina Marie) were "the first full-time parish Sisters with a diocesan stipend employed by the diocese."[115] Subsequently, Sister M. Doretta Leonard also served there, and like others, she taught doctrine classes in Cantonese, and once a month, she gave a talk to about one hundred women.[116] Because there were few churches at the time, people came from other parts of Kowloon to attend Mass and classes at St. Teresa's. Catechumens called Maryknoll Sisters there "the St. Teresa's Sisters."

When the Sisters moved to the long-anticipated convent in 1953, the entire M.C.S. building, which stood by its side, was devoted to teaching purposes. M.C.S. had reopened in 1946; and the Sisters took much effort in restoring the School building after the war. In the early 1950s, the Sisters applied to the government for a loan to build classrooms and playgrounds. A few years later, they made the same request for the erection of a new secondary school building on an adjacent lot.[117] Until 1958, Sister Ann Mary Farrell was principal of M.C.S. (later only of the Secondary Section when the School was separated into two sections). She served in the position for more than two decades. Under her leadership, M.C.S. obtained grant-in-aid status with its graduates entering the University of Hong Kong. Sister Ann Mary also started the Student Council, and was concerned that M.C.S. maintain its "moral and academic standards," which were expected by both Sisters themselves and the community.[118] By then, M.C.S. had become quite well known and expectations from local circles were high. Holy Spirit School was the Sisters' second school in Hong Kong. Its original location was 41 Robinson Road, and it moved to 140 Caine Road in 1930. It reopened in 1948 and changed its name to Maryknoll School, also with grant-in-aid status.

Like her predecessor, Sister Mary Imelda as regional superior wrote to the Motherhouse to ask for suitable personnel for the schools. In her February 1950 letter, she was precise in her request. She wanted a Sister to teach English and history in upper grades in M.C.S., and another Sister to teach biology and mathematics in Maryknoll School. Moreover, she needed three Sisters, who knew Chinese, to engage in the apostolate in the schools and to visit students' families.[119] Sister described the heavy burden of work—"The teachers' day is necessarily occupied with school work and attention to individual students. . . . Naturally some of the Sisters try to do all they can for the people in their free time, with the result that they are overworked and a little tense during rush seasons."[120] At the same time, there was "a crying need" for Sisters who could speak Chinese to visit the homes of the students. Or else, the visits were not useful. There were ever-growing needs in an expanding community. She stated, "We have been urged to do more for the people in home visiting and retreats at the convent for women and young girls."[121] "The fields are white for the harvest in Hong Kong," she said, "but the laborers are few."[122]

Not only did Maryknoll Sisters need additional personnel for their schools, but they also acquired more space for expansion. In October 1953, they secured a site on Blue Pool Road in Happy Valley. They planned to erect the new secondary school building and the convent on the compound, to release the pressure on the Caine Road premises accommodating over 260 students. As proposed, the building could take up to about 720 students, with more classrooms, special rooms, and an assembly hall. While the Sisters applied for a government loan, they understood it covered less than one half of the expenses. They had to take care of the balance. Subsequently, the local Church agreed to lend the remaining construction cost.[123] The total cost could accumulate to HK$1,000,000. The convent was to be a separate building and the cost was solely the responsibility of the Sisters.[124] Under the pressing circumstances, Sister Mary Imelda admitted she had a heavy workload. She remarked—"Sometimes I feel I am not equal to the demands—but somehow the more important things get done."[125] By early 1954, the Sisters were ready to go ahead with expansion on Blue Pool Road.[126]

In February 1954, the Sisters were planning a separation of the primary and secondary sections of M.C.S. This also meant that there was to be an additional principal for the primary section. In addition, there were the immediate needs of additional teaching staff. As Sister Mary Imelda put it—"in the order of urgency" one domestic science teacher, a French teacher (major in French), an English teacher for upper forms (major in English), a history teacher for upper forms (major in history), and two primary school teachers. As for Maryknoll School, she admitted that the demands were no less urgent, and asked for one housekeeper with a command of Chinese, a mathematics teacher for upper forms, a domestic science teacher, a teacher for geography and science, and three primary school teachers who had to arrive in advance to study Cantonese for one year before teaching.[127] One year later, the superior continued urging the Motherhouse for more Sister teachers. She believed that M.C.S. was still understaffed, as most of the Catholic English-speaking teachers preferred to take government positions, which offered better salaries and benefits. She seemed to panic, and said, "The situation is grave and a cause of great concern to me."[128] She made the following requests for M.C.S.: thirteen teachers for the primary school and three for the secondary section. For Maryknoll School, she asked for three teachers for the primary section and two teachers and a housekeeper for the secondary section.[129]

Besides teaching, the Sisters in M.C.S. were involved in religious instruction and home visits. A monthly summary of their work in 1956 showed that they were involved in Catholic Action, the Legion of Mary, Veritas Club, and Boys and Girls Club.[130] In 1957, Maryknoll School (precisely, its secondary section) moved to 123 Blue Pool Road, and was renamed Maryknoll Sisters School. For the moment, its primary section continued in the Caine Road premises until the Sisters obtained another adjacent lot, which was a level above at 336 Tai Hang Road.[131] On the Kowloon side, M.C.S. also operated in two sections, the Primary and Secondary. The Primary Section ran in double sessions under the Subsidized School Code, while the Secondary Section continued its grant-in-aid status. In 1960, the new building for the secondary section opened at 5 Ho Tung Road adjacent to the primary school, and marked the expansion of M.C.S. Indeed, the Sisters' work in the past decade provided a solid foundation for them to take up challenges in the 1960s.

CHAPTER FIVE

REFUGEE COMMUNITIES IN THE 1950S AND CHAI WAN

Set on the sides of towering mountains overlooking the beautiful Pacific Ocean, with the huts of the refugees clinging to the sides of the mountains, the sight is like one from a picture book. On a clear day one can see the ocean liners, small tankers, navy ships, submarines, ply their way amidst the smaller Chinese junks and saampaans away out on the horizon. The Sisters were happy on their first night in Chai Waan to be at last among the refugees whom they had come to help and amidst such beautiful God-made scenery.
Maryknoll Sisters, Chai Wan, Written in 1958[1]

While the Maryknoll Sisters began work in King's Park and Tung Tau Tsuen, they also had plans for Chai Wan (meaning "firewood bay") on Hong Kong Island. Like other resettlement areas, Chai Wan lacked almost everything. There was no water supply and electricity for inhabitants of squatter huts. There were no paved roads, nor any of the reclaimed land that appeared in the 1960s. With hills running toward the coastline, Chai Wan offered a spectacular view of the ocean, explaining why the parish was called Star of the Sea Church. In its raw state, the area was exposed to all sorts of possibilities. Scarcity, unemployment, and illness led to family and community problems. Running away from the mainland, newcomers faced tough beginnings and were willing to accept any opportunities available to them. The Sisters, therefore, had an open field. They moved with the squatters to Chai Wan, where they engaged in education, relief, social, and religious services. They traveled in the hillsides among the wooden shacks and lived among the poor. The American nuns witnessed the early history of postwar Chai Wan, which was waiting to be developed. Together with the Chinese people, they were pioneers in the area; both had much to learn and had many problems to face.

Chai Wan Resettlement Area

In the 1950s, there was an influx of refugees to Hong Kong. Unemployed, many of them lived on hillsides and any deserted land they managed to find. To deal with the pressing situation, the government allocated certain areas labeled as resettlement areas for squatters. Those people who had a white card to prove their status were able to move into new settlements. As the Sisters reported, settlements "were usually just a designated mountainous area, in which people set up their match-box-like wooden huts."[2] There were no plans for facilities and infrastructures to correspond with the move. Indeed, refugees were initial residents in resettlement areas, which seemed to be remote and inhospitable. In due course, "water was installed, roads cleared, markets built up, sanitary facilities provided"; but at the start, resettlement areas meant merely "existing."[3]

With a population of about seven thousand people, Chai Wan was one of such refugee communities. This was how it was described in the Maryknoll Sisters' chronicle of 1952—the government assigned an area that was "a former cemetery on the south side of the Gap Road between Shau Kei Wan and Stanley," where "evicted squatters and fire victims" could stay and "level off the tiny plots of mountain side, and then put up their huts."[4] The Sisters had many problems to overcome in the area, which was undeveloped, way off, and situated near the eastern end of Hong Kong Island. On the same day in February 1952 when Archbishop Antonio Riberi handed them the check for the King's Park Social Welfare Center, they also met with an official of the Hong Kong government. In the long discussion, K. M. A. Barnett, chairman of the Urban Council, suggested that they should work in Chai Wan right away. He pointed out the area on the hanging map to Sister Mary Imelda, superior of the Maryknoll nuns. He was willing to assign temporarily two wooden huts, one for starting a primary school and another for a convent. For the moment, the suggestion seemed acceptable; and the nuns had no time to lose. Accompanied by Maryknoll Father Thomas Malone and James Tinker Wakefield of the Resettlement Office, they visited the site the next day. It was on a hill near the beach, a location they thought superb. They were satisfied with the huts they were to use—the structures were 105 feet by 16 feet and were large by local standards. At least the floors were concrete, they thought, and the huts had windows on the sides and doors at the opposite ends.[5]

Barnett's suggestion matched earlier discussions Sister Mary Imelda had with Education Director D. J. S. Crozier, who supported the building of primary schools in areas like King's Park and Chai Wan. The Sisters considered education an urgent task, as they saw children roaming around and wasting time without any opportunity for normal schooling. Education was the only means to uplift the poor from poverty in the long run. Since nuns were not immediately available in Chai Wan, a Maryknoll priest was in charge. The Sisters moved into the area two months after Maryknoll Father Stephen B. Edmonds started the primary school in the transit hut. On July 1, Meng Tak School opened with an enrolment of 180.[6] Although the children came from different places in the interior, they were able to speak Cantonese; some of them learnt the dialect quickly after they came to Hong Kong. The school had several Chinese teachers. It operated on double sessions, morning and afternoon, and there were three classes to start with in each session, from Primary One to Primary Three.

Two months later, Maryknoll Sisters finally moved into Chai Wan. They were Irene Fogarty (M. Francis Jogues) and Dorothy Rubner (Barbara Marie). It was already 3 p.m. on the day of September 15 when they arrived; they were soon occupied:

[We] arrived in a downpour which flooded our 15 × 17' Convent with 2 inches of water. Fr. Edmonds came to ask us to help in distribution of clothing to recent fire-victims, the Catholic Paper came to take pictures of this; the Officials of the Area came to ask us what we were doing here—someone forgot to inform them of our new work—and the new stove refused to cook us our supper. But we were glad to be here.[7]

They were in keen demand in the new area. The situation was hectic, but they did not have much time to get settled and were to take over the work from Father Edmonds. As Sister Mary Imelda had planned, one Sister was responsible for the school and another for catechetical service. Sister Irene managed Meng Tak and taught religion classes while Sister Dorothy conducted catechumen classes and visited homes.[8] Because Edmonds and another Chinese priest were still staying in the transit hut, the nuns had found accommodations somewhere else. At the beginning, the women used two stone cottages built for refugees as the temporary convent, catechetical center, and community center.

In November the Sisters were able to move into the place in the rear of the transit hut, which was previously occupied by the priests.[9] The priests had vacated already and resided in the newly constructed chapel. Edmonds was the pastor of the area. This was the original deal Sister Mary Imelda had with the government: that the nuns use the wooden hut for the convent and school. But instead of the two huts that the government had earlier promised, they then lived and taught in the same wooden hut. Although they moved, they still kept the stone cottages for catechumen classes. For refugee work in Hong Kong, the Sisters had the most modest beginnings in Chai Wan. They lived with the squatters they came to help, and they lived in similar conditions. Their place was only "separated from the three temporary classrooms in the transit hut by a thin beaver board partition."[10] It was sleeping quarters, dining room, and recreation room for the nuns. There was no water supply, electricity, and telephone in the area. For a small amount of HK$90, they built a kitchen and bath outside the hut. They only used kerosene for light and cooking.

Writing to the Motherhouse in December, Sister Dorothy was already preparing for Christmas. Meng Tak students were to have their first party ever, each receiving "peanuts, candy, pencil, tiny toy, medal, handkerchief" and together performing a Christmas play.[11] Regarding the state of living, Sister Dorothy explained to Mother Mary Columba: "When we first moved here we lived in one of the cottages built for the refugees but as soon as Father [Edmonds] was able to move into his own Church and Rectory combination building (much like the King's Park set-up) we moved into Father's former quarters, which had originally been prepared for us."[12] Since Meng Tak originally had three grades in each session, the transit hut had three classrooms, one for each grade. A classroom could accommodate up to 36 students. The Sisters' place was further divided into two parts, their living quarters, which allowed for some privacy, and the teachers' room. Until May 1953, the transit hut served as their convent.

Meanwhile construction of the new convent and school building was under way. The Sisters' work in Chai Wan received attention from the Church and the N.C.W.C. In late 1952 and early 1953, important persons visited the site of the new building. Among them were Archbishop Antonio Riberi, Cardinal Francis Joseph Spellman (Archbishop of New York), Jesuit Father Patrick Joy, and N.C.W.C. executive director Monsignor Edward E. Swanstrom, who turned out to be long-time supporters of

Maryknoll. At that point, the N.C.W.C. was considering sending relief aid from the United States.[13] In May 1953 the Sisters moved again, to a two-story structure over-looking the site of the new school. A few days later, the ceremony of laying the corner-stone took place. Meng Tak was named in memory of Bishop James Anthony Walsh, late founder of the Maryknoll Fathers, and by then had more than 200 students.[14]

In their first year in Chai Wan, the Sisters managed despite changes in personnel. They suffered from illness, which was not uncommon in a newly developed mission area. As described—"Sickness which usually blesses a new foundation did not pass Chai Waan by."[15] Writing to the Motherhouse, Sister Mary Imelda expressed her worries for health conditions of the nuns in Hong Kong. Not only for those serving in Chai Wan, others also had problems, such as malaria and high blood pressure. Even the superior herself admitted that she was not well.[16] Eventually, Sisters Irene and Dorothy left because of health reasons. Others replaced them in Chai Wan— Sister Dominic Marie Turner shouldered the tiresome job of dealing with various government departments, while Sister M. Chanel Xavier was involved with mission work. In the summer of 1953, Sisters M. Ann Carol Brielmaier and Rose Duchesne Debrecht also served there for a short while, commuting from the convents on Caine Road and in Kowloon Tong respectively.

In catechumen classes and home visits, the Sisters came to know the people better, and to be very much aware of the family problems. In an afternoon doctrine class, a boy made a pessimistic remark despite his young age. "When asked where God was he promptly replied everywhere," the Sisters recalled, but considering "the question of where we all were, he thoughtfully decided it must be hell."[17] Misfortune was everywhere and happened everyday. On another occasion, three women were strug-gling whether they should sell their children, whom they were too poor to raise. One of them, a student of the catechumen class, admitted that she would receive HK$2,000 if she sold her one-year-old boy. The money was too tempting for her to resist, especially in the poverty her family was enduring.[18] Indeed, the world war had been most devastating for Chinese people. The Sisters told one of the stories:

> One afternoon when we were visiting the homes of our school children newly baptized, we dropped in to see a family living in a new cottage built by Catholic Social Welfare.
> The older of the two children is a girl of 13, and her little brother is 6. The father of the family was instructed at the Catholic Mission and baptized, together with his two children last Easter (1953). This man is out of work and his wife is supporting the family by going out to work as a servant every day. Whenever she can spare the time she comes to the Sisters for religious instruction.
> A photograph on the wall aroused our curiosity. It was a picture of the man of the family, Mr. Wong, dressed in an English sailor's uniform taken on board a battleship. In his youth, Mr. Wong had worked as an assistant in the galley of an English warship and had traveled back and forth to London twice. He told us of his happy days at sea, and how kind his English Quartermaster had been to him. The world war put an end to everything.[19]

There was also the story of a lonely old woman:

> When the Sisters started a class for catechumens, an old woman of 81, hobbling on a cane, said she wished to study, too. We welcomed her and invited her to come twice a

week for instructions. The old woman was most faithful in coming, but after a couple of weeks she asked for private instructions because she could not learn as fast as the younger women in her class. We agreed to this, and grandma came regularly every morning.

One day when we were trying to find out whether there were any obstacles to her baptism, Grandma told us the story of her life. As a young girl of 16, she was married to a young man in her native town. Shortly afterwards, she and her husband sailed for San Francisco where her father-in-law ran a restaurant. This was an entirely new world to her, of course, and not being able to speak English, she said she always stayed indoors so she would not meet any Americans. She was shy and afraid of strangers. She lived this way in San Francisco for some years and then returned to her native country.... Her husband died during the war years. One of her sons and his family were killed in an air raid; another son, still living, is miles away from China.

Grandma shares a hut with some friends now and supports herself by sewing buttons on shirts made in a nearby factory. Sometimes she sells chickens for a neighbor from house to house. As old as she is, her mind is clear and she can explain the doctrine better than many of the younger women we taught. She had the happiness of being baptized on Easter Sunday (1953) and is an edification to all by her simple faith and attendance at Mass every Sunday and feastdays, and quite often in spite of inclement weather.[20]

The Sisters were most probably the few Americans, whom the old lady felt comfortable to talk to, and this time, in a Chinese society.

Meng Tak School

In September 1953, Meng Tak School finally moved. Located in the resettlement area, the new school building was rather distinguishable from the surroundings. It came into use on September 1, and 480 children studied in the better classrooms. The address was Heng Wah Village, Chai Wan. Designed and supervised by Brother Albert, the Maryknoll architect, the structure, "all on one floor, of grey fieldstone, with green trimmings consisting of eight classrooms, two offices, convent and catechumenate section," was "easily the most outstanding building in the area, and frames a panoramic view seldom found except on postcards."[21] It could accommodate up to 640 pupils. The school building cost slightly over HK$128,000, and the equipment was about HK$16,000. Half of the expenses were paid by a government grant, and the rest by private donations. Since the left wing was the convent and the women's center, Maryknoll was responsible for the construction cost of that part of the building.[22] For the moment, Meng Tak was under the management of Sister Dominic Marie, who also taught religion, English, and music, with a staff of a Chinese male principal and fourteen lay teachers. Like before, the school operated on double sessions; and in September, it had 4 Primary One classes, 4 Primary Two classes, 2 Primary Three classes, and 2 Primary Four classes. The Sisters had already decided to ask for additional government subsidies to hire more teachers, and to add more classes the next year.[23]

Meng Tak was readily available to children who wanted to receive education. Under government subsidies, the fees were low enough for most poor families. Still, 40 percent of the students were exempt from tuition. The government paid the tuition for 10 percent of the students, Father Edmonds found donations for another 10 percent, and Maryknoll Sisters received private funds for the other 20 percent. Some students received free books. The children could also count on "a hot nourishing lunch" on school days.[24] Sometimes, private companies came and distributed supplies. The Colgate Toothpaste Company was one example, and each kid received a tube of toothpaste.[25] Through Father Paul Duchesne, the N.C.W.C. provided them with other necessities like bedding, clothing, and medicine. In addition, the school library was made possible through donations of local businessmen. Under subsidization, Meng Tak followed the Education Department syllabus. A vernacular school, all subjects were taught in Chinese, except for the English language. Religion classes followed the guidelines of the Hong Kong Catholic Church, and a set of five Chinese textbooks known as "Primary Catechism" was used.[26]

Shortly afterward, Mary Diggins (M. John Karen) and Marie Jean Theophane Steinbauer came to Chai Wan. They arrived in September and October 1953 respectively. The area was opening up; and when they came, there were workmen turfing the terraces to protect the slopes and planting cedar trees to improve the environment.[27] Sister Mary Diggins had been in Wuzhou, Guangxi Province. She subsequently left and stayed temporarily in Mauritius before returning to serve in Hong Kong. She took the place of Sister Chanel, who left for Macau, and was to be Maryknoll's Sister-in-charge in Chai Wan. Later on, she was able to make the acquaintance of families who were originally from Wuzhou. As she recalled, the Sisters went up to the squatter huts and recruited students for Meng Tak. Initially, there were more boys registered, but the Sisters were able to encourage the families to put their girls in school.[28] Sister Jean Theophane became the headmistress for Meng Tak and replaced Dominic Marie, who was assigned to Taiwan. A month later, in November, the official opening of the school took place. In Chinese society, important people must be present to make the event look formal and to give recognition to the organizers. Here, the guests came from the Church and the government—Bishop Lawrence Bianchi and Chairman Barnett gave the addresses, and Director Crozier also attended. Sister Mary was satisfied with the way the ceremony progressed. Nevertheless, she could not help noticing the amusing parts. "Everyone seemed pleased by the brevity of the affair, except the principal, who said that it was much too short," but the nun thought he was "a typical Chinese" who enjoyed long speeches and "was sorely tried that day, as each person's talk was only five or seven minutes."[29] The pupils had fun and "all got the giggles" when Barnett "twirled his mustache, and that tickled their funny bone."[30] In his speech, Barnett recalled how inaccessible Chai Wan had been two years ago. He described the area as having been as "wild and inhospitable." In the beginning, the hillside had been "only a rough, stony slope full of holes, pitfalls for the walker, traps to fall into, boulders on which to break your shins, and the whole covered with tough, long grass and scrub that you could scarcely push your way through."[31]

Indeed, Chai Wan had been an area of wilderness; newcomers came and built wooden shacks on the hillsides. People were willing to bear the adverse circumstances. Everyday, nuns climbed hundreds of steps to visit the homes of the squatters. Like the poor, they accepted difficulties in the area. While refugees began their new life in Hong Kong, the Sisters also took up the challenge of local services. In Chai Wan, people relied mainly on their own perseverance and hard work. The mission began among the community of the destitute, and firstly targeted children. Education caught the attention, and Meng Tak had a hopeful beginning. It was a school for the community, and teachers were able to maintain close relations with students visiting families regularly. Things were improving; by November a new road opened in front of Meng Tak, and the Sisters were expecting the opening of another road by the side of the school. In April 1954, the school added four more classes and had 620 pupils. With government support, its fees were among the lowest in Hong Kong.[32]

Days in the Mission

In August 1954, Sister Rose Bernadette Gallagher began her assignment in Chai Wan. She had served in Guangxi Province before, and recently recovered from malaria. After that, personnel became stable. Sisters Mary Diggins, Jean Theophane, and Rose Bernadette provided many years of service in the locality. The arrangement was an exceptional one—it did not take long for anyone to notice how very fast Sister Mary Diggins talked, both in English and Cantonese, and at the same time to be impressed by the excellent manners of Sister Rose Bernadette. In fact, Sister Mary was extraordinary in any circumstances, as she announced the details and development of her thoughts, which was her way of reasoning. She thought and talked simultaneously, so she spoke so quickly and did not cover up her ideas. Sometimes, other nuns got friendly with her, loved her frankness, and joked with her that she should "swallow" before she talked. Sister Rose Bernadette was sporty when she was a teenager and yet learned to be very refined in her manners because of her upbringing. The "tomboy" and "lady-like" images did not seem to come together, but she was surely a sportsperson and a gracious woman. Living under such tough circumstances, she was still able to keep her outstanding manners, a quality that was considered difficult by many missioners (see figure 5.1). Sisters Mary and Rose Bernadette were responsible for catechetical and welfare work, whereas Sister Jean Theophane managed Meng Tak.

Scarcity could pose a problem to the Sisters. Writing to Mother Mary Columba, Sister Mary made the requests. Like Sisters Mary Paul and Mary Imelda, who had written similar letters before, she listed the wanted items. Using aerogrammes, which cost less to send, she asked if there were any excess altar cloths and linens in the Motherhouse. Sister Mary admitted—"It's really begun to sound like a begging letter and I really didn't mean to start out that way, I was just going to mention the pictures that we don't have."[33] She looked for pictures of the Maryknoll founders and the mother general for the convent. The Sisters were in need of "some things" that were not available locally.[34] These things included stockings in the right sizes, balls of darning cotton, collar materials, facings, Rosary cord, and special shoes for Sister Jean Theophane. Also, the Sisters wanted to take language classes, which would be useful for their work. Later on, they were able to have Cantonese classes three times a week, to keep up with the language. Jean Theophane attended a refresher course in music, which was designed for teachers of vernacular primary schools.[35]

Figure 5.1   Sister Rose Bernadette Gallagher making a house visit in Chai Wan, ca. 1950s.
Source: Sisters Photo Collection, Maryknoll Mission Archives.

By September 1954, the Sisters had established a primary school and a women's center in the refugee settlement. Already, they were considering building an extension to the school.[36] The enrolment of Meng Tak rose to 649, with 2 girls for every 3 boys in class. It also added a new class of Primary Five. Among the students, Catholics were a small minority, only 70 of them. Out of the 22 teachers, 17 were baptized after the opening of the school. Besides education, the Sisters were involved in community welfare. The population of Chai Wan was already 10,000. The Sisters offered assistance to people for accommodation and house repairs, helped obtain hawker's licenses, and wrote recommendations for jobs. Also, they managed sewing classes for women so that the latter could acquire skills to earn money for the family. In some cases, they secured medical care for those in need. Through the government, they arranged dry rations and cooked food for the poor. As in King's Park, Father Duchesne, who chaired the N.C.W.C., sponsored relief aid in the resettlement area of Chai Wan. Besides bedding and clothing, the N.C.W.C. also supplied milk powder to about 100 families.

Catechetical service remained a focus of the Sisters' work. In the women's center, the Sisters worked with two lay catechists in offering doctrine instruction. Catholic Associations, the Legion of Mary, Our Lady Sodality for Women, the Immaculate Heart Sodality for Children, and Maryknoll School students provided volunteer service in the area. In September there were 120 catechumens, and by then the total number of women and children baptized was 182.[37] In another compound, Father Edmonds took care of the chapel and the men's center. Altogether the number of Catholics increased from only 40 in July 1952 to 500 in September 1954. By February 1955, there were 180 women receiving instructions. Sister Rose Bernadette had some enjoyable moments with catechumen classes. As she said, "Our work is going very nicely."[38] She remembered the charm of the "old ladies group":

> Of special delight, however, is the old ladies group—seventy years and above—that are struggling thru the doctrine thru the medium of the Jesus and I chart pictures. The answers they give are out of this world. We made the big mistake of telling them the names of Adam and Eve as our first parents, because every other person that the chart holds, is for them, Adam and Eve. Sister John Karen [Mary Diggins] was teaching the Blessed Trinity the other day and after repeating the Names of the Three Persons countless times asked back the doctrine. To the question, "How many Gods are there," and at the same time holding up one finger, Sister got the right answer. But when, "How many Persons in One God?" was asked a great silence fell upon the group; then one brave soul said, "Whatever Sister says!"[39]

Christmas of 1954 was particularly joyful for the three Sisters. There were gatherings, visits and parties. A week before Christmas, more than seventy people were baptized and received their First Holy Communion. At the same time, there was a reunion for those who were baptized the same day a year ago. The group stayed for the morning of December 19, while the Sisters were busy awaiting visitors from King's Park, children and teachers, in the afternoon. On December 22, the Christmas play was shown three times in a row, for pupils of morning and afternoon sessions, followed by parties, and for adults from the parish in the evening. There was also a party for Meng Tak teachers that day. On December 23, the jovial group of old ladies, in the catechumen class, came over for their party. They held "cups . . . decorated for them filled with soda water, a bag of candies and cookies, and a tangerine or two."[40] The Christmas gifts for them were a warm overcoat and a group photo. The Legion boys decorated the chapel. Midnight Mass was full of people but was orderly as babies were kept at home. On Christmas Day, the chapel was overcrowded and many stood outside looking in through the windows. The priests were expecting their new church the following year. As described, the parish was "growing by leaps and bounds."[41] On December 26, almost 100 children came for games on the playground. Afterward, the Sisters were completely exhausted.

Catechetical Work

From the beginning, the Sisters conducted catechetical work and visited homes. There were catechumen classes in the morning, afternoon, and evening. Usually late classes were most popular as women had to work during the daytime. Instructions lasted for about six months. Those who had some literacy studied separately from those who were illiterate, and had to memorize a set of eighty-six questions and answers. The seniors, the sick, and those with difficulties in learning studied the basic doctrine. After moving into the new Meng Tak building, Sunday school classes for

Table 5.1 Catechetical work from 1952 to 1957[a]

	1952 (3.5 months only)	1953	1954	1955	1956	1957
Visits to homes*	93	789	2,728	2,463	2,431	2,904
Visitors to convent	302	517	2,800	2,198	2,680	1,890
Doctrine classes*	81	933	1,764	2,461	2,719	3,383

Note: ᵃ "Chai Wan-1952," 1952, p. 2; "Chai Wan-1953," 1953, p. 3; "Chai Wan-1954," 1954, p. 3; "Chai Wan-1955," 1955, p. 3; "Chai Wan-1956," 1956, p. 2; "Chai Wan-1957," 1957, p. 2, Folder 6, Box 2, Chronicles, Maryknoll Mission Archives.
* By Sisters and lay persons.

children increased. A Chinese woman used to assist Sisters Mary and Rose Bernadette, having known the Sisters before in Guangxi; but shocked everyone by her sudden death from leukemia. Since catechumens increased dramatically, the Sisters soon hired a few lay catechists.[42] More people were baptized each year, and received First Holy Communion. In 1955, four groups were baptized, 292 of them, out of whom 245 women and children were taught by the Sisters. In 1956, 539 were baptized at 8 different times; and in 1957, 7 different feastdays were celebrated with 507 Baptisms.[43] The progress of catechetical work was remarkable especially in the first five years from 1952 to 1957 (see table 5.1).

The women's center had an extremely tight schedule every month. By 1958 the Catholic organizations were well formed. The Women's Blessed Mother Sodality grew from 26 participants in 1953 to 470 in 1958. It held monthly meetings for three different groups—old grandmothers, younger married women, and Swatonese-speaking women. There were also the Legion of Mary, beginning 1953; A Sodality for Young Post-First Communion Children, created in 1954; a group for young factory girls, created in 1957; and other post-Baptism classes and meetings.[44]

Despite progress, difficulties were always there. In 1958 the population of Chai Wan was mostly Cantonese with some Swatonese families. The government was tearing down squatter huts, and replacing them with seven-story estates on recently reclaimed land. There were many newcomers in Chai Wan. In order to make a living, the people worked very long hours a day, and many did not really have much spare time. "One of the biggest drawbacks to their studying of the doctrine is their very poverty itself"—the Sisters observed—"When they hardly know where their next bowl of rice is coming from, and work from dawn 'til late into the night hours, the people have neither the time nor the energy to come to class."[45] Therefore, Sister Mary insisted on home visits, and regarded it as the most effective way of attracting people to the Church and to attend classes.[46] In 1958, Maryknoll Father Michael McKeirnan temporarily replaced Edmonds as pastor in Chai Wan. Together with the priest and catechists, the Sisters visited every home during March and April. Home visiting, movie shows and talks were the means to draw in new catechumens.[47] The Church in Chai Wan was quite outgoing:

Movie and introductory doctrine talk night is planned. Then slips are passed out to the Catholics to introduce their Pagan friends and neighbors to the church. Twice since the beginning of 1958 two groups have come to the church through this effort, and 60 people signed up for doctrine. One time, in April 1958, the Fathers, Sisters and lay catechist went to each house giving out slips to invite the people to the Movie at the

Church. This was most successful, giving over a hundred pagans the chance to have contact with the Church. A movie... "Dust or Destiny," was used this particular time, (with commentary in Chinese) and this proved the best so far.[48]

The Sisters also organized yearly one-day retreats for women, and usually over a hundred attended. Good planning was necessary, and the retreats were held in the school on a holiday.[49] Space and quiet were precious for these women, considering their tiny, crowded living environment and busy working schedules. Temporarily free from their duties at home, they could have some time for themselves and reflect on their own spirituality. Such opportunities were rare in the hectic lifestyle in Hong Kong.

There was a consistent effort to keep in touch with Catholics after Baptism. In 1959, Sister Mary started a "Block System" to retain ties with Catholic families. It actually referred to home visits to the seven-story housing blocks. Each woman leader served six months visiting twenty to thirty Catholic families, and passing out information sheets of Church activities. She also took note of "any matter which Sister or Father should know—unbaptised babies, sickness."[50] The next year, the 45 women leaders increased to 67; they visited Catholic families in their own blocks.[51] In the 1950s, the parish in Chai Wan was growing rapidly. In 1960 the population of Chai Wan was 35,000, and the number of Catholics was 3,500.[52] By then, the Church had already faced "the pressing problem of instructing hundreds of catechumens at one time."[53] There was some urgency and no time to lose in training converts to become leaders among their people. The "Block System" aimed to serve such a purpose, in three ways—it developed leaders, formed a united Catholic community, and developed an awareness of local problems. The Church was promoting a long-term relationship with the neighborhood families. In November 1960, Sister Mary left Chai Wan for service in Kwun Tong, and Sister Teresa Leung (Marie Lucas) came to take over the Legion and Children of Mary.[54]

The Sisters had blended with the local community. Visitors to the convent were many. Sister Jean Theophane was enthusiastic about celebrating Chinese New Year, and she loved the "sputterings of tiny firecrackers everywhere."[55] On the first day of the New Year, the Church was crowded with people, usually women. Maryknoll Fathers had built a new Church to replace the old chapel. On the second day, visitors came to the convent to "wish" the Sisters luck and happiness for the new year. Visits to the Blessed Sacrament and the convent had become crucial parts of the women's festival activities. Since it was Chinese tradition to visit their relatives and most newcomers did not have near relatives in Hong Kong, they paid their respects instead to the nuns. Despite their poverty, the Sisters observed, the people looked for ways to be celebratory and joyful. That could be "a bit of bright ribbon fastened to a body pin for the little daughter, or a new saam [the Cantonese word for clothes] made from relief clothing."[56] They did not need to work for a few days, and they treasured the moments of joy and happiness. Everywhere, the Sisters saw, there were signs of festivity. As described, "Chinese New Year, new clothes of red, orange and purple shades; new red paper strips above and down each side of doors with characters, Chinese words, in black. Catholics have them also, but with Catholic sayings."[57]

Relief and Welfare

Nevertheless, people lived in terrible poverty. An American religious film, "And They found Him," had most of its scenes shot in the refugee settlement of Chai Wan. It depicted the severity of the local situation, but the reality was even worse. As Sister Mary wrote, people were "appallingly poor, more so than even the movie could bring out."[58] Most of them, men and women, were coolies. They made their living by harsh labor, which meant "breaking rocks into small pieces by hand, mason work carrying dirt, and toting heavy loads at the piers."[59] A coolie earned only fifty cents a day; and families lived at bare subsistence, often below that level. Since it was unsafe to leave their children at home for fear of accidents or fire, some women took their children with them when they begged for food from store to store. The people suffered from very deficient diet, and the hearts of the nuns sank when catechumens said they had no problem abiding by the law of abstinence simply because they rarely had meat for their meals.

As in King's Park, the N.C.W.C. had been sending relief supplies to Chai Wan since the very beginning. Maryknoll Fathers and Sisters were responsible for giving out all sorts of things, "butter, rice, milk-powder, oil, cornmeal, clothing, shoes, beans, flour, etc."[60] The poorest received supplies first; then the rest of the community. On top of this, the Sisters wrote letters for families in need. The letters were addressed to the government departments, applying for dry rations of rice, staple food, oil, salt, and wood, or in some cases, rice tickets for families whose fathers were unable to work. Another source of material aid was the Maryknoll Motherhouse. Shipped items included baby milk powder, baby vitamins, medicines, and clothing. Other American companies also sent in multivitamins and multipurpose food, which were particularly useful to pregnant women and nursing mothers who did not have enough nutrition.[61] Relief goods in 1956 and 1957 were of many kinds (as illustrated in table 5.2). In January 1957, the Sisters distributed rice to all families in Chai Wan, with each person getting six pounds of the supply.[62] During home visits, the Sisters also noticed those who were desperate for help. Among the community, there were "various degrees of poverty," and many sorts of problems resulting from it. Owing to limited resources, the Sisters "whispered" to some people and asked them to go to the convent in the evening. Comforters and blankets were too few and could only be given to those most in need, and that was "after nightfall so as to avoid having everyone see them."[63]

People needed help in many aspects and the Sisters worked zealously to help. The Sisters looked for jobs for those who came for assistance. These people could be cooks, coolies, amahs, seamstresses, and others, but the problem was really too big to solve. Writing recommendations for them was one way; contacting government departments was another. With the closing of the naval dockyard in the area and absorbing many more arrivals from China, unemployment worsened. Women and teenage girls worked in factories for eleven or twelve hours a day, and got very little in return. Therefore, the nuns organized a knitting group, so that women could work at home and earn more than they would have in factories. A knitted sweater paid HK$10–12. Indeed, the Sisters helped in all possible ways, asking on behalf of the people for anything from blood transfusions, exemption of medical fees, to

Table 5.2   Relief goods in Chai Wan in 1956 and 1957 [a]

1956 Food for Poor
Where sources given and amounts distributed are known
Jan. 4: Butter—¼ lb. to each person in Chai Wan NCWC
    12: Can of milk to each school child
March 1: Colgate toothpaste, to each school child
    7: Milk and butter to poorest
April 20: 400 cases of milk
    30: 6 lb. tin of butter to each Catholic
May 10: Distribute oil and milk
July 2: 150 cartons of butter
    14: 500 bags of rice
Aug. 11: 50 bags of cornmeal flour
    29: 500 bags of flour—NCWC
Oct. 7: 250 bags of rice
Nov. 10: 500 bags of cornmeal
    19: Distributed 3 lbs. rice to Catholics; 2 lbs. to non-Catholics
    26: Distributed 1,033 bundles of clothing
Dec. 19: Distributed milk powder, rice, blankets
1957
Jan. 13—600 bags of rice
March 9—300 bags of rice
April 2—150 bags of cornmeal
May 6—200 bags of cornmeal flour—bags themselves considered precious—we sell them for 50¢ for
    bed covers, underclothes and awnings and use money for the poorer ones
July 21—350 cartons of milk
Aug. 23—300 bags of flour
Oct. 31—100 cartons of milk
Nov. 15—60 bales of clothing
    18—200 bags of rice
Dec. 15—100 bags of broken rice

Note: [a] "Chai Wan 1956 Food for Poor," n.d. [December 1957?], 1 page, Folder 4, Box 8, South China Region: Hong Kong/Macau Region, 1921– , Maryknoll Mission Archives.

acquisition of stone cottages.[64] Some of their catechumens were in poor health conditions. Because the people lived at subsistence level and could not afford to lose their jobs, they were very hesitant to see the doctor even though they were sick. In one case, Sister Mary had no choice but to "escort" two women with signs of tuberculosis to the chest clinic in Happy Valley, Hong Kong Island.[65]

Most people lived in squatter huts, which could easily catch fire and were subject to all kinds of bad weather. In January and February 1955, fire broke out twice putting many families out on the street. To fire victims, who literally lost "everything" they had, the Church provided clothes, blankets, tinned food, food packages, and medical services.[66] The squatter huts were made of wooden boards and the wind and rain had no problem finding their way in (through the cracks). Sister Mary told the story: "On meeting a woman with a black eye one day . . . she told us that the face basin that was catching the rain water over the bed, during the night fell and struck her in the eye."[67] The whole bed, and the only bed they had, was thoroughly soaked; and so was the entire family. Actually, the worst came in September 1957 when Typhoon Gloria struck. More than 40 huts were destroyed and over 600 homes were in ruins.[68] The victims sought shelter in church, the Maryknoll women's center, and resettlement quarters. While the government provided free food to them for a week,

Maryknoll Fathers and Sisters offered some assistance for them to rebuild their homes. As the nuns observed—"In walking about visiting with the people, one can notice nothing but houses that have been blown every which way and are being held up only by a prayer."[69] They described a happening:

> We were passing the home of one of our Catholics, or I should say what was the home, as it lay in a heap on the ground, with not a pole standing. In true Chinese fashion and oriental courtesy, she said to us, "Please come in Sister and have a cup of tea." We wondered from under which board this cup of tea would be poured. This is indeed a period in which the refugees have everyone's deepest sympathy.[70]

Later on, with the support of the N.C.W.C., more stone cottages were built for the squatters in Chai Wan.

In fact, stone cottages were first erected in Chai Wan in 1954, for housing fifty Chaozhou families, who fled from the eastern part of Guangdong province and had stayed in air-raid tunnels (formerly built by the Japanese) for two years. Again, the endeavor was made possible through the support of the N.C.W.C. These people moved into the cottages, but they could only sleep on boards on the floor and could not afford beds. At least, they had some kind of shelter. While their living conditions improved, they were haunted by superstitions. According to the Sisters, Chaozhou people had a "great fear of devils," whom they believed were haunting their stone cottages because some of their babies either died or were still hospitalized. That same year, an addition of twenty families, this time fire victims from North Point, moved to Chai Wan. As recorded in the Sisters' chronicle, the government gave each family only "4 beams and a roof" and refused the Church's offer for "bricks for walls."[71] The luckier ones stayed in the stone cottages. This was said despite the fact that space was still limited and water could only be obtained from public faucets during fixed hours. Yet, Sister Mary considered stone cottages much better than "seven-story mountains" or the seven-story blocks, which the government was building in Chai Wan. Very soon, seven-story mountains would decorate the landscape and accommodate thousands of families who originally lived in squatter huts. After resettling the people in public housing, the government planned to demolish the vacated wooden shacks, estimated to number some 460. The number reflected only a portion of the entire squatter population, and the resettlement process was going to be a long one.[72] There was also a sampan shelter for fishing families.

In August 1958, Moira Riehl came to replace Mary Diggins temporarily as superior of the Sisters in Chai Wan. The latter had returned to the United States for her "decennial."[73] As winter would soon come, boxes of clothing donated from the United States reached Chai Wan. With the help of a few Catholic women, some of the clothing was bundled together and Meng Tak students each received a bundle during school dismissals.[74] The catechumen children were taught that it was always a blessing to be able to give. Therefore, during Christmas 1958, even the "POOR children collected $17 HK for POORER children—basket of food given to a non-Christian family."[75] As in King's Park, Sister Moira started a "noodle factory" to facilitate distribution of relief supplies. From Spring 1959 to Spring 1960, Chai Wan continued to receive food supplies. Some of the items for the year were—470 cases of powdered milk, 1,000 cases of rice, plus several cases of multipurpose food and vitamins.[76]

A Decade in Review

By 1960, the population of Hong Kong had grown to three million. Catholics numbered more than 158,000. Amidst poverty, society was progressing. This was how the Sisters described the colony in 1960—"Poverty is real and plentiful but somehow the poor do grow less poor, they are able to send their children to school, are able to celebrate festivals in traditional style, are able to stop grinding out a living despair."[77] Hong Kong had "an ever changing face," and "hardly any statement about it remains accurate for longer than five minutes."[78] With the rapidly changing situation, there were always different needs and demands. The quest for more diversified and professional social work became apparent. At the same time, benefits of welfare service had also been obvious. Catholic social service became extensive. In parishes, there were always welfare centers, clinics, and dispensaries. Also, there were Catholic institutions for specific needs.

The Church followed wherever the people went. In Hong Kong Island in 1960, there were twelve parishes. The Cathedral Parish, on Mid-Levels, was the largest, with 19,000 Catholics and 1,000 catechumens. On the Kowloon side, there were ten parishes. Serving Homantin, King's Park, and Kowloon Tong, St. Teresa's Parish had the largest Catholic population of over 20,000, and more than 2,000 catechumens. The New Territories were divided into ten districts.[79] Some data on religious personnel in July 1960 was: (1) 85 Diocesan priests; (2) 223 Non-Diocesan priests; (3) 102 Brothers, 45 of them were Chinese; (4) 628 Sisters, 294 of them were Chinese; 243 in schools, 79 in hospitals, and 78 in other charitable institutions; and (5) 130 lay catechists, of whom 61 were men and 69 women.[80]

There were institutions for different purposes, for the blind, the elderly, the infants and children. Altogether, the Church had 17 clinics, 5 general hospitals, 1 tuberculosis hospital, 1 maternity hospital, and 1 TB convalescent home. In order to organize all welfare staff for representation on committees, the Hong Kong Catholic Social Welfare Conference came into being. It also collaborated with the Catholic Relief Services of the N.C.W.C., and other donors for distribution of relief goods. Its establishment signified the desire to advance toward professional social work. In the 1950s, the professional status of social work was widely accepted to be low, "much lower than teaching," as both lacked qualified personnel.[81] Inadequate training opportunities and low salaries hindered the development of the social work profession. At the same time, "so much of the social work that is publicized is done in 'dole line' fashion . . . gives the general impression that there is not much professional skill required."[82] Therefore, not many people with some education wanted to be social workers.

In the early 1950s, Maryknoll Sisters ventured into organized social work. They were responding to the emergency resulting from the influx of refugees from China. Relief measures were lacking. Indeed, the fire in Tung Tau Tsuen set in motion housing, education, and welfare projects in King's Park, Tung Tau Tsuen, and Chai Wan. Relief and welfare were imperative, and the nuns were active agents in the community.

Besides efforts in different localities, the Sisters also devoted much energy to children and youth work, welfare of women, and development of social service in Hong Kong.

Even before the world war, they were aware that many children of poor families were unable to receive education. There were not enough schools to cater to local needs, and the problem was greatly aggravated in the 1950s. As a Sister recollected, whenever she asked if a child was attending school, the saddening answer was always "no." In 1950 both Maryknoll Convent School (M.C.S.) and Maryknoll School reactivated Boys and Girls Clubs, which offered some academic work for children without regular education. It was "a stop-gap solution" to the long line waiting for school places. Children, "who formerly roamed the streets begging or getting into mischief," were able to receive free tuition.[83] Since the Clubs could not be compared with normal schools, they targeted two objectives—teaching "basic knowledge and skills, to enable the children to face life with some degree of adequacy," and emphasizing "character development and a sense of civic responsibility."[84] The Clubs met for two hours a day, and each had at most thirty-five children, who were from six to sixteen years old. There were occasional picnics, outings, and beach camping. Every month, children were able to enjoy a delightful dinner; and during Christmas, they could celebrate with a party. One of the stories in the Boys and Girls Clubs was as follows:

> Among our poor children one can very quickly spot the child with an outstanding quality. Taat Meng, an eleven year old lad, shines in filial piety. There is a monthly dinner for the children and the first time Taat Meng had had such a feast in his whole eleven years. He was a thin little fellow and needed the food and so when I noticed him wrapping up almost the entire bowl of rice, I asked if he was not hungry. Yes, he was hungry but his mother, father and little brother were at home, having had nothing to eat all day, so he was going to share the rice with them. And so with every dinner or party, one would notice that the majority of rice, cookies, candy or fruit was tucked away in Taat Meng's pocket to bring home to his father and mother. He never shows signs of selfishness, is an intelligent child and likes to study, but there is no money to send him to school. His main worry, however, is that those at home are not getting enough to eat. So each time there is a dinner or party I always make sure that Taat Meng has an extra package of goodies for those at home.[85]

The Sisters also approached families of the children and attended to their needs. As described, they were usually "the poorest of the poor," afraid and not knowing where to ask for service. The Sisters paid home visits, and helped to solve hundreds of immediate problems, including financial difficulties. By 1960, M.C.S. retained three of the Clubs, while Maryknoll School ended the work after its move to Blue Pool Road. Similar clubs also sprang up in Hong Kong. In 1960 there were 204 of them and enrolment was 12,300. Nevertheless, education was still inadequate, as 50,000–60,000 children were on the waiting list for school.[86]

Besides children's work, the Sisters embarked on youth projects in local communities and their four schools, M.C.S., Maryknoll School, Lok Tak, and Meng Tak. Youth service was organized in the format of social group work. They included extracurricular activities, leadership training programs, handicraft courses, visits to society, and entertainment.[87] For special interest groups, young girls learned handicraft skills and equipped themselves with means to earn a living. Cultural and social functions offered opportunities for boys and girls to be away from the family, and to see other parts of Hong Kong. The Sisters aimed at developing the youth as leaders of their own community. Young people organized independent activities, and developed leadership qualities. Other than immediate concerns for relief, it was necessary to cultivate individuals as responsible members of society.

As always, women's work was a priority of Maryknoll Sisters. The Veritas Clubs began at M.C.S. in 1954, and were discussion groups for M.C.S. graduates and other working women, to prepare them to be leaders of the community. These groups had two objectives: (1) to create a meeting point for young women; and (2) to encourage their intellectual curiosity in social and community issues, to be beneficial to their future career and their relationship with society.[88] The meetings were in the evening, so that women could participate after work. Some of the topics of discussion were—"Woman: her nature, her role in the world, woman in history and individual women in the life of Christ"; "the states of womanhood, with papal documents as texts," on issues of marriage and virginity; social and political duties of women; and "broader social topics, presenting further social teachings of the Church."[89] In 1956, there were thirty-one members in the three discussion groups. They were nurses, teachers, social workers, and secretaries in business companies. Most of them were Catholics, and a few were Protestants.[90]

The methodology seemed to be appealing to the participants, who felt comfortable with the cordial and relaxed atmosphere, the mature manner in which they dealt with various issues, and the practicality of the discussion topics to their own situation.[91] They discussed happenings in everyday life, news items, and their role in society. Indeed, regular attendance after work hours called for sacrifice among the young women.[92] They wrote book reports and prepared newspaper clippings. They enjoyed the sense of attainment from active participation, and many continued discussions with their families. As observed—"The peak of achievement seemed to have been reached when some of our members were able to stand on their own feet and express their point of view in front of groups, including people who, to quote their own words, 'were older than themselves.' "[93] The Sisters believed that "this type of missionary work" was useful to the "intellectual, social and spiritual development" of women. It provided them with "an emotional sense of accomplishment," and contributed to "their development in intellectual concepts," "growth in social-mindedness," and "spiritual maturity."[94] By 1960, the Veritas Clubs reached a total number of over one hundred young women.[95]

Starting in 1957, there was the assignment of a trained Sister-social worker to Hong Kong, to explore possibilities for improvement in the field of social work. There were four aspects to her work—to assist other Sisters in welfare centers to communicate with other welfare agencies; to advise on the direction of Veritas Clubs; to organize Family Life groups of women and children; and to offer fresh and positive insights into the proper roles of family in society. It was simply hoped that as a trained social worker, Sister Mary Heath (Maria Crucis) could introduce new perspectives to Sisters in social service, and address the pressing needs of people in Hong Kong. Immediately after her arrival, she gave a number of talks to government employees. In subsequent years, she developed a cordial relationship with government departments. Arranged by the Social Welfare Department, Sister Mary Heath gave lectures on "The Nature and Scope of Social Work" to civil servants, who included police and custom inspectors. She was also in charge of weekly seminars on "Leadership for Life," which was targeted for the Youth Section of the Department. In 1959 she planned the "Introductory Course in Social Welfare" for the Social Welfare Department and Hong Kong Council of Social Service. Afterward, she continued to lecture for both agencies. In 1958, Sister Mary Heath was on the executive committee of the newly formed Hong Kong Catholic Social Welfare Conference, to devise a more professional approach to social work. Also, she served on the Child Welfare Committee of the Hong Kong Council of Social Service.[96] Subsequently, Family Life groups appeared in welfare centers in King's Park and Chai Wan, and continued with Veritas Clubs at M.C.S.

In the World Refugee Year of 1959–1960, the government decided to build a community center in one of the seven-story resettlement estate areas. The locality chosen was Wong Tai Sin. Maryknoll Sisters played a role in this government experiment, to see if problems created by the close living environment could be tackled and a sense of community belonging be promoted. They came to be in charge of the daycare nursery in Wong Tai Sin. The construction of seven-story blocks marked another stage in development of the resettlement areas. The policy signified the government's recognition that newcomers were there to stay, and its commitment to more long-term solutions to problems. As Hong Kong moved on to the next decade, more of these seven-story mountains were to appear in poor areas. The refugee communities looked different from before. The Sisters described the gradual change in government thinking and policies during the difficult years in the 1950s:

> Something about these 7-storey estates and how they came into being seems necessary. . . .
> Faced with the problem of planning for the refugees in 1949, '50, '51, Government hesitated for two main reasons.
>
> 1. It thought that as soon as the situation in China settled, the Communist regime would abandon its cruelty and the refugees could return home. They always had returned home after every crisis in the past which forced them to seek refuge in Hong Kong.
> 2. It seriously questioned the justice of diverting public funds, already insufficient to provide housing, schools and medical care for its own citizens, into meeting needs of one special group of new arrivals.
>
> Just to provide fireproof homes for the refugees, for instance, would cost more than Government had planned to spend all together on a badly needed airport, hospital, water reservoir and a scheme for reclaiming land, without which nothing at all could be done. Government hoped that some international body would come forward with funds for the refugees and so it waited and watched. By 1954 however, the spectacle of such extremes of misery, need and danger, outweighed all other considerations and Government acted. It committed itself to accept the refugees as an integral part of the community and plan accordingly. For housing, it had to build up rather than out, so it began constructing 7-storey H shaped blocks. The long arms of the H consist on each floor of 64 rooms and the cross piece contains 2 water taps, 6 flush toilets, 2 shower compartments (in which showering is done by the bucket and scoop method) and an open space for washing clothes.[97]

With the flood of refugees, the government reluctantly had to face reality. Newcomers lived in poverty and struggled for survival; they had to adapt to new circumstances and adverse living conditions. The government came to realize the great demands for housing, relief, welfare, and medical service in Hong Kong. It was unable to handle the situation and the presence of foreign missioners at this time was a godsend to those high authorities.

CHAPTER SIX

WONG TAI SIN, KOWLOON TSAI, AND SOCIAL SERVICES IN THE 1960S

About 2:00 a.m., September 1, 1962, Typhoon Wanda made it plain that this time Hong Kong lay directly in her path. The wind howled, and shrieked, and then the rains came. At 7:00 the next morning it really rained and howled in earnest. The number 10 typhoon signal which means "batten the hatches and be prepared for anything" was hoisted at 8:00 and we were supposed to be in the eye of the typhoon at 10:00 a.m. As you know, Mother, the hospital is surrounded by squatters in their makeshift huts that serve them as homes. Very soon these began to collapse. Throughout Mass, we could hear the tin of their roofs, which is held in place by rocks begin to blow and sail past the windows. Doors that were locked and bolted, were wrenched open by the wind, and the glass smashed. Putty was peeled away from the window frames by the wind and rain, and the panes of glass then just blew away and smashed. Electricity was off most of the day. Water just flows in around tightly closed windows and doors, so the mopping-up process is an unending one.

Maryknoll Sisters, Our Lady of Maryknoll Hospital,
Wong Tai Sin, September 1962[1]

In the 1960s, Hong Kong was struggling with poverty and developing its own industries. Working-class communities emerged, with families securing improved means of living. From a refugee community, Hong Kong gradually stood on its own feet. In the midst of poverty, there was always hope for a better tomorrow. Although people were poor, they realized they were becoming less poor; and that was where their confidence for the future lay. The provision of relief alone was no longer adequate to satisfy the growing desires of society. Apparently, newcomers were settling down and their families were looking for education, employment, and welfare opportunities. With expanding population, Hong Kong had become the fastest growing diocese in the world—by 1960 the number of Catholics increased steadily at between 10,000 and 15,000 every year.[2] As society took its form, Maryknoll Sisters began to consider a long-term social service program. In 1961 they established Our Lady of Maryknoll Hospital in Wong Tai Sin, as a significant move in offering ongoing service to the needy. At the same time, they ventured into new fields of casework and social work training. Building on their work in the past decade, they continued their role as a third force in society, serving the needs of the local community.

Our Lady of Maryknoll Hospital

Maryknoll Sisters had long thought of setting up and running a general hospital in Hong Kong. The first record of such a proposal was in 1953, and the suggested location was the Observatory Road in Tsimshatsui, Kowloon. At first, the government's Medical Department was also interested in the project.[3] Although the plan did not materialize, the Sisters knew that there were public demands for the hospital and that the authority was supportive of it. They continued to look for possibilities and sources of funding. In June 1957 the Sisters received the decision from the Far East Refugee Program (F.E.R.P.) of the American Foreign Service, "to make program funds available for the construction of a medical facility in Hong Kong."[4] The F.E.R.P. was willing to pay for the hospital building and equipment, and asked that the government provide the land and site preparation. It made its promise with the understanding that the hospital served the poor who left China after 1949, and should be situated close to refugee communities.[5] The F.E.R.P. was willing to sponsor the Maryknoll endeavor. Having secured financial support, the Sisters began negotiations with the F.E.R.P. on the size of the hospital, and with the government on the location.

Three months later, Maryknoll Sisters submitted their proposal to C. B. Burgess of the Colonial Secretariat. They planned to build a hospital with 50 beds, a large outpatient clinic and an extension in future that allowed for an expansion to 100 beds plus a training school for nurses. In the beginning, they estimated a yearly running cost of HK$300,000, which hopefully could depend on government subvention. Having discussed the matter with the Medical Department and Crown Lands Division of the Public Works Department, the Sisters reported that Wong Tai Sin was a suitable location.[6] In 1958, the prospect of a general hospital for the poor was encouraging.[7] The government was willing to grant land for construction of the hospital, and the F.E.R.P. allocated US$197,000 for the building and equipment. In the early stage, the Sisters needed 2 doctors, 9 nurses, a housekeeper, and a superior to serve in the hospital. They asked the Motherhouse for Sisters, who had taken the Canadian Medical Examinations and could practise locally, to be assigned to Hong Kong. The Sisters-personnel had to study Cantonese before opening the hospital.[8] In April, the government promised an annual subvention of HK$250,000 for the operation of the hospital, to be supplemented by an additional sum of HK$100,000 from the N.C.W.C.[9]

In the latter part of 1958, there was a change in leadership—Sister Barbara Mersinger (Rose Victor) replaced Sister Mary Imelda as superior of the Maryknoll Sisters in the South China Region, which included both Hong Kong and Taiwan. In 1961 Sister Mary Ignatia became superior of the Sisters, as well as administrator, in Our Lady of Maryknoll Hospital on Shatin Pass Road, Wong Tai Sin. That year was World Refugee Year; and Mother Mary Colman Coleman, then mother general of the Maryknoll Sisters' congregation, visited the hospital site. Finally, construction of the hospital building was completed. Construction was sluggish because the contractors had a few projects simultaneously in hand.[10] This was typical of the growing Hong Kong society. With limited funding, the Sisters were careful how they spent. They had new furnishings, but they also received old furniture from the Motherhouse and American donors. The Sisters unpacked provisions and asked a steel company to repair and repaint the furniture. It saved a lot of money to use the old beds, tables, and cabinets. The front hall was "a show case for hospital equipment as truckloads of equipment arrived, but no matter how cluttered the front foyer became it was soon swallowed up in the various departments."[11] The Sisters also received secondhand electrical appliances from the United States. For example, the old standing lamps were changed into local voltage, repaired, and painted. "They look beautiful and only $12.00 H.K. per lamp," Sister Mary Ignatia said, "If we bought a metal standing lamp it would be over $100.00 H.K."[12] The used X-ray equipment was modified to suit local needs. Subsequently, the Sisters asked a steel company to make pharmacy cabinets, which were the first of their kind in Hong Kong. It was advisable to use steel rather than wood furniture because of the humid weather.[13]

On August 16, 1961, the Sisters moved to the hospital building.[14] Led by Mary Ignatia, they were Sisters Monica Marie Boyle, Dominic Marie Turner, Marie Therese McCourtney, Mary Edna Brophy (M. Francis John), and Rose Goretti Ehm. Already at the hospital there was a man enquiring if his father could be admitted, reflecting desperate need for medical service in the locality. As the Sisters recollected—"He didn't really seem to believe us as we tried to explain that we weren't quite ready for admissions at this point."[15] Immediately, the nuns were tested as cholera had spread from China, through Macau, to Hong Kong. This time, the government was able to act fast and supply serum. Thousands of people were queuing up at government clinics for inoculations. Having obtained the serum from the Medical Department, the Sisters provided inoculations for children in their nursery in Wong Tai Sin. They joined the effort to prevent outbreak of an epidemic; and at the end, their efforts bore fruit. Deaths in Hong Kong were only fourteen.[16] In the new resettlement area, facilities awaited improvement, and there were always unexpected happenings, as described in the following event:[17]

> August 31st we had a typical Halloween. Earlier in the day the electricity had gone off. In vain we waited for a flicker of light. Nature added to the atmosphere with pelting rain and eerie winds, our candle light casting ghostly shadows about. At least we could count on sunlight the next day. The electrical problem was one not so readily solved and many a day we worked around this modern but slightly troublesome inconvenience.

In September two more Sisters arrived, Ruth Marie O'Donnell and Gloria Ruiz (Mara Jose).

On September 15, the outpatient clinic opened. The first patient arrived "bright and early at 7:30 A.M." In the ensuing months there was an average of 60–80 patients everyday. Other departments were still being planned. Painting secondhand equipment was another task. In the next two months, Sisters Helen Kenny (Mary Kenny) and Patricia Fitzmaurice (M. Thomas Ann) joined the overworked staff, who for the moment managed despite limited personnel and resources. While they planned to support all necessary medical care, the hospital was not yet fully equipped and was running only on a general basis until the special departments, which included dental clinic, minor surgery, X-ray, physiotherapy, and others, were in place. There were altogether four doctors, each providing an hour of service every week, and had known the nuns through work in other clinics and previous contacts. On those mornings without doctors, Sister Monica Marie, who was nursing director, shouldered the responsibilities.[18] Sister Gloria set up the laboratory, but in the early days she had no equipment other than a microscope. For some time, she worked on a borrowed table and watched over the carpenters as they fixed her laboratory counters and cabinets. Sister Ruth Marie, who was in charge of the pharmacy, was occupied with listing and sorting shipments of sample medicines from the United States, as well as stocking steel cabinets. With the help of students from the Maryknoll schools, she spent endless hours unpacking and cataloguing tons and tons of materials. In the morning, the Sister nurses were busy in the treatment and injection room, and with subsequent tidying up and sterilizing. In the afternoon, they unpacked medicines and supplies, and supervised the daily cleaning of the hospital. On Mondays and Thursdays, they distributed supplies to needy families, whom they met in the outpatient clinic. The items were mainly food commodities from the N.C.W.C., such as milk powder and cottonseed oil.[19] In addition, the Sisters took time out everyday to study Cantonese.

The opening ceremony of the hospital took place December 11, 1961. It was 18 months after the cornerstone was laid, and the Sisters already decided to expand the hospital to 150 beds. Initially, the hospital planned to have 63 beds for adults, 12 cots for children, and a general outpatient department. Although it had not yet accepted inpatients, it was to be equipped with facilities for surgery, midwifery, radiology, laboratory tests, and physiotherapy.[20] The Sisters were busy with installation of instruments for operating rooms and deliveries, and for the laundry. After it opened, the hospital became an instant attraction to visitors. There was a tour one Sunday, and many brought their families.[21] Some of them took the elevator for the first time. Other religious personnel also visited the hospital.

The inpatient department was scheduled to open on September 1, 1962, but that day, Typhoon Wanda struck Hong Kong. It became one of the worst disasters recorded in local history. Typhoon Signal Number 10 was hoisted, meaning that the storm was approaching very close to Hong Kong. That morning, "the wind howled, and shrieked," and "it really rained and howled in earnest."[22] Wind and rain destroyed squatter huts in the neighborhood, as the Sisters could hear tin plates of the roofs loosen and fly past the windows. Inside the hospital building, much was in disarray. "Putty was peeled away from the window frames," the Sisters described, "and the panes of glass then just blew away and smashed."[23] While windows and doors were tightly closed, water could still sneak in and mopping up became a tiresome process. Some women workers came back and helped with the work. One of them left in the afternoon, only to find her home had been washed away. Even the nurses reported for duty on this very first day, as they struggled up the long steep hill and in the typhoon.[24] They were thoroughly wet when they arrived. They spent the day, the next day, and the following days mopping. In the hospital, the nurses mopped, the Sisters mopped, and all the people mopped. On reflection, the Sisters thought—"the Lord really planned our Opening Day for us—after all the anticipation of the first patient—we had 150 wet, discouraged, homeless people living in the large OPD [outpatient department] waiting room for three days."[25] They were squatters whose huts were destroyed during the typhoon. They slept on mats and were willing to bear the crowded situation with so many people in the same room. For two days, they took shelter in the hospital until they found places to stay, either with their relatives or friends. At the same time, the Sisters were "a pretty tired and bedraggled crew."[26]

The Sisters had a tight schedule in the hospital. Sister nurses and midwives, as well as amahs and orderlies, were on duty. The hospital admitted its first inpatient, who was a typhoon victim. The woman was hit in the typhoon, but because of "the wholesale emergencies at the hospital" her wound was not properly cleaned before suturing, and she got an infection.[27] Sister Patricia took care of her afterward, and she recovered from the fever. Another patient suffered a slipped disc and was in traction. Close by, the parish school became a temporary shelter for over two thousand people whose village was destroyed by the storm. The Sisters visited the school and took with them people, who were wounded by flying pieces of wood and tin. After the typhoon, the injured received treatment for lacerations, sprains, and contusions in the hospital.[28] In September 1962 the first baby was born, a boy whose Chinese name meant "peaceful cloud."[29]

In the parish monthly in late 1962, Sister Mary Ignatia emphasized the needs of Wong Tai Sin, an immigrant community with a rapidly growing population. With the expected intake of 160,000 people in the near future, Wong Tai Sin could only rely on Our Lady of Maryknoll Hospital and a small clinic for medical service. Facilities were seriously inadequate to cater to the rapidly expanding population, who suffered from "malnutrition, vitamin deficiencies and parasitic diseases."[30] The hospital had 17 maternity beds, 33 medical-surgical beds, and 10 private beds for isolation patients. One year after opening the outpatient department, the Sisters already had 15,432 patients—1,881 men, 6,710 women, and 6,841 children.[31] The average number of patients treated daily was 200. Everyday, hundreds of people stood in line for hours to see the doctor. Demands were excessively more than the hospital could handle, and many were turned down even after queuing up for 10 to 12 hours. Subsequently, 200 numbered squares were painted on the sidewalks, but by 8 o'clock in the morning, all were filled.[32] The hospital managed a chest disease clinic, with a specialist coming for weekly visits. Owing to ever-growing needs, the hospital was already planning for its new extension. As a Sister described— "1,500 sick and aged refugees enter Hong Kong every month legally—while 16,000 others flee into Hong Kong [illegally] . . . our brand new hospital is but a tiny spot in the field of medical work to be done."[33] It also received donations of various kinds, on one occasion an ambulance from a group of Australians known as "Organ Grinders Association," whose name was written on the vehicle, and the Sisters had to find ways to remove the large characters if people were still to come to the hospital for surgery.[34]

By the end of 1962, the Sisters personnel increased to twelve, with the arrival of Maria Rieckelman (Maria Fidelis) and Pauline Gibbons (Paul Marie). Sister Maria became the administrator and superior, and Sister Pauline took up the post of supervisor of the outpatient department. Sister Maria had fallen victim to tuberculosis and left for treatment in Manila and the United States before she returned to Hong Kong. The Sisters staff included the administrator, a doctor, nurses, a medical technician, a pharmacist, and a physiotherapist.[35] In 1963 Sisters Mary Ignatia and Marie Therese left, and Sister Marya Zaborowski joined the staff.[36] Two years after the hospital opened, the types of work comprised medical, catechetical, and community-oriented services (see table 6.1).

Table 6.1   Types of work in the house in Wong Tai Sin (1963)

Catechetical	
1. Emergency baptisms	42
2. Catechumenate and catechetical classes	none reported
Medical	
3. Hospital	57,702 visits
	2,876 inpatients
	10,732 outpatients
4. Maternal care	4,444 visits
5. Child care	1,505 visits
Public Health Services	
6. Maternity classes	827 persons reached
7. Immunization	818 persons reached
8. Nutrition clinic	761 persons reached
Social Services	
9. Case work	31 individuals
10. Material relief through mass distribution	227 individuals
11. Senior Legion of Mary	7 members
Service to Civic Community	
12. Talks given	3
13. Workshops conducted	45
14. Technical guidance	10
Number of Sisters in the house	12

Source: "Our Lady of Maryknoll Hospital, Wong Tai Sin, Hong Kong: Types of Work in the House," 1963, 1 page, Folder 1, Box 9, South China Region: Hong Kong/Macau Region, 1921– , Maryknoll Mission Archives.

People in Wong Tai Sin had many worries. Poverty and malnutrition were common problems. The nutrition clinic supplied multipurpose food to the children. On one occasion, there was an 8-month-old baby who weighed only 9 lbs. When his mother took him to the hospital for the first time, he had two rotten teeth pushing out through his gums. In those days, many families fed their children with condensed milk, which contained too much sugar and preservatives and was not entirely nutritious. After many visits to the nutrition clinic, the baby eventually put on some weight, had some color in his cheeks, and had more normally colored black hair.[37] In September 1964, the first triplets were born in the hospital, and they belonged to a family living in one of the resettlement blocks. The unexpected imposed a great deal of financial pressure on the parents. However, the babies received much publicity, and thus, a number of gifts, including money, food, and clothing. A company was willing to supply the family with free milk powder.[38] For the moment, the family was able to manage. There were many other patients, who did not really need to see the doctor, but wanted better nutrition. Therefore, they received Metrecal, Calorid, or multipurpose food.

Another problem was shortage of water. People in hillside huts had to line up for hours for water. They could only get two buckets for two days' use. Each family in seven-story resettlement blocks had only a few minutes to get water, which meant two large cans (or ten gallons) of water. Old folks could not carry the water, and had to pay HK$5 to others for the water. With the limited supply, families were careful in their cooking. They used very little water for the vegetables (as they rarely had meat), and chose those vegetables that needed the least water for cooking. The problem worsened in 1963 and early 1964, with very little rain and water was only supplied for four hours every other day and later on every fourth day.[39] Owing to the exploding population, the government had a hard time meeting needs despite its efforts to build additional reservoirs. While restriction in water supply did not apply to hospitals, the Sisters had to cut back surgery to emergency cases in summer and later to selected urgent cases. Except for the seriously ill, patients got a bath only every other day. In order to minimize the amount of laundry, paper was used everywhere instead of linen. As the Sisters described their state of affairs:[40]

"Water, water, everywhere, and not a drop to drink," or wash with, or water plants with, or to do anything with for that matter, that you usually do with water. That is the present state of affairs, and we are all promising ourselves, that when we see the Heavens raining down water on us again... we will never, never, never, say anything against that heavenly substance. How true it is that you don't really appreciate the little things of everyday living until you don't have them. As you know, the rainfall has been much below the normal for this time of the year. We never do have water all 24 of the hours in each day, but that is the "normal" state of affairs here in this island colony. Now, however, with the population exploding as it is, the demand for water is much greater,... The restriction at first was four hours everyday, then four hours every other day, and now it is four hours every fourth day. This does not hold strictly on the hospital water supply, as we can get as much as we need for the running of the hospital. The Convent is separate however, and we have bid baths and showers good-bye. The patients now bathe every other day except for the acutely ill. We curtailed surgery to just emergency cases for the summer months, but as the ban continued, joined the other hospitals in the city to make it include urgent elective cases as well. Water is getting so that it is almost elastic. First it cleans food, then utensils, then floors, and then the outside steps and then waters the vegetables. It gets so that you are looking for some water to wash the water so that it will be cleaner for its next cleaning job.

This was the situation until May 1964, after which Typhoon Viola and ten more typhoons struck Hong Kong and ended the water shortage.

Stories in Wong Tai Sin

By 1964, Wong Tai Sin was one of the poorest and most densely populated areas in Hong Kong. With a growing population of almost half a million, it was overcrowded. Resettlement blocks and hillside shacks were everywhere. A more fatal problem to the neighborhood was the high risk of fire. Since squatter huts were made of wood and were closely packed together, once a fire broke out, it could destroy many homes. The use of kerosene for cooking and lighting meant that huts could easily catch fire. The new resettlement area, Chi Wan Shan (Mercy Cloud Village), was a government attempt to address the problem. Just behind the hospital, the resettlement blocks aimed to accommodate about 180,000 people.[41] Our Lady of Maryknoll was the only general hospital for this rapidly expanding community and neighborhood.

There were many stories about Wong Tai Sin. The hospital attracted media attention. In January 1964, the *Sing Tao Daily News* reported on the local situation.[42]

As families only had enough to feed themselves, they could not pay for expensive medicines. It was not exaggerating to say that a person was in a difficult situation if sick, and that she was miserable if pregnant. Not only did the sickness or pregnancy involve additional expenses, it also meant a loss in family income if the person was hospitalized. Therefore, the hospital charged patients a very low fee, only HK$4 for meals, medicines, and surgical care. Under the title of "Help the Sick-poor and the Maternity Patients," two of the stories were:

(1)

When a three year old Mei Lin was brought to this hospital the Sisters and nurses were shocked by her appearance as they all exclaimed, "What a pity." She was fast asleep at her mother's breast as we first observed her little body, thin as a bamboo stick and her stomach swollen with hunger. Prominent veins protruded from her neck and big sunken eyes had no light in them at all as they receded behind her prominent forehead. A truly living skeleton! At the sight of the poor baby it gave one chills all over. Because of severe poverty in families such as this, living conditions are very poor and malnutrition cannot be helped. No wonder then that Mei Lin lacked the proper nourishment and weighed only 15 lbs. These kind Sisters took upon themselves the responsibility of seeing her back to life again. Everyday they gave her injections of vitamins, and they provided nourishing food. Also they taught her how to walk and play games. This lucky little Mei Lin was as a small rose trying to bloom again in the warm climate of their love, so that she could breathe the sunlight in again and also see the dew and the mists again under this loving care, and finally to gain a completely new lease on life. Under such care she was able to sit up after three weeks, and her weight increased steadily. A few weeks later she was able to walk a bit.[43]

(2)

In another room a mature infant, only two lbs. when born and whose parents thought it could not live, was proof again that miracles happen under the good care and loving efforts of the good Sisters here. When the parents saw the baby after one month they cried tears of joy to see him so strong and alive, and they praised the Sisters for this job well done.[44]

By the end of 1964, the intake of the hospital rose to new heights. The outpatient department had 65,000 patients, the number of inpatients was 3,000, and the number of newborn babies was 1,000. In order to meet the growing needs, the Sisters opened the fourth floor, and increased the number of beds to 80.[45] With a staff of over 100, the outpatient department and wards were running at full capacity. That year, the government approved an extension to the hospital, which proposed to add 140 beds to the existing 80. Also, the government promised to provide an annual subvention at a maximum of two-thirds of HK$9,000 for each of the 180 third-class beds. The amount did not support forty other maternity, first-class, and second-class beds; for that the Sisters had to look elsewhere.[46] In the hospital there were then fifteen nuns,[47] and they themselves also recorded some mission stories:

(3)

"Perfect Rainbow," a very premature infant was born here over three months ago. Her mother had already lost twins and had only one living child. She had come to us because she wanted so much to have a healthy baby. However, as I said, the baby that was born to her was so tiny that it really frightened the mother. The infant was born with an obstructive type of liver diseases which made it gradually turn very yellow and then a deep bronze.... Over the first six weeks or so, our little "Rainbow" gained very little weight but she did take her feedings, and continued to live with very special handling on our part.... Her mother meanwhile had gone home, and while there became very ill and had to return to the hospital. After she was feeling better we began to take her down to visit her baby, and gradually she became less afraid of her smallness.... Slowly too the baby gained weight, and when it was 51/2 lbs. we allowed the mother to take her home.[48]

(4)

Fear loomed large in the eyes of the dear lady who waited her turn in the out-patient department some weeks ago. She actually drew back in terror when one of us Sisters approached her then. Weeks later, when she had grown to know us better we asked her why she was so afraid of us. She told us shyly that she thought we were foreign devils, but now she knew a different story. While in the hospital our surgeons relieved this lady of a tremendously huge cyst (abdominal).... She returned home last week, happy and grateful, ready to live a normal life again. She promises never to be afraid of American Sisters—or any Sisters—again. For our part, we know that we have made a friend who will pray for our needs to her dying day.[49]

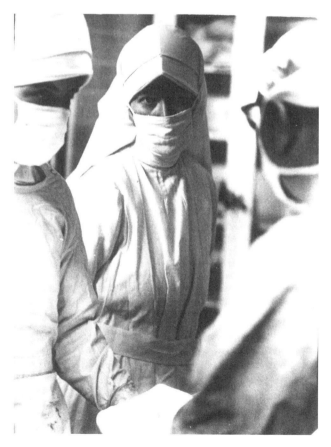

Figure 6.1   Sister Maria Rieckelman (middle) in Our Lady of Maryknoll Hospital, ca. 1965.

Source: Sisters Photo Collection, Maryknoll Mission Archives.

Until 1967, Sister Maria was administrator as well as superior of Sisters in the hospital (see figure 6.1). A medical doctor, she was deeply involved in planning the new wing, which allowed for a greater increase in the intake of patients. With expanding demands from the community, Sister Maria realized they were venturing into an open field. "Seeds and buds of apostolic contacts are here"—she said—"There is a large field in the daily work."[50] Finding it always difficult to get what they wanted, she realized people were initially suspicious of charity work. They tended to ask many questions about the Sisters providing medical care, but very soon, they were ready to cast away their doubts and were eager for the service. Sister Patricia was the surgeon in the hospital. She recognized that the hospital had aroused much attention in the area, and people were waiting anxiously for completion of the new wing. As she stated, "Small wonder that the New Wing looms large in everybody's thoughts."[51]

Sister Gloria, medical technologist, told a story. She recalled—"A nice man, with five children, refused to allow his family to be baptized. He came to the hospital, found he had cancer. After being here, he allowed his family to be baptized, then he was baptized himself. He died peacefully."[52] The outpatient department was cared for by Sister MaryLou Ann Rajdl (M. Ann David), a registered nurse, who came to the hospital in 1964. She was the department supervisor, and worked with a team of laboratory and X-ray technicians, an almoner, and a pharmacist. Every morning at 8 o'clock, when the outpatient clinic opened, there was already a long line waiting outside. Usually, people started to queue up around 6 o'clock. Sister MaryLou examined individual cases and gave the most needed the entrance discs, which were of different colors for different clinics. Although each doctor was supposed to see only thirty patients a day, she always persuaded him to see more. Sister MaryLou saw people at the nutrition clinic, listened to them and gave them necessary vitamins, which might be what they actually needed.[53] "The poor are used to being neglected," the Sisters explained, "but when they see true courtesy and kindness they recognize and respect it, and they appreciate the reasonableness of the arrangement."[54] In 1967 MaryLou became the hospital administrator, and Sister Joseph Lourdes Nubla who worked as her secretary remembered the heavy workload of running several departments at the same time, owing to the tight budget and resulting limited personnel.[55]

In charge of the pharmacy, Sister Ruth Marie was often occupied with her "supplies alley." She said, "I spend a lot of my time down in the supplies alley, separating the medical wheat from the chaff. We got a lot of sample medicines and . . . we get maximum value from it."[56] People also went to Sister Ruth Marie for food supplements, multipurpose food, Metrecal, Nutriment, and milk powder. Usually, doctors sent the undernourished to her. She taught them how to improve their diet, and to buy what was affordable and nourishing. She suggested peanut butter and bread for the children, and asked the people to add multipurpose food and Metrecal to their soup. The sick could not spend their time in the hospital; often, they delayed their own treatment because they could not afford a leave of absence from work. Most of them were living below subsistence levels, and the small amount they earned meant a great deal to them. They did not see the doctor until they were terribly sick, and many should have stayed longer in the hospital, "the very thing they wanted to avoid."[57] Chinese who were poor accepted their misery. As Sister Marya, head nurse, said, the Chinese were ready to believe that their life was one long suffering. The following described the daily scenes inside and outside the hospital:[58]

In front, hawkers spread their vegetables on the ground and market is open. Every noon, an old grandmother and 2 children eat their lunch on the threshold. Across the narrow alley, alongside the Clinic, a man sits on a stool and makes keys. When business is slack—and there's rarely a howling demand for keys—he watches people go by.

Between the key man and the clinic is the bookman. The bookman leaves his small, well-worn paper backs on the windows of the Clinic and rents them for 10¢ an hour. A 2 ft. wide canvas extends from the Clinic wall to protect the books and the crowd of children, sprawled on the ground reading. In case of rain, the canvas fills with water, which begins to seep at 5 minute intervals. With a bamboo pole, the man pushes the water up and out.

Near the key-man, under a lean-to roof, a night worker sleeps on a canvas bed, with children playing around. It is their home and it is a shamble—oil cans, grease cans, pots and pans, rice bowls, strings of noodles hanging from a wall, broken stools, and a plain wooden table in the midst of it all. Above everything, a beautiful old Chinese lantern hangs from the rusty tin roof.

Outside the injection room, another man carries on a thriving worm and fish business, worms in cellophane bags at 1¢, gold or black fish in plastic bags at 20¢.

Patients and others buy worms and fish as gifts for the children. These, with vegetables and other foodstuffs litter the floor of the waiting room.

There were also unusual moments, especially with the curfew during the riots in 1967:[59]

Holy Week here at Our Lady of Maryknoll Hospital was a bit unusual. Services had to be held in the afternoon since riots made a dusk-to-dawn curfew necessary. Most of the rioters were young students led on by some older men. The cause was said to be the five cents increase in ferry prices but it was evident that a more plausible reason lay hidden. Shops were broken into, goods looted, buses and cars overturned, fires started. Tear gas was used to disperse the mobs and the curfew kept the crowds off the street. Transportation was quite limited as buses and ferries stopped running. Many of our employees remained here at the hospital and every available bed was occupied. We were fortunate to have a few extras for them. Factories can be closed but a hospital must continue on a 24-hour schedule.

Looking back at their work, the Sisters realized that being listened to was actually most important to many of the patients, who came for help. The Sisters were asked—"What do you consider the most important work you do?" The response was: "Well, all day long I am busy. What seems to me to bring most people help is for the people to feel they can talk to me."[60]

Kowloon Tsai

In the 1960s, the Sisters began their work in Kowloon Tsai (or as they translated it into English "Nine Little Dragons"), for families in the Tai Hang Tung Resettlement Estate and those living in hillside huts on the west side of the railway tracks that separated the area from Kowloon Tong.[61] The two types of housing were packed into an area of about one-sixth of a square mile, but with a population of 120,000 people. The residents either lived in seven-story resettlement blocks or wooden shacks on hillsides. When the Sisters moved there in 1961, the convent took up one half of a one-story stone building, and the other half was the Maryknoll Fathers' clinic and catechumen rooms. As they described their place, it was "half Clinic and Catechumenate and half US."[62] They served in the clinic and chapel, which were supported by the Migration and Refugee Unit of the American government. Sponsorship of the American Unit lasted until the end of 1962. The chapel was named St. Peter in Chains, and the pastor was Maryknoll Father John McLoughlin.

In order to get to the chapel and the clinic, the Sisters had to walk down a dark, narrow alley. It had a half-covered drain, and dirty water flowed under the stone slabs. Its appearance was very different from its name, the Alley of Ten Thousand Fragrances, as the place used to be a swamp where lilies grew.[63] Although it was only five feet wide, it was the busiest alley. Neighbors raised pigs and dogs and grew a few vegetables. On narrow sidewalks, there were all sorts of activities going on. "Cooking, washing clothes, bathing children, eating, cottage industries, food stalls, peddlers, animals, toddlers, even sleeping" were often seen.[64] On the two-lane streets, the traffic was filled with "trucks, cars, bicycles with strident horns and clanging bells."[65]

In January 1961, Sisters Margaret Marie Jung and M. Doretta Leonard moved to Kowloon Tsai. The address of the convent was Lung Wah Street, Tai Hang Tung. Their ministry was primarily catechetical. There were about 7,000 Catholics in the area; out of those 4,000 were children. Immediately, the Sisters started house visits. They also provided catechetical classes, for 50, and First Holy Communion classes, for 250. For the Chinese New Year gathering, more than 200 elderly attended, all of them above 70 and the oldest over 90. At the same time, the Sisters organized the Sodalities for women and girls, and the Knights of the Blessed Sacraments for boys. Subsequently, they took over the parish Sunday school for about 400 children. As in Wong Tai Sin, the panic of cholera hit and people queued up for long hours for inoculations in the police station. In September, Sister Doretta was assigned to Kwun Tong, and Sister Ruth Evans (M. Margaret Veronica), who was also assigned to Kwun Tong, became a resident of Kowloon Tsai.[66] In October, Sister Pauline arrived to work in the clinic before being assigned to Wong Tai Sin. The clinic was a 20 feet by 20 feet room, further divided into three smaller rooms, with a doctor there for one evening every week, a nurse, and a registrar.[67] From October to December, the clinic served over 13,000 people, who paid a minimal fee of 40 cents.

Sister Margaret Marie stayed on in Kowloon Tsai, while the others subsequently left for other assignments. In the latter part of 1962, Sister Katherine Byrne (Philip Marie) joined the staff. That year, the area suffered from a fierce fire, which left nine hundred people homeless. Furthermore, there was tremendous damage caused by Typhoon Wanda. It took the government three months to clean up the debris. Despite the situation, the Sisters managed to continue with their work. With limited space, groups of catechumens and First Holy Communion children took shifts for doctrine classes in one single room. Sodality groups made the place more crowded on Sundays. Besides catechetical work, the Sisters provided medical care and expanded into social service. In 1962, the clinic handled about 32,460 cases.[68] As for social service, the Sisters started literacy classes for children who could not afford normal schooling. Many families were too poor to allow their children to go to school, it cost HK$5 a month for primary school tuition and HK$40 for secondary school tuition. The amount could take up to one-third of a family's income. Moreover, there were not enough school spaces for children. There were 24,000 primary school–aged children but only 1,000 spaces in a government school, 9,000 in Protestant rooftop schools (in the resettlement blocks), 350 in a Catholic school, and 2,500 in private schools. As said, "So many run wild."[69] Therefore, the Sisters arranged literacy classes and "took 20 retarded (from poverty, malnutrition) children for a slim course to prepare them 'to earn a bowl of rice.' "[70] During Christmas, former students of Maryknoll schools organized parties for nearby children.

In Kowloon Tsai, poverty was commonplace and missioners faced "a hundred challenges a day."[71] There were gambling and dope peddling. Many people suffered from dope addiction. Laborers did not have enough to eat, and took heroin or opium to give them the strength they needed. As the Sisters explained—"A man who smokes opium [believes he] can lift 250 lbs. and get a job. Without it, he cannot."[72] Soon, he got addicted. Running away from China, newcomers had to adapt to a new and difficult life. Many of them came from the countryside, and were then living in a crowded community. They stayed in small huts or the whole family shared a single room in the seven-story mountains. In the city, people lived very close to each other, and there was not enough space for families. The Sisters described—"Nothing in these peasant peoples' upbringing has prepared them for life in a cubicle, in a mountain of cubicles."[73] Without relatives or their lineage people to turn to, they were totally on their own. Families had a hard time raising their kids, providing their basic needs, not to say caring and disciplining them.

From early 1963 to 1965, Sister Katherine and Sister Agnes Cazale worked in Kowloon Tsai. In January 1963, Sister Katherine set up a new service termed "Well Baby Clinic." During its first ten months, about thirty-five babies, newborn to six months, were brought in to the clinic every week. They were weighed and given a checkup.[74] For registration, the mothers had to present birth certificates and immunization records. The mothers, who breast-fed their babies, received calcium, vitamins, and multi purpose food. If they bottle fed, they could buy one pound of milk powder for only HK$1. Sister also taught them how to supplement their diet in inexpensive ways. Soya bean milk was used to supplement milk, as it was rich in calcium and protein.[75] Sister Katherine had a clerk and a workwoman to assist her. As she said, "My young clerk enjoys weighing the babies. Everyone cheers the little 'premies' when they gain a few ounces."[76] The clinic also distributed used baby clothes. At the same time, almost one hundred people came to the clinic for care each day. The following was a description of one of the days of the nun:[77]

> The crowds had not yet assembled, but a few were there. 2 quiet, healthy children stood on a bench, interested in everything. One wore a very fancy short red silk dress (somebody's cast-off) over ankle length cotton Chinese trousers. Mothers, with babies on their backs, sat, some placid, some chattering, others visibly anxious. One woman, sat alone on a long bench, stiff and aloof, apparently her first visit.
> It was a cold day outside, but inside the small waiting room, the atmosphere was insufferable, filled with sweaty bodies, the smell of medications, and noise! There was a tired old man with a cane, mothers with babies with colds, a nurse taking temperatures,

babies crying, bigger brothers and sisters with shrill voices, cackling old women, grunts from old men, women singing or humming to quieten children, animated conversations going on among repeaters; "What's wrong with you, White Haired One?" "Eh?" "She asks what's wrong with you. Why do you come to see a doctor?" "Cough." This terminates the conversation. The old man stares into space again. One spoilt boy lies flat out on the narrow floor and refuses to move. Both parents yank him up. He collapses again, screaming at the top of his lungs. Mother yells, Father yells....

Outside little ones in wooden clogs and red shirts watched me as I write. I look up and smile at them. A mistake! They smile back, but keep returning for more smiles. They run up and down the narrow passage, voices shrill with excitement because I smile....

While Sister Katherine catered to the physical needs, Sister Agnes took care of catechetical work. Sister Agnes was responsible for training women catechists. She had regular meetings with women leaders, who then also taught other lay catechists. Her classes were usually at night, as the women had to work during the day. The working girls' Sodality also arranged group discussions, in which women talked about their problems both at work and at home and how to deal with them. Typical of the work of the Maryknoll Sisters, the service aimed to raise the self-esteem of women, to help them better face the challenges in society. In addition, Sister organized special sessions for young mothers, to see to their needs. She conducted home visits and responded to the calls of those who visited the catechetical center. Furthermore, she ran the Christian Family Living Program, and worked with Maryknoll Father Michael McKeirnan who became the new pastor.[78] More religious groups came into being—Legion of Mary, Sodality (Senior and Junior), Apostleship of Prayer, Eucharistic Crusade, Young Catholic Students, Children of Mary, and Young Christian Workers.[79] Chinese New Year parties continued to be held for the elderly, and English-language classes were offered in the evening. The types of work in Kowloon Tsai were demonstrated by the yearly statistics of 1963 (see table 6.2).

In 1964, the number of catechumens dropped from 400 to 500 a year to only 200.[80] The Sisters blamed materialism for the sudden decrease in catechumens. Child delinquency, stealing and vulgar language were common in families, whose parents were always out for work. Although Father McKeirnan ran a roof-top school for about 350 children, many did not have a chance to receive education. The community had many problems. Not an entirely safe neighborhood, a bomb was placed in the gambling den just opposite the Sisters' convent in 1965. It exploded and two "angry losers" were arrested. As the Sisters described, the explosion killed a few people and injured some, cracked their toilet, "besides frightening 100,000 people!"[81] From 1966 to 1968, Sister Agnes and Sister Marilyn Norris (M. Deirdre) served in Kowloon Tsai. Sister Anne Reusch (Alma Marie) joined them in 1968. In 1969 and 1970, Sisters Marilyn and Anne were the personnel there; and in 1971 and 1972, Sister Gloria joined them.[82] In 1972, the Sisters' house in Kowloon Tsai closed.

Maryknoll Sisters Social Service Program

The Sisters' social service program reflected the changing needs of Hong Kong society. In the early 1960s, they continued to supply relief goods for the poor. Nevertheless, they recognized that the community called for more long-term service.

Table 6.2   Types of work in the house in Kowloon Tsai (1963)

Educational	
1. TV English Classes	24 Students
2. Religion Classes	119 Students
Catechetical	
3. Catechumenate Classes	285 Children
	456 Adults
4. Classes for Already Baptized	626 Children
	132 Adults
5. Training Catechists	14 Trainees
Medical	
6. Clinic	24,647 Visits
7. Mobile Clinic	19,661 Visits
8. Child Care	1,034 Visits
9. Public Health Services	355 Persons reached
Social Services	
10. Counseling	123 Families
	1,921 Individuals
11. Junior Sodality	2 Groups, 70 Members
Senior Sodality	98 Members
12. Junior Legion of Mary	18 Members
Number of Sisters in the House	2

Source: "Kowloon Tsai, Hong Kong: Types of Work in the House," 1963, 1 page, Folder 7, Box 8, South China Region: Hong Kong/Macau Region, 1921– , Maryknoll Mission Archives.

By 1964 Sister Barbara, who was elected into the Congregation's General Council and was therefore succeeded by Rosalia Kettl as regional superior, admitted—"There is no longer an emphasis on material relief, though there is an amount of distribution going on by way of clothing and food supplies for the people in resettlement areas...."[83] The Sisters were shifting their focus, though for the time being, relief for the neighborhood was still necessary. Relief food and clothing were notable in terms of quantity and variety (see table 6.3).

Besides relief, the Sisters began to focus more attention on casework for individual families and children, and recreation-time work for youth. As described, "families began to get on their feet and the needs for distribution of welfare supplies dwindled; other needs called for other ways of helping."[84] Sister Mary Heath became the casework supervisor at the King's Park Social Welfare Center. With support of the government's Social Welfare Department, which paid for two trained caseworkers, the Center ventured into the new service. The idea was to provide more long-term aid to individuals and families, who were being referred to the Sisters. In 1964, Sister Barbara stated, their work "took on a new change, from the giving of material relief to supervising a Case Work Centre."[85]

In June 1963, the intake at the Center was 65.[86] The requests concerned family and child problems, housing, food, cash, employment, and nursery care. Cash grants were for general spending, old folks, house repairs, and physical examinations for emigration to the United States. Some of the clients came to the Center for

Table 6.3 Relief food and clothing, distributed during April 1, 1963–March 31, 1964 Maryknoll Sisters Catholic Welfare Center, Homantin-King's Park Resettlement Area

1. To residents of King's Park on a district basis
   Total families receiving the food—5,200

Item	Bulk Amount
Flour	212,000 lbs.
Cornmeal	57,200 lbs.
Dry Beans	54,500 lbs.
Bulgar Wheat	347,300 lbs.
Peanut Oil	3,000 gal.
Cottonseed Oil	24,000 gal.
Lard	16,000 gal.
Soy Bean Oil	6,680 gal.
Butter Oil	12,705 gal.
Noodles (wet)	748,800 lbs.
Clothing	60 bales (1,800 families received pieces)

2. To families given special tickets through the Casework Section of Center
   Total families receiving the food—500

Milk Powder	93,619 lbs.
Bulgar Wheat	50,400 lbs.
Cottonseed oil	1,200 gal.
Noodles (wet)	119,900 lbs.
Noodles (dry)	2,270 lbs. (1 lb. dry equals 3 lbs. wet)
Clothing	250 pieces (approx.) We keep a regular supply on hand for use of the case workers. About fifty families were given clothing during the year.

3. To institutions that requested noodles from our factory

Name	Amount
St. Joseph the Worker Chapel	117,250 lbs.
Precious Blood Sisters	56,000 lbs.
Wah Yan Boys Poor Club	7,900 lbs.
H.K. Society for the Blind	17,700 lbs.
Immaculate Conception Sisters	172,800 lbs.
Maryknoll Sisters	1,875 lbs.

4. To our Nursery and School at King's Park

Item	
Soy Bean Oil	310 gal.
Noodles (wet)	18,130 lbs.

Source: "Street Hawker: Maryknoll Sisters Social Service in Hong Kong 1960–1964," n.d. [1964?], p.12, Box 2A, South China Region: Hong Kong/Macau Region, 1921– , Maryknoll Mission Archives.

information, which covered quite a number of topics. They asked about labor laws, child welfare, and other personal problems, such as dope addiction. In the Center, staff activities included regular meetings, home visits, office interviews, phone calls, and letters for clients. Although many cases were carried over to following months, different requests came up each month. For example, in July the casework was not entirely the same—52 of the cases were carried forward from June, but 93 of them were new applications.[87] Clients asked for help for foster care, schooling, and medical care. They received grants for school fees, books, uniforms, maternity needs, hawkers license, and even for the payment of a high-interest loan (see table 6.4).

Table 6.4 Statistics in King's Park in the ten months of 1963/1964

I Intake
New applications—455; Average monthly intake: First five months—70–80; Last five months—20–30

II Requests and Financial Grants Given

Request	Total Number	Total Cash Grants
1. Housing This includes paying for tax, rent or repair. Also requests to arrange with government for housing.	42	HK$907.50
2. Food Requests for special weekly food grants of noodles, oil, wheat and milk. Grants are reviewed and renewed if needed every three months.	111 (reapplications are not included)	
3. Employment Includes requests to pay for license and capital to hawk food; locate work or arrange for vocational training.	62	$345.00
4. Nursery care	89	
5. Other child care requests This includes foster homes, institutions or hostel care for both boys and girls.	14	
6. Disturbed child behavior	15	
7. Marital and other disturbed relationships	4	
8. Emigration to the U.S.	3 (Requests from our Sisters in the U.S. are not ordinarily handled by the case work section)	
9. General family maintenance	58	$20,422.14
10. Travel expenses	6	
11. Medical care and maternity fee	17	$168.50
12. Legal advice	4	
13. Schooling This includes school fees, books, uniforms	29	$550.00
14. Pay off high-interest loan	1	$300.00

Source: Modified from "Street Hawker: Maryknoll Sisters Social Service in Hong Kong 1960–1964," pp. 8–9.

For casework service there were problems that needed to be solved. The Sisters had to look for assistance for needy families on both short-term and long-term bases. They created a "Guide for Determining Grants" and offered financial help to cater to specific needs of the people. The objective was to allow families to have a reasonable standard of living, rather than just giving them token sums of money. For the first ten months, the intake was not that large, and the Sisters were able to abide by the policy. Nevertheless, they were aware of the difficulties ahead, if the service became more widely known and more people asked for help. It meant huge sums of money if there was a large intake in future. As the Sisters described, it was "not an academic question in Hong Kong," whether "to help a few families in a substantial way or to help many families just meet minimum needs."[88] In matters of urgency, the voluntary agencies could only give whatever possible to many people.

Very often, the Sisters tackled behavior problems of children whose parents, both of them, worked and had little time for the family. Delinquency extended to young children who were only eight years old. Situations were "getting quite out of hand," for example, "out over night, gamble, steal, truant from school, and no amount of beating (and they get plenty of this) from their parents" had an effect on them.[89] Parents had an extremely tough time accepting what had become of their sons and daughters. Solutions to the problems were neither easy nor quick. Usually, the Sisters referred children to clubs where they could spend their hours after school. Those with emotional difficulties received treatment at the Child Guidance Clinic at the University of Hong Kong. The Sisters also assisted families financially so that mothers could stay at home. Moreover, children whose mothers died or left the family were under the care of foster homes. When compared with foster homes in the United States, the Sisters admitted that the Hong Kong situation was rather different. Foster parents were clients on financial support, and their living conditions were far from satisfactory. Nevertheless, it was better than leaving the children without care and discipline.[90]

In King's Park, the Center organized evening activities for teenagers who graduated from Lok Tak (Primary) School. It cooperated with the Federation of Youth Groups and received support from the Social Welfare Department. Aside from King's Park Center, the Sisters at St. Teresa's Parish engaged in club activities for children and young adults, as well as some family counseling. In Kwun Tong, the Sisters arranged activities for children on the rooftop of a resettlement block. Moreover, Sisters of the parishes organized Young Christian Student Groups, Young Christian Worker Groups, and the Christian Family Movement Group, as attempts to deal with delinquency and family issues.[91]

Development of Social Work Training

Besides casework that provided close attention to individual and family needs, the Sisters also launched a program for training social workers. King's Park Center offered fieldwork placement for social work students of Chinese University and University of Hong Kong. At the same time, Caritas, the Diocesan Catholic charities organization, had close relations with Maryknoll Sisters. In the early 1960s, Sister Mary Heath was responsible for setting up and teaching in Caritas' social work training center. Caritas sent its students for practical work at King's Park; and for supervision of its students, it hired a qualified social worker to work there. On a community-wide basis, Sister Mary assumed an active role in developing social casework and social work training. She had regular meetings with the teaching and supervising staff of social work at Chinese University. She also lectured on casework in the University. In addition, she sat on the executive committees of the Hong Kong Council of Social Services and the Hong Kong Social Workers Association. Appointed by the government, she was a member of the Social Work Training Advisory Committee. Through these affiliations, she engaged in projects and discussions on training local social workers. Sister Mary promoted the idea of social work as a career for young people, and prepared recruitment material for distribution in schools. Moreover, she took part in the organizational reforms of the Council of

Social Services. The Sister met with Legislative Council members and discussed community needs before the government initiated its policies.[92]

On the Diocesan level, Sister Mary was the general administrator of all casework centers of Caritas.[93] This represented part of "a new development," in which Maryknoll Sisters supervised Caritas casework programs throughout the Diocese.[94] They were responsible for Caritas's social work training program, as well as those university students who practised at Caritas' social work centers. In the mid-1960s, Caritas set up a number of centers throughout Hong Kong, and its students were able to conduct placement work in its own centers. Specifically, the Sisters took charge of its new casework center on Caine Road and the proposed center, which was to be situated next to St. Teresa's Church on Waterloo Road.[95] The new center in the St. Teresa's Church site was to replace the casework center situated in Maryknoll's Social Welfare Center in King's Park, and Sister Susan Gubbins (Susan Marie) who arrived in 1967 became responsible for this center. Established in December 1957, Caritas as a Diocesan organization had well-defined objectives. It was (1) to run all the social welfare institutions set up by the Diocese; (2) to offer welfare service to needy families; (3) to be responsible for food distribution in the community; (4) to take care of undernourished children; (5) to solicit funds locally and abroad for development of Catholic social service; (6) to develop moral and charitable welfare, vocational training, and relief services; and (7) to promote social work as a possible career among Catholics.[96]

By the mid-1960s, Caritas had a few social centers, a general hospital, and schools. Its centers were located in different localities—Tsuen Wan and Shek Kip Mei in Kowloon; and Kennedy Town, Aberdeen and the upcoming Central Diocesan Building next to the Cathedral on Caine Road on Hong Kong Island. Although it had the financial support of the Diocese, it was still short of funding; activities were organized to raise funds. Other religious communities were responsible for their own expenses if they took up social service. As described, they were "asked not to compete with the Caritas fund raising efforts in the Diocese."[97] Instead, religious communities belonged to the Catholic Social Welfare Conference, which was formed by the Bishop as a coordinating body for all Catholic activities under the direction of religious orders, congregations, lay organizations, and clubs. It was different from Caritas which organized social welfare activities for the Diocese. The aims of the Conference were to provide official representation of Catholic activities, to coordinate and promote social welfare activities, and to build up relations between the government's Social Welfare Department and voluntary Catholic institutions.[98] In the 1960s, Hong Kong society was moving toward better standards of living, higher expectations, and greater civil awareness. What the Church and missioners had in mind was not only to help people solve their immediate problems, but to achieve greater objectives in the long run.

CHAPTER SEVEN

KWUN TONG AND CHAI WAN IN THE 1960S

Our Christmas was a royal welcome to the Christ Child....
The playlets and dances culminated in the ever new and ever dear Christmas tableau.
And not even the first shepherds were more enthralled than our little ones were. But their
reverent attendance at the Nativity did not cool their fun in the classroom parties where
cookies, a pound of candy for each class of forty five children, and imprudently "all the milk
they could drink." I forgot for the nonce that the children had never in all their lives had
"all they could" of anything, and I watched with awe as the sixth grade boys guzzled bottle
after bottle of that perfectly innocuous non-fat powdered milk. Coming out of my trance
when I heard two boys saying, "This is my twelfth bottle" I quietly removed temptation from
them lest there be an explosion of some sort!

Sister Anne Clements (Mary Famula), Holy Spirit School,
Kwun Tong, Christmas 1963[1]

The 1960s was a decade of change, which came in multiple numbers and in rapid speed. Whilst Maryknoll Sisters served in various aspects of relief, service, and welfare, they underwent significant revisions in the objectives of their mission, as generated by Vatican Council II (1962–1965), a landmark in the history of the Roman Catholic Church. Even before the event, the Sisters already paid much attention to the destitute and disadvantaged. The Council allowed missioners to involve in noninstitutional tasks, meaning they could work in their own individual capacities in places in need of help, giving them more freedom and opportunities to respond to the local wants. Mission for the poor became the emphasis of Vatican Council II.

On the other side of the world, Hong Kong was developing its own industries and people could earn a living through hard labor in newly erected factory buildings. The Sisters reached out to newly emerged working-class areas of Kwun Tong, while continuing their work in Chai Wan. The second half of the 1960s also witnessed the upsurge of revolutionary tide on the mainland, which swept across the boundary to Hong Kong. Hope, anxieties, fears, and worries described mixed feelings of the society in the turbulent decade. Both people and the Sisters encountered different circumstances and challenges.

Working-Class Community of Kwun Tong

Hong Kong turned into an industrial city and its economic performances were promising, but at the same time, the society was open to many uncertainties.

Forty percent of the labor force, about one and a half million, engaged in export-oriented industries, that of cotton garments and plastic products. The blooming economy allowed people to have more opportunities to improve their livelihood. In three years, salaries of workers increased within the range of seven to forty percent. Skilled workers were able to earn HK$9–24 a day; semiskilled workers HK$8–11.50 a day; and the unskilled HK$4–10 a day.[2] Paid on a daily basis, most of them worked even on Sundays and holidays so as to obtain extra income. More than one family member had to work in order to meet the cost of living. While there were still many problems in society, things were progressing and that gave hope. As the Sisters observed—"Dole lines are disappearing from the scene," and people were getting on their own feet. With jobs, people could "pay their way more and a sense of human dignity and independence . . . replaced their desperate mentality."[3]

Kwun Tong was nonexistent when Maryknoll Sisters first arrived in Hong Kong in the 1920s.[4] In fact, it emerged as a factory area only in the 1960s. Some of the industrial entrepreneurs as well as poor laborers, both of whom fled from China, began their new life and career in Kwun Tong. The Sisters described the scene:

> Kwun Tong is an agglomeration of tired, old mountains, and of man-made plateaus; of flat land and of valleys scooped out of mountains; of towering apartments and of squatters' huts. It is a thick growth of steel and cement, of bamboo scaffoldings and builders' shacks; of clattering factories and clamourous tenements; of banks and shops and of itinerant hawkers' stands; of noise and confusion and smell; of people—hundred[s] and thousands of them—people everywhere!
>
> In Kwun Tong's 40 acres with its population of 500,000 there is always the background of people and the sounds they make. Just beyond the ragged rows of factories built helter-skelter on land reclaimed from the sea are the arrogantly ugly tanks of an oil company, spread in disproportionate profusion where living space is so limited. Between the reclaimed sea flats and the mountains, buildings are everywhere. The whole area is in a state of becoming and this is accompanied by a shattering din. The thumping, screeching, rolling and swishing of factory machines, whine and moan of concrete mixers, the pounding of pile drivers, the hammering and clinging of the builders, the cries of hawkers, the blaring of uncounted radios and the voices of thousands of people going about the prosy routine of their daily existence in inescapable proximity to one another.[5]

Kwun Tong exhibited signs of a vibrant economy. With chances ahead of them, people were confident. The Hong Kong community was rather young. As the 1961 census showed, forty-five percent of the population were under age 14; fifteen percent between 15 and 24; thirty percent between 25 and 54; and only ten percent were over 55.[6] The youthful population provided a powerful force for development of indigenous industries.

In 1959 Maryknoll Father Edward Krumpelmann, asked for assistance of the Sisters in running a clinic in the area. Working in Kwun Tong, he was well aware of the demand for medical service in the poor neighborhood. He hoped the Sisters' clinic could replace the existing one, which was managed by Maryknoll Fathers but was closing down. Our Lady of Maryknoll Hospital was still in planning, and some of its assigned staff could be spared to take up the task. In November, Sisters Monica Marie Boyle and Helen Kenny opened the clinic in one of the resettlement blocks.

It was situated in Orchid House (the name of the block). Their diary recorded their first impression of the new working environment:

> A few years before, it was rocky and mountainous. Now the ground was level, mountains were being moved and factories and apartment houses were sprouting all around. We walked over ditches on the planks, broken earth and newly dug foundations but could not find the site of the new clinic in "Orchid House." Finally Orchid House was located and we went up one flight in this five story apartment building to room number one to our new clinic. The room was quite small with a tiny kitchen which later became the kitchen and injection room alternatively. A small verandah looks out on the harbor.[7]

Their place was small, and they were waiting for furniture from the Maryknoll Fathers' clinic. The local Precious Blood Sisters also helped them with their initial needs. While the government had planned to erect factories and housing for 300,000 people by 1961, it requested the clinic of the Maryknoll Sisters to provide emergency treatment to injured workers in factory accidents. Since resources were limited, the nuns had to learn to cope with a situation that was far from being optimal. "As the cabinets, desks and files began to enter the room," they remarked, "the room began to shrink until one wondered just where the patients would stand."[8] The walking area was only 6 × 4 feet, and the Sisters called it the "bargain basement." Gradually, their intake of patients grew, and they treated about thirty-five cases a day. On one weekday a doctor was on duty, and the day before the number of people lined up for registration could reach 120.[9] While the Sisters only spoke Cantonese, they were lucky to have the assistance of a laywoman who knew a few dialects and could communicate with non–Cantonese speaking patients. A year later, in 1960, the clinic moved to Lily House. The address was Catholic Mission Clinic, Maryknoll Sisters, Ground Floor, Lily House, 293 Ngau Tau Kok Road.[10] When the Hospital opened in Wong Tai Sin in 1961, the two Sisters moved to their original assignments there.

In November 1960, Sister Mary Diggins left Chai Wan and began to work in Kwun Tong.[11] Sisters Anne Clements and Joanne Bastien (M. Anne Noel) later joined in. They moved to a building, which was used as a dormitory for factory workers. In September 1961 Sister Ruth Evans, who resided in the Kowloon Tsai convent, was assigned to Kwun Tong.[12] Also, Sister Doretta Leonard moved from Kowloon Tsai to Kwun Tong. The neighborhood was developing quickly. Besides Orchid House, Lily House, and other Houses that used flowers as names, the government was building an additional number of resettlement estates in the area. As Mary Diggins said, they were "24 huge blocks of concrete tenements, grey inside and out with no gilding of the lily." These new blocks were H-shaped and were distinguished by their "cement walls, and dank stairways, smelly close-walled alley-ways."[13] In those days, the seven-story blocks were the popular choices of the government as it only took sixteen weeks to build them from piling to completion.[14] When Sister had been in Chai Wan, she showed no liking for these blocks; now, she seemed to think poorly of the resettlement estates in Kwun Tong also:

> Even the names lack imagination—A, B, C etc. Arrived at "Z" (Zed to us) the blocks now in the making will bear the fascinating double names AA, BB, CC etc. After double Ized (ZZ) there will be triple letters—AAA, BBB, CCC etc.

> Every block is identical to every other block being distinguished by a huge black letter, its name. Each Block is shaped like an H—opening out onto a cement court which gives light and is in practice, an outsize garbage disposal unit. The bar of the H is the sanitary facilities, ... Outside stairways lead up to the roof. Presumably humans aren't able to walk up more than eight flights, as all the blocks are just seven storeys plus a roof. ...
> In spite of the ugliness of it all, the people are friendly and receptive.[15]

Nevertheless, she admitted that Hong Kong had experienced "the most stupendous refugee incursion in the world." The government at least provided "shelter, employment, security and schools, however ugly, for these astronomical numbers of people in this microscopic space."[16] In the seven-story blocks, each family crowded together—ate, slept, and entertained themselves—in a small room of $9 \times 12 \times 8$ feet. According to statistics, an adult had at most 24 square feet of living space, and a child at most 12 square feet.[17] The toilets were communal. As for cooking, the family took care of their own outside their room along the verandah. Laundry was stretched out on bamboo poles hanging out into the air on every floor. When Hong Kong faced water shortages, the government supplied tap water during fixed hours only; and that stretched the patience of people to the limits. At public taps, the rule was usually three hours of water every two days. As the Sisters saw: "They use kerosene cans and stand in the broiling sun in queues a mile long waiting their turn at the single tap. As most people can afford two kerosene cans, only, besides having no place to store the water, that much water must last for two days for cooking, bathing and for any cleaning that is done."[18] Surely, public housing was a sight, with so many people in such limited space.

The government was moving ahead with reclamation—removing nearby mountains and dumping soil into the sea—then building resettlement blocks on the new land. Even the Sisters remarked that the scene from their convent, located on the fifth floor of the factory dormitory, changed completely within a few years. They used to enjoy a splendid view of the ocean, which was just at their feet. Very soon, they could only see the multistory buildings on land that had been nonexistent before. Activities were all out there—"I can see without stretching, twenty-three pile-drivers and cement mixers. ...within my eye span are thirteen trucks speeding along the four roads converging at our corner. ...without changing my position, I can see the scaffoldings of three large buildings going up across the street from us."[19] There was the noise of buses, speeding cars, taxis, hums of engines from factories, drills, and of course thousands and thousands of people in the area. In the youthful community, thousands were children under ten years old. Crowding and energy described Kwun Tong.

The Sisters started ministry in the area and engaged in catechetical service. Sisters Mary and Doretta used rooms in a seven-story resettlement block, Block F, for catechetical classes and sodality meetings. The location soon became the center of activities of Maryknoll. Sister Joanne also attended to the clinic there, and Father Krumpelmann directed the making and distribution of noodles and bread.[20] With three lay catechists, the nuns arranged doctrine instructions for huge crowds of people. In one Baptism group, there were almost three hundred women and over three hundred children.[21] There were night classes for factory workers, who could only have time after work and supper, and classes were also available on Sundays. Women workers participated in the activities. For example, Sister Mary started the Young Christian Worker Group; and every week, Sister and the women met and discussed their work problems, social questions, and religion. Yearly retreats were also part of the program. In order to get to know more about the community, the nuns arranged home visits and gained some knowledge of the local situation.

To deal with the problem of unattended children, as parents went to work and kids were left alone without proper care, Sister Mary started a nursery on the ground floor and rooftop of Block F, which registered a few hundred children. This was a response to a tragedy in which a fire broke out; a child died and other children were severely burnt. It happened when both parents were out for work, the six-year-old "big sister" was cooking with charcoal, the "paper, clothing, wooden bedstead were aflame," and the children could not escape because the steel door was locked (so as to prevent them from wandering around in the neighborhood).[22] A neighbor called the police, who broke in, but it was already too late. With the supervision of Sister Katherine Byrne, the students of Maryknoll schools helped to set up the nursery, providing care for children not yet entering Primary One, whose parents worked during daytime and could not afford to pay for kindergarten.[23] Eventually, a laywoman was hired as manager under Sister Mary's direction. Other members of the staff included teachers, cleaning women, and a cook. Every day, the kids came and had three meals in the nursery—milk and bread in the morning; rice, meat, and a vegetable around noon; and noodles in the late afternoon. As the nursery only asked for a small fee, Catholic Relief Services supplied most of the food to the neighborhood. This was some kind of help to families. One child said to Sister: "Mother told me to eat all I could [in the nursery] so that I could leave more for the rest at home."[24]

Under the supervision of Sister Joanne, who was a nurse, Maryknoll managed two clinics in Kwun Tong, one in Lily House in the mornings and another one in Block F in the afternoons. With the help of a worker and a social worker, and more frequent visits of doctors, the Lily House clinic was able to take care of 1,000 patients a month and Block F clinic 3,000 patients a month. At Block F clinic, about 250 TB patients visited daily for treatment.[25] Despite their illness, most TB patients continued to live with their families, as there was not enough space in the hospital to make the necessary accommodation. Like the situation in Our Lady of Maryknoll Hospital in Wong Tai Sin, people spent many hours lining up for medical care. As described: "Patients that are to be seen from 2 PM onwards are already in line sitting on their infinitesimal stools at seven thirty AM."[26] Therefore, Sister Joanne marked the ground outside the clinic from one to one hundred for people to line up, to maintain some kind of order. She had some favorite visitors, and one of them was "Ah Poh" (the Cantonese word for old grannie):[27]

> Sister . . . has a crush on several of her old grannies. . . . She is a tiny mite shaking up and down, always coming to the clinic at the wrong time, but Sister . . . cannot resist her because of her bilingualism! She comes in with a "Hullo, good-by" and is as uninhibited and friendly as a child. At Church when the usher came along for collection she stood up to shake hands with him. When Father Reilly was in the act of making an impressive gesture during a sermon, up hops Ah Poh (grannie) and shakes his hand.

Very commonly, her patients included street hawkers:[28]

> One of Sister's patients helps her husband sell vegetables by going about the streets calling out their wares. One day Sister scolded the woman for leaving her four weeks old twins at home alone. With the eleventh month's old baby on her back, her two-year-old

daughter who can neither sit nor walk without toppling over in her arms, the woman quite reasonably asked, "How can I carry four?" But she hastened to reassure Sister that the twins would come to no harm. There was no bed for them to fall off of.

The old clinic room in Lily House lasted until January 1963, after which all people received treatment in Block F clinic. In Block F, Sister took care of TB patients in the mornings and general cases in the afternoons.[29]

Through the years, Christmas celebrations were fond memories. Had she been asked, Sister Mary Diggins would have agreed that the Christmas of 1962 was incredible. In her usual straightforward manner, she wrote: "Well, here we are with another Christmas gone into eternity.... thank God, there is only one Christmas a year.... would be terrible if we had one [Christmas] a month,...."[30] There were four Midnight Masses—one in the school classroom, one in the auditorium, and two others on rooftops of seven-story blocks. The four sites were packed with adults. From the industrial department in Kowloon Tong, the Sisters received a white vestment as a gift and used it for Mass. On the morning of December 25, there were eight Masses altogether, attended by mothers and children. After Mass, the Sisters had "lauds," "mail and packages."[31] For the children of Kwun Tong, Christmas was surely the big event. Sister Anne Clements recorded the happenings in a Christmas party in 1963:[32]

Our Christmas was a royal welcome to the Christ Child. The teachers managed everything themselves, even to assembling parts of a demolished ship to make an iron stage, and then after all was over, marking each part and putting all away for next year. One of them painted and carved out of tin a really beautiful outdoor crib. The girl teachers, using old crinolines and bits of cloth from here and there, made charming little dancing costumes. The stage curtains were drapes donated by one of Hong Kong's posh hotels—old drapes to them, but resplendently new and gorgeous to us....

The playlets and dances culminated in the ever new and ever dear Christmas tableau. And not even the first shepherds were more enthralled than our little ones were. But their reverent attendance at the Nativity did not cool their fun in the classroom parties where cookies, a pound of candy for each class of forty five children, and imprudently "all the milk they could drink." I forgot for the nonce that the children had never in all their lives had "all they could" of anything, and I watched with awe as the sixth grade boys guzzled bottle after bottle of that perfectly innocuous non-fat powdered milk. Coming out of my trance when I heard two boys saying, "This is my twelfth bottle" I quietly removed temptation from them lest there be an explosion of some sort!

The parents had bags of goodies to take home and a chance to draw for a prize. There were only eighty prizes for the throng, but it was such fun to hope you had the lucky number that the hundreds that did not get one of the eighty prizes had a good time too. It is all very simple, but these people work seven days a week and have no recreation so our silly little games are a delight to them, and we enjoy their really great enjoyment.

By the end of 1963, the Sisters had settled down and were involved in a number of endeavors in Kwun Tong (see table 7.1).

Movement and activities characterized the Kwun Tong resettlement estates. Every day, the community shared a busy and vigorous life. Someone described a morning at the food stall as:[33]

The five, seven-storey grey blocks, with their deck-like verandahs, on every floor, and their deep gutters of mildewed filth surrounding them, form a shapeless background for

Table 7.1   Types of work in the house in Kwun Tong (1963)

Education

1. Elementary school	2 schools	
	2,307 students	
2. Domestic science classes	36 girls	

Catechetical

3. Catechumentate classes	43 baptisms
	309 children
	874 adults
4. Classes for already baptized	729 children
	223 adults
5. Training Catechists	4 trainees

Medical

6. Clinic	6,103 outpatients
	64,518 visits
7. Pubic health service: TB Clinic	411 persons reached

Social Services

8. Counseling women	1,836 visits
9. Visits to homes	3,836 visits
10. Day nursery and play center	294 children
11. Case work	86 individuals
	268 families
12. Self-help projects	12 families
13. Material relief	376 families
14. Choir	92 members
15. Junior sodality	62 members
Senior sodality	3 groups, 246 members
16. Young Christian Students	2 groups, 19 members
17. Girls club	59 members
18. Boys club	86 members
19. Teenagers club	36 members
20. Retreats held	5 times, 286 attended

Services to Civic Community

| 21. Technical guidance | 85 |

| *Number of Sisters in the House* | 5 |

Source: Statistics on types of work done by Sisters in the Holy Spirit Convent, Kwun Tong, Hong Kong, 1963, 1 page, Folder 5, Box 2, South China Region: Hong Kong/Macau Region, 1921– , Maryknoll Mission Archives.

the "plaza" which has become a bustling outdoor restaurant. The bustle and movement are soundless, except for the shuffling of thousands of feet in soft Chinese slippers, the burbling of boiling things, the sizzle of deep fat frying, the grunts that do for speech.

There are smells too—of hot peanut oil, of tangy sauces, of stagnant gutters, of people—babies in stale wet cloths, of sweaty little boys, of men going off to work in yesterday's work clothes, and of foods galore.

Through the grey half-light of that early hour, one glimpses the stalls and eating places through the masses of people, mostly men and women on their way to work; ditch diggers, street cleaners, dirt carriers, vendors of cigarettes and newspapers, and hawkers who peddle their wares in more affluent areas. They jostle each other as they all try to get near the food of their choice. They eat and drink hungrily, standing, hurriedly, smacking their lips with appreciation. They wipe their months on their sleeves and hurry off, making room for the swarms of children squirming in and out of the throng, looking for some favorite delicacy. . . . They look on longingly at the new shiny tin stall with two holes in it, one for frying the succulent, long, golden, non-sweet crullers, so popular with them all, the other for steaming the fat, white dumplings, which burst open when done to reveal the riches of garlic, pork and vegetables within. . . .

The crowd is not noisy. Chinese take their eating seriously. In spite of the fact that they can make an ordinary discussion among three people sound like a riot they eat in solemn silence.

Kwun Tong was then composed of several sections; at the center were large apartment buildings used as private homes, hostels, and home industries. The Sisters' convent was in one of the apartment buildings; a room was used as a chapel, another as a dining room, and the other as a recreation room. By the middle of the 1960s, the Sisters had moved from their original accommodation in the workers' dormitory to a new place on Tung Yan Street. Sister Doretta had already left for parish work at St. Teresa's Church; and Sisters Agnes Chow (Marian Agnes), Margaret Marie Jung, Pauline Gibbons (Paul Marie), and Margaret Kirkendall (Miriam John) were newly assigned to the area. Subsequently, there were further personnel changes with the arrival of Dorothy Rubner (Barbara Marie) and Christina Marie Jung.[34] In the focal point of the community, the nuns could notice swift development. On the other side of the Sisters' building were nicer apartments, rented for higher prices. There were also twenty-four H-shaped resettlement estates, three squatter villages, and a middle-income resettlement area of seven blocks. In addition, two new resettlement areas were opening up. At last, there were countless home factories, many of which were in the apartment buildings and were legalized under government permits.[35]

Holy Spirit School and Our Lady of China School

Besides caring for spiritual and immediate needs of the people, the Sisters recognized the necessity of education for the children, as a long-term means to help the less fortunate improve their future livelihood. The Sisters, since their earlier years in Hong Kong, had been devoted to education. In other resettlement areas—King's Park and Chai Wan—they already established vernacular primary schools, which accepted students from immigrant families. In 1961, Holy Spirit School and Our Lady of China School opened in Kwun Tong. Unlike Lok Tak and Meng Tak, these two schools did not have their own buildings. Instead, they were situated on the ground floors of seven-story blocks, and the sites were on the government leases to the Catholic Diocese.[36] Sister Anne Clements was principal and supervisor of Holy Spirit School, and Sister Ruth Evans was her counterpart in Our Lady of China School.

When Holy Spirit School opened in September 1961, there were 1,128 students in 24 classes, with 29 teachers and 5 custodians. It was located on the ground floor of Block U of the Kwun Tong resettlement estates. Although the building was classified as residential, the custodial staff made tremendous efforts in converting the ground floor to a school. They painted all the classrooms, covered dangerous gutters, planted flowers, decorated the place, and erected statues. With staff, children, and families gathering in a new environment, cooperation, dedication, and trust of everyone were significant.[37] There were two sessions, morning school and afternoon school. Coeducational, the school collected an annual fee of HK$50 from each student in ten installments.[38]

In September 1963, Holy Spirit expanded to accept more than 1,400 students in 32 classes. One year later, the enrolment increased to about 1,610 children in

36 classes. The numbers of staff increased to 43 teachers and 7 custodians.[39] A vernacular primary school, Sister Anne described its aims as "Spiritual, Scholastic, Cultural, Practical." Religious education was part of the curriculum. Religious observances were provided with daily prayers and bimonthly Masses. Both Chinese and English languages were taught. For the Chinese classes, the agenda was to instill in the little minds appreciation of their own culture. Teachers had to progress rather slowly in the teaching of English. They used fewer textbooks, as students needed more time and effort in learning the language. There was also a special sewing room for girls, and bulletin boards were used to disseminate information and to exhibit students' homework. Besides the regular curriculum, the school had to teach most basic personal hygiene and cleanliness. Students wore uniforms, to be neat and properly dressed, so as to feel at ease in school. Although these were rather simple matters, they were not easy for children in the poor neighborhood.

In school, every class had its monitor, who was responsible for helping teachers and maintaining orderliness and discipline. He or she developed a sense of responsibility and leadership, and qualities of conscientiousness and dependability. Parents had the opportunity to attend classes and to see for themselves how subjects were taught. During the school year, teachers met several times with parents to discuss needs of the children.[40] Apart from classes, the school arranged entertainment events, in which students performed and their families attended. The entertainment could be music, dance, and plays. Usually the occasions took place on "a home-made stage in the school grounds," like the iron stage (made of the parts of a demolished ship) Sister Anne described in her Christmas essay in 1963.[41] Every year, the entire school went off for a picnic.

Children in Kwun Tong came from working-class families, and had nobody to refer to when their parents were out during the day. Schooling gave them at least some discipline, moral direction, and a sense of acknowledgment. In a school in the resettlement area, character building was crucial. The intention was to provide encouragement to students, hopefully to arouse their "own interest in self-improvement" in future.[42] Teachers made use of awards and punishment to maintain attendance in classes. A class was rewarded with a one-day excursion if it achieved complete attendance for thirty days. By 1964 the Sisters were able to achieve "almost perfect attendance" in the majority of classes.[43] Nevertheless, some students had their problems. Sister Anne was particularly concerned about five boys, who ran away from school. Like others, they lived in seven-story blocks. Their parents worked for long hours a day, and had no time for them. Some children did not see parents the whole day. Parents were still at work in the evening. In an area troubled by gambling, opium smuggling, and crime, young people could be subjected to bad influences. As Sister recalled, a family chained their son to the steel door to prevent him from wandering in the neighborhood. He finally made use of the opportunity of going to the bathroom and ran away. Some parents locked their children at home when they were out for work. With five to nine people living in one room, there was hardly any space or quiet time for the children to study and do their homework.[44]

While Holy Spirit School was bidding farewell to its first batch of graduating students, a typhoon caused huge destruction. On August 8, 1964 Typhoon Ida hit, leading to a landslide with tons of mud pouring into classrooms:[45]

> A tremendous landslide originating at a P.W.D. [Public Works Department] work project site, well to the rear of the school, took place last night [August 8] slightly after midnight. Tens of thousands of tons of mud and dirt inundated the entire School, which comprises the entire ground floors of double Block U; as well as the outside playground and walks. Tons of dirt and water ripped into classrooms, through doors and windows. Not a classroom was spared. This morning, nine hours after the land-slide, thousands of gallons of water and silt were still pouring into classrooms, before, eventually, finding their way out again. Mud, at some classrooms was piled as high as windows. Access to the school was almost impossible.

Around 1:20 a.m. on August 9, the school was buried. At 7 a.m., the night watch-man went over to the convent, and the Sisters hurried to the site and could not believe their own eyes. Literally—they described—"the mountain had descended in a wall of mud rolling right through the school grounds and piling up to the second floor of our seven story building."[46] The unbelievable happened:[47]

> The ocean of mud flowed from a great height and with great force. It struck the seven floor building as high as the second floor and stayed there, but the opening offered by the school yard made a river bed and through the school yard and on both sides of the building the moving mountain rolled, taking with it walls and doors and windows and furniture.
>
> Rain poured in from both sides washing away blackboards and bulletin boards.
>
> To the left of the building at about a thirty foot drop in the large Government play-ground, dirt piled up there to a height of about fifty feet.

In the mud, the Sacred Heart statue was standing high up with arms stretching out. Definitely a sight! Inside the classrooms, mud and water was 6 to 9 feet high, and furniture was either buried or floating. Outside the doors and windows, hundreds and thousands of tons of mud blocked entry into the school. Therefore, Sister Anne estimated at least two weeks of work to remove the mud, and a-hundred-percent loss in furniture and equipment. She was writing letters for help. Immediate actions were necessary, and these included the purchase of furniture and equipment, repair of walls, replacement of facilities, and ordering of textbooks.[48]

"We literally inherited the earth"—that was the feeling of those in Kwun Tong.[49] They expected to spend months "fighting with a mountain." Removal of mud and replacement of furniture and equipment were time consuming. Since the school year started in September, Sister Anne had to find other ways to run classes. She did not want to suspend for a year, as it meant an end to school life for some children, who would have no alternatives but to work in factories to earn money for the family. Sister was determined to start the school somewhere else, even if teachers had to use loudspeakers for class. When Holy Spirit started its new term in September, teachers and students gathered on rooftops (of Blocks U and Q) and in five borrowed class-rooms of Our Lady of China School. There was rearrangement of lessons so that school could begin in its temporary places. In three shifts, the staff managed to continue eight classes for 1,620 students in limited space on rooftops. At Block U, two teachers taught two classes simultaneously and spoke face-to-face, but students learned to behave. Over Block Q, students used church pews as desks and chairs in two rooms. In another room, they used ping-pong tables instead.[50] By March 1965, Holy Spirit was free from the problems of the landslide, though a minor mudslide occurred two months later. The school continued to expand, and later occupied the rooftops of both wings of Block U as well.[51]

Sister Ruth Evans, the principal of Our Lady of China School, was fortunate that Block S was not struck by a mudslide. Our Lady of China was situated in Block S, and was able to escape the disaster. By 1963, Our Lady of China had thirty-one classes and thirty-seven teachers. It prepared students for the very competitive secondary school entrance examinations. A few succeeded in the exam, while some suffered from the greatest problem of being overage, and the authority was stringent on age requirement. In the fifth and sixth grades, more practical classes were provided. Boys learned carpentry and girls had needlework. There was also a percussion band in school. On Saturday mornings, band, carpentry, needlework, and physical training classes were all going on at the same time. Therefore, there was "a lot of moving around, to the high glee of the children."[52] At Christmas, the school had its program in the outside court of the seven-story H-shaped block. On the rooftop, the school had its chapel where 30 children received their first Holy Communion.

Chai Wan Moves into the 1960s

As Chai Wan moved into the 1960s, the community was equally affected by industrialization efforts in Hong Kong. About 38,000 people lived there—25,000 people lived in resettlement estates and 13,000 in huts.[53] The government planned to open a major road along the coast to Shaukiwan, to ease the pressure of traffic on then the only road to Chai Wan. A city growing up within a city, Chai Wan continuously changed its appearance.[54] The seven-story mountains gave a new look to the area. They were the government's solution to the growing population and the need to provide better housing against fire hazards. Each of the blocks could accommodate about 2,500 people, with 40 rooms on each floor. With "the proximity to one's neighbor, the noise and general confusion of living in this atmosphere, the lack of family privacy," there were many problems in the neighborhood. Nevertheless, it was better than staying in hillside shacks and suffering from rainstorms and all sorts of difficulties. In the resettlement area, new bus lines came into being. Shops appeared on ground floors of the blocks, and gave convenient access to goods of necessity. On the rooftops, primary school kids went to school. In such crowded living conditions, no space could be lost.

The greatest change lay among people themselves, who came "through a period of great poverty, stress and mental adjustment to a precarious and fitful existence."[55] Although problems of employment remained, there were feelings of hope and vigor. People realized that so long as they struggled hard, they could improve their life. They were able to afford "little things in the home—a radio, a sewing machine."[56] They worked long hours a day to earn as much as they could. While men had more than one job, women either worked outside or took with them materials to do at home. Usually, both parents were out for work; but if the mother was at home, she was definitely working with "plastic flowers, gloves, beads, embroideries." For small sums of money, she was busy sewing beads on sweaters. Children helped, sorting and stringing the beads. Even three-year-old kids joined the labor. The family strove to be occupied—"Everybody is intent on getting as much work as possible done, so that they can get more money."[57] As Mary Diggins said, women were "the backbone of Chinese society," as they struggled so hard to support and unite their families. Most times, men not women deserted the families in harsh conditions.[58]

In 1961, Rosalia Kettl replaced Mary Diggins as superior of the Sisters in Chai Wan. Sister Marie Jean Theophane Steinbauer remained principal of Meng Tak School. Sisters Rose Bernadette Gallagher and Teresa Leung (Marie Lucas) were involved in catechetical work. Sister Teresa remembered climbing hundreds of steps on the hill to visit the squatter huts.[59] By then, Chai Wan had a Catholic population of about 3,500. This gave the impression of being a busy city parish, which occupied the central hillside. One Mass followed closely on another. Crowds of people went to Confession and received Holy Communion.[60] That year, a catechetical center opened on the ground floor of a seven-story block. The place held doctrine instructions, and on Saturdays, the Sisters borrowed some rooms from the Maryknoll Fathers' new primary school, which was on the same floor, for afternoon sessions. "A catechetical set-up in such a thickly populated area" was a great advantage; doctrine classes increased rapidly in enrolment and were held from 8:30 to 11:00 in the morning and 2:00 to 4:00 in the afternoon.[61] The numbers of Baptisms, First Holy Communion, and Confirmation were notable (see table 7.2). At the same time, the Sisters organized sodalities for women, working girls, schoolchildren, and future catechists. They started the election of officers, who conducted the sodality meetings.[62] The elected, enjoying a sense of respect and dignity in their Church community, seemed to like the responsibilities.

There was another attempt. It was the training, through theory and practice, of women catechists. Catholic Action initiated the program, considering the possibility of allowing these women to instruct many future catechumen groups. At first, there were only twelve participants, who had some education and some free time. They were taking courses on how to teach catechumens, to employ more lively methods, and to use pictures for the illiterate. For practice, the trainees taught one or a few catechumens at home once a week, using theories and methods learned in class. Several of them already ran some preschool "home schools" for kids, and thus, were more ready to exert influence in their neighborhood.

Before Sister Mary Diggins left Chai Wan, she started the Block System, which meant that trained women leaders led home visits to Catholic families in the seven-story

Table 7.2 Catechetical activities in Chai Wan (1961–1963)[a]

Year	Number of Catholics	Baptisms	First Holy Communion	Confirmation
1961	3,500	350	100+	100+
1962	around 4,000	200+	200+	247
1963	over 5,000	400+	not recorded	250

Note: [a] "Chai Wan," 1961, 1 page; "Chai Wan—1962," 1962, 1 page; "Chai Wan—1963," 1963, 1 page, Folder 6, Box 2, Chronicles, Maryknoll Mission Archives.

blocks. The efforts continued, now under the direction of Sister Rose Bernadette, and involved more than eighty volunteers. By 1963 the project grew in scale: 9 leaders for 88 Swatonese families and 92 leaders for 990 Cantonese families, altogether 1,078 families.[63] The Block System operated on the principle that every Catholic could become a leader in the community and attend to the needs of other fellow Catholics. It proved to be quite workable and practical in Chai Wan. A group of women became block leaders, and each had a designated area, usually covering ten to fifteen Catholic families. Once a month, they visited their areas and were made aware of any unattended problems. As people were living so close to each other, visits were convenient opportunities to retain ties between the Church and converts, and to remind people of parish activities. Some issues the Sisters were concerned about were: "new babies unbaptized, children unprepared for First Holy Communion, laxity in their duties as Catholics, bad marriages etc."[64] Every time, the families were given a timetable of religious events, Masses, and feasts of the month. A block leader performed her duties for six months, learning to be conscious of her responsibilities.

There were consistent efforts to reach out to families in the neighborhood. In a Chinese setting, the best way to approach parents was to offer some kind of help for the children.[65] Since most women worked, there was not much time for the family. Therefore, when the Sisters organized preparatory groups for the kids, the efforts were very well received. For working girls, sewing classes were an attraction. So were Sister Rose Bernadette's "charm courses," which taught them proper social and dining manners, to be of use in the more complicated Hong Kong society. Other items on the agenda were folk dancing lessons, picnics, and outings. The Sisters started the Christian Family Movement by arranging retreats with couples and having informal meetings with them afterward to discuss their practical problems. "They love our meetings," Sisters explained, as those were their "only social life."[66] After one of the meetings—"the women stayed on and talked for $1^1/_2$ hrs. None of these have been to Grammar School, but they have all absorbed a lot by being in H.K. They have become very alert. One woman hawker has learned a lot. She has confidence and talks very well."[67] There were also tea parties for non-Christians. There were fun activities, as Sister Teresa organized a "wrapping up packages" group to shoulder some work of the catechists. As there were always gifts and prizes to be prepared for Baptism, the birth of new babies, Sunday school kids, and First Communion classes, the energy of some young girls was channeled toward this task. In the process, they enjoyed the "glamor in pretty bows and colorful wrapping paper."[68]

Sister Mary Ellen Mertens (M. Benjamin), or Sister Molly as she preferred to be called, worked with factory girls. In 1966 she sent out a letter from Chai Wan, sharing some of her thoughts. She told the story of a teenage girl:[69]

> I have gotten to know our people quite well now and feel that we share with them their joys, cares, burdens of everyday life. I'm thinking especially of my young friend, Lam Wai Ying. On my way to the bus stop one day, this wide-eyed 12-year-old girl appeared at my elbow. "Gou Leung (Chinese way of addressing unmarried women), would you help me find a school?"
>
> As it turned out, Wai Ying had *never* opened a book in her life; she could not even write her own name. As you can expect, it was not easy to find a school that would accept a 12-year-old kindergarten student. Of course we're only in the beginning stages

presently, but Wai Ying has already acquired a bit of self-confidence and ease in social relationships.

In a working-class neighborhood like Chai Wan, children did not receive adequate attention. As the Sisters observed—"It is not uncommon to find children either locked out of the house for the day, or locked in as is often the case with very small children."[70] A seven-year-old child was already responsible for taking care of younger siblings, cooking, and preparing food for the family. With parents working long hours a day, children learned to be very independent though they suffered from "lack of home training." The Sisters organized a children's sodality known as the "Pure Heart of Mary Sodality" where basic religious and moral values were taught. The children also enjoyed games and interesting projects. Very well received, these meetings were divided into several age groups. Even though the kids did not have much, they learned to give of the little they had. One of the stories was as follows:[71]

> Along these lines was the project of donating a dearly loved toy or possession to the Christ Child during Advent to be given to the sick children treated at Our Lady of Maryknoll Hospital. The toy did not need to be new—it just needed to be a loved possession. At the entrance of the catechetical room was a large box tied with a big red bow, and on the box a picture of little children holding up their toys to Our Lord. The caption under the picture read: "That which is given to another is given to Our Lord, Himself." The day of sacrifice had come for the children of the "Pure Heart of Mary" Sodality—and how they knew it. Furtive glances cast at the box and a clutch at bulging pockets portrayed the struggle. We watched while one little youngster came in, cast an appealing look at the box, and then ran out. This was repeated twice, when on the re-bound, all went from the pocket to the box in one burning flame of marbles, a toy, a feather—and other prized possessions. It was all or nothing. Some little youngsters not having a toy bought some little trinket with the ten cents allowed for a morning snack… and added to the joy of giving—a new experience—that of hunger for love's sake.
>
> But, it was a proud and happy day when representatives from each group accompanied Sister Rose Bernadette to personally present their gifts to our hospital Sisters, to be given to sick children.

In 1967 Chai Wan had approximately 55,000 estate-dwellers. The government was reclaiming the waterfront, and building multistory blocks on the land. In newer blocks, apartment rooms were bigger, with individual verandahs for families.[72] People were moving into Chai Wan. With the flood of newcomers, there were accompanying problems as well. There were concerns of "low moral standards, drinkers, smokers and the like."[73] Among the low-income group, any unexpected illness of one parent could produce terrible consequences to the family for a long time. Borrowing money with high interest rates was common. At the same time, children needed more recreational facilities, which were not readily available despite the moving of families to this developing area. The Sisters recorded some stories of the neighborhood:[74]

(1)

Once a month, Sister Marie Lucas [Teresa Leung] holds a meeting with the Children of Mary factory girls. This group is more difficult to work with as the girls have little or no education, and do not readily enter into discussion or planned projects. In an attempt to further develop them along cultural lines, guest speakers were invited to speak to them. Miss Rose Yeung, prominent in social welfare circles, shared with the girls her trip to the Holy Land; slides were shown and conditions there were compared with what the girls have knowledge of here. Miss Loh, our Catholic nurse at the Church clinic gave an informative exposition on teen-age problems with proper attitudes that should accompany them. If outwardly the work seems unrewarding, we are beginning to see the first fruits of these months of dedicated effort on Sister's part. Four of the group have been married during the year; all have had Church weddings. When there is a wedding due or just taken place, a party held for the new bride with presents bought by the members, and an atmosphere of good fun prevails. It is a powerful incentive to all the girls to follow this good example set by one of their members.

(2)

Wong Shuk Lin, a young woman most recently out of China came in to study the doctrine. The first few weeks went along nicely, then tragedy struck. Early one morning she came to class crying bitterly because in complete distress of mind and soul she had sold her two-day old baby boy for ready money on which to live. Upon presenting herself at Social Welfare seeking help, it was reported to them that she had sold her child for some HK$250.00. She was severely reprimanded and told that if she did not get the child back within two weeks, she would be in danger of imprisonment for this illegal action. Sister Mary Rosalia counselled her to speak to the family that bought the child, return the money and get the child as quickly as possible. Further, Sister knowing the family would not give the child up readily, wrote Social Welfare asking for a little longer period in which to negotiate this transaction.... Herein lay another anxiety as Wong Shuk Lin had spent $80.00 of it around the time of the child's birth and now was penniless. Our Maryknoll Sisters' Secondary School at Blue Pool Road came to the rescue with a donation of a few hundred dollars to be used for the poor; what better way to use a part of it than to redeem this son, radiantly happy now, and so grateful to God and to all those who helped her find this lost peace.

(3)

One of our Catholic women, Wan Nim Chan, had been childless for several years after her marriage. She and her husband decided to adopt [a] child...merely two days old...they called her Little Victory.... The first eight years were filled with much happiness, but just three months ago a serious turn of events was felt in the home. Little Victory's oldest sister, studying in the same school with her, began to fill her little mind with glowing tales of home; how rich her own family was, all the advantages there would be to coming home and living with them. How her parents missed her and the like. The child, confused in mind, by the repeated onslaught of words began thinking she wanted to return home. She became disobedient on occasions to her adopted parents, rebellious and sulky. The showdown came when Wan Nim Chan came in and told Sister Rose Bernadette of her intention to return the child.... After much talking, it was decided to have a showdown with the oldest sister who was the cause of all this trouble. The result was the sister acknowledged her fault and promising never again to torment the child. The session ended with Little Victory openly professing her love for her adopted parents and promising obedience to them. Thus by bringing a problem to the fore, a serious mistake was avoided.

Sisters' Profiles in the 1960s

Maryknoll was a church for the poor, with the saying "You make your path by walking it."[75] Everywhere Maryknoll Sisters looked upon the poor as heralds who pointed to the light of their lives.[76] When the pioneers founded the mission, China was the dream of overseas adventure. Indeed the "secret of the China myth" had revealed itself to the missioners—the people did not need the Sisters as much as the Sisters needed them.[77] As missioners, the nuns went outside their own environment to foreign cultures, to the deprived. From going beyond themselves to others, they gradually realized that they themselves benefited most. Dreams and myths turned out to be different, but more fascinating than they originally anticipated: "the real objective of their often perilous journeys was not to change the world, or even a small portion of it, but to go beyond themselves and do something important in life."[78] Throughout the years, Maryknollers were independent, outgoing, and joyous women who shouldered their own responsibilities. Penny Lernoux observed, as others would: "The ability to laugh even in the most awful circumstances is a Maryknoll trait, and it helped the Sisters survive one of the most turbulent periods in their history, when they were uprooted from China—which had been Maryknoll's *raison d'être*...."[79]

In Hong Kong, the work of the Sisters was of different kinds (see figure 7.1). While they lived and worked with the poor, catering to local needs, they soon

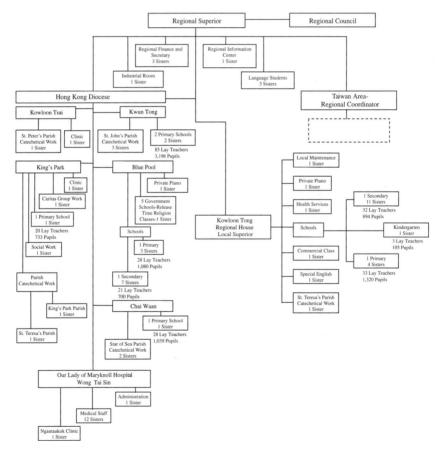

Figure 7.1 Plan of organization (1966–1967) of the South China Region.

Source: Modified from "1966–1967 South China Region Hong Kong-Taiwan Areas: Plan of Organization, Houses and Work," n.d. [1967?], Folder 7, Box 5, Regional Correspondence: South China, Maryknoll Mission Archives.

developed their vision of social services. They served the poor, working classes, and the disabled. In 1959 they began professional social work when Sister Mary Heath joined the Maryknoll Sisters' Social Welfare Center in King's Park. From 1963 to 1965, she was supervisor of Caritas Social Service training courses. She also took charge of Caritas Casework Service. Soon others became involved: Sister Susan Gubbins oversaw the Caritas Youth Center and Sister Jane Umberg concentrated on community development.[80] As chaplain and collaborator, Sister Molly Mertens joined the Young Christian Workers Movement. In the late 1960s, Sister Moira Riehl established the Blind Study Center in the basement of the Regional Center House (Maryknoll convent) on Flint Road. The Blind Study Center later grew to become the Association of the Blind.[81]

When Our Lady of Maryknoll Hospital opened in Wong Tai Sin, it aimed to serve low-income families. Not only did they offer medical services, but the objective of the Sisters was also to "pioneer in ways to broaden the scope of comprehensive health care in the hospital and community."[82] Therefore, Sister Dominic Marie Turner organized the Medical Social Work Department in 1962. In 1964 Sister Barbara Mersinger organized Our Lady of Maryknoll Medical and Welfare Association, which raised funds for the Hospital and the Sisters' welfare projects. In order to provide ongoing care for discharged patients, Sisters Mary Louise Higa (Regina Therese) and Marilyn Norris started the Community Nursing Program in 1970. The Maryknoll Sisters set up the School of Nursing for Enrolled Nurses in 1971. Besides the hospital, there were also other ways to promote health consciousness of the society. In 1969, Sister Therese Howard (Mary Howard) was the first Catholic to sit on the Medical Committee of the Hong Kong Council of Christian Service. Moreover, she took part in the Hong Kong Catholic Marriage Advisory Council together with programs of Birthright and Natural Family Planning.[83]

The Sisters continued catechetical work in parish and resettlement areas. In Kowloon Tong, they were involved in full-time catechetical work in St. Teresa's Church. They worked with lay catechists, providing instruction throughout the day, visiting homes, and offering religious classes to schools in the neighborhood. Occasionally, the Sisters provided doctrine instruction to students in King George School, Kowloon Junior Government School, and St. Teresa's Primary School. Preparing catechumens for Baptism, they had around 20–50 people baptized at every feast. Each year, the Sisters instructed over 1,000 converts in the parish. Others were under the care of lay catechists. The new converts were from all walks of life—"These range from the poorest living on the sidewalks to a prominent Chinese actress, whose baptism rated two columns with pictures in the local paper."[84] Factory workers attended evening lessons. It required determination on the part of catechumens, as they came around 7:30 p.m. and returned home late at 9 p.m. Baptism was "not the end of work," as there were post-Baptism lessons, sodalities, and marriage counseling.

At the same time, the Sisters paid daily visits to Kwong Wah Hospital, which was nearby on Waterloo Road. It was a Chinese hospital under government supervision of nonreligious background, but it welcomed nuns' visits. Each morning, two Sisters and one lay catechist visited the baby ward. They looked after Baptisms of dying babies. As described: "Here one sees poor little things, just holding on to life until the saving waters are poured on their foreheads. It is considered bad luck in China if anyone dies in the house, so most of the mites are brought in at death's door and a pitiful lot they are."[85] There were two or three Baptisms each day, and the numbers increased in hot weather to four or five. If the baby managed to live, the Sisters visited the family and spread the doctrine. Also assisting the Sisters was the Legion of Mary, whose members were students of Maryknoll schools. There were over 100 of these student-volunteers, who visited patients and followed up cases. Some of them even accompanied the Sister to weekly visits to prisons, and talked about religion with the inmates.

By 1966, the Maryknoll Sisters took up catechetical work in five centers—in Kowloon Tong and in four resettlement areas. Altogether, twelve Sisters were involved and were competent in Cantonese. The work in "direct catechetical field" included:[86]

(1) Arranging religious instruction for women catechumens and their children, preparing them for Baptism, and later consolidating their faith through post-Baptism classes.

(2) Offering doctrine instruction to Catholic children of non-Catholic schools, both before and after their First Holy Communion and Confirmation.

(3) Paying home visits to Catholics and non-Christians.

(4) Providing welfare to non-Christians, who learned about the Church through existing institutions such as schools.

(5) Interviewing those who approached the Church for material help, or as a result of family and social difficulties.

(6) Organizing and running sodalities, discussion groups, and advanced religious classes for women.

(7) Training lay catechists and volunteers, so that they could contribute to teaching catechumens, organizing visits, and parish work.

(8) Counseling women of the parish, to help them with their practical, emotional, and spiritual needs.

(9) Conducting a periodical census in the parish.

(10) Supervising lay teachers of religious classes in Catholic primary schools.

In the latter half of the 1960s, the Sisters paid much attention to social fields, that is, work in community centers, community services, and youth groups. The agenda was:

(11) Supervising community services, which included day nurseries, kindergartens, and evening adult classes.

(12) Managing youth and adult recreational centers.

(13) Offering interest classes for women, like sewing, cooking, "charm," and English.

(14) Arranging discussion groups for women and teenagers.

(15) Referring women, who sought help, to social agencies.

Catechetical work in Hong Kong was expanding and moving toward greater professionalism. As the Sisters envisaged, there was development in two areas, which were "catechetical-social work" and "catechetical-teacher training." The training of a catechetical-social worker meant the combination of "catechetical training, catechetics, methodology for adults, psychology, theology, Scripture, doctrine" and "leadership training, group dynamics, guidance, counseling, sociology, community service."[87] The training of a catechetical-teacher also involved studies of education, child psychology, methodologies, and administration. For catechists, the emphasis was to address different demands of people, and to recognize development of individuals as whole persons. On the diocesan level, the Church recognized the need to train parish catechists both before and during employment. It also trained volunteers, who were teachers of religion in schools and parishes, and leaders in the community. On the parish level, the Sisters supervised catechetical work, and lay catechists were able to shoulder more responsibilities. There was also leadership training for Church workers. In parish schools, the Church provided training for teachers and organized extracurricular activities for students. It also set up community centers in the localities.[88] There was the idea of apostolic training—"The emphasis in all catechetical work is to imbue each Catholic with his or her place in the Church as an apostle to those about them bringing to them the riches of the Faith which they have embraced."[89]

In the latter part of the 1960s, the Cultural Revolution taking place in China began to show its effects on Hong Kong. The Red Guards—teenagers who had supported Mao Zedong in launching the Cultural Revolution—were finally suppressed and some of them were sent to the villages to live with peasant families. Mostly boys, from the age of seventeen to nineteen, they swam from Guangdong Province to Hong Kong, and were termed the "freedom swimmers," who sought opportunities to go to Western countries. Sister M. Julia Hannigan provided these refugees with English classes, as they wanted to go abroad to study or work. They needed to file an application with the International Rescue Committee if they wanted to go to the United States, and in two exceptional cases, Sister tried to find sponsors for them. One of the sponsors was a priest in the United States. Many of them eventually ended up in the United States, some went to Canada as well.[90]

CHAPTER EIGHT
CONCLUSION

... by the time Vatican Council II came along.... I realized more and more that our own techniques were in great need of change and that we weren't here just to evangelize but we were here to be evangelized ourselves. My idea first had been, we were those who would bring Christ to the people who didn't know him. And, it was a great revelation when I realized that Christ was already with them.

We began to think more of how we could be serving the local church rather than being members of foreign groups. And yet, it took a long time before I really thought of myself as a foreigner because you were becoming so immersed in the Chinese culture, you kind of accepted the fact that you were being all changed to Chinese and being as much like them as you could. There were many occasions when a student would speak out against Americans. I would sit and listen thinking to myself, "Well, I'm American" and then when I would have a chance to speak, I'd say, "Well, you know I'm one of the people you're talking about." "Oh no, Sister, you're different." So, I think you don't look upon yourself as being so foreign, ...

"Rose, do you realize how Chinese you are?" And I said, "Yes, I think I do." I said, "You're probably going to say that I have a reserve of a non-American kind of person." ... However, I think our own Maryknoll girls have taken on so much of our way of behaving that, we have ended up changing them at the same time that we in part have been changed by our association with them.

Sister Rose Duchesne Debrecht
Hong Kong, July 19, 1981[1]

One day in August 2000 the author met with Maryknoll Sisters at their convent in Kowloon Tong, to start the first interview with the women for this book. The location was a two-story structure adjacent to the Primary Section of Maryknoll Convent School. The first building behind the Boundary Street gate, visitors would assume that it was part of the school had they not taken notice of the Convent sign. At the doorway visitors rang the bell and waited to be admitted to the Convent, commonly referred to as the Boundary Street House. This house has been the quarters of the Maryknoll Sisters since the mid-1970s. Its high ceilings produce a solemn atmosphere, but the structure itself and the primary school form a cluster of "russet tiled roofs topping a patchwork exterior in shades of *café au lait*," an imitation of the motherhouse in New York State, and what was more, the images of a children's book.[2] Dedicated and committed to their work, the Sisters often project a spirit of cheerfulness and confidence. They have been independent and outgoing, assuming a great deal of responsibilities. As Jean-Paul Wiest points out, one of the requirements for its candidates in the earliest days of Maryknoll was that they should be able to show a sense of humor and be cheerful in any kind of work they were engaging in.[3] Penny Lernoux says: it was "a Maryknoll trait" that the missioners were able to laugh even in very difficult circumstances.[4]

So, too had Hong Kong people survived turbulent years and continued to generate much energy. In the first half of the twentieth century, Hong Kong encountered trade problems, war threats, and uncertainty surrounding its precious colonial status. It soon survived Japanese occupation in the 1940s, political and social disturbances in the 1950s and 1960s, and built on its industrial economy in the 1970s. By the 1980s, it was already a prosperous city with up-to-date education, medical, and social facilities. Basically an immigrant community after World War II, it cultivated its own identity and tried to understand its roles in a rapidly changing world. It rose from humble beginnings and became cosmopolitan. In transition for its turnover to China in 1997, Hong Kong underwent tremendous political and confidence crises. Faced with problems of different sorts throughout decades, it continued to demonstrate impressive vitality and strength. A Chinese society, Hong Kong turned a new page of its history as it reintegrated with the motherland, the greater Chinese but somewhat dissimilar hinterland.

The story of Maryknoll Sisters in Hong Kong was closely intertwined with local development. Maryknoll grew and matured with the Chinese people, whose concerns were those of the nuns as well. With the trust of the government, the missioners embarked on their effort for relief and reform. The foreign mission transformed to become part of society; the Hong Kong people also benefited from cross-cultural exchanges. Besides providing basic support to the community, the Sisters continued to work for the disadvantaged and neglected, and to promote civil and social awareness. They were there to cater to local needs, and in the process, excelled as professionals in their own specialties. In conclusion, this chapter emphasizes evolutionary aspects of the nuns' work throughout the years, both in theory and in actual implementation. It also assesses their roles as professional women and their relations with the local society.

Evolution of the Maryknoll Congregation's Missionary Objectives

History revealed the evolutionary nature of the Maryknoll Sisters' work. As missioners, they went outside their own environment and served in a foreign culture.[5] Through passage of time, they expanded the scope of their activities. Their work, objectives, and principles underwent reconsideration and revision. Drafted in 1917 and promulgated in 1925, the first Maryknoll Constitutions stated that the Sisters be sent to "pagans in heathen lands" for two specific purposes—"personal sanctification" of themselves, through the three vows of poverty, chastity, and obedience, as the primary objective; and the conversion of others to Christianity, through the cooperation with Maryknoll Fathers and other foreign missionary bodies, as the secondary objective.[6] As the nuns were assigned to their mission fields, they were expected to embrace "a spirit of perfect detachment" and to be ready to go to any designated countries.[7] Again the 1931 Constitution called for converting "pagans in heathen lands" and "Asiatics in Christian countries," and responding to the reality of mission fields. It allowed missioners to engage in necessary income-earning tasks, so as to enable them to continue their work.[8] The mission could be in "schools, dormitories, private instruction, catechetical instruction, [the] formation of native sisters, hospitals, dispensaries, creches, [the] care of orphans, the blind and maimed, and the aged, village and neighborhood visitation, industrial work and so forth."[9] They were encouraged to use the native languages when communicating with local people and in public prayers. Becoming official probably after that year's General Chapter, the 1937 Constitution resembled closely the 1931 edition, except it changed the wording to "the conversion of pagans in non-Christian countries and of Asiatics or other racial groups in Christian countries."[10] "Heathen lands" was replaced by "non-Christian countries," and besides Asiatics, "other racial groups" were also of concern.

After World War II the first edition of the Constitutions appeared in 1952, and continued to consider "the sanctification of its members" the "general end," though no longer putting it as "the primary end." The "special end" was "the spread of the Faith and the salvation of souls...in non-Christian countries; and in Christian countries, especially among Asiatics and other racial groups."[11] In 1954 the Congregation became a Pontifical Institute and its name was changed to "Maryknoll Sisters of St. Dominic." That year, the Constitutions recorded the change and included the decree of pontifical approval. The general end remained the sanctification of the nuns, but added the phase "to promote the glory of God."[12] There was no change to the special end.

In the midst of Vatican Council II (1962–1965), the 1964 General Chapter mandated the revisions to be included in the 1965 Constitutions. According to the 1965 Constitutions, the general end was the same as listed in the 1954 edition. As for the special end, the emphasis was "primarily in non-Christian and de-Christianized countries," "to give witness to Christ, to proclaim the Gospel message, to strengthen and re-vitalize the Church."[13] Unlike previous editions, the 1965 Constitutions did not employ "conversion" and "the salvation of souls" in the objectives. Vatican Council II was to change many aspects of the life of the nuns. It was a landmark in Roman Catholic history, emphasizing service for the poor. Since the Council, the Sisters could engage in non-institutional tasks, more closely working with ordinary people as they already had been doing. They also changed to wearing simple suits and veils, then finally to ordinary clothes, and could choose to return to their own baptismal names instead of using the given religious names.[14] More importantly, from considering conversion the primary goal, the Roman Catholic Church came to see that God was already present in foreign places before Christian missioners arrived. Therefore, conversion was not necessarily the objective of foreign missioners. In Hong Kong, as elsewhere, the Maryknoll Sisters placed much emphasis on improving the livelihood of the people, and supporting individuals to become better persons.

As a response to Vatican Council II, Maryknoll convened the Special Chapter of Affairs, which lasted for four months from October 1968 to February 1969. "Background Papers and Enactments" of the Chapter, entitled *Missions Challenge Maryknoll Sisters*, outlined their reflections upon the challenges to theology, their missionary role and work, and the place of the Church in contemporary society. The Chapter acknowledged "growing awareness of the rapidity" of changes taking place, and responsibility to look for the means for adaptation and renewal for mission.[15]

The nuns emphasized the need to respond to the revelation in theological thought, regarding the meaning of human beings and their relations with God, and to the evaluation of mission, in light of the needs of the communities being served. The "Kingdom of God" then centered on two words—"justice" and "peace," which formed the catchphrases and names of many committees of the Catholic Church since the 1960s. On this basis, the Maryknoll Sisters were to speak out against matters that infringed upon such principles.[16]

Working in foreign lands, they were to be "transcultural missioners," while unavoidably bringing "their own background and value system as part of themselves," could "only fulfill their role as enablers" if they could be "deeply attuned to the culture of the people with whom they live" and be "truly sensitive to the point of view of these people, their values, and their aspirations."[17] They were "to act as catalysts and enablers of local responsibility and community self-development," and to understand that their priority was to train locals to take their place and not to duplicate positions of the local people.[18] This is to say, they worked in areas lacking in their expertise, and in the process, helped train local professionals who could then take up their tasks. As the document indicated, conversion was not necessarily the objective of the missioners—"Mission is not only the help which the Church in one continent gives the Church in another. Neither is it the effort of Christians to increase their Church membership."[19] The Congregation was "a collaborator" with all groups, secular or religious, to work for the welfare and unity of the people.[20] Its end was to reveal God's love, to promote missionary dynamism, and to encourage missionary awareness for other people.

The 1970 Constitution, entitled *Searching and Sharing: Mission Perspectives*, reiterated the decision of Vatican Council II, to build a church for the poor—"It must be clear to all men that we take our stance unconditionally with the poor in the true gospel sense: the spiritually dehumanized, socially oppressed, culturally marginalized, or economically deprived."[21] It urged "identifying with the poor" and developing "human community through mutual sharing and deeper understanding of the ultimate meaning of life."[22] The nuns should move beyond their barriers, culture, territories, economics, society, and religion, to answer their missionary vocation.[23] They continued to be social activists as they were "to participate in the development of peoples, focusing on the realities of human dignity, the rights of man, freedom, responsibility, duty, work, and social harmony."[24] Evangelization acquired a new meaning, which spoke of liberating people from the restrictions of their surroundings so that they were able to realize themselves.[25]

The spirit of "global mission" was explicit in the 1975 Constitution, *Maryknoll Sisters in Mission*, as the missioners were to serve all people in a world in need.[26] The Sisters emphasized importance of global awareness and development of global vision. When they outlined their basic ministries, they deliberately addressed "the root causes of injustice," "the poor, oppressed and the alienated," and "people to whom the gospel has not yet been proclaimed." They sought to "foster deeper interfaith and intercultural dialogue," and to "foster living Christian communities with a special focus on the emergence of leaders from these communities."[27] In 1978, the revised edition defined "mission as a total way of life," concentrating on "solidarity with the poor," "inculturation," "mutual evangelization," "Christian unity," and "witness of

Christian community." Ministry in the United States was a part of Maryknoll's global mission. There were special emphases on the poor, women, and with the relaxation of the political atmosphere in China, a presence in China as well. The Constitutions of 1985 described mission for the poor, abandoned, oppressed, those suffering from injustices, women and refugees. The Sisters called for "dialogue of life & inter-religious dialogue," "struggle for justice," "interrelatedness of world issues," and "women shaping the world."[28]

In the 1990 Constitutions, the Sisters talked about "mission as cross cultural" and "multiculturalism." They put forth the idea of "wholistic evangelization," which meant "liberation, inculturation, & dialogue, human development and reverence for creation."[29] In other words, they embraced much broader definitions of mission and evangelization. Their mission meant "showing Christ's compassion to others," not necessarily converting people to Christianity.[30] Evangelization meant development of the whole person, and was a mutual experience as the Sisters believed they also saw Christ in the people they served. Throughout the years, they progressed to different interpretations of relations between the foreign mission and the local community.

Contemporary Years

Until 1971 Maryknoll Sisters' mission in Hong Kong belonged to the South China Region, which also included Taiwan. From 1946 to 1958, Sister Mary Imelda Sheridan was regional superior. From 1958 to 1964 Sister Barbara Mersinger took up the post; and from 1964 to 1971 Sister M. Rosalia Kettl was the superior. In 1970 the South China Region divided into the Hong Kong and Taiwan areas, each of which was responsible for its own administrative matters. In 1971 Hong Kong and Taiwan became separate Regions; and the territory alone became the Hong Kong Region (see figure 8.1). In 1982 Hong Kong and Macau belonged to the Hong Kong/Macau Region.[31]

Maryknollers always referred to the "Maryknoll Spirit" as the leading philosophy. The nuns should embrace an "apostolic spirit," as Mother Mary Joseph once said, and she described the Maryknoll Spirit—"As one lamp lights another nor grows less, so nobleness enkindleth nobleness."[32] It was supposed to be "a foreign mission spirit," to "seek those lost sheep of the fold." The following became a famous quotation of hers:

> We have tried from the beginning to cultivate a spirit which is extremely difficult and which for a long time might have been misunderstood even by those who were nearest to us, and that is, the retention of our own natural dispositions, the retention of our own individuality, having in mind, of course, that all of these things should be corrected where radically wrong, and all of it supernaturalized. . . . Each one of us, in her own work, with her own particular little sweetness or attractiveness, is to be used by God as a particular tool to do particular work and to save particular souls.[33]

In the 1960s, Vatican Council II broadened missionary perspectives. Maryknollers previously spoke of seeking pagans and converting them to Christianity. Nowadays, they consider themselves guests of a foreign place or government.[34] As Sister Mary Lou Martin said: "In general, missioners accompany the local people rather than

Figure 8.1 Maryknoll Sisters in a retreat in the convent on Waterloo Road in 1974; also present were the Jesuits.

Source: Sisters Photo Collection, Maryknoll Mission Archives.

initiate political/social changes."[35] As described in the papers of the 1968–1969 Chapter, they were "enablers" in mission to help local people fully realize themselves. The Maryknoll Spirit of "going beyond oneself," "reaching out to the unfortunate," and "showing Christ to others" filled the hearts of these women. Their continued presence in Hong Kong reflected the strong sentimental ties Maryknoll had with the place, which became a permanent part of their global mission. In 1971, there were seventy-one Sisters and eight houses in Hong Kong. Four years later, the Convent, which was built in the early 1950s and overlooked the swimming pool, was vacated. The "new convent" was created by renovating the former Industrial Department. In 1981 there were forty-eight Sisters and nine houses in Hong Kong; in 1991 there were twenty-eight Sisters and six houses; and in 2001 there were twelve Sisters and four houses.[36]

Vatican Council II allowed missioners to venture into noninstitutional tasks, and to serve the needs of people more closely—the work the Sisters had already been doing in Hong Kong. Encouraged by what they had done, they continued their mission for the disadvantaged. The nuns lived and worked in the neighborhood of the poor and less fortunate. Two Sisters worked for a short time in factories, so as to understand better the state of being of workers; and subsequently established the Young Workers Center in a resettlement estate in Sau Mau Ping in the early 1970s. In the meantime, Ann Marie Emdin and Teresa Dagdag moved into a temporary housing area in Shun Lee village, the former working with the Helping Hand for the elderly and the latter with the Young Workers Federation. Some of the nuns also lived in the working-class settlements in Fuk Wah village, Ngau Tau Kok, and Kwun Tong during different intervals in the 1970s and 1980s.[37]

The Sisters paid special attention to minority groups, who required support and care. In the early 1980s Arlene Trant taught at the School for the Deaf, and Alice Wengrzynek (Alice Rose) joined the International Assistance in Development program for the mentally retarded. The latter had opportunities to travel to China and other Asian countries, to understand more about the situation of the mentally retarded and how to be of service to them. She was a volunteer for the Home of Loving Faithfulness, a place for severely mentally retarded children.[38] In addition, Paulette Yeung (Paulette Marie) took part in the planning of Harmony House, a place for abused women. Working with the Association for the Promotion of Public Justice, Kathleen Hughes (Miriam Pacis) fought for the interests of the low-income population. Ruth Evans, Miedal Stone, and others worked in an elderly home in Yuen Long; and together, they occupied a one-room quarter there in the 1980s. Like residents of the home, the nuns themselves shared a room that was slightly more than one hundred square feet, and yet they described the work there as constituting a very happy time of their life. Sister Miedal had considerable experience taking care of the elderly, as she used to deliver meals to them before in different localities, calling it "meat on feet."[39]

For many years, Moira Riehl worked for the blind in the Blind Study Center, which she set up on the Maryknoll Convent School (M.C.S.) compound on the side of Flint Road. Aware of the difficulties of the Vietnamese refugees in Hong Kong, Martha Bourne (Martha Mary) visited the refugee detention centers where she provided necessary service in the late 1980s and early 1990s. She taught English, arranged classes and outside visits, and catered to the needs of those living in the closed camps.[40] In the 1990s, Helene O'Sullivan (M. Helene) reached out to prostitutes in working-class districts of Yaumati and Shamshuipo. This service was a pioneering work at the time. Together with a Columban nun, they tried to win the trust of the women as they went out on the streets. After a long search, they opened a center in Yaumati that offered counseling in family and drug issues, as well as assistance in case the women were arrested and had problems with the law. As Sister Helene remembered, knowing those women and establishing a personal relationship with them was important in her work.[41] In addition, many of the Maryknoll Sisters took up volunteer work of different types—prison visitation, the Samaritan hotline for the suicidal, program for AIDS patients, and committee work to tackle drug abuse.

In the 1970s and 1980s the Sisters engaged in ministry with secondary school and university students. Besides Maryknoll schools, Maryknoll Sisters also took up positions in other educational structures. Two of them served as principal during the first years of Kit Sam Secondary School in Wang Tau Hom in the 1970s. This vernacular school was set up by the Immaculate Heart of Mary nuns who had close relations with Maryknoll. Together with the Jesuits, the Maryknoll Sisters had built Adam Schall Hostel for students of United College, the Chinese University of Hong Kong. The priests were responsible for the men's wing, and the nuns took care of the women's wing. For some years, Joan Delaney (Albertus Marie) taught at United College; Joan Toomey (Lourdes Marie) was a lecturer at Lingnan College, another tertiary institute, and was responsible for the diploma courses for business and computer studies.[42]

At the same time, Sisters continued their parish work in a number of localities. In the early 1980s, Doretta Leonard was involved in parish ministry at St. Stephen's Church in Ha Kwai Chung. In the 1990s, Susan Glass and Alice Wengrzynek served in Saints Peter and Paul Church in Yuen Long and the former also worked for Rosary Church in Hung Shui Kiu. Michelle Reynolds remained occupied with parish activities in Rosary Church and St. Jerome's Church in Tin Shui Wei.[43] Concerned about the well-being of migrant workers, Marilu Limgenco was involved in the Filipino ministry. On the diocesan level, Mary Lou Martin was instrumental in planning courses and facilitating training for lay catechists in the 1970s and 1980s. Maryknoll was also supportive of pastoral activities of the diocese, and the vacated Convent building housed the Diocesan Pastoral Center. Joan Ling was director of the Center, which arranged youth and pastoral programs, retreats, and weekly lectures.[44]

Maryknoll Sisters also participated in long-term projects to cultivate social awareness and sensitivity. In 1972 Rose Bernadette Gallagher initiated the Asian/Pacific Meeting of Women Religious (A.M.O.R.) as well as a number of surveys for the religious community in Hong Kong and Macau.[45] In 1978 Sister Helene started the Center for the Progress of Peoples, which focused on social issues, human rights and peace concerns in Asia.[46] Gradually, the Center developed its hotline and the publication *Asia Link*. Its name was changed to Asian Center for the Progress of Peoples in 1990. In 1986 the Hong Kong Diocese set up the Catholic Institute for Religion and Society (C.I.R.S.), "to assist Catholics and other interested parties to prepare, attitudinally, pastorally, and culturally for the political turnover of Hong Kong to China in 1997."[47] Mary Lou Martin served as one of the three executive directors. The C.I.R.S. encouraged Catholics and other people to combine their social awareness with their faith in Christ. It also helped Hong Kong Catholics to be more aware of their Chinese identity.[48]

During different spans of time, the Sisters took up communications work on both Diocesan and institutional levels. In 1979 Sister Joanna Chan (Miriam Joanna) was in charge of the Diocesan Audio-Visual Center for the Hong Kong Diocese, and she produced catechetical material for educational purposes. In the second half of the 1980s, Sister Martha worked with the Union of Catholic Asian News (U.C.A.N.) conducting interviews and writing for *Asia Focus*. In the late 1980s and early 1990s, Rose Duchesne Debrecht also served as editor and librarian for U.C.A.N. Both of them represented U.C.A.N. on separate occasions at the A.M.O.R. Meeting outside Hong Kong. In 1990 Betty Ann Maheu (Antoine Marie) began work at the Holy Spirit Study Centre, where she became the English editor for *Tripod*, the internationally renowned bimonthly focusing on religious issues in China. Also, she wrote for *China Bridge* of the *Sunday Examiner*, the English-language weekly newspaper for the Diocese. Regularly, Mary Lou Martin wrote and had her articles translated for *Kung Kao Po*, the Chinese-language Diocesan paper; occasionally she contributed to *Tripod*. In different intervals in the 1980s and 1990s, Mary Lou Teufel (Maryam) was on the editorial committee of *Asia Link*, Miriam Xavier Mug joined the staff of the Holy Spirit Study Centre, and Dorothy Rubner worked for the *Sunday Examiner*.[49]

An Evaluation of the Sisters' Work from 1921 to 1969

Maryknoll as an Institutional Force

Before Vatican Council II allowed missioners to engage in noninstitutional tasks, meaning they could work outside their own religious groups and provide service that they saw needed in local communities, Maryknollers basically shouldered responsibilities within their own establishment, namely in their schools, hospital, clinics, and social welfare centers in resettlement areas. The only exception was that some of them were involved in parish ministry in St. Teresa's Church, and that was not the creation of the nuns. Within the Maryknoll establishment, the first endeavor was the Industrial Department with the Sisters designing the hand-embroidered silk vestments and supervising Chinese women with the tasks. The decision to start this mail-order business arose from the urgent need of finding a source of income to sustain the house in Hong Kong. Indeed, it turned out to be profitable and lasted until the early 1970s as the death of Sister Teresa Yeung meant that there was nobody else to take care of the Department. Originally, the Industrial Department was a try-and-see move. It was only after Sister Mary Paul and Mother Mary Joseph visited China in 1924 and realized some religious communities in the interior were engaging in the vestment business to finance their own expenses, that the local superior decided to give it a try.

With the success of the Industrial Department and the Sisters' marketing efforts by returning to the United States to solicit orders, Maryknoll was able to use the money earned to set up a kindergarten in the Convent. Portuguese parents had been looking for up-to-standard English-language education for their children. As the kindergarten was small and did not put so much pressure on the pool of personnel (as in the case of a school), Sister Mary Paul was quite willing to respond to demands of the Portuguese community. At that time, she believed that the Sisters had inadequate knowledge of the local system and the number of trained teachers was insufficient to start a school in Hong Kong. Beyond her imagination, the kindergarten expanded quickly to become a school, which came to be known as Maryknoll Convent School (M.C.S.), and by coincidence M.C.S. fitted into the request from the local Catholic Church to establish a school in Kowloon Tong to correspond with the opening of St. Teresa's parish. With the urging of the bishop in 1929, Maryknoll finally decided that education was their long-term commitment in the colony. Having said that, the nuns were still wondering in 1930 whether they could continue two schools in Hong Kong, or whether Holy Spirit (established in 1927) was to consolidate with their school in Kowloon Tong. By the completion of the school building in Kowloon Tong in 1937, both M.C.S. and Holy Spirit were recognized for their high standards, and signified the beginning of the Maryknoll establishment in Hong Kong.

The decision to establish themselves as a community in Hong Kong was not the original plan of the Maryknoll pioneers. Nor was the development of the mission premeditated, but was an answer to the need of maintaining the house in Hong Kong, as a serving post for the interior, and was a response to the demands of the local Catholic Church and people. What the Sisters did in Hong Kong was very different from Maryknollers in China. From the start evangelization was not the prior objective of their work, though it was an accompanying one. There were high percentages of non-Catholics in their schools, and by the 1960s Catholic students took up less than one half of their school enrolment. Although the Hong Kong Diocese grew rapidly in the 1950s and 1960s, the Sisters began their work in the resettlement areas with the main tasks of providing relief and service to people, while at the same time they conducted catechumen classes and church activities. To help people secure basic standards of living, meaning some kind of shelter, food for the families and medical care, was the top item on their agenda. Evangelization was a secondary concern. Their "organized relief work" really took off after the fire in Tung Tau Tsuen in 1951, and Sister Mary Imelda immediately looked for an area to begin the stone cottages project to accommodate the 17,000 homeless victims. Eventually the government was willing to assign an area in King's Park and Homantin Village to the nuns, to start the housing plan and social welfare center. The nuns established vernacular schools in resettlement areas, to offer education to poor children as the means to help them escape from their poverty. From 1921 to 1969, Maryknollers adapted very well to local circumstances, and before Vatican Council II emphasized service for the poor and the need to respond to local demands, these American nuns had already been doing so for many years. The evolutionary aspect of their mission was obvious: from education, to relief, social welfare, medical care, and elaborate social service. Their willingness to see mission among ordinary people, and to live with and learn from the Chinese, explained the success of their endeavors in Hong Kong.

Until the 1960s the nuns constituted an institutional force in society, with they themselves following strictly the orders of superiors and concentrating on their own schools, hospital, clinics, and centers, which all bore the name of Maryknoll. Maryknoll was able to fill different openings in society in different periods of time, offering expertise that was lacking. The provision of sound English-language education, relief supplies and service, and medical support were all very well received. While many responsibilities should have been shouldered by local authorities, the government was incapable of satisfying desires of different sectors of society, and meeting fundamental needs of an exploding population. The poverty of the community at large posed many opportunities for missioners, Catholic and Protestant alike, to make themselves useful. Thus they were able to gain acceptance from local people. Fulfilling some of the responsibilities of the government and working among the poor, Maryknoll acted as a "third force" in society and contributed to the resolution of conflicts. Through their service, they acted as a mediator between the "first force" of the government and the "second force" of the Chinese population. Despite the fact that they were a foreign congregation, the American nuns were equally sensitive to problems of local citizens. More importantly, they were in better positions to negotiate with the government (as they were offering services the government should be responsible for), and to look for donations (from the N.C.W.C., C.R.S., the Motherhouse, and the well-to-do). It was highly desirable that the Maryknoll establishment develop and expand amidst poverty and uncertainty. By the turn of the 1970s, the Sisters responded to Vatican Council II and became engaged in tasks outside their own establishment. By then, Hong Kong society was getting on its feet, its industry was prospering, people were more confident of themselves, and various types of service were available. As an institutional force, Maryknoll had performed its role, and from the 1970s onward, the mission was to embark on a new course of history.

Liberation of the Maryknoll Women

During these years, the image of the Maryknoll Sisters was that they were young, energetic, and highly educated. Belonging to a group of women only, they had the freedom to occupy any position so long as they proved their abilities and the superior approved of the appointment, without the consideration of sexual biases found in ordinary companies, schools, institutions, and government departments. From this perspective, they were able to shoulder responsibilities as "equally capable individuals" and to realize their own potential and talents. The nuns took up positions of school principals, hospital administrators, and directors of welfare centers. Within their establishment, they found their dignity as intelligent and capable women. In fact, their workload had been so heavy that they often faced the question of "what more they could do" rather than of "what they could do." As the study of Sister Joan Chatfield shows (mentioned in chapter one), most Maryknollers entered the Congregation because they wanted to go abroad for service. From the beginning of their religious life, adventure overseas was their dream, and in those early days, the nuns did not expect to return home because foreign mission was for life. It was only after World War II that those who came to Hong Kong could return home every ten years, and through the passage of time, the restriction tended to become less harsh. The missioners had to be prepared before they embarked on their long, if not lifelong, journey overseas. From the very first start, a daring and independent character was what one might expect from these missionary women. Mission provided the nuns with what they wanted—the kind of "equal employment opportunities"—which were only later emphasized in the women's liberation movements in the 1960s.

While they enjoyed the freedom to live as "capable individuals," they endured sacrifices, leading a highly disciplinary life. Before the changes adopted by Vatican Council II, the Sisters had to follow more rules and restrictions. The vow of obedience, in practice, demanded strict adherence to the orders of the local Superior, rigid daily schedules, and habits and veils. Ever since the days of their training, the women lived by very tight timetables every day. The time slots for morning Mass, prayers, household labor, and recreation were simply unchangeable. In Hong Kong Sister Mary Paul made sure that such discipline, closely observed in the Motherhouse, was also in force under her leadership. Therefore, she decided the items on the daily routine of the nuns, down to every detail. She even told the nuns how much time they should spend on language learning, and how much time they needed for rest and exercise. Mary Paul was famous for asking the women to take a short siesta every day (a practice not found in the U.S. motherhouse), given the hot and humid weather of Hong Kong. In later years, her successors did not think of other alternatives but to continue what she had put in place. The practice lasted until the late 1960s, and newcomers usually had difficulty adjusting to the schedule, as they were not used to sleeping in the afternoon. In Hong Kong, leadership of the local superior left an impression on the minds of every woman. Mary Paul had very strong ideas, and to some, it helped to "keep the group going." Many years later, the nuns could still tell that she required the women to allocate some time for a walk "on the green."[50] With a commanding character, Mary Paul made an imposing presence in the house. None dared to speak when she gave her orders, and none dared to disobey her. Her days were termed the "Manchu Dynasty," considering her authoritative leadership, and her successors were "carbon-copies" of her. The vow of obedience meant a lot of restrictions on the life of the religious, though they were able to realize themselves in their work in society, as respected teachers, doctors, nurses, and directors.

The conventional image of nuns, even in contemporary society, was that they played a subservient role to the priests. Although this was true when considering that the priests were in charge of parishes and religious services, the Maryknoll Sisters in Hong Kong assumed an independent role in their work. Sister Mary Paul made the decisions regarding Maryknoll schools, and Sister Mary Imelda initiated the idea of building stone cottages for the fire victims of Tung Tau Tsuen. Although the nuns had the support of priests in their endeavors, they acted in their capacity as leaders of their own community. Unlike those in China before the 1950s (who were already considered outgoing compared to other religious women of the time), the Maryknoll nuns in the colony were not under the guidance of the Maryknoll Fathers. Even those working in the parishes of the Maryknoll Fathers administered their own social welfare centers, women centers, clinics, and nurseries, and all were under the Sisters' establishment. The Sister-teachers had minimal contact with the Maryknoll Fathers. Many of the nuns, who worked in resettlement areas, had previous experience in mission fields in the interior, but had to leave China after the Communist takeover. They brought with them Francis X. Ford's "Jiaying method" of direct evangelization, in the sense that they lived close to the people, conducted home visits, and reached out to both converted and non-Catholics.[51] The experience in China prepared them for an independent role in direct apostolate in Hong Kong. Their image should be that of a group of outgoing, assimilative, and professional women.

Cross-Cultural Exchanges

In their constitutions, the Maryknoll Sisters stress the importance of cultural awareness and respect for different cultures. Nowadays, new members who complete their formation (or pass their training) are required to spend their first ten years serving in a culture other than their own. Although the requirement might prevent potential candidates who wish to work in their native land from joining Maryknoll, it aims to cultivate among the women a sense of appreciation for traditions and history of other peoples. The emphasis on foreign mission has always been a unique aspect of this Catholic congregation, characteristic of its history since the earliest days. Knowing very little about Chinese society and people before they embarked on their journey abroad, the Maryknoll pioneers and the later arrivals made tremendous effort in learning the language and making themselves useful to the Hong Kong community. To various degrees, the women adjusted to the local society, some of them were more fluent in Cantonese and some could more easily make friends with the local people and families. Interviewing the Sisters, I heard them saying quite a number of times— "As Americans, we know nothing"—there was so much to learn about Chinese mentality, their social behavior and culture. Having witnessed Hong Kong's difficult years, the Sisters were most impressed with the hard work of the Chinese, their ability to endure suffering and devotion to their families. Working in resettlement areas, missioners had the opportunity to improve their Cantonese and other dialects they learned in the interior or in the first year of language study in Hong Kong. A story often quoted by the nuns was that Rose Bernadette Gallagher, who spent much time with the people in Chai Wan, unconsciously spoke in Cantonese over a long-distance call until the other side reminded her to speak in English instead. Arriving in Hong Kong in 1946, Rose Duchesne Debrecht was disappointed to know that she was going to teach in English to M.C.S. students. Nevertheless, having lived in Hong Kong for over fifty years by now, her Cantonese is as good as any local people. Two other Sisters, Mary Diggins and Mary Lou Martin literally shocked many people by not only how very fast they spoke in English, but in Cantonese as well. While the nuns celebrated Western festivals, they also made special arrangement for the Lunar New Year in their houses. Chinese food, customs, and language had become part of their life, and that continued after many of them returned to the United States for service and retirement.

Cross-cultural exchanges were a two-way process, with the Chinese being aware of and some getting used to the presence of the American nuns in workplaces, schools, parishes, and other localities. Fleeing from China, refugees arrived in Hong Kong with very few belongings and had nothing to hold onto, without savings, recognized degrees, qualifications, friends, and relatives. The immigrant community in the 1950s and 1960s produced a very pragmatic mentality among the people, while they struggled to the best of their ability to uplift themselves from their own poverty. The Chinese worked round the clock and even children contributed to the effort. The little more (material relief/care/respect) they could have meant a lot to them, given that the poor were often ignored and many times mistreated. Together with the Chinese, Maryknoll Sisters settled in the newly designated resettlement areas, which were at the beginning bare fields without roads, electricity, and water supply. Both were pioneers in newly opening-up land. With provision of relief and social service in the locality, the Sisters were able to remove initial suspicion and win acceptance from the people. Chinese always prize education, as a means for their children to secure better jobs and to acquire better living; and with the education they provided, the Maryknoll nuns could easily obtain the respect of families and the community. As Jeanne Houlihan (Joel Marie), who taught at M.C.S. for many decades and was the last Sister to serve as principal, thought back, the Confucian philosophy (its emphasis on education), the Chinese parents' trust in Maryknoll and government approval were like a "three-pronged tool," which gave the nuns the opportunity to move forward with education work.[52] In the second half of the 1960s, the women changed to wearing suits and simplified veils, and in 1969 to wearing ordinary clothes. Before this change, their appearance in full habits and veils in schools, hospital, clinics, and poor neighborhoods made an impression on those who came into contact with them. As the nuns recalled, the Chinese had always been very polite to them, and in reaching out to the people, they were able to promote a better understanding of the Church and themselves as foreign missioners.

While the nuns were promoting changes in the communities they served, they were in turn changed by their association with the Chinese people. Agnes

McKeirnan (Rose Eileen) taught at M.C.S. from the 1960s to the 1990s. She thought that her responsibility was to encourage the students to express their opinions and to cultivate independent thinking. As missioner, she hoped that the Maryknoll spirit could pass on to her Chinese students as well, making each of them a "giver" to other people.[53] The American spirit came through the Sisters, Corinne Rost believed, and was that of a "fun-loving" and "joyful" spirit.[54] From the perspective of the nuns, these were American and Christian values that they shared with the teenagers. At the same time, the Sister-teachers also acquired Chineseness in their manners, expressions, and thinking, in the many years of relationship with the students. As Sister Rose Duchesne admitted, "I think our own Maryknoll girls have taken on so much of our way of behaving that, we have ended up changing them at the same time that we in part have been changed by our association with them."[55] In other areas of their service, the nuns had close contacts with local people and took on many of the Chinese values and ways of behavior. Learning much about old Chinese customs and social relationships from the elderly she served, Sister Miedal believed that she would do things in a Chinese way unconsciously. She would ask a third person to solve the problem indirectly so as to uphold the dignity of the other person.[56] Having worked for many years at Our Lady of Maryknoll Hospital, MaryLou Ann Rajdl also established long-term relationships with Chinese families. Deeply interested in Chinese culture, she tried to integrate her American and Chinese identities, and described herself as a "Buddhist Catholic nun."[57] In the many years of service to the community, the nuns had very fond memories of Chinese people, and it was the love of the people they served that provided them the strength, courage, and faith to continue their mission in Hong Kong. If they had been asked, they would agree that they were always in love with the Chinese people.

Appendix I: Statistics on Maryknoll Sisters Who Were in Hong Kong from 1921 to 2004*

Year	Number of Sisters	Year	Number of Sisters
1921	6	1956	50
1922	6	1957	57
1923	12	1958	66
1924	14	1959	66
1925	17	1960	64
1926	13	1961	72
1927	25	1962	73
1928	27	1963	76
1929	18	1964	83
1930	22	1965	86
1931	21	1966	82
1932	25	1967	76
1933	25	1968	76
1934	22	1969	72
1935	23	1970	70
1936	23	1971	64
1937	28	1972	63
1938	25	1973	56
1939	24	1974	51
1940	28	1975	49
1941	28#	1976	52
1942	28+	1977	52
1943	0	1978	45
1944	0	1979	46
1945	13	1980	48
1946	24	1981	48
1947	22	1982	44
1948	24	1983	35
1949	28	1984	38
1950	31	1985	38
1951	38	1986	39
1952	43	1987	35
1953	43	1988	34
1954	42	1989	33
1955	44	1990	32

* The statistics came from the Lists of Personnel of the Maryknoll Sisters from 1921 to 2004. Each figure shows the number of Sisters who were in Hong Kong *in that certain month* of the year in which the list was drawn. Refer to Boxes 1–5, Lists: Sisters Personnel; and Box 14, Lists: Address Directories 1997– , Maryknoll Mission Archives.

Year	Number of Sisters	Year	Number of Sisters
1991	28	1998	18
1992	28	1999	13
1993	26	2000	12
1994	23	2001	12
1995	23	2002	13
1996	21	2003	14
1997	21	2004	14

[#] The number of Sisters in Hong Kong when the colony fell to the Japanese on Christmas Day 1941.

[+] The number of Sisters in Hong Kong before repatriation and their departure from the colony in 1942.

Appendix II: List of Maryknoll Sisters Who Were in Hong Kong from 1921 to 2004[*]

Bachmann, Marian
Balicki, Nina
Bastien, Joanne (M. Anne Noel)
Basto, Candida Maria
Bone, Nancy (Rose Virginia)
Bourguignon, Marie de Lourdes
Bourne, Martha (Martha Mary)
Boyle, Monica Marie
Brachtesende, M. Amata
Bradley, M. Jane Imelda
Bresnahan, Mary Thomas
Brielmaier, M. Ann Carol
Britz, Helen Elizabeth (M. Gerald)
Brophy, Mary Edna (M. Francis John)
Brusati, M. Brian
Byrne, Katherine Teresa (Philip Marie)
Cain, M. de Ricci
Carvalho, Cecilia Marie
Cavagnaro, Maria Ynez
Cazale, Agnes (Maria Petra)
Chan, Joanna (Miriam Joanna)
Chin, Rose (Rose Miriam)
Chou, Agnes (Marian Agnes)
Clements, Anne (M. Famula)
Collins, M. Cornelia
Conlon, M. Matthew
Connally, Carol Helen (Maura Thomas)
Connolly, Marie Thomas
Conroy, Elizabeth Therese
Coughlin, M. Patricia
Coupe, M. Eucharista
Coveny, Angela Marie
Cruickshank, Mary Cecilia
Cruise, Mary Dolores

Cunningham, Henrietta Marie
Cusack, Mercedes
Dagdag, Teresa
Davis, M. Francis
de Felice, Rosemary
Debrecht, Rose Duchesne
Delaney, Joan Frances (Albertus Marie)
Devine, Marie Noel Chabanel
Devlin, Gabriel Marie
Diggins, Mary (M. John Karen)
Doherty, Grace C. (M. Tarsicius)
Doherty, Rose Thomas
Donnelly, Joan (Marie Gerald)
Donnelly, M. St. Bernard
Edwards, Diane (Regina Hostia)
Ehm, Rose Goretti
Elliott, Joan Eileen (Marilyn Martin)
Emdin, Ann Marie
Evans, Ruth (M. Margaret Veronica)
Farrell, Ann Mary
Farrell, Elinor Marie
Fernandez, Lourdes
Fitzmaurice, Patricia Marie (M. Thomas Ann)
Flagg, Virginia (Stella Marie)
Flynn, M. Berchmans
Fogarty, Irene (M. Francis Jogues)
Foley, Mary Lawrence
Fortin, Anne Marie
Franz, Eileen (Marea Consuela)
Frey, Norma
Froehlich, Mary Barbara
Furey, M. Christella
Gallagher, Rose Bernadette

[*] In the late 1960s, Maryknoll Sisters could choose to return to their baptismal names instead of using their religious names. For Sisters whose names changed in archival records owing to this reason, their religious names are listed in brackets after their baptismal names. Refer to Boxes 1–5, Lists: Sisters Personnel; and Box 14, Lists: Address Directories 1997–, Maryknoll Mission Archives.

Gardner, Frances Marion
Garvey, Rita Mary
Gibbons, Paul Marie (Pauline Marie)
Giglio, Mary
Gunning, Angela Maureen
Glass, Susan Carolyn
Grondin, Marie Marcelline
Gubbins, Mary Susan (Susan Marie)
Guerrieri, Antonia Maria
Guidera, M. Dominic
Hannigan, M. Julia
Harrington, M. Raphael
Hayden, M. St. Teresa
Healy, Marie Antoine
Heaney, M. Dolorita
Heath, Mary (Maria Crucis)
Higa, Mary Louise (Regina Therese)
Higgins, Agnes Virginia
Holman, Janet
Hom, May Anne
Hopfinspirger, M. Marcia
Houlihan, Jeanne (Joel Marie)
Howard, Therese Alvera (M. Howard)
Hughes, Kathleen (Miriam Pacis)
Issac, Josephine Marie
Jacobsen, Patricia (M. Patricia Francis)
Jaramillo, Maria Corazon
Johnson, Virginia Therese
Junas, Mary Ann
Jung, Christina Marie
Jung, Margaret Marie
Kane, Joseph Marie
Karlon, M. Madeleine Sophie
Kelly, M. St. Dominic
Kenny, Helen Marie (M. Kenny)
Kettl, M. Rosalia
Killoran, M. Mark
Kirkendall, Margaret (Miriam John)
Knoerl, Elizabeth
Kuper, M. Augustine
Kwok, Irene
Lee, Catherine Mary
Lee, Elizabeth
Leifels, Mary Rose
Leonard, M. Doretta
Leung, Teresa Suk Ching (Maria Lucas)
Lewandoski, M. Anne Charles
Limgenco, Marilu
Ling, Joan (Joan Miriam)
Lipetzky, Marie Ann (Victoria Marie)
Lotito, M. Francis Venard
Lucier, M. Francisca

Maheu, Betty Ann
Manning, Santa Maria
Makra, M. Lelia
Marquez, Grace
Martin, Mary Louise (Regina Marie)
McCourtney, Marie Therese
McKeirnan, Agnes (Rose Eileen)
McKenna, Mary Paul
McNally, M. Ignatia
Mersinger, Barbara Rose (Rose Victor)
Mertens, Mary Ellen (M. Benjamin)
Meyer, M. Beatrice
Miller, Marilyn (Marie James)
Moffat, Mary Monica
Mug, Miriam Xavier
Murphy, Maria Regis
Norris, Marilyn (M. Deirdre)
Nubla, Joseph Lourdes
Oberle, M. Dolorosa
O'Connor, Maura Bernadette
O'Donnell, Ruth Marie
O'Hagan, M. Joan Catherine
O'Leary, M. Angelica
O'Neil, M. Cecile
O'Regan, Sonja
O'Sullivan, Helene (M. Helene)
Pardini, M. Daniel Joseph
Perkes, Theresa (Marina)
Perlewitz, Miriam Francis
Plante, Theresa (Eugene Marie)
Quinlan, M. Liguori
Quinn, M. Clement
Rajdl, MaryLou Ann (M. Ann David)
Reardon, M. Regina
Regan, Rita Marie
Remedios, Bernardine
Reusch, Anne (Alma Marie)
Reynolds, M. Camillus
Reynolds, Michelle
Rhatigan, Elizabeth Agnes
Riconda, M. Ruth
Rieckelman, Maria (Maria Fidelis)
Riehl, Moira
Riehle, M. Edith
Rietz, Marion Cordis
Riordan, M. Regina
Rizzardi, M. Gonzaga
Roethle, M. Andrea
Rost, Marie Corinne
Rowe, Catherine
Rubner, Dorothy (Barbara Marie)
Ruiz, Gloria (Mara Jose)

Ryan, Joan Marie
Schmitt, Miriam
Schmitt, Rosalie (M. John Mark)
Shepherd, Margaret (Rose Martin)
Sheridan, Mary Imelda
Silva, M. Reginald
Skehan, Rose Olive
Smyth, Margaret Rosario
Stapleton, Beatrice Ann   (Matthew Marie)
Steinbauer, Marie Jean Theophane
Steinhoff, M. William Regis
Stone, Miedal
Sullivan, Rose Madeleine
Swent, M. Giles
Tam, M. Bernadette
Teufel, Mary Louise (Maryam)
Toomey, Joan (Lourdes Marie)
Trant, Arlene
Turner, Dominic Marie

Umberg, Jane
Unitas, Anthony Marie
Vaccaro, M. John Bernard
Valde, Adelaida
Veile, M. Luella
Venneman, M. Albert
Walenty, Barbara Ann (Rose Barbara)
Walsh, M. Dorothy
Weber, M. Rosalie
Welscher, M. Agnes Christine
Wengrzynek, Alice
Wenzel, M. Richard
Wilson, M. Edward Marmion
Wittman, M. Xaveria
Wong, Marie Carmel
Xavier, M. Chanel
Yeung, Maria Teresa
Yeung, Paulette Marie
Zaborowski, Marya

Notes

Abbreviations Used in Notes

Maryknoll Sisters Archives, Maryknoll Mission Archives, Maryknoll, New York

CHRONICLES-MMA	Chronicles, Maryknoll Mission Archives
CONSTITUTIONS-MMA	Constitutions, Maryknoll Mission Archives
CWPP-MMA	Creative Works and Personal Papers, Maryknoll Mission Archives
DIARIES-MMA	Diaries, Maryknoll Mission Archives
LISTS-MMA	Lists: Sisters Personnel, Maryknoll Mission Archives
LISTS (1997–)-MMA	Lists: Address Directories 1997–, Maryknoll Mission Archives
MCHP-MMA	Maryknoll China History Project, Oral Histories-Typed Transcripts, Maryknoll Mission Archives
MMA	Maryknoll Mission Archives
MMJC-MMA	Mother Mary Joseph Collection, Maryknoll Mission Archives
PNWWII-MMA	Personal Narratives of WWII: South China, Maryknoll Mission Archives
RCSC-MMA	Regional Correspondence: South China, Maryknoll Mission Archives
RC-MMA	Regional Records: Hong Kong-Macau Region, Maryknoll Mission Archives
SCR-MMA	South China Region: Hong Kong/Macau Region, 1921–, Maryknoll Mission Archives

Hong Kong Catholic Diocesan Archives, Hong Kong

IV-HKCDA	Section IV: Territorial Subdivision, Hong Kong Catholic Diocesan Archives
V-HKCDA	Section V: Mission Personnel, Hong Kong Catholic Diocesan Archives
VI-HKCDA	Section VI: Catholic Social Commitments, Hong Kong Catholic Diocesan Archives

Public Records Office, Hong Kong

PRO-HK	From Its Collection

Chapter One   Introduction

1. Maryknoll Heritage Exhibit, Maryknoll Sisters Center, Maryknoll, New York, visited by the author in July and August 2001.
2. Penny Lernoux, *Hearts on Fire: The Story of the Maryknoll Sisters* (Maryknoll: Orbis Books, 1993), p. 47.
3. Sister Miriam Xavier Mug, "Maryknoll Sisters, Hong Kong-Macau Region: A History—1921–1998" (Unpublished, March 2000), p. 1.
4. Jean-Paul Wiest, *Maryknoll in China: A History, 1918–1955* (Armonk: M.E. Sharpe, 1988), p. 31.
5. An example of such an endeavor was the collection of Joshua A. Fogel's essays in his edited volume *The Cultural Dimension of Sino-Japanese Relations: Essays on the Nineteenth and Twentieth Centuries* (Armonk: M.E. Sharpe, 1995). The first part of the book deals with Chinese studies in Japan, and the second part mainly describes Japanese individuals and groups in China. In his preface, Fogel acknowledges the contribution of Akira Iriye's "international history" concept (p. vii). Other studies of the cultural dimension of Sino-foreign relations are John Charles Pollock's *A Foreign Devil in China: The Story of Dr. L. Nelson Bell—An American Surgeon in China* (Minneapolis: World Wide Publications for Billy Graham Evangelistic Association, 1971); and Robert A. Bickers' *Britain in China: Community, Culture and Colonialism, 1900–1949* (Manchester: Manchester University Press, 1999).
6. Akira Iriye, "Culture and International History," in *Explaining the History of American Foreign Relations*, ed. Michael J. Hogan and Thomas G. Paterson (Cambridge: Cambridge University Press, 1991), p. 220. Examples of such works are Warren I. Cohen, *The Chinese Connection: Roger S. Greene, Thomas W. Lamont, George E. Sokolsky and American-East Asian Relations* (New York: Columbia University Press, 1978); Emily S. Rosenberg, *Spreading the American Dream: American Economic and Cultural Expansion, 1890–1945* (New York: Hill and Wang, 1982); James Reed, *The Missionary Mind and American East Asian Policy, 1911–1915* (Cambridge, Mass.: Council on East Asian Studies, Harvard University, 1983); David L. Anderson, *Imperialism and Idealism: American Diplomats in China, 1861–1898* (Bloomington: Indiana University Press, 1985); Carolle J. Carter, *Mission to Yenan: American Liaison with the Chinese Communists, 1944–1947* (Lexington: University Press of Kentucky, 1997); and Eileen P. Scully, *Bargaining with the State from Afar: American Citizenship in Treaty Port China, 1844–1912* (New York: Columbia University Press, 2001).
7. Iriye, "Culture and International History," p. 220. In his idea of "international history," countries should be considered "cultures when looking at their international affairs" (p. 216).
8. John K. Fairbank, ed., *The Missionary Enterprise in China and America* (Cambridge, Mass.: Harvard University Press, 1974).
9. Ellsworth C. Carlson's *The Foochow Missionaries, 1847–1880* (Cambridge, Mass.: East Asian Research Center, Harvard University, 1974) was an example of a favorable appraisal of the contribution of missionaries in China. An example of a critical account of missionary activities was Sidney A. Forsythe's *An American Missionary Community in China, 1895–1905* (Cambridge, Mass.: East Asian Research Center, Harvard University, 1971).
10. Examples are: Frederick W. Drake, "Bridgman in China in the Early Nineteenth Century," *American Neptune*, Vol. 46, No. 1 (1986), pp. 34–42; Wayne Flynt and Gerald W. Berkley, *Taking Christianity to China: Alabama Missionaries in the Middle Kingdom 1850–1950* (Tuscaloosa: University of Alabama Press, 1997); Loren W. Crabtree, "Andrew P. Happer and the Presbyterian Missions in China, 1844–1891," *Journal of Presbyterian History*, Vol. 62, No. 1 (1984), pp. 19–34. Studies on missionary women are: Carol Berg, "Margaret Thomson in China, 1917–1939," *The Historian*, Vol. 53, No. 3 (Spring 1991), pp. 455–72; and Mary Carita Pendergast, *Havoc in Hunan: The Sisters of Charity in Western Hunan, 1924–1951* (Morristown: College of St. Elizabeth Press, 1991).

11. Examples are: Ruth V. Hemenway, *A Memoir of Revolutionary China, 1924–1941,* edited with an Introduction by Fred W. Drake (Amherst: University of Massachusetts Press, 1977); John S. Service, ed., *Golden Inches: The China Memoir of Grace Service* (Berkeley: University of California Press, 1989); E. G. Ruoff, ed., *Death Throes of a Dynasty: Letters and Diaries of Charles and Bessie Ewing, Missionaries to China* (Kent, Ohio: Kent State University Press, 1990); and Edward V. Gulick, *Teaching in Wartime China: A Photo-Memoir, 1937–1939* (Amherst: University of Massachusetts Press, 1995).

12. Daniel H. Bays, ed., *Christianity in China: From the Eighteenth Century to the Present* (Stanford: Stanford University Press, 1996). A study on individual Chinese's reactions to foreign missionaries on local settings is: Jessie G. Lutz and Rolland Ray Lutz, *Hakka Chinese Confront Protestant Christianity, 1850–1900: With the Autobiographies of Eight Hakka Christians, and Commentary* (Armonk: M.E. Sharpe, 1998).

13. Patricia Neils, ed., *United States Attitudes and Policies toward China: The Impact of American Missionaries* (Armonk: M.E. Sharpe, 1990).

14. In *China and the Christian Colleges, 1850–1950,* Jessie Gregory Lutz argued that conflicts existed between the evangelization goals and educational tasks of the foreign missionaries. Read Jessie Gregory Lutz, *China and the Christian Colleges, 1850–1950* (Ithaca: Cornell University Press, 1971). As Lutz elaborates: "The demands of the Chinese environment rather than studies in mission methodology first persuaded missionaries to found schools, translate Western works, and compile dictionaries. One consequence was that individuals who were already devoting much of their time and energy to educational work continued to consider that work decidedly secondary to evangelist activities. ... The evangelists assumed the superiority of their work, so that educational missionaries were constantly on the defensive and felt obliged to give great emphasis to the evangelistic goals of their education" (p. 12).

15. Philip West, *Yenching University and Sino-Western Relations, 1916–1952* (Cambridge, Mass.: Harvard University Press, 1976).

16. Works on the early Catholic mission in China include: Bertram Wolferstan, *The Catholic Church in China: From 1860 to 1907* (St. Louis: B. Herder, 1909); Marion Alphonse Habig, *Pioneering in China: The Story of the Rev. Francis Xavier Engbring, O.F.M., First Native American Priest in China, 1857–1895: With Sketches of His Missionary Comrades* (Chicago: Franciscan Herald Press, 1930); and Alan Richard Sweeten, *Christianity in Rural China: Conflict and Accommodation in Jiangxi Province, 1860–1900* (Ann Arbor: Center for Chinese Studies, University of Michigan, 2001).

17. Xiaoxin Wu, "A Case Study of the Catholic University of Peking during the Benedictine Period (1927–1933)" (Ed.D. diss., University of San Francisco, 1993).

18. Robert Edward Carbonneau, "Life, Death, and Memory: Three Passionists in Hunan, China and the Shaping of an American Mission Perspective in the 1920s. (Vols. I & II) (Coveyou Walter, Seybold Clement, Holbein Godfrey)" (Ph.D. diss., Georgetown University, 1992).

19. Sue Bradshaw, "Religious Women in China: An Understanding of Indigenization," *Catholic Historical Review*, Vol. 68, No. 1 (1982), pp. 28–45.

20. An example is: Frederick B. Hoyt, "Protection Implies Intervention: The U.S. Catholic Mission at Kanchow," *The Historian,* Vol. 38, No. 4 (August 1976), pp. 709–27.

21. Thomas A. Breslin, *China, American Catholicism, and the Missionary* (University Park: Pennsylvania State University Press, 1980), p. 112.

22. Jeroom Heyndrickx, ed., *Historiography of the Chinese Catholic Church: Nineteenth and Twentieth Centuries* (K.U. Leuven: Ferdinand Verbiest Foundation, 1994). Read Bernard Hung-kay Luk's article, "History of the Catholic Church in Hongkong," pp. 397–406.

23. The graduate works include: Li Ng Suk-Kay, "Mission Strategy of the Roman Catholic Church of Hong Kong, 1949 to 1974" (M.Phil. thesis, University of Hong Kong, 1978); Louis Ha, "The Foundation of the Catholic Mission in Hong Kong, 1841–1894" (Ph.D. diss., University of Hong Kong, 1998); and John Kang Tan, "Church, State and

Education during Decolonization: Catholic Education in Hong Kong during the Pre-1997 Political Transition" (Ph.D. diss., University of Hong Kong, 2000).

24. Wang Gungwu, ed., *Xianggangshi xinbian (Hong Kong History: New Perspectives)* Vols. 1–2 (Hong Kong: Joint Publishing (H.K.) Co., 1997). The chapter is in the second volume: Li Zhigang, "Tianzhujiao yu Jidujiao zai Xianggang de chuanbo yu yingxiang" [The Work and the Impact of the Catholic Church and the Protestant Churches in Hong Kong], pp. 739–82.

25. Stephen Uhalley, Jr. and Xiaoxin Wu, eds., *China and Christianity: Burdened Past, Hopeful Future* (Armonk: M.E. Sharpe, 2001).

26. Father Sergio Ticozzi, ed., *Historical Documents of the Hong Kong Catholic Church* (Hong Kong: Hong Kong Catholic Diocesan Archives, 1997).

27. Tian Yingjie [Sergio Ticozzi], ed., *Xianggang Tianzhujiao zhanggu* (The Historical Anecdotes of the Hong Kong Catholic Church), trans. You Liqing (Hong Kong: Holy Spirit Study Centre, 1983).

28. Beatrice Leung and Shun-hing Chan, *Changing Church and State Relations in Hong Kong, 1950–2000* (Hong Kong: Hong Kong University Press, 2003).

29. Jane Hunter, *The Gospel of Gentility: American Women Missionaries in Turn-of-the-Century China* (New Haven: Yale University Press, 1984), p. xvi.

30. Patricia R. Hill, *The World Their Household: The American Woman's Foreign Mission Movement and Cultural Transformation, 1870–1920* (Ann Arbor: University of Michigan Press, 1985).

31. Kathleen L. Lodwick, *Educating the Women of Hainan: The Career of Margaret Moninger in China, 1915–1942* (Lexington: University Press of Kentucky, 1995).

32. Maria Cristina Zaccarini, *The Sino-American Friendship as Tradition and Challenge: Dr. Ailie Gale in China, 1908–1950* (Bethlehem, Pa.: Lehigh University Press, 2001).

33. Dana L. Robert, *American Women in Mission: A Social History of Their Thought and Practice* (Macon: Mercer University Press, 1996).

34. There were a number of publications on the life of Catholic Sisters in China. Examples of such were: Ann Colette Wolf, *Against All Odds: Sisters of Providence Mission to the Chinese, 1920–1990* (Saint Mary-of-the Woods: Sisters of Providence, 1990); Maria Scatena, "Educational Movements That Have Influenced the Sister Teacher Education Program of the Congregation of the Sisters of Providence, 1840–1940" (Ph.D. diss., Loyola University of Chicago, 1987); Nora M. Clarke, *"The Governor's Daughter Takes the Veil": Sister Aloysia Emily Bowring, Canossian Daughter of Charity, Hong-Kong 1860–1870* (Hong Kong: Canossian Missions Historic Archives, 1980); Sister Mary Just, *Immortal Fire: A Journey through the Centuries with the Missionary Great* (St. Louis: Herder, 1951); Mother Mary of St. Austin, *Fifty-Six Years a Missionary in China: The Life of Mother St. Dominic, Helper of the Holy Souls* (London: Burns, Oates & Washbourne, 1935); and Henry Mazeau, *The Heroine of Pe-Tang: Helene de Jaurias, Sister of Charity, 1824–1900* (New York: Benziger Brothers, 1928).

35. Pendergast, *Havoc in Hunan*.

36. Sue Bradshaw, "Catholic Sisters in China: An Effort to Raise the Status of Women," in *Women in China: Current Directions in Historical Scholarship*, ed. Richard W. Guisso and Stanley Johannesen (Youngstown: Philo Press, 1981), pp. 201–13; Bradshaw, "Religious Women in China."

37. Sister Rose Duchesne Debrecht, Interview by Sister Virginia Unsworth, July 19, 1981, p. 14, MCHP-MMA.

38. Tak-Wing Ngo, "Colonialism in Hong Kong Revisited," in *Hong Kong's History: State and Society under Colonial Rule*, ed. Tak-Wing Ngo (London: Routledge, 1999), p. 2.

39. Ibid., pp. 2, 3, 5, and 6.

40. Chan Wai Kwan, *The Making of Hong Kong Society: Three Studies of Class Formation in Early Hong Kong* (New York: Oxford University Press, 1991).

41. These works include: Wong Siu-Lun, *Emigrant Entrepreneurs: Shanghai Industrialists in Hong Kong* (Hong Kong: Oxford University Press, 1988); Jung-fang Tsai, *Hong Kong in*

Chinese History: Community and Social Unrest in the British Colony, 1842–1913 (New York: Columbia University Press, 1993); Carl T. Smith, *A Sense of History: Studies in the Social and Urban History of Hong Kong* (Hong Kong: Hong Kong Educational Publishing Co., 1995); Wang Gungwu, ed., *Xianggangshi xinbian*; Jung-fang Tsai, *Xianggangren zhi Xianggangshi 1841–1945 (The Hong Kong People's History of Hong Kong)* (Hong Kong: Oxford University Press, 2001); and Lau Yee-cheung and Wong Man-kong, eds., *Xianggang shehui yu wenhuashi lunji (Studies in the Social and Cultural History of Hong Kong)* (Hong Kong: United College, Chinese University of Hong Kong, 2002).

42. Chan Lau Kit-ching, *From Nothing to Nothing: The Chinese Communist Movement and Hong Kong, 1921–1936* (Hong Kong: Hong Kong University Press, 1999); Chan Lau Kit-ching, "The Perception of Chinese Communism in Hong Kong, 1921–1934," *China Quarterly*, No. 164 (2000), pp. 1044–61; Cindy Yik-yi Chu, "The Chinese Communists, Hong Kong, and the Sino-Japanese War," *American Journal of Chinese Studies*, Vol. 7, No. 2 (October 2000), pp. 131–46; Yik-yi Chu, "Overt and Covert Functions of the Hong Kong Branch of the Xinhua News Agency, 1947–1984," *The Historian*, Vol. 62, No. 1 (Fall 1999), pp. 31–46.

43. Hugh D. R. Baker, "Social Change in Hong Kong: Hong Kong Man in Search of Majority," *China Quarterly*, No. 136 (1993), pp. 864 and 874.

44. Janet W. Salaff, *Working Daughters of Hong Kong: Filial Piety or Power in the Family?* (Cambridge: Cambridge University Press, 1981; New York: Columbia University Press, 1995); Chan Ka Yan, "Joss Stick Manufacturing: A Study of a Traditional Industry in Hong Kong," *Journal of the Hong Kong Branch of the Royal Asiatic Society*, Vol. 29 (1989), pp. 94–120.

45. Nicole Constable, *Christian Souls and Chinese Spirits: A Hakka Community in Hong Kong* (Berkeley: University of California Press, 1994).

46. Sally Blyth and Ian Wotherspoon, eds., *Hong Kong Remembers* (Hong Kong: Oxford University Press, 1996).

47. For example, James Hayes, a retired civil servant, provides vivid descriptions of rural society and culture in the post–World War II decades in *Friends & Teachers: Hong Kong and Its People 1953–87* (Hong Kong: Hong Kong University Press, 1996).

48. D. D. Waters, "The Country Boy Who Died for Hong Kong," *Journal of the Hong Kong Branch of the Royal Asiatic Society*, Vol. 25 (1985), pp. 210–15; Dan Waters, "Hong Kong Hongs with Long Histories and British Connections," *Journal of the Hong Kong Branch of the Royal Asiatic Society*, Vol. 30 (1990), pp. 219–56; Carl T. Smith, "The German Speaking Community in Hong Kong 1846–1918," *Journal of the Hong Kong Branch of the Royal Asiatic Society*, Vol. 34 (1994), pp. 1–55; Carl T. Smith, "The Hong Kong Amateur Dramatic Club and Its Predecessors," *Journal of the Hong Kong Branch of the Royal Asiatic Society*, Vol. 22 (1982), pp. 217–51.

   Christian missionary schools were crucial to the educational development of Hong Kong, and aroused much scholarly research. Examples are: David Walter Vikner, "The Role of Christian Missions in the Establishment of Hong Kong's System of Education" (Ed.D. diss., Columbia University Teachers College, 1987); W. J. Howard, "Diocesan Boys School Seventy Years Ago," *Journal of the Hong Kong Branch of the Royal Asiatic Society*, Vol. 24 (1984), pp. 318–24; Anna Lee, "To the Dragon Gate: Adventist Schools in South China and Hong Kong (1903–1941)," *Adventist Heritage*, Vol. 8, No. 1 (1983), pp. 52–60.

49. An example is: Anita M. Weiss, "South Asian Muslims in Hong Kong: Creation of a 'Local Boy' Identity," *Modern Asian Studies*, Vol. 25, No. 3 (1991), pp. 417–53.

50. Gordon Mathews, "Hèunggóngyàhn: On the Past, Present, and Future of Hong Kong Identity," *Bulletin of Concerned Asian Scholars*, Vol. 29, No. 3 (July–September 1997), pp. 3–13.

51. John Mark Carroll, "Empires' Edge: The Making of the Hong Kong Chinese Bourgeoisie" (Ph.D. diss., Harvard University, 1998).

52. Kam-yee Law and Cheung-wai Wong, "More Than a Primitive Imperialism: The Colonial Government and the Social Relief of Hong Kong in the Early Twentieth Century," *Journal of Contemporary China*, Vol. 6 No. 16 (1997), pp. 513–30; Zhou Hong, "The Origins of Government Social Protection Policy in Hong Kong: 1842–1941" (Ph.D. diss., Brandeis University, 1992).

53. M. Castells, L. Goh, and R. Y.-W. Kwok, *The Shek Kip Mei Syndrome: Economic Development and Public Housing in Hong Kong and Singapore* (London: Pion, 1990).

54. Anthony Sweeting mentions the chaotic policymaking of the colonial government in *A Phoenix Transformed: The Reconstruction of Education in Post-War Hong Kong* (Hong Kong: Oxford University Press, 1993). In the midst of acute housing problems in the 1950s, Alan Smart notes, the government tolerated the existence of squatter areas in Hong Kong. Read his article, "The Development of Diamond Hill from Village to Squatter Area: A Perspective on Public Housing," *Asian Journal of Public Administration*, Vol. 8, No. 1 (1986), pp. 43–63.

55. Sister Miriam Xavier, "Maryknoll Sisters, Hong Kong-Macau Region"; and Father Peter Barry, "Maryknoll in Hong Kong, 1918 to the Present," Paper presented at the Seminar on "Church History of Hong Kong" of the Centre of Asian Studies, University of Hong Kong, September 22–24, 1993.

56. Joan Chatfield, "First Choice: Mission: The Maryknoll Sisters, 1912–1975" (Ph.D. diss., Graduate Theological Union, 1983).

57. Ibid., p. 60, table 2: 1.

58. Ibid., pp. 7–8.

59. Lernoux, *Hearts on Fire,* p. xxi.

60. Some of the works of Sister Maria del Rey Danforth were: *Pacific Hopscotch* (New York: Charles Scribner's Sons, 1951); *Safari by Jet: Through Africa and Asia* (New York: Charles Scribner's Sons, 1962); and *No Two Alike: Those Maryknoll Sisters!* (New York: Dodd, Mead & Co., 1965).

61. Sister Jeanne Marie Lyons, *Maryknoll's First Lady* (New York: Dodd, Mead & Co., 1964); Sister Camilla Kennedy, *To the Uttermost Parts of the Earth: The Spirit and Charism of Mary Josephine Rogers* (Maryknoll: Maryknoll Sisters, 1987).

62. Sister Mary Victoria (written by Sister Maria del Rey Danforth), *Nun in Red China* (New York: McGraw-Hill Book Co., 1953); Sister M. Marcelline Grondin, *Sisters Carry the Gospel* (Maryknoll: World Horizon Reports, Maryknoll Publications, 1956); and Sister Mary Francis Louise Logan, *Maryknoll Sisters: A Pictorial History* (New York: E.P. Dutton & Co., 1962).

63. Bradshaw, "Catholic Sisters in China," pp. 206–09.

64. Ibid., p. 207.

65. Patricia Hughes Ponzi, "The Maryknoll Sisters in South China, 1920–1938" (M.A. thesis, St. John's University, 1980).

66. Kathleen Kelly, "Maryknoll in Manchuria, 1927–1947: A Study of Accommodation and Adaptation" (Ph.D. diss., University of Southern California, 1982).

67. Sister Mary Ann Schintz, "An Investigation of the Modernizing Role of the Maryknoll Sisters in China" (Ph.D. diss., University of Wisconsin-Madison, 1978).

68. Ibid., p. 515.

69. Wiest, *Maryknoll in China.* The book was a product of the Maryknoll China History Project, which produced 10,000 pages of transcribed material now stored in the Maryknoll Mission Archives in Maryknoll, New York. The book received excellent scholarly reviews, and demonstrated the importance of oral history.

70. Ibid., p. xiv.

71. Sister Miriam Xavier, "Maryknoll Sisters, Hong Kong-Macau Region"; and Cindy Yik-yi Chu, "From the Pursuit of Converts to the Relief of Refugees: The Maryknoll Sisters in Twentieth-Century Hong Kong," *The Historian*, Vol. 65, No. 2 (Winter 2002),

pp. 353–76. A slightly different version of Chu's article was published under the title "Maryknoll Sisters in Twentieth-Century Hong Kong," in *China Reconstructs*, ed. Cindy Yik-yi Chu and Ricardo K.S. Mak (Lanham: University Press of America, 2003), pp. 179–99. Also read Father Barry, "Maryknoll in Hong Kong, 1918 to the Present."

72. Rev. James Smith and Rev. William Downs, "The Maryknoll Mission, Hong Kong 1941–1946," *Journal of the Hong Kong Branch of the Royal Asiatic Society,* Vol. 19 (1979), pp. 27–148.

73. Bill Surface and Jim Hart, *Freedom Bridge: Maryknoll in Hong Kong* (New York: Coward-McCann, 1963).

74. Reverend Richard J. Cushing, *New Horizons: Thoughts Occasioned by the Thirtieth Anniversary of the Founding of the Maryknoll Sisters 1912–1942* (Boston: Society for the Propagation of the Faith, 1942), p. 25; Murray A. Rubinstein, "China in Maryknoll: The Sinologically-Related Holdings of the Catholic Foreign Mission Society of America," *Newsletter for Modern Chinese History* (Jindai Zhongguo shi yanjiu tongxun), Vol. 13 (March 1992), p. 179.

75. Angelyn Dries, *The Missionary Movement in American Catholic History* (Maryknoll: Orbis Book, 1998), pp. 43–57.

76. Wiest, *Maryknoll in China*, p. 20.

77. Later Rogers attended Boston Normal School where she got her diploma.

78. Sister Jeanne Marie, *Maryknoll's First Lady*, pp. 31–32.

79. Sister Betty Ann Maheu, "Mother Mary Joseph," in *Maryknoll Convent School 1925–2000,* ed. Aloysius Lee (Hong Kong: Maryknoll Convent School, 2000), p. 23.

80. Sister Jeanne Marie, *Maryknoll's First Lady*, pp. 34–35.

81. Ibid., pp. 35–41.

82. Wiest, *Maryknoll in China*, p. 25.

83. Ibid, pp. 25–27.

84. Sister Mary Francis Louise, *Maryknoll Sisters*, p. 7.

85. Sister Jeanne Marie, *Maryknoll's First Lady*, pp. 85–86; Sister Camilla, *To the Uttermost Parts of the Earth*, pp. 24–25.

86. Sister Camilla, *To the Uttermost Parts of the Earth*, p. 25.

87. Sister Jeanne Marie, *Maryknoll's First Lady*, pp. 104–05.

88. Dries, *The Missionary Movement in American Catholic History*, p. 77.

89. Sister Camilla, *To the Uttermost Parts of the Earth*, p. 33.

90. Ibid., p. 34.

91. Ibid., p. 47; Robert, *American Women in Mission,* pp. 352–53.

92. Robert, *American Women in Mission,* pp. 358–59.

93. Sister Camilla, *To the Uttermost Parts of the Earth*, p. 51.

94. Ibid.

95. Sister Camilla, *To the Uttermost Parts of the Earth*, p. 52.

96. *Tentative Constitutions of the Foreign Mission Sisters of St. Dominic (Third Order), Congregation of the Immaculate Conception, at Maryknoll, Ossining, New York* (drafted in 1917, in use in 1925), p. 1, CONSTITUTIONS-MMA.

97. Ibid., p. 55.

98. Ibid., p. 4.

99. Ibid., pp. 8–18.

100. Ibid., p. 18.

101. Ibid., p. 19.

102. Ibid., p. 1.

103. Cushing, *New Horizons*, pp. 28–29.

104. Sisters Mary Lou Martin and Agnes Chou, Interview by Cindy Yik-yi Chu in Maryknoll Convent, Boundary Street, Kowloon, Hong Kong, August 12, 2000.

105. Sister Miriam Xavier, "Maryknoll Sisters, Hong Kong-Macau Region," p. 1.

Chapter Two   Early Arrival, 1921–1937

1. Sister Mary Paul McKenna (Hong Kong) to Mother Mary Joseph Rogers (Maryknoll Sisters' Motherhouse), February 1, 1922, 3rd page, Folder 1, Box 1, RCSC-MMA.
2. Sister Mary Imelda Sheridan, "A History of the South China Region 1921–1958" (written in 1959), p. 2, Folder 1, Box 1, SCR-MMA.
3. Ibid.
4. According to Sister Joan Chatfield: "The early missioners went to the Orient with little thought of returning. It would be several years before an organized program of home visits would be established whose structure was seen as part of the mission education of the United States as well as rest, respite and renewal for the missioner." As she elaborates on the program: "The initial *decennial* program began in 1946 with Sisters returning every tenth year for an ordered time of study and home visit. The interim *furlough* program, following Vatican Council II, allowed more flexibility regarding opportunities for enrichment, study and prayer. The current *renewal* program, initiated in 1974, allows a four months' return to the United States each five years under Regional funds with the approval of the Central Governing Board." Read Joan Chatfield, "First Choice: Mission: The Maryknoll Sisters, 1912–1975" (Ph.D. diss., Graduate Theological Union, 1983), pp. 34 and 229, n. 21 (emphases in original).
5. Sister Mary Imelda, "A History of the South China Region," p. 2; Reverend George C. Powers, *The Maryknoll Movement* (Maryknoll: Catholic Foreign Mission Society of America, 1926), p. 115; Sister Therese Howard, "Mission to the Middle Kingdom: 75 Years Ago the First Group of Maryknoll Sisters Set Sail for China," *Sunday Examiner*, November 1, 1996, p. 8, Folder 14, Box 6, CWPP-MMA.
6. Sister Mary Imelda, "A History of the South China Region," pp. 2–3; Holy Spirit Study Centre, *Tianzhujiao nuxiuhui dui Zhongguo jiaohui he shehui de gongxian [The Contribution of the Catholic Sisters' Congregations to the Church and Society of China]* (Hong Kong: Holy Spirit Study Centre, 1997), p. 11.
7. Penny Lernoux, *Hearts on Fire: The Story of the Maryknoll Sisters* (Maryknoll: Orbis Books, 1993), p. 46.
8. Sister Mary Paul McKenna, Interview by Sister Joanna Chan, April 10, 1980, p. 3, MCHP-MMA.
9. R. L. Jarman, ed., *Hong Kong Annual Administration Reports 1841–1941*, Archive ed., Vol. 4: 1920–1930 (Farnham Common, 1996), pp. 26–27.
10. S. G. Davis, *Hong Kong in Its Geographical Setting* (London: Collins, 1949), p. 215.
11. Jarman, *Hong Kong Annual Administration Reports*, Vol. 4, p. 50.
12. *Maryknoll Mission Letters—China* (New York: Macmillan Co., 1927), Vol. II, p. 124.
13. Father Sergio Ticozzi, ed., *Historical Documents of the Hong Kong Catholic Church* (Hong Kong: Hong Kong Catholic Diocesan Archives, 1997), p. 220.
14. Interview of Sister Mary Paul, April 10, 1980, p. 3.
15. Sister Mary Imelda Sheridan, Interview by Sister Jeanne Marie Lyons, December 1956, p. 1, File Box A-1, MMJC-MMA.
16. Sister Mary Paul to Mother Mary Joseph, November 3, 1921, 4 pages, Folder 1, Box 1, RCSC-MMA.
17. Sister Mary Paul to Mother Mary Joseph, November 8, 1921, 8 pages, Folder 1, Box 1, RCSC-MMA.
18. Sister Mary Paul to Mother Mary Joseph, November 26, 1921, 4 pages, Folder 1, Box 1, RCSC-MMA.
19. Report of Proceedings of the Public Works Committee at a Meeting held on February 5, 1920, p. 48, Legislative Council Sessional Papers 1920–1940, Hong Kong Government Reports Online (1853–1941), University of Hong Kong.
20. Interview of Sister Mary Paul, April 24, 1980, p. 13.
21. Interview of Sister Mary Paul, April 10, 1980, p. 4.

22. Ibid.
23. Interview of Sister Mary Paul, April 10, 1980, p. 6.
24. Interview of Sister Mary Paul, April 24, 1980, p. 18.
25. Sister Mary Paul to Mother Mary Joseph, February 1, 1922, 1st page, Folder 1, Box 1, RCSC-MMA.
26. *Tentative Constitutions of the Foreign Mission Sisters of St. Dominic (Third Order), Congregation of the Immaculate Conception, at Maryknoll, Ossining, New York, U.S.A.* (drafted in 1917; First Constitutions in use after General Chapter of 1925), p. 25.
27. Sister Mary Paul to Mother Mary Joseph, February 1, 1922, 2nd page.
28. Interview of Sister Mary Paul, April 10, 1980, p. 2.
29. Sister Mary Paul to Mother Mary Joseph, January 31, 1922, 2nd page, Folder 1, Box 1, RCSC-MMA.
30. Interview of Sister Mary Paul, April 24, 1980, p. 18.
31. Sister Mary Paul to Mother Mary Joseph, February 1, 1922, 5th page.
32. Father Superior James Anthony Walsh to Father James Edward Walsh (Hong Kong), December 16, 1921, 1 page, Folder 1, Box 1, RCSC-MMA.
33. Sister Mary Paul to Mother Mary Joseph, January 31, 1922, 2nd page.
34. Sister Mary Paul to Mother Mary Joseph, June 28, 1922, 2 pages, Folder 1, Box 1, RCSC-MMA.
35. Interview of Sister Mary Paul, April 24, 1980, p. 17; Sister Mary Paul to Mother Mary Joseph, October 2, 1922, 1 page, Folder 1, Box 1, RCSC-MMA.
36. Interview of Sister Mary Paul, April 10, 1980, p. 2.
37. Sister Mary Paul to Mother Mary Joseph, December 21, 1922, pp. 3–4, Folder 1, Box 1, RCSC-MMA.
38. Ibid., pp. 4–5.
39. Sister Mary Ann Schintz, "An Investigation of the Modernizing Role of the Maryknoll Sisters in China" (Ph.D. diss., University of Wisconsin-Madison, 1978), p. 327.
40. Sister Mary Imelda, "A History of the South China Region," p. 3. The word "procure" was used in the Sisters' correspondence and writings. As Jean-Paul Wiest explains: "This word, borrowed from the French, is a term commonly used by Catholic missionary societies. It refers to a house or office in some convenient location to which missioners can look for service in procuring needed supplies, exchanging checks, and so forth. A procure also serves, when large enough, as a hostel for passing missioners." See Jean-Paul Wiest, *Maryknoll in China: A History, 1918–1955* (Armonk: M.E. Sharpe, 1988), p. 60 footnote.
41. Sister Miriam Xavier Mug, "Maryknoll Sisters, Hong Kong-Macau Region: A History—1921–1998" (Unpublished, March 2000), p. 1; Interview of Sister Mary Paul, April 10, 1980, p. 3.
42. Sister Mary Eunice Tolan and Sister Mary Incarnata Farrelly, comp., *Maryknoll Distaff—1922* (Unpublished, 1970), p. 24, MMA.
43. Sister Mary Imelda, "A History of the South China Region," p. 5.
44. *Personnel*, 1922, p. 3, Folder 3, Box 1, LISTS-MMA.
45. *Personnel*, 1923, p. 3, Folder 3, Box 1, LISTS-MMA.
46. Sister Mary Paul to Mother Mary Joseph, December 21, 1922, pp. 1–3, Folder 1, Box 1, RCSC-MMA.
47. Sister Mary Paul to Mother Mary Joseph (through Father Superior), January 15, 1923, p. 2, Folder 2, Box 1, RCSC-MMA.
48. Interview of Sister Mary Paul, April 10, 1980, p. 9.
49. Ibid., p. 8.
50. Ibid.
51. Interview of Sister Mary Paul, April 10, 1980, pp. 7–9.
52. Sister Miriam Xavier, "Maryknoll Sisters, Hong Kong-Macau Region," p. 1.

53. Sister Mary Imelda, "A History of the South China Region," p. 5; "Kowloon—Later Kowloon Tong" (A report giving the general background and development of the central mission at Kowloon, Hong Kong, 1921–1942), 1st page, Folder 2, Box 2, SCR-MMA.

54. Sister Miriam Xavier, "Maryknoll Sisters, Hong Kong-Macau Region," p. 1; Sister Mary Paul to Mother Mary Joseph, January 15, 1923, pp. 6–7; Interview of Sister Mary Paul, April 10, 1980, p. 9.

55. Interview of Sister Mary Paul, April 10, 1980, p. 10.

56. Sister Miriam Xavier, "Maryknoll Sisters, Hong Kong-Macau Region," p. 1.

57. Mother Mary Joseph to Sister Mary Paul, March 6, 1923, p. 1, Folder 2, Box 1, RCSC-MMA.

58. Sister Jeanne Marie Lyons, *Maryknoll's First Lady* (New York: Dodd, Mead & Co., 1964), p. 143.

59. Ibid., pp. 143–44.

60. Lernoux, *Hearts on Fire*, p. 46.

61. Ibid., p. 47.

62. Sister Maria Teresa Yeung, Interview by Sister Jeanne Marie Lyons, October 12, 1956, 1 page, File Box A-1, MMJC-MMA.

63. Sister Betty Ann Maheu, "Mother Mary Joseph," in *Maryknoll Convent School 1925–2000*, ed. Aloysius Lee (Hong Kong: Maryknoll Convent School, 2000), p. 27.

64. Sister Barbara Hendricks, "The Legacy of Mary Josephine Rogers," *International Bulletin of Missionary Research*, Vol. 21, No. 2 (April 1997), p. 5 (of 12 pages of printouts made available through the Academic Search Elite database).

65. Ibid., p. 6.

66. For Jean-Paul Wiest's description of the "Kaying Method" (Jiaying method), read *Maryknoll in China*, pp. 99–109.

67. Sister Mary Francis Louise Logan, *Maryknoll Sisters: A Pictorial History* (New York: E.P. Dutton & Co., 1962), p. 24.

68. Ibid., pp. 24–26; Lernoux, *Hearts on Fire*, p. 47.

69. Interview of Sister Mary Paul, April 10, 1980, p. 1.

70. Interview of Sister Mary Paul, April 24, 1980, p. 15.

71. Ibid.; Sister Mary Liguori Quinlan, "Embroidery and Vestments and Church Linens, Hong Kong, Kowloon Tong, Maryknoll," n.d., 1st page, Folder 1, Box 2, SCR-MMA.

72. Sister Mary Liguori, "Embroidery and Vestments and Church Linens," 1st page.

73. Ibid., 3rd page.

74. Ibid., 2nd page.

75. Ibid.

76. Sister Mary Liguori, "Embroidery and Vestments and Church Linens," 2nd and 3rd pages.

77. Sister Mary Reginald Silva, "History, Organization and Management of Cassock Department, Hong Kong," n.d., pp. 1–3, Folder 1, Box 2, SCR-MMA.

78. Bishop Dominic Pozzoni, Vicar Apostolic, to A. G. M. Fletcher, Colonial Secretary, April 24, 1923, 1 page; Father Superior James Anthony Walsh to Bishop Pozzoni, July 13, 1923, 1 page, Folder 1, Box 43: Religious Sisters Congregations—Maryknoll Sisters, V-HKCDA.

79. Wiest, *Maryknoll in China*, pp. 157–58.

80. Copy of the Agreement attached to the letter from Sister Mary Paul to Mother Mary Joseph, October 7, 1924, p. 1, Folder 3, Box 1, RCSC-MMA.

81. "Concerning Kowloon Hospital—Extracts from *South China Morning Post*—'Correspondence' Columns," enclosed with the letter from Sister Mary Paul to Mother Mary Joseph, November 19, 1924, Folder 3, Box 1, RCSC-MMA.

82. Ibid.

83. Ibid.

84. Ibid.

85. Interview of Sister Mary Paul, March 4, 1981, pp. 8–9.

86. Lernoux, *Hearts on Fire*, p. 48.

87. Catholic Foreign Mission Society of America, *Maryknoll: Hong Kong Chronicle* (Hong Kong: Catholic Foreign Mission Society of America, 1978), p. 5.

88. "Concerning Kowloon Hospital—Extracts from *South China Morning Post*—'Correspondence' Columns," enclosed with the letter from Sister Mary Paul to Mother Mary Joseph, November 19, 1924.

89. "Selected Letters, Mother Mary Joseph to Sisters in South China, 1923–1948," n.d., p. 2, Folder 3, Box 1, RCSC-MMA.

90. Mother Mary Joseph to Sister Mary Paul, March 25, 1925, 1st page, Folder 4, Box 1, RCSC-MMA.

91. Schintz, "Modernizing Role of the Maryknoll Sisters," p. 314.

92. Sister Mary Paul to Mother Mary Joseph, January 15, 1923, pp. 5–6.

93. Ibid., p. 6 (emphases in original).

94. Sister Mary Paul to Mother Mary Joseph, April 6, 1923, pp. 1–2, Folder 2, Box 1, RCSC-MMA.

95. Sister Mary Paul to Bishop Pozzoni, February 22, 1923, 2 pages, and February 23, 1923, 1 page, Folder 1, Box 43, V-HKCDA.

96. Father Peter de Maria was a strong advocate of expansion in educational services. See Thomas F. Ryan, S.J., *The Story of a Hundred Years: The Pontifical Institute of Foreign Missions, (P.I.M.E.), in Hong Kong, 1858–1958* (Hong Kong: Catholic Truth Society, 1959), pp. 153–54.

97. Victor F. S. Sit, *Xianggang fazhan dituji (Hong Kong: 150 Years, Development in Maps)* (Hong Kong: Joint Publishing (H.K.) Co., 2001), pp. 94–95.

98. Sister Mary Paul to Mother Mary Joseph, May 9, 1923, p. 1, Folder 2, Box 1, RCSC-MMA; Schintz, "Modernizing Role of the Maryknoll Sisters," p. 316.

99. Interview of Sister Mary Paul, April 21, 1980, p. 12; Wiest, *Maryknoll in China*, pp. 50–51.

100. Sister Mary Paul to Mother Mary Joseph, May 9, 1923, pp. 1–2.

101. Ibid., p. 2.

102. Ibid., pp. 2–3.

103. Bishop Pozzoni to Fletcher, May 16, 1923, 1 page, and June 30, 1923, 2 pages, Folder 1, Box 10: St. Teresa's Church, IV-HKCDA; Letter from A. E. Wright, Pro-Director of Public Works, to Colonial Secretary, June 5, 1923, HKRS 58-1-114-46 "Application of Roman Catholic Mission for Three Areas near Kowloon Tong for Erection of Church, Training School, Girls' School and Houses for Portuguese," PRO-HK.

104. Sister Mary Paul to Mother Mary Joseph, May 7, 1924, p. 1, Folder 2, Box 1, RCSC-MMA.

105. Sir Claud Severn, Colonial Secretary, to Governor, September 23, 1924, HKRS 58-1-114-46, PRO-HK; Severn to Reverend John Spada, Pro-Vicar Apostolic of Hong Kong, September 24, 1924, 1 page, Folder 1, Box 10, IV-HKCDA.

106. Spada to Severn, October 29, 1924, 1 page; hand-drawn map related to the previous letter, November 18, 1924; Severn to Spada, December 1, 1924, 1 page, Folder 1, Box 10, IV-HKCDA.

107. Sister Mary Paul to Mother Mary Joseph, January 15, 1925, p. 2, Folder 4, Box 1, RCSC-MMA; Interview of Sister Mary Paul, April 24, 1980, p. 16.

108. Sister Mary Paul to Mother Mary Joseph, January 15, 1925, p. 3.

109. Ibid.

110. *Maryknoll Convent School 1925–2000*, pp. 31–32.

111. Sister Rosalie Weber, Interview by Sister Joanna Chan, July 31, 1981, p. 3, MCHP-MMA.

112. Sister Mary Paul to Father Superior, April 5, 1927, 4 pages, Folder 4, Box 1, RCSC-MMA.

113. Sister Mary Paul to Mother Mary Joseph, August 24, 1928, p. 1, Folder 5, Box 1, RCSC-MMA.
114. Ibid.
115. Ibid.
116. Raymond Kerrison, *Bishop Walsh of Maryknoll: A Biography* (New York: G.P. Putnam's Sons, 1962), p. 172.
117. *Maryknoll Distaff—1927*, p. 10, MMA.
118. Hendricks, "The Legacy of Mary Josephine Rogers," p. 6 (taken from printouts).
119. Ibid., citing Mother Mary Joseph, "Mission Policy," August 17, 1929, Folder 1 (a), Box 12, Mother Mary Joseph Rogers Papers, MMA.
120. *Personnel*, 1929, p. 7, Folder 4, Box 1, LISTS-MMA.
121. Hendricks, "The Legacy of Mary Josephine Rogers," p. 6 (taken from printouts).
122. Mother Mary Joseph shared Ford's view of the active role of the Sisters in direct apostolate. Ford experimented with his idea in Yangjiang before he was assigned to Jiaying in 1925. In the 1930s, the Maryknoll Sisters in Jiaying took an active role in visiting the villages. Wiest, *Maryknoll in China*, pp. 101–05.
123. Bishop Henry Valtorta, Vicar Apostolic to Colonial Secretary, May 18, 1928, 1 page; Colonial Secretary to Valtorta, June 26, 1928, 1 page; Valtorta to Colonial Secretary, July 3, 1928, 1 page, plus attached map, Folder 1, Box 10, IV-HKCDA; Letter from Wright to Colonial Secretary, October 5, 1928, HKRS 58-1-145-18 "Kowloon Inland Lot No. 2153: Application from Right Rev. Bishop Valtorta to Purchase an Area at the Junction of Prince Edward Road and Waterloo Road," PRO-HK.
124. Bishop Valtorta to Colonial Secretary, July 3, 1928, 1 page, Folder 1, Box 10, IV-HKCDA; Letter from Wright to Colonial Secretary, October 5, 1928, HKRS 58-1-145-18 "Kowloon Inland Lot No. 2153," PRO-HK.
125. Ryan, *The Story of a Hundred Years*, pp. 197–98.
126. Bishop Henry Valtorta to Sister Mary Paul, May 6, 1929, 1 page, Folder 5, Box 1, RCSC-MMA.
127. Sister Mary Lawrence Foley to Sister Mary Paul, October 17, 1929, pp. 1–2, Folder 5, Box 1, RCSC-MMA.
128. Ibid., p. 2.
129. Ibid., p. 4.
130. Letters from G. P. de Martin, Director of Education to Colonial Secretary, June 27 and July 26, 1930, HKRS 58-1-158-39 "Kowloon Inland Lot No. 1419: Application from Father Spada to Purchase an Area at the Junction of Waterloo Road and Boundary Street for the Erection of a Girls' School," PRO-HK.
131. Letter from the Governor to Lord Passfield, October 21, 1930, 2 pages, CO 129/528/4 "Sale of Land to Maryknoll Sisters for use as a girls' school," Hong Kong Collection, Main Library, University of Hong Kong.
132. Sister Mary Paul to Mother Mary Joseph, January 7, 1931, 2 pages, Folder 6, Box 1, RCSC-MMA.
133. Luk Hung-kay, *A History of Education in Hong Kong*, Report Submitted to Lord Wilson Heritage Trust (Hong Kong: n.p., 2000), pp. 43–52.
134. Sister Mary Imelda, "A History of the South China Region," p. 7.
135. Sister Mary Paul to Mother Mary Joseph, April 17, 1931, pp. 1–2, Folder 6, Box 1, RCSC-MMA.
136. Sister Mary Paul to Mother Mary Joseph, September 22, 1932, 1 page, Folder 6, Box 1, RCSC-MMA.
137. Sister Mary Paul to Mother Mary Joseph, October 27, 1933, 1 page, Folder 1, Box 2, RCSC-MMA.
138. Sister Mary Paul to Mother Mary Joseph, April 25, 1933, p. 2, Folder 1, Box 2, RCSC-MMA.

139. A list of the qualifications and experience of the Maryknoll Sisters teaching at Maryknoll Convent School and Holy Spirit School] n.d. (1939?), 6 pages, Folder 4, Box 2, RCSC-MMA; Sister M. de Ricci Cain, Interview by Sister Virginia Unsworth, November 20, 1980, personal data sheet, MCHP-MMA.

140. An Ordinance to provide for the Incorporation of the Regional Superior in Hong Kong of the Foreign Mission Sisters of St. Dominic commonly known as Maryknoll Sisters, (or in short, "Foreign Mission Sisters of St. Dominic" Incorporation Ordinance), No. 20 of 1934 of the Legislative Council of the Colony of Hong Kong, July 27, 1934.

141. Sister Mary Paul to Mother Mary Joseph, April 17, 1931, p. 2.

142. Sister Mary Paul to Mother Mary Joseph, March 22, 1934, p. 1, and attached newspaper clipping, Folder 1, Box 2, RCSC-MMA.

143. Sister Mary Paul to Mother Mary Joseph, May 29, 1935, p. 1, Folder 2, Box 2, RCSC-MMA.

144. *Maryknoll Convent School 1925–2000*, p. 76.

Chapter Three   Difficult Years, 1937–1951

1. Sister Santa Maria Manning, "Hong Kong Happenings," n.d., p. 1, Folder 9, Box 1, PNWWII-MMA.

2. R. L. Jarman, ed., *Hong Kong Annual Administration Reports 1841–1941*, Archive ed., Vol. 5: 1931–1939 (Farnham Common, 1996), p. 303.

3. Sister Miriam Xavier Mug, "Maryknoll Sisters, Hong Kong-Macau Region: A History— 1921–1998" (Unpublished, March 2000), p. 44.

4. Penny Lernoux, *Hearts on Fire: The Story of the Maryknoll Sisters* (Maryknoll: Orbis Books, 1993), pp. 48–49.

5. Ibid., p. 48.

6. Ibid.

7. Sister Mary Gemma Shea, Interview by Sister Joanna Chan, July 9, 1980, p. 5, MCHP-MMA.

8. Ibid., p. 6.

9. Sister Mary Paul McKenna, Interview by Sister Joanna Chan in Maryknoll, New York, June 25, 1980, pp. 6, 9, MCHP-MMA.

10. Sister Mary Imelda Sheridan, "A History of the South China Region 1921–1958" (written in 1959), p. 16, Folder 1, Box 1, SCR-MMA.

11. An essay on the history of the Maryknoll Sisters in Hong Kong from 1921 through the war years, n.d., pp. 2–3, Folder 9, Box 1, PNWWII-MMA.

12. Sister Mary Imelda, "A History of the South China Region," pp. 16–17.

13. Sister Santa Maria Manning, "A Brief History of Five Decades of Maryknoll Convent School," dated February 1975, p. 1, Folder 2, Box 5, SCR-MMA.

14. Ibid., p. 2; Sister Mary Ann Schintz, "An Investigation of the Modernizing Role of the Maryknoll Sisters in China" (Ph.D. diss., University of Wisconsin-Madison, 1978), p. 321.

15. "Grant Code," dated September 1941, p. 1; "Grant Code Part IV," p. 1, Folder 1, Box 5, SCR-MMA.

16. Aloysius Lee, ed., *Maryknoll Convent School 1925–2000* (Hong Kong: Maryknoll Convent School, 2000), p. 34; An essay on the history, p. 2.

17. "Grant Code Part IV," p. 1.

18. Ibid. p. 3

19. Ibid.

20. Lernoux, *Hearts on Fire*, p. 87.

21. Sister Jeanne Marie Lyons, *Maryknoll's First Lady* (New York: Dodd, Mead & Co., 1964), p. 235.

22. Catholic Foreign Mission Society of America, *Maryknoll: Hong Kong Chronicle* (Hong Kong: Catholic Foreign Mission Society of America, 1978), p. 26.
23. Lernoux, *Hearts on Fire*, p. 87; Sister Jeanne Marie, *Maryknoll's First Lady*, pp. 235–36.
24. Sister Jeanne Marie, *Maryknoll's First Lady*, pp. 240–41.
25. Sister Mary Imelda, "A History of the South China Region," p. 21.
26. Sister Santa Maria, "Hong Kong Happenings," p. 1.
27. HKRS 112-1-1 "Provisional Lists of British and Foreign (Other Than Japanese) Casualties, Prisoners of War and Internees in Hong Kong Compiled in the Month Following the Surrender of British Forces to the Japanese," n.d. (December 1941), PRO-HK.
28. Sister Santa Maria, "Hong Kong Happenings," p. 1.
29. Ibid., p. 2.
30. An essay on the history, p. 6.
31. Ibid., pp. 5–6.
32. Sister Santa Maria, "Hong Kong Happenings," p. 3.
33. Ibid.
34. Ibid.; Sister Mary Imelda, "A History of the South China Region," p. 21.
35. Sister Santa Maria, "Hong Kong Happenings," pp. 3–4.
36. Ibid., p. 4.
37. An essay on the history, p. 17a.
38. HKRS 112-1-1 "Provisional Lists of British and Foreign (Other Than Japanese) Casualties, Prisoners of War and Internees in Hong Kong."
39. Sister Santa Maria, "Hong Kong Happenings," p. 5.
40. An essay on the history, p. 12.
41. Sister Mary Imelda, "A History of the South China Region," p. 22.
42. Sister Santa Maria, "Hong Kong Happenings," p. 4.
43. Ibid., p. 5.
44. Ibid., p. 4.
45. Sister Cecilia Marie Carvalho, "Conditions in HongKong after the Outbreak of the War," n.d., p. 4, Folder 9, Box 1, PNWWII-MMA.
46. An essay on the history, p. 19.
47. Ibid.
48. *Maryknoll Distaff—1942–1951*, p. 12, MMA.
49. Geoffrey Charles Emerson, "Behind Japanese Barbed Wire: Stanley Internment Camp, Hong Kong, 1942–1945," *Journal of the Hong Kong Branch of the Royal Asiatic Society*, Vol. 17 (1977), p. 30.
50. List of "Sisters Who Were Stationed in Hong Kong at the Beginning of World War II—Dec. 1942," n.d., Folder 1, Box 1; News Release to N.C.W.C., December 17, 1941, pp. 1–2, Folder 9, Box 1, PNWWII-MMA.
51. Sister Santa Maria, "Hong Kong Happenings," p. 5.
52. Sister Cecilia Marie, "Conditions in Hong Kong after the Outbreak of the War," p. 5.
53. Sister Santa Maria, "Hong Kong Happenings," p. 5.
54. Sister Mary Amata Brachtesende, "Thoughts—As They Come," n.d., p. 4, Folder 9, Box 1, PNWWII-MMA.
55. Emerson, "Behind Japanese Barbed Wire," pp. 31–32.
56. "The Story of the Internment Camp," n.d., p. C-3, Folder 9, Box 1, PNWWII-MMA.
57. Reverend James Smith and Reverend William Downs, "The Maryknoll Mission, Hong Kong 1941–1946," *Journal of the Hong Kong Branch of the Royal Asiatic Society*, Vol. 19 (1979), p. 78.
58. Canadians and Australians belonged to the British category; and during internment, there were also other Europeans. Emerson, "Behind Japanese Barbed Wire," pp. 31–33; Bernice Archer and Kent Fedorowich, "The Women of Stanley: Internment in Hong

Kong, 1942–45," *Women's History Review*, Vol. 5, No. 3 (1996), p. 390, n. 2; Smith and Downs, "The Maryknoll Mission, Hong Kong," p. 77.

59. A. D. Blackburn, "Hong Kong, December 1941–July 1942," *Journal of the Hong Kong Branch of the Royal Asiatic Society,* Vol. 29 (1989), p. 82.
60. Sister Mary Amata, "Thoughts—As They Come," p. 5.
61. Sister Frances Marion Gardner, "Hong Kong War Experience," n.d., p. 9; Sister Mary Liguori Quinlan, "Kowloon Tong, December 8th, 1941 – Stanley June 29th, 1942," n.d., p. 5, Folder 9, Box 1, PNWWII-MMA.
62. Sister Frances Marion, "HongKong War Experience," p. 9.
63. Sister Mary Liguori, "Kowloon Tong, December 8th, 1941 – Stanley June 29th, 1942," p. 6.
64. Ibid.
65. Sister Mary Amata, "Thoughts—As They Come," p. 5.
66. Sister Santa Maria, "Hong Kong Happenings," p. 6.
67. Sister Mary Liguori, "Kowloon Tong, December 8th, 1941 – Stanley June 29th, 1942," p. 6.
68. Sister Santa Maria, "Hong Kong Happenings," p. 6.
69. Sister Mary Liguori, "Kowloon Tong, December 8th, 1941 – Stanley June 29th, 1942," pp. 6–7.
70. Sister Santa Maria, "Hong Kong Happenings," p. 6.
71. Sister Mary Gonzaga Rizzardi, "Repatriation Account," n.d., p. 3, Folder 9, Box 1, PNWWII-MMA.
72. Sister Mary Amata, "Thoughts—As They Come," p. 5 (emphasis in original, underlined in original text).
73. Ibid.
74. Sister Beatrice Ann Stapleton (Matthew Marie), "Repatriation Account," n.d., p. 8, Folder 9, Box 1, PNWWII-MMA.
75. Sister Frances Marion, "HongKong War Experience," p. 12.
76. Ibid.
77. Ibid.
78. Sister Mary Amata, "Thoughts—As They Come," p. 5.
79. "The Story of the Internment Camp," p. C5; Sister Mary Imelda, "A History of the South China Region," p. 22.
80. "The Story of the Internment Camp," pp. C7–C8.
81. Ibid., p. C8.
82. Ibid., p. C9.
83. Sister Mary Amata, "Thoughts—As They Come," p. 5.
84. Sister Cecilia Marie, "Conditions in HongKong after the Outbreak of the War," pp. 5–6.
85. Sister Candida Maria Basto to the Officer in Charge, Internment Camp Office, Hong Kong, March 6, 1942, 1 page, Folder 1, Box 43, V-HKCDA.
86. Bishop Henry Valtorta to The Foreign Section, Imperial Japanese Government, Hong Kong, March 24, 1942, 1 page, Folder 1, Box 43, V-HKCDA.
87. Sister Mary Clement Quinn, "Co-Prosperity and the New Order Comes to Hongkong," pp. 1–2, Folder 9, Box 1, PNWWII-MMA.
88. Ibid., p. 2.
89. Ibid.
90. Sister Mary Clement, "Co-Prosperity and the New Order Comes to Hongkong," pp. 2–5.
91. Ibid., pp. 3–6.
92. Sister Frances Marion, "HongKong War Experience," p. 13.
93. Sister Mary Amata Brachtesende, Interview by Sr. Virginia Johnson in Maryknoll, New York, July 8, 1981, p. 26, MCHP-MMA.
94. Sister Mary Paul McKenna, "Report of Foreign Mission Sisters of St. Dominic (Maryknoll Sisters), Hong Kong" (dated August 10, 1942) enclosed in the letter from Sister Mary Paul (Hong Kong) to Mother Mary Joseph (Maryknoll Sisters' Motherhouse), August 14, 1942, pp. 1–2, Folder 9, Box 1, PNWWII-MMA.

95. Emerson, "Behind Japanese Barbed Wire," p. 33; Smith and Downs, "The Maryknoll Mission, Hong Kong," p. 110.

96. Sister Mary Christella Furey, "On the Outside Looking in," n.d. (1943?), p. 4, Folder 9, Box 1, PNWWII-MMA.

97. Letter from Maryknoll Bishop Adolph J. Paschang to Sister Mary Paul, September 1, 1942, 1 page, Folder 1, Box 43, V-HKCDA.

98. Sister Mary Paul to Bishop Valtorta, September 10, 1942, 1 page, Folder 1, Box 43, V-HKCDA.

99. Sister Mary Eucharista Coupe, "My Impressions of Hong Kong after Leaving Camp," n.d., p. 1, Folder 9, Box 1, PNWWII-MMA.

100. Ibid., p. 2.

101. Ibid.

102. Sister Mary Eucharista, "My Impressions," p. 4.

103. Sister Mary Paul to Mother Mary Joseph, October 25, 1945, p. 1, Folder 9, Box 2, RCSC-MMA.

104. Sister Mary Paul to Mother Mary Joseph, November 30, 1945, pp. 1–2, Folder 9, Box 2, RCSC-MMA.

105. Sister Mary Paul to Brigadier D. M. MacDougall, Chief of Civil Affairs, November 16, 1945, pp. 1–3; Sister Mary Paul to Major-General F. W. Festing, General Officer Commanding, November 19, 1945, pp. 1–3, Folder 9, Box 2, RCSC-MMA.

106. Sister Mary Paul to Festing, November 19, 1945, p. 2.

107. Sister Mary Paul to Mother Mary Joseph, November 30, 1945, pp. 1–2.

108. Ibid., p. 2.

109. Sister Mary Paul to Mother Mary Joseph, December 13, 1945, p. 1, Folder 9, Box 2; Sister Mary Paul to Mother Mary Joseph, January 9, 1946, p. 1, Folder 3, Box 3, RCSC-MMA.

110. Sister Mary Paul to Mother Mary Joseph, January 11, 1946, p. 1, Folder 3, Box 3, RCSC-MMA.

111. Ibid.

112. Sister Mary Paul to Sister M. Regina Reardon (Maryknoll Sisters' Motherhouse), January 15, 1946, 1 page; Purchase Order from Sister Mary Paul to Sister M. Andre Seiler (Maryknoll Sisters' Motherhouse), January 16, 1946, 2 pages; Duplicates of Orders Previously Sent from Sister Mary Paul to Sister M. Andre, January 16, 1946, 2 pages, Folder 3, Box 3, RCSC-MMA.

113. Sister Mary Paul to Mother Mary Joseph, March 29, 1946, p. 2, Folder 3, Box 3, RCSC-MMA.

114. Chronicle, September 26–December 31, 1945, Kowloon Tong Convent, p. 4, Folder 1, Box 5: Chronicles—Asia, South China (War Years) 1942–1968, CHRONICLES-MMA.

115. *Silver Jubilee of St. Teresa's Church 1932–1957* (Hong Kong: St. Teresa's Church, 1957), no page number; Chronicle 1946, Kowloon Tong Convent, p. 1, Folder 2, Box 2: Hong Kong Chronicles, CHRONICLES-MMA.

116. Sister Marie Corinne Rost, Interview by Cindy Yik-yi Chu in Maryknoll Sisters Center, Maryknoll, New York, July 24, 2001.

117. Sister Santa Maria, "A Brief History of Five Decades of Maryknoll Convent School," p. 2.

118. "Maryknoll Convent School, Inspection Report 1947/48," dated December 7, 1948, Folder 1, Box 5, SCR-MMA.

119. Sister Miriam Xavier, "Maryknoll Sisters, Hong Kong-Macau Region," p. 26; Lee, ed., *Maryknoll Convent School 1925–2000*, p. 39.

120. Sister Mary Imelda, "A History of the South China Region," p. 31.

121. Personnel List, 1946, p. 11, Folder 3, Box 2, LISTS-MMA.

122. Sister Rose Duchesne Debrecht, Interview by Sister Virginia Unsworth in Hong Kong, July 19, 1981, p. 6, MCHP-MMA.
123. Ibid., pp. 9–10.
124. Ibid., p. 18.
125. Ibid., p. 12.
126. Ibid.
127. HKRS 156-1-323 "No. 140 Caine Road on Inland Lot No. 2300: Application from the Maryknoll Sisters for the Recovering of No. 140 Caine Road for the Purpose of a School," PRO-HK.
128. Maryknoll School, Caine Road Diaries, August 1948, pp. 1–2, Folder 6, Box 31: Hong Kong, DIARIES-MMA.
129. Maryknoll School, Caine Road Diaries, September 1948, p. 1, Folder 6, Box 31, DIARIES-MMA.
130. Ibid., pp. 1, 3.
131. Sister Mary Francis Louise Logan, *Maryknoll Sisters: A Pictorial History* (New York: E.P. Dutton & Co., 1962), pp. 138–42.
132. Ibid., p. 142.
133. Sister Mary Imelda, "A History of the South China Region," p. 32.

Chapter Four   Extreme Poverty of the 1950s, King's Park and Tung Tau Tsuen

1. "Refugee Work in Hong Kong," 1954, p. 1, Folder 3, Box 8, SCR-MMA.
2. Peter Hodge, "Social Policy: An Historical Perspective as Seen in Colonial Policy," *Journal of Oriental Studies*, Vol. 11, No. 2 (1973), pp. 218–19.
3. Thomas F. Ryan, S. J., *Catholic Guide to Hong Kong* (Hong Kong: Catholic Truth Society, 1962), p. vii.
4. Report on the Catholic Social Welfare Center in King's Park, July 12, 1953, p. 1, Folder 1, Box 8, SCR-MMA.
5. Personnel List, April 1, 1953, p. 2, Folder 4, Box 2, LISTS-MMA.
6. Sister Agnes Cazale's letter to family, January 27, 1952, p. 3, Box 88: Agnes Cazale—Personal Letters to Parents, CWPP-MMA.
7. Ibid.
8. T. D. Vaughan and D. J. Dwyer, "Some Aspects of Postwar Population Growth in Hong Kong," *Economic Geography*, Vol. 42, No. 1 (January 1966), p. 42.
9. Sister Agnes' aerogramme to family, July 20, 1956, 1st page, Box 88, CWPP-MMA.
10. Vaughan and Dwyer, "Some Aspects of Postwar Population Growth in Hong Kong," p. 43.
11. Sister Agnes' aerogramme to family, January 18, 1953, 2nd page, Box 88, CWPP-MMA.
12. D. J. Dwyer, "Urban Squatters: The Relevance of the Hong Kong Experience," *Asian Survey*, Vol. 10, No. 7 (1970), p. 609.
13. Catholic Action began in 1931 and attempted to coordinate various social and welfare activities of the lay community. It included Catholic groups, which were formed to offer service to the needy and less fortunate people.
14. Sister Mary Imelda Sheridan, "A History of the South China Region 1921–1958" (written in 1959), p. 33, Folder 1, Box 1, Publicity Department, "Sisters' Work among the Refugees," October 26, 1953, p. 1, Folder 5, Box 8, SCR-MMA.
15. Sister Miriam Xavier Mug, "Maryknoll Sisters, Hong Kong-Macau Region: A History—1921–1998" (Unpublished, March 2000), p. 9.
16. Ibid.
17. Publicity Department, "Sisters' Work among the Refugees," p. 1.
18. Ibid.

19. "A Brief History of the Maryknoll Sisters in Chai Waan, Hongkong (Work Begun, 1952)," 1958, p. 1, Folder 4, Box 8, SCR-MMA.

20. "The Emergency (Resettlement Areas) Regulations, 1952," approved by the Legislative Council on June 11, 1952, pp. 1–2, Folder 2, Box 12: Assistance to Refugees, VI-HKCDA.

21. "Extract from Urban Council Meeting," August 4, 1964, HKRS 70–6–927 "King's Park Development," PRO-HK; Hal Empson, *Mapping Hong Kong: A Historical Atlas* (Hong Kong: Government Information Services, 1992), pp. 184–85, Plate 4–7 (1947) and pp. 186–87, Plate 4–8 (1964).

22. Report on the Catholic Social Welfare Center in King's Park, p. 1.

23. Sister Moira Riehl, "History of King's Park," May 3, 1958, p. 1, Folder 1, Box 8, SCR-MMA.

24. Sister Mary Imelda Sheridan (Hong Kong) to Mother Mary Columba Tarpey (Maryknoll Sisters' Motherhouse), January 8, 1952, p. 2, Folder 8, Box 3, RCSC-MMA.

25. History of the Catholic Welfare Center, King's Park, n.d. [1953 or 1954], p. 1, Folder 1, Box 8, SCR-MMA.

26. Catholic Foreign Mission Society of America, *Maryknoll: Hong Kong Chronicle* (Hong Kong: Catholic Foreign Mission Society of America, 1978), p. 177.

27. Sister Moira, "History of King's Park," p. 1.

28. Ibid., pp. 1–2.

29. Report on the Catholic Social Welfare Center in King's Park, p. 3.

30. Ibid.; Excerpt of the Report on the Catholic Social Welfare Center in King's Park (to Bishop Fulton Sheen), July 12, 1953, pp. 1–2, Folder 1, Box 8, SCR-MMA.

31. Sister Moira, "History of King's Park," p. 2.

32. Publicity Department, "Tung Tau Village Women's Centre, Kowloon," n.d. [1952?], p. 1, Folder 3, Box 8, SCR-MMA.

33. Sister Agnes' aerogramme to family, May 18, 1952, 2 pages, Box 88, CWPP-MMA.

34. Sister Agnes' aerogramme to family, March 5, 1952, 1st page, Box 88, CWPP-MMA.

35. Sister Agnes' aerogramme to family, January 18, 1953, 2 pages, Box 88, CWPP-MMA.

36. Sister Agnes' aerogramme to family, August 1, 1954, 1 page, Box 88, CWPP-MMA.

37. Hu Yueh, "The Problem of the Hong Kong Refugees," *Asian Survey*, Vol. 2, No. 1 (1962), p. 28.

38. Sister Miriam Xavier, "Maryknoll Sisters, Hong Kong-Macau Region," pp. 11–12.

39. "Refugee Work in Hong Kong," received in the Motherhouse with Sister Mary Imelda's letter of May 15, 1952, 1 page, Folder 8, Box 3, RCSC-MMA.

40. Report on the Catholic Social Welfare Center in King's Park, p. 1.

41. Ibid.

42. Ibid.

43. Sister Mary Imelda to Mother Mary Columba, February 12, 1952, p. 1, Folder 8, Box 3, RCSC-MMA.

44. Report on the Catholic Social Welfare Center in King's Park, pp. 6–7. Archbishop Antonio Riberi was expelled from China in 1951. Piero Gheddo, *Lawrence Bianchi of Hong Kong*, trans. Catholic Truth Society (Hong Kong: Catholic Truth Society, 1992), p. 114.

45. Sister Mariel, "Catholic Welfare Committee of China," *Catholic Review*, May 1947, pp. 1–4, Folder 1, Box 12, VI-HKCDA.

46. Report on the Catholic Social Welfare Center in King's Park, p. 2; Sister Mary Imelda to Mother Mary Columba, February 12, 1952, pp. 1–2.

47. Sister Miriam Xavier, "Maryknoll Sisters, Hong Kong-Macau Region," p. 11; Sister Moira Riehl, "Response to Questionnaire on Community Welfare Centers," May 23, 1955, p. 3, Folder 1, Box 8, SCR-MMA.

48. Report on the Catholic Social Welfare Center in King's Park, p. 5.

49. Ibid.

50. Ibid.
51. "Maryknoll Sisters and Refugee Work in Kowloon and Hong Kong," September 19, 1954, p. 2 (King's Park), Folder 3, Box 8, SCR-MMA.
52. Report on the Catholic Social Welfare Center in King's Park, p. 2.
53. "Standard of Living of Poorer Families" [October 1954?], Folder 1, Box 8, SCR-MMA.
54. Report on the Catholic Social Welfare Center in King's Park, p. 3.
55. "General Survey of Work at King's Park, June 1st–December 31st, 1953," n.d. [1953?], p. 2, Folder 1, Box 8, SCR-MMA.
56. Report on the Catholic Social Welfare Center in King's Park, p. 3.
57. Sister Moira, "Response to Questionnaire on Community Welfare Centers," p. 2.
58. "General Survey of Work at King's Park, June 1st–December 31st, 1953," pp. 1–2.
59. Report on the Catholic Social Welfare Center in King's Park, p. 5.
60. As Sister Miriam Xavier Mug points out, "Nairn Road was a short dirt road that petered out a bit beyond the church." Subsequently, King's Park and Homantin underwent redevelopment and Nairn Road became Princess Margaret Road. Sister Miriam Xavier, "Maryknoll Sisters, Hong Kong-Macau Region," pp. 11–12.
61. Sister Marie Thomas Connolly, Interview by Cindy Yik-yi Chu in Maryknoll Sisters Center, Maryknoll, New York, July 28, 2001.
62. Personnel List, October 1, 1955, p. 17; Personnel List, April 1, 1956, p. 18; Personnel List, October 1, 1956, p. 18; Personnel List, April 1, 1957, p. 18; Personnel List, October 1, 1957, p. 17; Personnel List, April 1, 1958, p. 18; Personnel List, October 1, 1958, p. 19; Personnel List, April 1, 1959, p. 18; Personnel List, April 1, 1960, p. 20; Personnel List, November 1, 1960, p. 20, Folder 5, Box 2, LISTS-MMA.
63. Very Rev. John Romaniello, "Catholic Relief Services," *Catholic Hong Kong: A Hundred Years of Missionary Activity* (Hong Kong: Catholic Press Bureau, 1958), p. 150.
64. "Maryknoll/Welfare Center, King's Park, Financial Report for the Year ended 31st December, 1957," n.d. [1957?], 2 pages, Folder 1, Box 8, SCR-MMA.
65. Ibid.
66. Catholic Foreign Mission Society of America, *Maryknoll: Hong Kong Chronicle*, p. 215.
67. "Maryknoll/Welfare Center, King's Park, Financial Report for the Year ended 31st December, 1957," 2 pages.
68. Sister Miriam Xavier, "Maryknoll Sisters, Hong Kong-Macau Region," pp. 11–12; "Brief Chronological History of the Maryknoll Sisters' Catholic Welfare Centre—Homantin, King's Park, Kowloon," 1959, Folder 1, Box 8, SCR-MMA.
69. "Report on Current Activities," June 5, 1959, p. 1, Folder 1, Box 8, SCR-MMA.
70. Ibid.
71. Document attached with the letter from Sister Mary Imelda to Bishop Lawrence Bianchi, March 18, 1955, p. 1, Folder 2, Box 12: Other Churches in Kowloon, IV-HKCDA.
72. Excerpt of the Report on the Catholic Social Welfare Center in King's Park, p. 1.
73. Report on the Catholic Social Welfare Center in King's Park, p. 4.
74. Ibid.
75. Sister Moira, "Response to Questionnaire on Community Welfare Centers," p. 1.
76. Interview of Sister Marie Thomas, July 28, 2001.
77. Sister Moira, "History of King's Park," p. 3.
78. "Report on Current Activities," p. 1.
79. Excerpt of the Report on the Catholic Social Welfare Center in King's Park, p. 2.
80. Ibid.
81. "General Survey of Work," n.d. [1953?], p. 1, Folder 1, Box 8, SCR-MMA.
82. Publicity Department, "King's Park Settlement Area," April 1954, Folder 1, Box 8, SCR-MMA.
83. "Standard of Living of Poorer Families," October 1954, Folder 1, Box 8, SCR-MMA.
84. Report on the Catholic Social Welfare Center in King's Park, p. 7.

85. Ibid., p. 4.
86. "Report on the Social Service Program of the Maryknoll Sisters' Catholic Welfare Centre, King's Park-Homantin Resettlement Area-Hong Kong, Year Ending December 31, 1957," n.d. [1957?], 2 pages, Folder 1, Box 8, SCR-MMA.
87. Sister Moira Riehl, "Response to Questionnaire on Community Welfare Centers," pp. 2–3.
88. Ibid., pp. 4–5.
89. Sister Miriam Xavier, "Maryknoll Sisters, Hong Kong-Macau Region," p. 32.
90. Sister M. Joseph Kim Hom, "A Report on the Catechetics in King's Park, Hong Kong," June 17, 1964, p. 1, Folder 1, Box 8, SCR-MMA.
91. "Response to Questionnaire on Community Welfare Centers," p. 2.
92. Ibid., p. 4.
93. Sister Miriam Xavier, "Maryknoll Sisters, Hong Kong-Macau Region," p. 9; Personnel List, September 8, 1954, p. 20; Personnel List, April 1, 1955, p. 20; Personnel List, October 1, 1955, p. 17; Personnel List, April 1, 1956, p. 18; Personnel List, October 1, 1956, p. 18; Personnel List, April 1, 1957, p. 18; Personnel List, October 1, 1957, p. 17; Personnel List, April 1, 1958, p. 18, Folders 4 and 5, Box 2, LISTS-MMA.
94. "Maryknoll Sisters and Refugee Work in Kowloon and Hong Kong," pp. 1–2 (Tung Tau Tsuen).
95. "Brief History of the Work of the Maryknoll Sisters in Tung Tau Resettlement Area, Kowloon City, Hong Kong, Founded October 2, 1952," April 1958, p. 2, Folder 3, Box 8, SCR-MMA.
96. Ibid., pp. 7–8.
97. Sister Mary Ignatia McNally (Tung Tau Tsuen) to Mother Mary Columba, February 9, 1955, 2 pages, Folder 6, Box 4, RCSC-MMA.
98. "Brief History of the Work of the Maryknoll Sisters in Tung Tau Resettlement Area, Kowloon City, Hong Kong, Founded October 2, 1952," p. 5.
99. Ibid., p. 8.
100. Ibid., p. 9; Sister Agnes Cazale (Maria Petra), Interview by Cindy Yik-yi Chu in King's Park Annex, Kowloon, Hong Kong, June 20, 2002.
101. Sister Mary Ignatia to Mother Mary Columba, July 20, 1955, 2 pages, Folder 6, Box 4, RCSC-MMA.
102. Sister Moira, "History of King's Park," p. 3.
103. Report on the Catholic Social Welfare Center in King's Park, p. 2.
104. Sister Moira, "History of King's Park," p. 3.
105. Ibid.
106. Sister Moira, "History of King's Park," pp. 4–5.
107. Ibid., pp. 5–6.
108. Sister Mary Imelda to Mother Mary Columba, January 8, 1952, pp. 1–2, Folder 8, Box 3, RCSC-MMA.
109. Ibid., p. 2.
110. Mother Mary Columba to Sister Mary Imelda, March 28, 1952, p. 1, Folder 8, Box 3, RCSC-MMA.
111. Sister Mary Imelda to Sister Mary Annette Kelley (Maryknoll Sisters' Motherhouse), February 8, 1952, 1 page, Folder 8, Box 3, RCSC-MMA.
112. "Suggestions for Training the Sister-Apostle: The Sister Missioner in the Direct Apostolate," n.d. [February 15, 1952?], p. 4, Folder 8, Box 3, RCSC-MMA.
113. Ibid., p. 6.
114. *Silver Jubilee of St. Teresa's Church 1932–1957* (Hong Kong: St. Teresa's Church, 1957), no page number.
115. Sister Miriam Xavier, "Maryknoll Sisters, Hong Kong-Macau Region," p. 33.
116. Sister M. Doretta Leonard, Interview by Cindy Yik-yi Chu in Maryknoll Convent, Boundary Street, Kowloon, Hong Kong, December 27, 2001.

117. HKRS 229-1-103 "Application from Maryknoll Convent School, Kowloon for Interest-Free Loan," 1953–1960, PRO-HK.

118. Aloysius Lee, ed., *Maryknoll Convent School 1925–2000* (Hong Kong: Maryknoll Convent School, 2000), p. 46.

119. "Request for Personnel" (1 page) enclosed in the letter from Sister Mary Imelda to Mother Mary Columba, February 22, 1950, 1 page, Folder 6, Box 3, RCSC-MMA.

120. Sister Mary Imelda to Mother Mary Columba, February 22, 1950.

121. Ibid.

122. Ibid.

123. Sister Mary Imelda to Mother Mary Columba, October 30, 1953, 1 page, Folder 5, Box 4, RCSC-MMA; Memo from Peter Donohue, Pro-Director of Education to Financial Secretary, December 14, 1956, pp. 1–3, HKRS 229-1-184 "Application for Interest-Free Loan from Maryknoll Convent Secondary School, Blue Pool Road, Hong Kong," PRO-HK.

124. Sister Mary Imelda to Mother Mary Columba, October 9, 1953, p. 2, Folder 1, Box 4, RCSC-MMA.

125. Ibid.

126. Sister Mary Imelda to Mother Mary Columba, February 19, 1954, p. 1, Folder 2, Box 4, RCSC-MMA.

127. Ibid.

128. Sister Mary Imelda to Mother Mary Columba, March 7, 1955, p. 1, Folder 3, Box 4, RCSC-MMA.

129. Ibid.

130. Maryknoll Convent Diary, Kowloon Tong, Hong Kong, February 1956, p. 5, Folder 4, Box 33: Kowloon, Hong Kong, DIARIES-MMA.

131. Sister Miriam Xavier, "Maryknoll Sisters, Hong Kong-Macau Region," p. 19.

Chapter Five   Refugee Communities in the 1950s and Chai Wan

1. "A Brief History of the Maryknoll Sisters in Chai Waan, Hong Kong," 1958, p. 2, Folder 4, Box 8, SCR-MMA.

2. Ibid., p. 1.

3. Ibid.

4. "Chai Wan-1952," 1952, p. 1, Folder 6, Box 2: Hong Kong Chronicles, CHRONICLES-MMA.

5. "A Brief History of the Maryknoll Sisters in Chai Waan, Hong Kong," p. 1; Sister Mary Imelda Sheridan (Hong Kong) to Mother Mary Columba Tarpey (Maryknoll Sisters' Motherhouse), March 1, 1952, p. 1, Folder 8, Box 3, RCSC-MMA.

6. "A Brief History of the Maryknoll Sisters in Chai Waan, Hong Kong," pp. 1–2.

7. "Chai Wan-1952," 1952, p. 1.

8. "Refugee Work in Hong Kong," enclosed with Sister Mary Imelda's letter to Mother Mary Columba of May 1, 1952, p. 2, Folder 8, Box 3, RCSC-MMA; Sister Miriam Xavier Mug, "Maryknoll Sisters, Hong Kong-Macau Region: A History—1921–1998" (Unpublished, March 2000), p. 15.

9. "A Brief History of the Maryknoll Sisters in Chai Waan, Hong Kong," pp. 2–3; "Chai Wan Refugee School," September 1953, p. 1, Folder 9, Box 4, RCSC-MMA.

10. "Chai Wan Refugee School," p. 1.

11. "Chai Wan-1952," p. 1.

12. Sister Dorothy Rubner (Barbara Marie) to Mother Mary Columba, December 13, 1952, Folder 1, Box 7, RCSC-MMA.

13. "A Brief History of the Maryknoll Sisters in Chai Waan, Hong Kong," p. 2.

14. Ibid., p. 3; "Maryknoll Sisters' Report of Maryknoll Primary School, Chai Wan," enclosed in the letter from Sister Mary Imelda to Mother Mary Columba, November 5,

1953, p. 1, Folder 5, Box 4; Sister Mary Imelda to Mother Mary Columba, May 17, 1953, p. 1, Folder 1, Box 4, RCSC-MMA.

15. "A Brief History of the Maryknoll Sisters in Chai Waan, Hong Kong," p. 3.

16. Sister Mary Imelda to Mother Mary Columba, May 17, 1953, p. 1; Sister Mary Imelda to Mother Mary Columba, November 5, 1953, p. 1.

17. Chai Wan Diaries, October 1953, p. 5, Folder 1, Box 34: Hong Kong, DIARIES-MMA.

18. Chai Wan Diaries, April 1954, p. 1, Folder 2, Box 34, DIARIES-MMA.

19. "Chai Wan Refugee School," p. 3.

20. Ibid.

21. "A Brief History of the Maryknoll Sisters in Chai Waan, Hong Kong," p. 3.

22. "Maryknoll Sisters' Report of Maryknoll Primary School, Chai Wan," p. 2.

23. Ibid., pp. 1–2; Chai Wan Diaries, September 1953, p. 1, Folder 1, Box 34, DIARIES-MMA.

24. "Maryknoll Sisters' Report of Maryknoll Primary School, Chai Wan," p. 2.

25. Chai Wan Diaries, March 1956, p. 1, Folder 3, Box 34, DIARIES-MMA.

26. "A Brief History of the Maryknoll Sisters in Chai Waan, Hong Kong," p. 4.

27. Chai Wan Diaries, September 1953, p. 1, Folder 1, Box 34, DIARIES-MMA.

28. Sister Mary Diggins (M. John Karen), Interview by Cindy Yik-yi Chu in Maryknoll Sisters Center, Maryknoll, New York, July 31, 2001.

29. Letter from Sister Mary Diggins (M. John Karen) to Mother Mary Columba, November 15, 1953, 1 page, Folder 1, Box 7, RCSC-MMA.

30. Ibid.

31. Copy of K. M. A. Barnett's speech on November 11, 1953, 1 page, enclosed in the letter from Sister Mary Diggins to Mother Mary Columba, November 15, 1953.

32. Chai Wan Diaries, November 1953, p. 4, Folder 1, Box 34, DIARIES-MMA; "A Brief History of the Maryknoll Sisters in Chai Waan, Hong Kong," p. 4.

33. Aerogramme from Sister Mary Diggins to Mother Mary Columba, November 15, 1953, Folder 1, Box 7, RCSC-MMA.

34. Sister Mary Diggins to Mother Mary Columba, February 6, 1954, Folder 1, Box 7, RCSC-MMA.

35. "Credits Earned by Sisters," September 1955, Folder 1, Box 7, RCSC-MMA.

36. "A Brief History of the Maryknoll Sisters in Chai Waan, Hong Kong," p. 4.

37. "Maryknoll Sisters and Refugee Work in Kowloon and Hongkong," September 19, 1954, pp. 1–2 (Chai Wan, Hong Kong), Folder 9, Box 4, RCSC-MMA.

38. Sister Rose Bernadette Gallagher to Mother Mary Columba, February 6, 1955, Folder 1, Box 7, RCSC-MMA.

39. Ibid.

40. Sister Mary Diggins to Mother Mary Columba, January 2, 1955, Folder 1, Box 7, RCSC-MMA.

41. Ibid.

42. "A Brief History of the Maryknoll Sisters in Chai Waan, Hong Kong," p. 7.

43. "Chai Wan-1955," 1955, p. 3; "Chai Wan-1956," 1956, p. 2; "Chai Wan-1957," 1957, p. 2, Folder 6, Box 2, CHRONICLES-MMA.

44. "A Brief History of the Maryknoll Sisters in Chai Waan, Hong Kong," p. 8.

45. Ibid., pp. 8–9.

46. Ibid., p. 8.

47. "Chai Wan," 1958, 1 page, Folder 6, Box 2, CHRONICLES-MMA.

48. "A Brief History of the Maryknoll Sisters in Chai Waan, Hong Kong," p. 9.

49. Ibid.

50. "Chai Wan," 1959, 1 page, Folder 6, Box 2, CHRONICLES-MMA.

51. "Chai Wan," 1960, 1 page, Folder 6, Box 2, CHRONICLES-MMA.

52. Ibid.

53. "Summary of Parish Work and Maryknoll Sisters' Primary School at Chai Waan, Hongkong," n.d. [1965?], p. 1, Folder 4, Box 8, SCR-MMA.
54. "Chai Wan," 1960, 1 page.
55. Sister Jean Theophane Steinbauer to Sister Maria Pia Remmes and Sisters in Maryknoll Motherhouse, February 9, 1959, 1 page, Folder 1, Box 7, RCSC-MMA.
56. Ibid.
57. "Chai Wan-1955," 1955, p. 1.
58. Sister Mary Diggins, "Chai Waan," November 1958, p. 1, Folder 4, Box 8, SCR-MMA.
59. Ibid.
60. "A Brief History of the Maryknoll Sisters in Chai Waan, Hong Kong," p. 10.
61. Ibid., pp. 10–11.
62. Chai Wan Diaries, January 1957, p. 3, Folder 3, Box 34, DIARIES-MMA.
63. Sister Mary Diggins, "Chai Waan," p. 4.
64. "A Brief History of the Maryknoll Sisters in Chai Waan, Hong Kong," p. 10; "Chai Wan-1957," p. 1.
65. Chai Wan Diaries, May 1954, p. 5, Folder 2, Box 34, DIARIES-MMA.
66. "Chai Wan-1955," p. 1.
67. Sister Mary Diggins, "Chai Waan," p. 1.
68. "Chai Wan-1957," p. 2.
69. Chai Wan Diaries, September 1957, p. 4, Folder 3, Box 34, DIARIES-MMA.
70. Ibid.
71. "Chai Wan-1954," 1954, pp. 1–2.
72. Sister Mary Diggins, "Chai Waan," p. 1; "Summary of Mission Work and Maryknoll Sisters' Primary School at Chai Waan, Hongkong, from March, 1958 to March, 1959," June 1959, p. 1, Folder 4, Box 34, DIARIES-MMA; Sister Mary Imelda to Mother Mary Columba, February 10, 1956, p. 2, Folder 4, Box 4, RCSC-MMA.
73. "Annual Report for the Year Ending December 31, 1958," 1958, p. 3; "Annual Report for the Year Ending December 31, 1959," 1959, p. 1, Folder 6, Box 2, CHRONICLES-MMA.
74. Chai Wan Diaries, September 1958, pp. 1, 4, Folder 4, Box 34, DIARIES-MMA.
75. "Chai Wan," 1958, 1 page.
76. "Relief Goods Received from March 1959–1960," May 19, 1960, 1 page, Folder 4, Box 34, DIARIES-MMA.
77. "Borrowed Light: A Report on the Work of the Maryknoll Sisters in the Field of Social Service in Hong Kong—1950–1960," 1960, p. 1, Folder 5, Box 2, SCR-MMA.
78. Ibid.
79. "The Catholic Population of Hong Kong (June 30, 1960)," Folder 5, Box 2, SCR-MMA.
80. "Personnel of the Hong Kong Diocese (Per July 1st, 1960)," Folder 5, Box 2, SCR-MMA.
81. "Borrowed Light," p. 7.
82. Ibid.
83. Joe Veiga, "Maryknoll Sisters in Hongkong," October 17, 1953, p. 2, Folder 9, Box 4, RCSC-MMA.
84. "Borrowed Light," p. 9.
85. "A Few Short Incidents That Have Happened in the Poor School (Boys and Girls' Club)," 1954, pp. 1–2, Folder 9, Box 4, RCSC-MMA.
86. "Borrowed Light," p. 9.
87. "Youth Work, Hong Kong," November 27, 1957, 5 pages, Folder 4, Box 2, SCR-MMA.
88. "Veritas Clubs 1954–1955, Maryknoll Convent School, Kowloon Tong," April 22, 1955, pp. 1–2, Folder 1, Box 5, SCR-MMA.
89. Ibid., p. 1.
90. "Discussion Groups at M.C.S., Kowloon Tong, Hong Kong: An Evaluation," March 12, 1956, p. 2, Folder 1, Box 5, SCR-MMA.

91. Ibid.
92. "Veritas Clubs 1954–1955, Maryknoll Convent School, Kowloon Tong," p. 2.
93. "Discussion Groups at M.C.S., Kowloon Tong, Hong Kong," p. 3.
94. Ibid., p. 4.
95. "Borrowed Light," p. 15.
96. Ibid.
97. "Borrowed Light," p. 16.
98. "Chai Wan 1956 Food for Poor," n.d. [December 1957?], 1 page, Folder 4, Box 8, SCR-MMA.

Chapter Six   Wong Tai Sin, Kowloon Tsai, and
Social Services in the 1960s

1. "Typhoon Wanda," n.d. [September 1962?], 1 page, Folder 1, Box 9, SCR-MMA.
2. Thomas F. Ryan, S.J., *Catholic Guide to Hong Kong* (Hong Kong: Catholic Truth Society, 1962), p. viii.
3. Sister Mary Imelda Sheridan (Hong Kong) to Mother Mary Columba Tarpey (Maryknoll Sisters' Motherhouse), December 14, 1953, p. 1; Mother Mary Columba to Sister Mary Imelda, January 5, 1954, 1 page, Folder 2, Box 4, RCSC-MMA.
4. Andrew J. Posey, Jr. (Refugee Program Officer, Hong Kong) to Sister Mary Imelda, June 20, 1957, p. 1, Folder 7, Box 4, RCSC-MMA.
5. Ibid.
6. Sister Mary Imelda to Hon. C.B. Burgess, O.B.E., Colonial Secretariat, Hong Kong, October 28, 1957, pp. 1–2, Folder 7, Box 4, RCSC-MMA.
7. Sister Mary Imelda to Mother Mary Columba Tarpey, January 17, 1958, p. 2, Folder 5, Box 4, RCSC-MMA.
8. Ibid.
9. Sister Mary Imelda to Mother Mary Columba, April 16, 1958, 1 page, Folder 7, Box 4, RCSC-MMA.
10. Sister Mary Ignatia McNally (Hong Kong) to Sister Mary Mercy Hirschboeck (Maryknoll Sisters' Motherhouse), April 11, 1961, 2 pages, Folder 2, Box 7, RCSC-MMA.
11. History/Report/Diary (August 16–December 31, 1961), 1961, 3 pages, Folder 1, Box 9, SCR-MMA.
12. Sister Mary Ignatia to Sister Mary Mercy Hirschboeck, February 21, 1961, 2 pages, Folder 2, Box 7, RCSC-MMA.
13. Sister Mary Ignatia to Mother Mary Colman Coleman, July 23, 1961, 2 pages, Folder 2, Box 7, RCSC-MMA.
14. "Our Lady of Maryknoll Hospital—1961," 1961, 1 page, Folder 1, Box 9, SCR-MMA.
15. History/Report/Diary (August 16–December 31, 1961), 3 pages.
16. Ibid.; Sister Ruth Marie O'Donnell, Interview by Cindy Yik-yi Chu in Maryknoll Sisters Center, Maryknoll, New York, July 22, 2001.
17. "Diary—August 16, 1961–March 19, 1962, Our Lady of Maryknoll Hospital, Wong Tai Sin," April 12, 1962, p. 1, Folder 18, Box 31: Hong Kong Diaries, DIARIES-MMA.
18. Sister Mary Ignatia to Mother Mary Colman Coleman, October 8, 1961, 2 pages, Folder 2, Box 7, RCSC-MMA.
19. "Diary—August 16, 1961–March 19, 1962, Our Lady of Maryknoll Hospital, Wong Tai Sin," p. 1; History/Report/Diary (August 16–December 31, 1961), 3 pages.
20. "Speech to be given by the Director of Medical and Health Services at the Opening Ceremony of Our Lady of Maryknoll Hospital on Monday, 11th December, 1961," p. 1, Folder 1, Box 9, SCR-MMA.
21. Sister Mary Ignatia to Mother Mary Colman Coleman, January 12, 1962, 2 pages, Folder 2, Box 7, RCSC-MMA.
22. "Typhoon Wanda," 1 page.

23. Ibid.
24. "Maryknoll Sisters Cope with the Population Explosions in Hong Kong," enclosed in the letter from Sister Anne Clements (Mary Famula) to Mother Mary Colman Coleman, n.d. [1966?], p. 26, Folder 6, Box 2, SCR-MMA.
25. "Typhoon Wanda," 1 page.
26. Ibid.; "Diary—April 1, 1962–April 1, 1963, Our Lady of Maryknoll Hospital, Wong Tai Sin," n.d. [1963], p. 2, Folder 18, Box 31, DIARIES-MMA.
27. Sister Mary Ignatia to Mother Mary Colman Coleman, September 4, 1962, 2 pages, Folder 2, Box 7, RCSC-MMA.
28. Ibid.; "Typhoon Wanda," 1 page.
29. "Annual Report for the Year Ending December 31, 1962, Our Lady of Maryknoll Hospital, Wong Tai Sin," December 31, 1962, p. 3, Folder 12, Box 2: Hong Kong Chronicles, CHRONICLES-MMA.
30. Sister Mary Ignatia, "Wong Tai Sin, Hong Kong," 1962, 1 page, Folder 1, Box 9, SCR-MMA.
31. Ibid.
32. "Diary—April 1, 1962–April 1, 1963, Our Lady of Maryknoll Hospital, Wong Tai Sin," n.d. [1963], p. 1; Sister Maria Del Rey Danforth, "Hong Kong Hospital," December 1962, 5 pages, Folder 1, Box 9, SCR-MMA.
33. Sister Mary Ignatia, "Wong Tai Sin, Hong Kong," 1 page.
34. "Diary—April 1, 1962–April 1, 1963, Our Lady of Maryknoll Hospital, Wong Tai Sin," p. 3.
35. Sister Maria Del Rey, "Hong Kong Hospital," 5 pages.
36. "Our Lady of Maryknoll Hospital—1962," 1962, 2 pages; "Our Lady of Maryknoll Hospital—1963," 1963, 1 page, Folder 1, Box 9, SCR-MMA.
37. History/Report/Diary (April 1963–March 1964), 1964, p. 4, Folder 1, Box 9, SCR-MMA.
38. "Our Lady of Maryknoll Hospital—1964," 1964, 1 page, Folder 1, Box 9, SCR-MMA.
39. Ibid.; "April 1, 1963–March 31, 1964, Our Lady of Maryknoll Hospital, Wong Tai Sin," n.d. [1964], p. 3, Folder 18, Box 31, DIARIES-MMA.
40. "April 1, 1964–March 31, 1965, Our Lady of Maryknoll Hospital, Wong Tai Sin," n.d. [1965], p. 1, Folder 18, Box 31, DIARIES-MMA.
41. History/Report/Diary (April 1963–March 1964), pp. 4–5.
42. "Excerpt of article from the Sing Tao Daily News, Sunday, January 5, 1964," 1964, 2 pages, Folder 1, Box 9, SCR-MMA.
43. Ibid.
44. Ibid.
45. Christmas 1964 Letter from Sister Dominic Marie Turner, December 1964, 1 page, Folder 1, Box 9, SCR-MMA.
46. *Annual Report of the Medical Development Plan Standing Committee (21st March, 1964–31st March, 1965)* (Hong Kong: Government Printer, 1965), pp. 13–14, Folder 1, Box 9, SCR-MMA.
47. "Our Lady of Maryknoll Hospital—1964," 1964, 1 page, Folder 1, Box 9, SCR-MMA.
48. Mission Stories by Sister Maria Rieckelman (Maria Fidelis), December 1, 1964, p. 1, Folder 1, Box 9, SCR-MMA.
49. Ibid., p. 2.
50. "Maryknoll Sisters Cope with the Population Explosions in Hong Kong," pp. 26–27.
51. Ibid., p. 26.
52. Ibid., p. 27.
53. Sister MaryLou Ann Rajdl (M. Ann David), Interview by Cindy Yik-yi Chu in Maryknoll Sisters Center, Maryknoll, New York, July 25, 2001.
54. "Maryknoll Sisters Cope with the Population Explosions in Hong Kong," p. 27.
55. Sister Joseph Lourdes Nubla, Interview by Cindy Yik-yi Chu in Maryknoll Sisters Center, Maryknoll, New York, August 5, 2001.
56. "Maryknoll Sisters Cope with the Population Explosions in Hong Kong," p. 28.

57. Ibid., p. 29.
58. Ibid., p. 30.
59. "Diary—April 1, 1966–March 31, 1967, Our Lady of Maryknoll Hospital, Wong Tai Sin," n.d. [1967], p. 1, Folder 18, Box 31, DIARIES-MMA.
60. "Maryknoll Sisters Cope with the Population Explosions in Hong Kong," p. 30.
61. Sister Miriam Xavier Mug, "Maryknoll Sisters, Hong Kong-Macau Region: A History—1921–1998" (Unpublished, March 2000), p. 9; "1961 Diary, Kowloontsai," April 30, 1962, p. 1, Folder 19, Box 31, DIARIES-MMA.
62. "Kowloon Tsai—1961," 1961, 1 page, Folder 7, Box 8, SCR-MMA.
63. Sister Miriam Xavier, "Maryknoll Sisters, Hong Kong-Macau Region," p. 10; "Kowloon Tsai—1963," 1963, 1 page, Folder 7, Box 8, SCR-MMA; "Maryknoll Sisters Cope with the Population Explosions in Hong Kong," p. 22.
64. "Maryknoll Sisters Cope with the Population Explosions in Hong Kong," p. 22.
65. Ibid.
66. "Kowloon Tsai—1961," 1961, 1 page.
67. Ibid.
68. "Kowloon Tsai—1962," 1962, 1 page, Folder 7, Box 8, SCR-MMA.
69. Ibid.
70. Ibid.
71. "Maryknoll Sisters Cope with the Population Explosions in Hong Kong," p. 22.
72. Ibid.
73. Ibid.
74. Sister Agnes Cazale (Maria Petra) to Sister Jessie Lucier (M. Francisca), November 19, 1963, Folder 7, Box 8, SCR-MMA.
75. "Maryknoll Sisters Cope with the Population Explosions in Hong Kong," p. 23.
76. Excerpt from a report written by Sister Katherine Byrne (Philip Marie), "Cheers in the Well Baby Clinic," 1963, pp. 9–10, Folder 7, Box 8, SCR-MMA.
77. "Maryknoll Sisters Cope with the Population Explosions in Hong Kong," p. 23.
78. Ibid., p. 24.
79. "Kowloon Tsai—1963," 1963, 1 page.
80. "Kowloon Tsai—1964," 1964, 1 page, Folder 7, Box 8, SCR-MMA.
81. "Kowloon Tsai—1965," 1965, 1 page, Folder 7, Box 8, SCR-MMA.
82. Personnel List, 1969, p. 31; Personnel List, 1970, p. 40; Personnel List 1971, Hong Kong; Personnel List, 1972, Hong Kong, Folders 6–9, Box 3, LISTS-MMA.
83. Sister Barbara Mersinger (Rose Victor), "Summary of Developments in South China Region for the Last Sexennial Period—1958/1964," April 17, 1964, p. 6, Folder 5, Box 2, SCR-MMA.
84. "Maryknoll Sisters Cope with the Population Explosions in Hong Kong," p. 16.
85. Sister Barbara, "Summary of Developments in South China Region for the Last Sexennial Period—1958/1964," p. 8.
86. "Casework Section—Statistical Report for June 1963," 1963, 1 page, Folder 1, Box 8, SCR-MMA.
87. "Casework Section Statistics—July 1963," 1963, pp. 1–2, Folder 1, Box 8, SCR-MMA.
88. "Street Hawker: Maryknoll Sisters Social Service in Hong Kong 1960–1964," n.d. [1964?], p. 10, Box 2A, SCR-MMA.
89. Ibid.
90. Ibid.
91. "Street Hawker: Maryknoll Sisters Social Service in Hong Kong 1960–1964," pp. 10–11.
92. "Maryknoll Sisters Cope with the Population Explosions in Hong Kong," p. 16.
93. Ibid.
94. "Street Hawker: Maryknoll Sisters Social Service in Hong Kong 1960–1964," p. 13.
95. Ibid., pp. 13–15.
96. Ibid., p. 13.

97. Ibid.
98. "Street Hawker: Maryknoll Sisters Social Service in Hong Kong 1960–1964," p. 14; Constitution of the Hong Kong Catholic Social Welfare Conference, July 1, 1961, p. 1, Folder 2, Box 12: Assistance to Refugees, VI-HKCDA.

Chapter Seven   Kwun Tong and Chai Wan in the 1960s

1. Sister Anne Clements (Mary Famula), "Christmas in Kwun Tong, 1963," 1963, 1 page, Folder 7, Box 7, RCSC-MMA.
2. "Street Hawker: Maryknoll Sisters Social Service in Hong Kong 1960–1964," n.d. [1964?], p. 1, Box 2A, SCR-MMA.
3. Ibid.
4. Sister Miriam Xavier Mug "Maryknoll Sisters, Hong Kong-Macau Region: A History—1921–1998" (Unpublished, March 2000), p. 10.
5. "Maryknoll Sisters Cope with the Population Explosions in Hong Kong," enclosed in the letter from Sister Anne Clements to Mother Mary Colman Coleman, n.d. [1966?], p. 24, Folder 6, Box 2, SCR-MMA.
6. "Street Hawker: Maryknoll Sisters Social Service in Hong Kong 1960–1964," p. 1.
7. "Kuntong Mission, Hong Kong, South China Region, November 1959 to June 1960," August 23, 1960, p. 1, Folder 5, Box 34: Hong Kong, DIARIES-MMA.
8. Ibid.
9. "Kuntong Mission, Hong Kong, South China Region, November 1959 to June 1960," pp. 1–2.
10. Sister Miriam Xavier, "Maryknoll Sisters, Hong Kong-Macau Region," p. 10; *Personnel*, November 1, 1961, p. 19; *Personnel*, November 1, 1962, p. 21; *Personnel*, November 1, 1963, p. 23, Folder 1, Box 3, LISTS-MMA.
11. "Chai Wan," 1960, 1 page, Folder 6, Box 2: Hong Kong Chronicles, CHRONICLES-MMA.
12. Sister Miriam Xavier, "Maryknoll Sisters, Hong Kong-Macau Region," pp. 10 and 21; "Kowloon Tsai—1961," 1961, 1 page, Folder 7, Box 8, SCR-MMA.
13. Sister Mary Diggins (M. John Karen), "Yearly Diary for Maryknoll Sisters, Holy Spirit Convent, Kwun Tong, Kowloon, Hongkong, South China Region, Covering the Year March 1961–March 1962," May 21, 1962, pp. 1–2, Folder 5, Box 34, DIARIES-MMA.
14. James Ronald Firth, "The Work of the Hong Kong Housing Authority," *Journal of the Royal Society of Arts*, Vol. 113, No. 5103 (February 1965), p. 177.
15. Sister Mary Diggins, "Yearly Diary for Maryknoll Sisters, Holy Spirit Convent, Kwun Tong, Kowloon, Hongkong, South China Region, Covering the Year March 1961–March 1962," p. 2.
16. Ibid.
17. Letter written by Sister Anne Clements, February 10, 1964, 2 pages, Folder 6, Box 8, SCR-MMA; Keith Hopkins, "Public and Private Housing in Hong Kong," in *The City as a Centre of Change in Asia*, ed. D. J. Dwyer (Hong Kong: Hong Kong University Press, 1972), p. 203.
18. "Maryknoll Sisters' Diary, Holy Spirit Convent, Kwun Tong, Kowloon, Hongkong, March 1962–March 1963," n.d. [1963], p. 1, Folder 5, Box 34, DIARIES-MMA.
19. "Kwun Tong, March 1963–March 1964," May 25, 1964, p. 1, Folder 5, Box 34, DIARIES-MMA.
20. Sister Mary Diggins, "Yearly Diary for Maryknoll Sisters, Holy Spirit Convent, Kwun Tong, Kowloon, Hongkong, South China Region, Covering the Year March 1961–March 1962," p. 3.
21. "Maryknoll Sisters Cope with the Population Explosions in Hong Kong," p. 25.

22. Ibid.
23. Sister Miriam Xavier, "Maryknoll Sisters, Hong Kong-Macau Region," p. 10.
24. Sister Mary Diggins, "Yearly Diary for Maryknoll Sisters, Holy Spirit Convent, Kwun Tong, Kowloon, Hongkong, South China Region, Covering the Year March 1961–March 1962," p. 8.
25. Ibid, p. 5.
26. Ibid.
27. Sister Mary Diggins, "Yearly Diary for Maryknoll Sisters, Holy Spirit Convent, Kwun Tong, Kowloon, Hongkong, South China Region, Covering the Year March 1961–March 1962," pp. 5–6.
28. Ibid., p. 6.
29. "Maryknoll Sisters' Diary, Holy Spirit Convent, Kwun Tong, Kowloon, Hongkong, March 1962–March 1963," p. 2.
30. Sister Mary Diggins (M. John Karen) to Mother Mary Colman Coleman, December 27, 1962, 1st page, Folder 7, Box 7, RCSC-MMA.
31. Ibid.
32. Sister Anne Clements, "Christmas in Kwun Tong, 1963," 1963, 1 page.
33. Sister Anne Clements, "The Plaza—Block U," 1965, 3 pages, Folder 6, Box 8, SCR-MMA.
34. "Annual Report for the Year Ending December 31, 1965, Kwun Tong," February 20, 1966, 1 page; "Annual Report for the Year Ending December 31, 1966, Kwun Tong," February 16, 1967, 1 page; "Annual Report for the Year Ending December 31, 1967, Kwun Tong," February 27, 1968, 1 page; "Annual Report for the Year Ending December 31, 1968, Kwun Tong," February 1969, 1 page, Folder 8, Box 2, CHRONICLES-MMA.
35. "Kwun Tong, March 1965–1966," June 8, 1966, pp. 1–2, Folder 5, Box 34, DIARIES-MMA.
36. Sister Miriam Xavier, "Maryknoll Sisters, Hong Kong-Macau Region," pp. 20–21.
37. Sister Anne Clements, "Report of Holy Spirit School, 1961–1964," June 15, 1964, pp. 1–5, Folder 6, Box 8, SCR-MMA.
38. Application for registration of Holy Spirit School in Kwun Tong signed by Sister Anne Clements (Mary Famula), February 24, 1961, 3 pages, Folder 11, Box 1, RC-MMA.
39. Sister Anne Clements, "Report of Holy Spirit School, 1961–1964," pp. 1–5.
40. Ibid., pp. 3–4.
41. Ibid., p. 3.
42. Ibid., p. 1.
43. Ibid.
44. Letter written by Sister Anne Clements, February 10, 1964, 2 pages.
45. Sister Anne Clements, "Typhoon Ida—Report of School Damage & Destruction," submitted to the Education Department, August 9, 1964, 1st page, Folder 6, Box 8, SCR-MMA.
46. Sister Anne Clements to Mother Mary Colman Coleman, received on August 15, 1964, p. 1, Folder 6, Box 8, SCR-MMA.
47. Ibid.
48. Sister Anne Clements, "Typhoon Ida—Report of School Damage & Destruction," 1st page.
49. Sister Anne Clements to the Publicity Department (Maryknoll Sisters' Motherhouse), Christmas 1964, 1st page, Folder 7, Box 7, RCSC-MMA.
50. Ibid., 1st and 2nd pages; Sister Anne Clements to Pauline MacGuire, Catholic Relief Services, Hong Kong, October 6, 1964, 2nd page, Folder 7, Box 7, RCSC-MMA.
51. Certificate of registration of Holy Spirit School in Kwun Tong, February 9, 1965, 1 page, Folder 11, Box 1, RC-MMA.
52. Sister Ruth Evans (M. Margaret Veronica) to Publicity Department (Maryknoll Sisters' Motherhouse), Christmas 1964, 2 pages, Folder 7, Box 7, RCSC-MMA.

53. "Chai Wan," 1961, 1 page, Folder 6, Box 2, CHRONICLES-MMA.
54. "Summary of Parish Work and Maryknoll Sisters' Primary School at Chai Waan, Hongkong," n.d. [1965?], pp. 7–8, Folder 4, Box 8, SCR-MMA.
55. Ibid., p. 8.
56. "Maryknoll Sisters Cope with the Population Explosions in Hong Kong," p. 20.
57. Ibid.
58. Sister Mary Diggins, Interview by Cindy Yik-yi Chu in Maryknoll Sisters Center, Maryknoll, New York, July 31, 2001.
59. Sister Teresa Leung (Marie Lucas), Interview by Cindy Yik-yi Chu in Maryknoll Sisters Center, Maryknoll, New York, July 22, 2001.
60. "Summary of Parish Work and Maryknoll Sisters' Primary School at Chai Waan, Hongkong," [1965], p. 8.
61. "Summary of Parish Work and Maryknoll Sisters' Primary School at Chai Wan, Hong Kong from March 1961 to March 1962," n.d. [1962], p. 7, Folder 4, Box 34, DIARIES-MMA.
62. "Summary of Parish Work and Maryknoll Sisters' Primary School at Chai Waan, Hongkong" [1965], p. 10.
63. "Chai Wan—1963," 1963, 1 page, Folder 6, Box 2, CHRONICLES-MMA.
64. "Summary of Parish Work and Maryknoll Sisters' Primary School at Chai Waan, Hongkong," [1965], p. 10.
65. "Maryknoll Sisters Cope with the Population Explosions in Hong Kong," p. 21.
66. Ibid.
67. Ibid.
68. "Summary of Parish Work and Maryknoll Sisters' Primary School at Chai Wan, Hong Kong from March 1961 to March 1962," [1962], p. 4.
69. Letter from Sister Mary Ellen Mertens (M. Benjamin), n.d. [1966?], 1 page, Folder 1, Box 7, RCSC-MMA. She addressed to Maria del Rey Danforth, the famous Sister-journalist who had written many popular books on the Maryknoll Sisters. The works of the latter were probably one of the reasons why so many applications flooded Maryknoll in the 1950s.
70. "Summary of Parish Work and Maryknoll Sisters' Primary School at Chai Waan, Hongkong," [1965], p. 9.
71. Ibid., p. 10.
72. Ibid., pp. 11 and 13; Leo U. Murray, *Chai Wan Social Needs Study: A Report of a Survey Carried Out among Organizations and Residents in the Chai Wan District of Hong Kong* (Hong Kong: Hong Kong Council of Social Service, September 1967), Part I, pp. 5–6.
73. "Summary of Parish Work and Maryknoll Sisters' Primary School at Chai Waan, Hongkong" [1965], p. 13.
74. Ibid., pp. 13–14.
75. Penny Lernoux, *Hearts on Fire: The Story of the Maryknoll Sisters* (Maryknoll: Orbis Books, 1993), p. xii.
76. Ibid., pp. xxvi, xxxii.
77. Ibid., p. xxxii.
78. Ibid., p. xxi.
79. Lernoux, *Hearts on Fire*, p. 2. At the very beginning, Mother Mary Joseph stressed the importance of "cheerfulness" in the Sisters' missionary work. Read Sister M. Marcelline Grondin, *Sisters Carry the Gospel* (Maryknoll: World Horizon Reports, Maryknoll Publications, 1956), pp. 84–87.
80. Sister Miriam Xavier, "Maryknoll Sisters, Hong Kong-Macau Region," p. 27; Sister Susan Gubbins, Interview by Cindy Yik-yi Chu in Maryknoll Sisters Center, Maryknoll, New York, August 2, 2001.
81. Sister Moira Riehl received the MBE (a Member of the British Empire) award in recognition of her contribution to the blind in 1981.

82. Sister Miriam Xavier, "Maryknoll Sisters, Hong Kong-Macau Region," p. 24.
83. Ibid., pp. 24–26.
84. "Mission Work in Hong Kong," n.d. [1960?], p. 3, Folder 5, Box 2, SCR-MMA.
85. Ibid., p. 6.
86. "Hong Kong: Catechetical Work, Past, Present, Future," 1966, pp. 1–2, Folder 6, Box 2, SCR-MMA.
87. Ibid., p. 3.
88. Ibid., pp. 1–2.
89. Ibid., p. 3.
90. Sister M. Julia Hannigan, Interview by Cindy Yik-yi Chu in Maryknoll Sisters Center, Maryknoll, New York, July 27, 2001.

Chapter Eight   Conclusion

1. Sister Rose Duchesne Debrecht, Interview by Sister Virginia Unsworth in Hong Kong, July 19, 1981, pp. 6–7, 13–14, 30–31, MCHP-MMA.
2. Aloysius Lee, ed., *Maryknoll Convent School 1925–2000* (Hong Kong: Maryknoll Convent School, 2000), p. 76.
3. Jean-Paul Wiest, *Maryknoll in China: A History, 1918–1955* (Armonk: M.E. Sharpe, 1988), p. 31.
4. Penny Lernoux, *Hearts on Fire: The Story of the Maryknoll Sisters* (Maryknoll: Orbis Books, 1993), p. 2.
5. Sisters Mary Lou Martin and Agnes Chou, Interview by Cindy Yik-yi Chu in Maryknoll Convent, Boundary Street, Kowloon, Hong Kong, August 12, 2000.
6. *Tentative Constitutions of the Foreign Mission Sisters of St. Dominic (Third Order), Congregation of the Immaculate Conception, at Maryknoll, Ossining, New York, U.S.A.* (drafted in 1917; First Constitutions in use after General Chapter of 1925), p. 1, CONSTITUTIONS-MMA; Lernoux, *Hearts on Fire*, p. 143.
7. *Tentative Constitutions of the Foreign Mission Sisters of St. Dominic*, p. 55.
8. *Constitution of the Foreign Mission Sisters of St. Dominic, Maryknoll, New York*, October 25, 1931, p. 1, CONSTITUTIONS-MMA.
9. Ibid., p. 56.
10. *Constitution of the Foreign Mission Sisters of St. Dominic, Maryknoll, New York*, 1937, p. 1, CONSTITUTIONS-MMA.
11. *Constitutions of the Foreign Mission Sisters of St. Dominic, Congregation of the Immaculate Conception, Maryknoll, New York*, March 7, 1952, p. 1, CONSTITUTIONS-MMA.
12. *Constitutions of the Maryknoll Sisters of St. Dominic, Congregation of the Immaculate Conception, Maryknoll, New York*, December 12, 1954, p. 1, CONSTITUTIONS-MMA.
13. *Constitutions of the Maryknoll Sisters of St. Dominic, Congregation of the Immaculate Conception, Maryknoll, New York*, May 12, 1965, p. 1, CONSTITUTIONS-MMA.
14. Lernoux, *Hearts on Fire*, pp. 139–44.
15. *Missions Challenge Maryknoll Sisters: Background Papers and Enactments, Special Chapter of Affairs, October 7, 1968 to February 5, 1969*, foreword (no page number), CONSTITUTIONS-MMA.
16. Ibid., pp. 7–8, 10.
17. Ibid., pp. 14–15.
18. Ibid., p. 16.
19. Ibid., p. 18.
20. Ibid., p. 25.
21. Maryknoll Sisters, *Searching and Sharing: Mission Perspectives*, 1970, p. 7, CONSTITUTIONS-MMA.

22. Sister Camilla Kennedy, comp., "(Chart of the) Historical Perspective of the Nature and Scope of the Maryknoll Sisters," June 1992, 1st page, CONSTITUTIONS-MMA; *Searching and Sharing*, pp. 10–11; Lernoux, *Hearts on Fire*, p. 143.

23. *Searching and Sharing*, p. 5.

24. Ibid., p. 7.

25. Ibid., p. 6.

26. *Maryknoll Sisters in Mission*, December 1975, CONSTITUTIONS-MMA.

27. Ibid., p. 30.

28. Sister Camilla comp., "(Chart of the) Historical Perspective of the Nature and Scope of the Maryknoll Sisters," 2nd page; *Constitutions: Maryknoll Sisters of St. Dominic*, May 1985, p. 4, CONSTITUTIONS-MMA.

29. Sister Camilla comp., "(Chart of the) Historical Perspective of the Nature and Scope of the Maryknoll Sisters," 2nd page.

30. Interview of Sister Mary Lou and Sister Agnes, August 12, 2000.

31. Sister Miriam Xavier Mug, "Maryknoll Sisters, Hong Kong-Macau Region: A History—1921–1998" (Unpublished, 2000), pp. 44–45.

32. Sister Camilla Kennedy, *To the Uttermost Parts of the Earth: The Spirit and Charism of Mary Josephine Rogers* (Maryknoll: Maryknoll Sisters, 1980), p. 51.

33. Ibid.

34. Lernoux, *Hearts on Fire*, p. 143; Sister Mary Lou Martin, Interview by Cindy Yik-yi Chu in Maryknoll Convent, Boundary Street, Kowloon, Hong Kong, August 22, 2000.

35. Interview of Sister Mary Lou, August 22, 2000.

36. Personnel, 1971, Folder 8, Box 3; Personnel, September 12, 1981, pp. 7–8, Folder 4, Box 4; Personnel, September 30, 1991, pp. 6–7, Folder 6, Box 5, LISTS-MMA; Personnel, May 21, 2001, pp. 11–12, Box 14, LISTS (1997–)-MMA.

37. Sister Miriam Xavier, "Maryknoll Sisters, Hong Kong-Macau Region," pp. 13–14, 28–32.

38. Sister Alice Wengrzynek (Alice Rose), Interview by Cindy Yik-yi Chu in Maryknoll Sisters Center, Maryknoll, New York, August 8, 2001.

39. Sister Miedal Stone, Interview by Cindy Yik-yi Chu in Maryknoll Sisters Center, Maryknoll, New York, July 21, 2001.

40. Sister Martha Bourne (Mary Martha), Interview by Cindy Yik-yi Chu in Maryknoll Sisters Center, Maryknoll, New York, August 3, 2001.

41. Sister Helene O'Sullivan (M. Helene), Interview by Cindy Yik-yi Chu in Maryknoll Sisters Center, Maryknoll, New York, August 8, 2001.

42. Sister Joan Toomey (Lourdes Marie), Interview by Cindy Yik-yi Chu in Maryknoll Sisters Center, Maryknoll, New York, August 5, 2001.

43. Sister Miriam Xavier, "Maryknoll Sisters, Hong Kong-Macau Region," pp. 13–14, 22.

44. Ibid., p. 35.

45. Sister Rose Bernadette Gallagher, Interview by Cindy Yik-yi Chu in Maryknoll Sisters Center, Maryknoll, New York, August 4, 2001.

46. Sister Miriam Xavier, "Maryknoll Sisters, Hong Kong-Macau Region," pp. 29–30.

47. Ibid., p. 35.

48. Interview of Sister Mary Lou, August 22, 2000.

49. Sister Miriam Xavier, "Maryknoll Sisters, Hong Kong-Macau Region," pp. 37–38; Sister Betty Ann Maheu (Antoine Marie), Interview by Cindy Yik-yi Chu in King's Park Annex, Kowloon, Hong Kong, May 10, 2002.

50. Sisters M. Ann Carol Brielmaier and Margaret Shepherd (Rose Martin), Interview by Cindy Yik-yi Chu in Maryknoll Convent, Boundary Street, Kowloon, Hong Kong, July 1, 2002.

51. Jean-Paul Wiest describes in detail Father Francis X. Ford's "Kaying Method" (Jiaying method) in his book *Maryknoll in China* (pp. 99–109).

52. Sister Jeanne Houlihan (Joel Marie), Interview by Cindy Yik-yi Chu in Maryknoll Sisters Center, Maryknoll, New York, August 7, 2001.

53. Sister Agnes McKeirnan (Rose Eileen), Interview by Cindy Yik-yi Chu in Maryknoll Sisters Center, Maryknoll, New York, July 20, 2001.
54. Sister M. Corinne Rost, Interview by Cindy Yik-yi Chu in Maryknoll Sisters Center, New York, July 24, 2001.
55. Interview of Sister Rose Duchesne, July 19, 1981, p. 31.
56. Interview of Sister Miedal, July 21, 2001.
57. Sister MaryLou Ann Rajdl (M. Ann David), Interview by Cindy Yik-yi Chu in Maryknoll Sisters Center, Maryknoll, New York, July 25, 2001.

BIBLIOGRAPHY

Archives and Collections

Maryknoll Mission Archives, Maryknoll, New York.
Hong Kong Catholic Diocesan Archives.
Public Records Office, Hong Kong.
Hong Kong Collection, Main Library, University of Hong Kong.
Hong Kong Government Reports Online (1853–1941), University of Hong Kong.
Archives on the History of Christianity in China, Hong Kong Baptist University Library.
Map Library of Hong Kong Central Library.

Interviews

Interviews conducted by the author with 34 Maryknoll Sisters in Hong Kong and Maryknoll, N.Y., between August 2000 and July 2002.

Official Publications, Reports, Directories, and Published Documents

Catholic Diocese of Hong Kong. *Catholic Directory and Calendar for 1947*. Hong Kong: Nazareth Press, 1947.
———. *Catholic Directory and Calendar for 1948*. Hong Kong: Nazareth Press, 1948.
———. *Catholic Directory and Calendar for 1949*. Hong Kong: Nazareth Press, 1949.
———. *Catholic Directory and Calendar for the Holy Year 1950*. Hong Kong: Nazareth Press, 1950.
———. *Catholic Directory and Calendar for the Year 1951*. Hong Kong: Nazareth Press, 1951.
———. *Catholic Directory and Calendar for the Year 1952*. Hong Kong: Nazareth Press, 1952.
———. *Catholic Directory and Calendar for the Year 1953*. Hong Kong: Nazareth Press, 1953.
———. *Catholic Directory and Year Book for the Year of Our Lord 1954*. Hong Kong: Catholic Truth Society, 1954.
———. *Hong Kong Catholic Directory and Year Book for the Year of Our Lord 1955*. Hong Kong: Catholic Truth Society, 1955.
———. *Hong Kong Catholic Directory and Year Book for the Year of Our Lord 1956*. Hong Kong: Catholic Truth Society, 1956.
———. *Hong Kong Catholic Directory and Year Book for the Year of Our Lord 1957*. Hong Kong: Catholic Truth Society, 1957.
———. *Hong Kong Catholic Directory and Year Book for the Year of Our Lord 1958*. Hong Kong: Catholic Truth Society, 1958.
———. *Hong Kong Catholic Directory and Year Book for the Year of Our Lord 1959*. Hong Kong: Catholic Truth Society, 1959.
———. *Hong Kong Catholic Directory and Year Book for the Year of Our Lord 1960*. Hong Kong: Catholic Truth Society, 1960.

Catholic Diocese of Hong Kong. *Hong Kong Catholic Directory and Year Book for the Year of Our Lord 1961*. Hong Kong: Catholic Truth Society, 1961.

————. *Hong Kong Catholic Directory and Year Book for the Year of Our Lord 1962*. Hong Kong: Catholic Truth Society, 1962.

————. *Hong Kong Catholic Directory and Year Book for the Year of Our Lord 1963*. Hong Kong: Catholic Truth Society, 1963.

————. *Hong Kong Catholic Directory and Year Book for the Year of Our Lord 1964*. Hong Kong: Catholic Truth Society, 1964.

————. *Hong Kong Catholic Directory and Year Book for the Year of Our Lord 1965*. Hong Kong: Catholic Truth Society, 1965.

————. *Hong Kong Catholic Directory and Year Book for the Year of Our Lord 1966*. Hong Kong: Catholic Truth Society, 1966.

————. *Hong Kong Catholic Directory and Year Book for the Year of Our Lord 1967*. Hong Kong: Catholic Truth Society, 1967.

————. *Hong Kong Catholic Directory and Year Book for the Year of Our Lord 1968*. Hong Kong: Catholic Truth Society, 1968.

————. *Hong Kong Catholic Directory and Year Book for the Year of Our Lord 1969*. Hong Kong: Catholic Truth Society, 1969.

————. *Hong Kong Catholic Directory and Year Book for the Year of Our Lord 1970*. Hong Kong: Catholic Truth Society, 1970.

————. (Pamphlets of) *Exhibition of Catholic Church*. Hong Kong: Catholic Church, 1990.

————. *Xianggang Tianzhujiaohui yibai wushi zhounian jinian tekan (The Special Bulletin for the 150th Anniversary of the Catholic Church in Hong Kong)*. Hong Kong: Catholic Church, 1991.

Catholic Foreign Mission Society of America. *Maryknoll: Hong Kong Chronicle*. Hong Kong: Catholic Foreign Mission Society of America, 1978.

Catholic Hong Kong: A Hundred Years of Missionary Activity. Hong Kong: Catholic Press Bureau, 1958.

Empson, Hal. *Mapping Hong Kong: A Historical Atlas*. Hong Kong: Government Information Services, 1992.

Ha, Louis. *110 Years in the Grace of Our Lord*. Hong Kong: Catholic Cathedral of the Immaculate Conception, 1999.

Hong Kong. *A Problem of People*. Hong Kong: Government Press, 1956.

————. *Aims and Policy for Social Welfare in Hong Kong*. Rev. ed. Hong Kong: Government Printer, 1965.

————. *Review of Policies for Squatter Control, Resettlement and Government Low-Cost Housing 1964*. Hong Kong: Government Printer, 1964.

Hong Kong. Census and Statistics Department. *Hong Kong Statistics, 1947–1967*. Hong Kong: Government Printer, 1969.

Hong Kong. Government Information Services. *Building Homes for Hong Kong's Millions: The Story of Resettlement*. Hong Kong: Government Printer, 1963.

————. *The Hong Kong Housing Authority*. Hong Kong: Government Printer, 1963.

Hong Kong. Housing Board. *Report of the Housing Board for the Period 1.4.66 to 31.3.67*. Hong Kong: Government Printer, 1967.

Hong Kong. Resettlement Department. *Hong Kong Annual Departmental Report by the Commissioner for Resettlement for the Financial Year 1954–55*. Hong Kong: Government Printer, 1955.

————. *Hong Kong Annual Departmental Report by the Commissioner for Resettlement for the Financial Year 1955–56*. Hong Kong: Government Printer, 1956.

————. *Hong Kong Annual Departmental Report by the Commissioner for Resettlement for the Financial Year 1956–57*. Hong Kong: Government Printer, 1957.

————. *Hong Kong Annual Departmental Report by the Commissioner for Resettlement for the Financial Year 1957–1958*. Hong Kong: Government Printer, 1958.

————. *Hong Kong Annual Departmental Report by the Commissioner for Resettlement for the Financial Year 1958–59*. Hong Kong: Government Printer, 1959.

————. *Hong Kong Annual Departmental Report by the Commissioner for Resettlement for the Financial Year 1959–60*. Hong Kong: Government Printer, 1960.

————. *Hong Kong Annual Departmental Report by the Commissioner for Resettlement for the Financial Year 1960–61*. Hong Kong: Government Printer, 1961.

————. *Hong Kong Annual Departmental Report by the Commissioner for Resettlement for the Financial Year 1961–62*. Hong Kong: Government Printer, 1962.

————. *Hong Kong Annual Departmental Report by the Commissioner for Resettlement C. G. M. Morrison for the Financial Year 1962–63*. Hong Kong: Government Printer, 1963.

————. *Hong Kong Annual Departmental Report by the Commissioner for Resettlement D. C. Barty, O.B.E. for the Financial Year 1963–64*. Hong Kong: Government Printer, 1964.

————. *Hong Kong Annual Departmental Report by the Commissioner for Resettlement J. T. Wakefield for the Financial Year 1964–65*. Hong Kong: Government Printer, 1965.

————. *Hong Kong Annual Departmental Report by the Commissioner for Resettlement D. C. Barty, O.B.E., M.A., J.P. for the Financial Year 1965–66*. Hong Kong: Government Printer, 1966.

————. *Hong Kong Annual Departmental Report by the Commissioner for Resettlement D. C. Barty, O.B.E., M.A., J.P. for the Financial Year 1966–67*. Hong Kong: Government Printer, 1967.

————. *Hong Kong Annual Departmental Report by the Commissioner for Resettlement J. P. Aserappa, B.A., J.P. for the Financial Year 1967–68*. Hong Kong: Government Printer, 1968.

————. *Hong Kong Annual Departmental Report by the Commissioner for Resettlement J. P. Aserappa, B.A., J.P. for the Financial Year 1968–69*. Hong Kong: Government Printer, 1969.

————. *Hong Kong Annual Departmental Report by the Commissioner for Resettlement J. P. Aserappa,, J.P. for the Financial Year 1969–70*. Hong Kong: Government Printer, 1970.

Hong Kong. Working Party on the Development of Medical Services. *Development of Medical Services in Hong Kong*. Hong Kong: Government Printer, 1964.

Hong Kong Council of Social Service. *Meeting the Social Challenge: A Survey of the Work of Voluntary and Government Social Service Organizations in Hong Kong*. Hong Kong: Council of Social Service, 1953.

Jarman, R. L., ed. *Hong Kong Annual Administration Reports 1841–1941*. Archive ed. Vol. 4: 1920–1930. Farnham Common, 1996.

————. *Hong Kong Annual Administration Reports 1841–1941*. Archive ed. Vol. 5: 1931–1939. Farnham Common, 1996.

————. *Hong Kong Annual Administration Reports 1841–1941*. Archive ed. Vol. 6: 1940–1941/42. Farnham Common, 1996.

Maryknoll Mission Letters—China, Vols. I and II (New York: Macmillan Co., 1927).

Maunder, Wynne Frederick. *Hong Kong Housing Survey, 1957*. Hong Kong: Special Committee on Housing, 1957.

Murray, Leo U. *Chai Wan Social Needs Study*. Hong Kong: Hong Kong Council of Social Service, 1967.

Our Lady of Maryknoll Hospital: Tenth Anniversary, 1961–1971. Hong Kong: Our Lady of Maryknoll Hospital, 1971.

Silver Jubilee of St. Teresa's Church 1932–1957. Hong Kong: St. Teresa's Church, 1957.

Tian Yingjie [Sergio Ticozzi], ed. *Xianggang Tianzhujiao zhanggu* (The Historical Anecdotes of the Hong Kong Catholic Church), trans. You Liqing. Hong Kong: Holy Spirit Study Centre, 1983.

Ticozzi, Sergio, ed. *Historical Documents of the Hong Kong Catholic Church.* Hong Kong: Hong Kong Catholic Diocesan Archives, 1997.

Vicariate Apostolic of Hong Kong. *The Catholic Directory of the Vicariate-Apostolic of Hongkong for the Year 1921.* Hong Kong: Catholic Church, 1921.

———. *Catholic Directory: With the Compliments of the Season, 1931.* Hong Kong: Nazareth Press, 1931.

———. *Catholic Directory: With the Compliments of the Season, 1932.* Hong Kong: Nazareth Press, 1932.

———. *Catholic Directory for the Year 1937.* Hong Kong: Catholic Church, 1937.

———. *Souvenir Number of the Golden Jubilee of the Catholic Cathedral in Hong-Kong 1888–8th December-1938: Catholic Directory of the Vicariate Apostolic of Hong-Kong and Calendar for 1939.* Hong Kong: Catholic Church, 1939.

———. *Catholic Directory and Calendar for 1940.* Hong Kong: Nazareth Press, 1940.

———. *Catholic Directory and Calendar for 1941.* Hong Kong: Nazareth Press, 1941.

Books

Anderson, David L. *Imperialism and Idealism: American Diplomats in China, 1861–1898.* Bloomington: Indiana University Press, 1985.

Banham, Tony. *Not the Slightest Chance: The Defence of Hong Kong, 1941.* Hong Kong: Hong Kong University Press, 2003.

Bays, Daniel H., ed. *Christianity in China: From the Eighteenth Century to the Present.* Stanford: Stanford University Press, 1996.

Bickers, Robert A. *Britain in China: Community, Culture and Colonialism, 1900–1949.* Manchester: Manchester University Press, 1999.

Blyth, Sally and Ian Wotherspoon, eds. *Hong Kong Remembers.* Hong Kong: Oxford University Press, 1996.

Breslin, Thomas A. *China, American Catholicism, and the Missionary.* University Park: Pennsylvania State University Press, 1980.

Bush, Lewis. *The Road to Inamura.* London: Robert Hale, 1961.

Carlson, Ellsworth C. *The Foochow Missionaries, 1847–1880.* Cambridge, Mass.: East Asian Research Center, Harvard University, 1974.

Carter, Carolle J. *Mission to Yenan: American Liaison with the Chinese Communists, 1944–1947.* Lexington: University Press of Kentucky, 1997.

Castells, M., L. Goh and R. Y.-W. Kwok. *The Shek Kip Mei Syndrome: Economic Development and Public Housing in Hong Kong and Singapore.* London: Pion, 1990.

Chan Lau, Kit-ching. *From Nothing to Nothing: The Chinese Communist Movement and Hong Kong, 1921–1936.* Hong Kong: Hong Kong University Press, 1999.

Chan, Wai Kwan. *The Making of Hong Kong Society: Three Studies of Class Formation in Early Hong Kong.* New York: Oxford University Press, 1991.

Clarke, Nora M. *"The Governor's Daughter Takes the Veil": Sister Aloysia Emily Bowring, Canossian Daughter of Charity, Hong-Kong 1860–1870.* Hong Kong: Canossian Missions Historic Archives, 1980.

Cohen, Warren I. *The Chinese Connection: Roger S. Greene, Thomas W. Lamont, George E. Sokolsky and American-East Asian Relations.* New York: Columbia University Press, 1978.

Constable, Nicole. *Christian Souls and Chinese Spirits: A Hakka Community in Hong Kong.* Berkeley: University of California Press, 1994.

Cushing, Richard J. *New Horizons: Thoughts Occasioned by the Thirtieth Anniversary of the Founding of the Maryknoll Sisters, 1912–1942.* Boston: Society for the Propagation of the Faith, 1942.

Danforth, Maria del Rey. *Pacific Hopscotch.* New York: Charles Scribner's Sons, 1951.

———. *Nun in Red China.* New York: McGraw-Hill Book Co., 1953.

———. *Safari by Jet: Through Africa and Asia.* New York: Charles Scribner's Sons, 1962.

————. *No Two Alike: Those Maryknoll Sisters!* New York: Dodd, Mead & Co., 1965.

Davis, S. G. *Hong Kong in Its Geographical Setting.* London: Collins, 1949.

Dries, Angelyn. *The Missionary Movement in American Catholic History.* Maryknoll: Orbis Books, 1998.

Dwyer, Denis John, ed. *Asian Urbanization: A Hong Kong Casebook.* Hong Kong: Hong Kong University Press, 1971.

Endacott, G. B. *Hong Kong Eclipse.* Edited and with Additional Material by Alan Birch. Hong Kong: Oxford University Press, 1978.

Fairbank, John K., ed. *The Missionary Enterprise in China and America.* Cambridge, Mass.: Harvard University Press, 1974.

Flynt, Wayne and Gerald W. Berkley. *Taking Christianity to China: Alabama Missionaries in the Middle Kingdom 1850–1950.* Tuscaloosa: University of Alabama Press, 1997.

Fogel, Joshua A. *The Cultural Dimension of Sino-Japanese Relations: Essays on the Nineteenth and Twentieth Centuries.* Armonk: M.E. Sharpe, 1995.

Ford, Francis Xavier. *Stone in the King's Highway: Selections from the Writings of Bishop Francis Xavier Ford (1892–1952).* With Introductory Memoir by Raymond A. Lane. New York: McMullen Books, 1953.

Forsythe, Sidney A. *An American Missionary Community in China, 1895–1905.* Cambridge, Mass.: East Asian Research Center, Harvard University, 1971.

Gheddo, Piero. *Lawrence Bianchi of Hong Kong.* Translated by Catholic Truth Society. Hong Kong: Catholic Truth Society, 1992.

Gittins, Jean (Hotung). *I Was at Stanley.* Hong Kong: n.p., 1946.

Grondin, M. Marcelline. *Sisters Carry the Gospel.* Maryknoll: World Horizon Reports, Maryknoll Publications, 1956.

Gulick, Edward V. *Teaching in Wartime China: A Photo-Memoir, 1937–1939.* Amherst: University of Massachusetts Press, 1995.

Habig, Marion Alphonse. *Pioneering in China: The Story of the Rev. Francis Xavier Engbring, O.F.M., First Native American Priest in China, 1857–1895, With Sketches of His Missionary Comrades.* Chicago: Franciscan Herald Press, 1930.

Hayes, James. *Friends & Teachers: Hong Kong and Its People 1953–87.* Hong Kong: Hong Kong University Press, 1996.

Hemenway, Ruth V. *A Memoir of Revolutionary China, 1924–1941.* Edited with an Introduction by Fred W. Drake. Amherst: University of Massachusetts Press, 1977.

Heyndrickx, Jeroom, ed. *Historiography of the Chinese Catholic Church: Nineteenth and Twentieth Centuries.* K. U. Leuven: Ferdinand Verbiest Foundation, 1994.

Hill, Patricia R. *The World Their Household: The American Woman's Foreign Mission Movement and Cultural Transformation, 1870–1920.* Ann Arbor: University of Michigan Press, 1985.

Hogan, Michael J. and Thomas G. Paterson, eds. *Explaining the History of American Foreign Relations.* Cambridge: Cambridge University Press, 1991.

Holy Spirit Study Centre, *Tianzhujiao nuxiuhui dui Zhongguo jiaohui he shehui de gongxian (The Contribution of the Catholic Sisters' Congregations to the Church and Society of China).* Hong Kong: Holy Spirit Study Centre, 1997.

Hopkins, Keith, ed. *Hong Kong: The Industrial Colony—A Political, Social and Economic Survey.* Hong Kong: Oxford University Press, 1971.

Hui, Che-shing. *Hong Kong's Resettled Squatters: The Final Report on the 1957 Sample Survey of Resettlement Estates.* Hong Kong: n.p., 1959.

Hunter, Jane. *The Gospel of Gentility: American Women Missionaries in Turn-of-the-Century China.* New Haven: Yale University Press, 1984.

Jarvie, I. C., ed. *Hong Kong: A Society in Transition.* London: Routledge, 1969.

Kelly, Ian. *Hong Kong: A Political-Geographic Analysis.* Basingstoke: Macmillan, 1987.

Kennedy, Camilla. *To the Uttermost Parts of the Earth: The Spirit and Charism of Mary Josephine Rogers.* Maryknoll: Maryknoll Sisters, 1987.

Kerrison, Raymond. *Bishop Walsh of Maryknoll: A Biography.* New York: Putnam, 1962.

Lau Yee-cheung and Wong Man-kong, eds. *Xianggang shehui yu wenhuashi lunji (Studies in the Social and Cultural History of Hong Kong)* Hong Kong: United College, Chinese University of Hong Kong, 2002.

Lee, Aloysius, ed. *Maryknoll Convent School 1925–2000.* Hong Kong: Maryknoll Convert School, 2000.

Lernoux, Penny. *Hearts on Fire: The Story of the Maryknoll Sisters.* Maryknoll: Orbis Books, 1993.

Leung, Beatrice and Shun-hing Chan. *Changing Church and State Relations in Hong Kong, 1950–2000.* Hong Kong: Hong Kong University Press, 2003.

Lodwick, Kathleen L. *Educating the Women of Hainan: The Career of Margaret Moninger in China, 1915–1942.* Lexington: University Press of Kentucky, 1995.

Logan, Mary Francis Louise. *Maryknoll Sisters: A Pictorial History.* New York: E.P. Dutton & Co., 1962.

Luk Hung-kay. *A History of Education in Hong Kong.* Report Submitted to Lord Wilson Heritage Trust. Hong Kong: n.p., 2000.

Lutz, Jessie Gregory. *China and the Christian Colleges, 1850–1950.* Ithaca: Cornell University Press, 1971.

Lutz, Jessie G. and Rolland Ray Lutz. *Hakka Chinese Confront Protestant Christianity, 1850–1900: With the Autobiographies of Eight Hakka Christians, and Commentary.* Armonk: M.E. Sharpe, 1998.

Lyons, Jeanne Marie. *Maryknoll's First Lady.* New York: Dodd, Mead & Co., 1964.

Mazeau, Henry. *The Heroine of Pe-Tang: Helene de Jaurias, Sister of Charity, 1824–1900.* New York: Benziger Brothers, 1928.

Miners, Norman. *Hong Kong Under Imperial Rule, 1912–1941.* Hong Kong: Oxford University Press, 1987.

Morris, Jan. *Hong Kong: Epilogue to an Empire.* London: Penguin Books, 1997.

Mother Mary of St. Austin. *Fifty-Six Years a Missionary in China: The Life of Mother St. Dominic, Helper of the Holy Souls.* London: Burns, Oates & Washbourne, 1935.

Neils, Patricia, ed. *United States Attitudes and Policies toward China: The Impact of American Missionaries.* Armonk: M.E. Sharpe, 1990.

Ngo, Tak-Wing, ed. *Hong Kong's History: State and Society under Colonial Rule.* London: Routledge, 1999.

Pendergast, Mary Carita. *Havoc in Hunan: The Sisters of Charity in Western Hunan 1924–1951.* Morristown: College of St. Elizabeth Press, 1991.

Pollock, John Charles. *A Foreign Devil in China: The Story of Dr. L. Nelson Bell—An American Surgeon in China.* Minneapolis: World Wide Publications for Billy Graham Evangelistic Association, 1971.

Powers, George C. *The Maryknoll Movement.* Maryknoll: Catholic Foreign Mission Society of America, 1926.

Pryor, E. G. *Housing in Hong Kong,* 2d ed. Hong Kong: Oxford University Press, 1983.

Reed, James. *The Missionary Mind and American East Asian Policy, 1911–1915.* Cambridge, Mass.: Council on East Asian Studies, Harvard University, 1983.

Robert, Dana L. *American Women in Mission: A Social History of Their Thought and Practice.* Macon: Mercer University Press, 1996.

Roland, Charles G. *Long Night's Journey into Day: Prisoners of War in Hong Kong and Japan, 1941–1945.* Waterloo: Wilfrid Laurier University Press, 2001.

Rosenberg, Emily S. *Spreading the American Dream: American Economic and Cultural Expansion, 1890–1945.* New York: Hill and Wang, 1982.

Ruoff, E. G., ed. *Death Throes of a Dynasty: Letters and Diaries of Charles and Bessie Ewing, Missionaries to China.* Kent: Kent State University Press, 1990.

Ryan, Thomas F., *The Story of a Hundred Years: The Pontifical Institute of Foreign Missions, (P.I.M.E.), in Hong Kong, 1858–1958.* Hong Kong: Catholic Truth Society, 1959.

———. *Catholic Guide to Hong Kong.* Hong Kong: Catholic Truth Society, 1962.

Salaff, Janet W. *Working Daughters of Hong Kong: Filial Piety or Power in the Family?* Cambridge: Cambridge University Press, 1981; New York: Columbia University Press, 1995.

Scully, Eileen P. *Bargaining with the State from Afar: American Citizenship in Treaty Port China, 1844–1942.* New York: Columbia University, 2001.

Service, John S., ed. *Golden Inches: The China Memoir of Grace Service.* Berkeley: University of California Press, 1989.

Sister Mary Just. *Immortal Fire: A Journey through the Centuries with the Missionary Great.* St. Louis: Herder, 1951.

Sit, Victor F. S. *Xianggang fazhan dituji (Hong Kong: 150 Years, Development in Maps).* Hong Kong: Joint Publishing (H.K.) Co., 2001.

Smith, Carl T. *A Sense of History: Studies in the Social and Urban History of Hong Kong.* Hong Kong: Hong Kong Educational Publishing Co., 1995.

Snow, Philip. *The Fall of Hong Kong: Britain, China and the Japanese Occupation.* New Haven: Yale University Press, 2003.

Stericker, John. *A Tear for the Dragon.* London: Arthur Barker, 1958.

Surface, Bill and Jim Hart. *Freedom Bridge: Maryknoll in Hong Kong.* New York: Coward-McCann, 1963.

Sweeten, Alan Richard. *Christianity in Rural China: Conflict and Accommodation in Jiangxi Province, 1860–1900.* Ann Arbor: Center for Chinese Studies, University of Michigan, 2001.

Sweeting, Anthony. *A Phoenix Transformed: The Reconstruction of Education in Post-War Hong Kong.* Hong Kong: Oxford University Press, 1993.

Tsai Jung-fang. *Hong Kong in Chinese History: Community and Social Unrest in the British Colony, 1842–1913.* New York: Columbia University Press, 1993.

Tsai Jung-fang. *Xianggangren zhi Xianggangshi 1841–1945 (The Hong Kong People's History of Hong Kong).* Hong Kong: Oxford University Press, 2001.

Uhalley, Stephen, Jr. and Xiaoxin Wu, eds. *China and Christianity: Burdened Past, Hopeful Future.* Armonk: M.E. Sharpe, 2001.

Walsh, James E. *Zeal for Your House.* Huntington: Our Sunday Visitor, 1976.

Wang Gungwu, ed. *Xianggangshi xinbian (Hong Kong History: New Perspectives).* Vols. 1–2. Hong Kong: Joint Publishing (H.K.) Co., 1997.

West, Philip. *Yenching University and Sino-Western Relations, 1916–1952.* Cambridge, Mass.: Harvard University Press, 1976.

Wiest, Jean-Paul. *Maryknoll in China: A History, 1918–1955.* Armonk: M.E. Sharpe, 1988.

Wolf, Ann Colette. *Against All Odds: Sisters of Providence Mission to the Chinese 1920–1990.* Saint Mary-of-the-Woods: Sisters of Providence, 1990.

Wolferstan, Bertram. *The Catholic Church in China: From 1860 to 1907.* St. Louis: B. Herder, 1909.

Wong, Siu-Lun. *Emigrant Entrepreneurs: Shanghai Industrialists in Hong Kong.* Hong Kong: Oxford University Press, 1988.

Wright-Nooth, George (with Mark Adkin). *Prisoner of the Turnip Heads: Horror, Hunger and Humour in Hong Kong, 1941–1945.* London: Leo Cooper, 1994.

Zaccarini, Maria Cristina. *The Sino-American Friendship as Tradition and Challenge: Dr. Ailie Gale in China, 1908–1950.* Bethlehem, Pa.: Lehigh University Press, 2001.

Dissertations and Theses

Barry, Peter James. "A Brief History of the Missionary Work of the Maryknoll Fathers in China." M.A. thesis, National Taiwan University, Taipei, 1977.

Bhalla, Madhu. "Americans and Chinese: A Study of Culture as Power, 1930s and 1940s." Ph.D. diss., Queen's University at Kingston, Canada, 1990.

Carbonneau, Robert Edward. "Life, Death, and Memory: Three Passionists in Hunan, China and the Shaping of an American Mission Perspective in the 1920s." Ph.D. diss., Georgetown University, 1992.

Carroll, John Mark. "Empires' Edge: The Making of the Hong Kong Chinese Bourgeoisie." Ph.D. diss., Harvard University, 1998.

Chatfield, Joan. "First Choice: Mission: The Maryknoll Sisters, 1919–1975." Ph.D. diss, Graduate Theological Union, 1983.

Ha, Louis. "The Foundation of the Catholic Mission in Hong Kong, 1841–1894." Ph.D. diss., University of Hong Kong, 1998.

Kelly, Kathleen. "Maryknoll in Manchuria, 1927–1947: A Study of Accommodation and Adaptation." Ph.D. diss., University of Southern California, 1982.

Li Ng, Suk-Kay. "Mission Strategy of the Roman Catholic Church of Hong Kong, 1949 to 1974." M. Phil. thesis, University of Hong Kong, 1978.

Ponzi, Patricia Hughes. "The Maryknoll Sisters in South China, 1920–1938." M.A. thesis, St. John's University, 1980.

Rajdl, Marylou A. "Inculturation: A Challenge to Christian Life in Hong Kong." M.A. diss., Mundelein College, 1984.

Scatena, Maria. "Educational Movements That Have Influenced the Sister Teacher Education Program of the Congregation of the Sisters of Providence, 1840–1940." Ph.D. diss., Loyola University of Chicago, 1987.

Schintz, Mary Ann. "An Investigation of the Modernizing Role of the Maryknoll Sisters in China." Ph.D. diss., University of Wisconsin-Madison, 1978.

Tan, John Kang. "Church, State and Education during Decolonization: Catholic Education in Hong Kong during the Pre-1997 Political Transition." Ph.D. diss., University of Hong Kong, 2000.

Vikner, David Walter. "The Role of Christian Missions in the Establishment of Hong Kong's System of Education." Ed.D. diss., Columbia University Teachers College, 1987.

Wu Xiaoxin. "A Case Study of the Catholic University of Peking during the Benedictine Period (1927–1933)." Ed.D. diss., University of San Francisco, 1993.

Zhou Hong. "The Origins of Government Social Protection Policy in Hong Kong: 1842–1941." Ph.D. diss, Brandeis University, 1992.

Articles and Unpublished Papers

Archer, Bernice and Kent Fedorowich. "The Women of Stanley: Internment in Hong Kong, 1942–45." *Women's History Review* Vol. 5, No. 3 (1996): 373–99.

Baker, Hugh D. R. "Life in the Cities: The Emergence of Hong Kong Man." *China Quarterly* No. 95 (1983): 469–79.

———. "Social Change in Hong Kong: Hong Kong Man in Search of Majority." *China Quarterly* No. 136 (1993): 864–77.

Barry, Peter. "Maryknoll in Hong Kong, 1918 to the Present." Paper Presented at the Seminar on "Church History of Hong Kong" of the Centre of Asian Studies, University of Hong Kong, September 22–24, 1993.

Bays, Daniel H. "Foreign Missions and Chinese Christians, 1850–1950: Towards Autonomy." May 1995. Archives on the History of Christianity in China, Hong Kong Baptist University Library.

Berg, Carol. "Margaret Thomson in China, 1917–1939." *The Historian* Vol. 53, No. 3 (Spring 1991): 455–72.

Blackburn, A. D. "Hong Kong, December 1941–July 1942." *Journal of the Hong Kong Branch of the Royal Asiatic Society* Vol. 29 (1989): 77–93.

Bradshaw, Sue. "Catholic Sisters in China: An Effort to Raise the Status of Women." In *Women in China: Current Directions in Historical Scholarship,* ed. Richard W. Guisso and Stanley Johannesen, 201–13. Youngstown: Philo Press, 1981.

———. "Religious Women in China: An Understanding of Indigenization." *Catholic Historical Review* Vol. 68, No. 1 (1982): 28–45.

Chan, Ka Yan. "Joss Stick Manufacturing: A Study of a Traditional Industry in Hong Kong." *Journal of the Hong Kong Branch of the Royal Asiatic Society* Vol. 29 (1989): 94–120.

Chan Lau Kit-ching. "The Perception of Chinese Communism in Hong Kong, 1921–1934." *China Quarterly* No. 164 (2000): 1044–61.

Chu, Cindy Yik-yi. "Overt and Covert Functions of the Hong Kong Branch of the Xinhua News Agency, 1947–1984." *The Historian* Vol. 62, No. 1 (Fall 1999): 31–46.

———. "The Chinese Communists, Hong Kong, and the Sino-Japanese War." *American Journal of Chinese Studies* Vol. 7, No. 2 (October 2000): 131–46.

———. "From the Pursuit of Converts to the Relief of Refugees: The Maryknoll Sisters in Twentieth-Century Hong Kong." *The Historian* Vol. 65, No. 2 (Winter 2002): 353–76.

———. "Maryknoll Sisters in Twentieth-Century Hong Kong." In *China Reconstructs*, ed. Cindy Yik-yi Chu and Ricardo K. S. Mak, 179–99. Lanham: University Press of America, 2003.

Crabtree, Loren W. "Andrew P. Happer and the Presbyterian Missions in China, 1844–1891." *Journal of Presbyterian History* Vol. 62, No. 1 (1984): 19–34.

Drake, Frederick W. "Bridgman in China in the Early Nineteenth Century." *American Neptune* Vol. 46, No. 1 (1986): 34–42.

Dudley, Marion. "Hong Kong Prison Camp." New York: n.p., 1942.

Dwyer, D. J. "Urban Squatters: The Relevance of the Hong Kong Experience." *Asian Survey* Vol. 10, No. 7 (1970): 607–13.

Emerson, Geoffrey Charles. "Behind Japanese Barbed Wire: Stanley Internment Camp, Hong Kong 1942–1945." *Journal of the Hong Kong Branch of the Royal Asiatic Society* Vol. 17 (1977): 30–42.

Firth, James Ronald. "The Work of the Hong Kong Housing Authority." *Journal of the Royal Society of Arts* Vol. 113, No. 5103 (February 1965): 175–95.

Hendricks, Barbara. "The Legacy of Mary Josephine Rogers." *International Bulletin of Missionary Research* Vol. 21, No. 2 (April 1997): 72–80.

Howard, Therese. "Mission to the Middle Kingdom: 75 Years Ago the First Group of Maryknoll Sisters Set Sail for China." *Sunday Examiner*. November 1, 1996, 8.

Howard, W. J. "Diocesan Boys School Seventy Years Ago." *Journal of the Hong Kong Branch of the Royal Asiatic Society* Vol. 24 (1984): 318–24.

Hoyt, Frederick B. "Protection Implies Intervention: The U.S. Catholic Mission at Kanchow." *The Historian* Vol. 38, No. 4 (August 1976): 709–27.

Hu Yueh. "The Problem of the Hong Kong Refugees." *Asian Survey* Vol. 2, No. 1 (1962): 28–37.

Johnson, Sheila K. "Hong Kong's Resettled Squatters: A Statistical Analysis." *Asian Survey* Vol. 6, No. 11 (November 1966): 643–56.

Law, Kam-yee and Cheung-wai Wong. "More Than a Primitive Imperialism: The Colonial Government and the Social Relief of Hong Kong in the Early Twentieth Century." *Journal of Contemporary China* Vol. 6, No. 16 (1997): 513–30.

Law, Stephen H. L. "Social Commitments of the Catholic Church in Hong Kong—Education." Paper Presented at the Seminar on "Catholic Archives Records" Organized by the Hong Kong Catholic Diocesan Archives and Hong Kong Catholic Social Communications Office, January 5, 1995.

———. "Social Commitments of the Catholic Church in Hong Kong—Welfare Services." Paper Presented at the Seminar on "Catholic Archives Records" Organized by the Hong Kong Catholic Diocesan Archives and Hong Kong Catholic Social Communications Office, January 5, 1995.

Lee, Anna. "To the Dragon Gate: Adventist Schools in South China and Hong Kong (1903–1941)." *Adventist Heritage* Vol. 8, No. 1 (1983): 52–60.

Lutz, Jessie G. "Chinese Christianity and China Missions: Works Published since 1970." *International Bulletin of Missionary Research* Vol. 20, No. 3 (July 1996): 98–106.

Mathews, Gordon. "Hèunggóngyàhn: On the Past, Present, and Future of Hong Kong Identity." *Bulletin of Concerned Asian Scholars* Vol. 29, No. 3 (July–September 1997): 3–13.

McKeirnan, M. "Field Trip to Maryknoll House, Stanley by the Hong Kong Royal Asiatic Society Dec. 8, 1984." *Journal of the Hong Kong Branch of the Royal Asiatic Society* Vol. 23 (1983): 1–6.

Mug, Miriam Xavier. "Maryknoll Sisters, Hong Kong-Macau Region: A History— 1921–1998." Unpublished, March 2000.

Ng, Norman Yen Tak. "The Early Population of Hong Kong: Growth, Distribution and Structural Change, 1841–1931." Hong Kong: Department of Geography, Chinese University of Hong Kong, 1984.

Rieckelman, Maria. "My Pilgrimage in Mission." *International Bulletin of Missionary Research* Vol. 25, No. 4 (October 2001): 169–73.

Rivera, Paul R. "The Yangjiang Incident of November 1927: The Maryknoll Mission Enterprise and the Chinese Nationalist Revolution of 1925–1927." *Southeast Review of Asian Studies* Vol. 19 (1997): 47–64.

———. " 'Field Found!': Establishing the Maryknoll Mission Enterprise in the United States and China, 1918–1928." *Catholic Historical Review* Vol. LXXXIV, No. 3 (July 1998): 477–517.

Rubinstein, Murray A. "China in Maryknoll: The Sinologically-Related Holdings of the Catholic Foreign Mission Society of America." *Newsletter for Modern Chinese History* (Jindai Zhongguo shi yanjiu tongxun) Vol. 13 (1992): 179–90.

Sinn, Elizabeth. "The Study of Local History in Hong Kong: A Review." *Journal of the Hong Kong Branch of the Royal Asiatic Society* Vol. 34 (1994): 147–69.

Smart, Alan. "The Development of Diamond Hill from Village to Squatter Area: A Perspective on Public Housing." *Asian Journal of Public Administration* Vol. 8, No. 1 (1986): 43–63.

Smith, Carl T. "The Hong Kong Amateur Dramatic Club and Its Predecessors." *Journal of the Hong Kong Branch of the Royal Asiatic Society* Vol. 22 (1982): 217–51.

———. "The German Speaking Community in Hong Kong 1846–1918." *Journal of the Hong Kong Branch of the Royal Asiatic Society* Vol. 34 (1994): 1–55.

Smith, James and William Downs. "The Maryknoll Mission, Hong Kong 1941–1946." *Journal of the Hong Kong Branch of the Royal Asiatic Society* Vol. 19 (1979): 27–148.

Stewart, G. O. W. "Post-War Development in Hong Kong." *Asian Review* Vol. 58 (April 1962): 128–31.

Vaughan, T. D. and D. J. Dwyer. "Some Aspects of Postwar Population Growth in Hong Kong." *Economic Geography* Vol. 42, No. 1 (January 1966): 37–51.

Waters, D. D. "The Country Boy Who Died for Hong Kong." *Journal of the Hong Kong Branch of the Royal Asiatic Society* Vol. 25 (1985): 210–15.

———. "Hong Kong Hongs with Long Histories and British Connections." *Journal of the Hong Kong Branch of the Royal Asiatic Society* Vol. 30 (1990): 219–56.

Weiss, Anita M. "South Asian Muslims in Hong Kong: Creation of a 'Local Boy' Identity." *Modern Asian Studies* Vol. 25, No. 3 (1991): 417–53.

Wong, Timothy Man-kong. "A Survey of English and Chinese Source Materials Related to the History of Christianity in Hong Kong." *Ching Feng* Vol. 41, No. 1 (March 1998): 1–40.

Periodicals

The Field Afar
Kung Kao Po
Maryknoll
The Rock
Sunday Examiner

Index